CLEARING THE PLAINS

CLEARING

DISEASE, POLITICS OF STARVATION, AND THE LOSS OF ABORIGINAL LIFE

THE PLAINS

JAMES DASCHUK

U OF R PRESS

Printed and bound in Canada at Friesens.
The text of this book is printed on 100% post-consumer recycled paper with earth-friendly vegetable-based inks.

Cover and text design: Duncan Campbell, University of Regina Press.
Editor for the Press: David McLennan, University of Regina Press.
Copy editor: Dallas Harrison.
Index by Judy Dunlop.
Maps by Diane Perrick, University of Regina Press.
Cover photo: "Cree Indian, Maple Creek, Saskatchewan, 1884." Reproduced with the permission of Natural Resources Canada 2012, courtesy of the Geological Survey of Canada (Photo 615 by T. C. Weston).

Library and Archives Canada Cataloguing in Publication

Daschuk, James W. (James William), 1961–
Clearing the Plains : disease, politics of starvation, and the loss of Aboriginal life / James Daschuk.

(Canadian Plains studies, 0317-6290 ; 65)
Includes bibliographical references and index.
Issued in print and electronic formats.
ISBN 978-0-88977-296-0 (bound).—ISBN 978-0-88977-340-0 (pbk.)
ISBN 9780889772977 (pdf).—ISBN 978-0-88977-246-5 (ebook)

1. Indians of North America—Canada, Western—History. 2. Indians of North America—Diseases—Canada, Western—History. 3. Indians of North America—Health and hygiene—Canada, Western—History. 4. Indians of North America—Government policy—Canada—History. 5. Canada, Western— Colonization—Health aspects—History. 6. Canada, Western—Ethnic relations— History. I. Title. II. Series: Canadian plains studies ; 65

E78.C2D36 2013   971.2'00497   C2013-901819-0

10   9

University of Regina Press, University of Regina
Regina, Saskatchewan, Canada, S4S 0A2
TEL: (306) 585-4758 FAX: (306) 585-4699
WEB: www.uofrpress.ca

We acknowledge the financial support of the Government of Canada through the Canada Book Fund for our publishing activities, and the Creative Industry Growth and Sustainability program which is made possible through funding provided to the Saskatchewan Arts Board by the Government of Saskatchewan through the Ministry of Parks, Culture and Sport. We acknowledge the support of the Canada Council for the Arts for our publishing program.

CONTENTS

ACKNOWLEDGEMENTS

THIS PROJECT BEGAN AS MY DOCTORAL DISSERTATION AT THE University of Manitoba two decades ago, and I am indebted to many people and institutions that have helped me over the years. Dr. Mary Black Rogers opened up her home and the vast anthropological collection of her husband, Dr. E. S. Rogers, to me as a young graduate student. Dr. Jack Bumsted set me on the path by finding me work as a research assistant to Dr. Kue Young, then of the Faculty of Medicine at U of M. The Social Sciences and Humanities Research Council of Canada provided me with a doctoral fellowship as I began this study. Many friends and colleagues, particularly Dr. Renée Fossett and Scott MacNeil, kept me going during the years when this study took shape. Joy Flynn and Grant Taylor were kind enough to provide their cabin on the White Bear First Nation, where much of the dissertation was written. As I completed my dissertation, my graduate school friend and colleague, Dr. Paul Hackett, hired me as a research associate in the Faculty of Medicine at U of M, allowing me to spend almost two years immersed in the fascinating records of the Hudson's Bay Company Archives.

The second phase of this project was completed during my years with the Saskatchewan Indian Federated College (now First Nations University of Canada) and the University of Regina. Dr. David Reed Miller, Professor Emeritus at FNUV, was instrumental in the completion of this task. His encyclopedic knowledge, his collegiality, and his kindness have served to guide me in countless ways over the years. I am lucky to know him. I am very grateful to Dr. Greg Marchildon, Canada Research Chair in Public Policy and Economic History at the Johnson-Shoyama Graduate School of Public Policy, for providing me with the opportunity to spend an entire year studying the history of climate change and its impact on the indigenous communities of the region. I also thank Greg for suggesting the Canadian Plains Research Center Press (now the University of Regina Press) as a publisher for this project.

Dr. Ralph Nilson, former Director of the Indigenous People's Health Research Centre in Regina, gave me a home on campus as the manuscript took shape. I would also like to thank Dr. Craig Chamberlin, Dean of the Faculty of Kinesiology and Health Studies at U of R, and Dr. Bonnie Jeffery, Director of the Saskatchewan Population Health Evaluation and Research Unit (SPHERU), for their generous support in the editing of the final manuscript and Dallas Harrison for pruning it down to a manageable size and to David McLennan for editing it. Thanks also to Brian Mlazgar (now retired) at the Canadian Plains Research Center for his patience in the completion of this project.

I would not have been able to undertake this study without the help of the staff of many libraries and archives, including Library and Archives Canada, the Hudson's Bay Company Archives, the Saskatchewan Archives Board, the Glenbow Archives, the Dr. John Archer Library at the University of Regina, and the late Ken Aitkin and his staff at the Prairie History Room of the Regina Public Library. My friends at First Nations University Library, especially Belle Young and Rob Nestor, made numerous trips there as enjoyable and they were productive. My friends and colleagues at the Network in Canadian History of Environment (NICHE) have contributed to the work in a number of ways. I also thank my friend Doran Degenstein, the Executive Director of the Fort Whoop-Up National Historic Site in Lethbridge for his sage advice on many occasions.

Additionally, I would like to acknowledge the University of Regina's Humanities Research Institute for funding support, and Christina Winter, Copyright Officer with the Dr. John Archer Library at the University of Regina, for her help with securing permissions to reproduce some of the images that appear in this text. I cannot overstate my gratitude to my friend, Bruce Walsh, Director of the University of Regina Press. His vision, skill and support have been the key to the success of this project and I hope he continues to shake up academic publishing in this country for a long time to come.

Finally, and most importantly, I would like to thank my spouse, Giselle Marcotte, and my daughters, Dominique, Sophie, and Marie-Eve, for their support and patience over the many years that it took to complete this project. I dedicate this book to them.

INTRODUCTION

FOR DECADES, CANADIANS HAVE ENJOYED AN ANNUAL ACKNOWL-
edgement of their collective success. Canada consistently places
among the top nations in the world according to the UN Human
Development Index. In its report for 2007–08, only Iceland, Norway,
and Australia ranked higher than Canada in the criteria considered
by the United Nations.[1] Yet also a regular story is the dismal condition
of Canada's indigenous people in comparison with its mainstream
population. The gap between these populations is so wide that official
communications of the Assembly of First Nations, the largest aboriginal
organization in the country, state that Canada's indigenous population
would rank sixty-third on the same index, the equivalent of Panama,
Malaysia, or Belarus.[2] On average, indigenous Canadians can expect
to die between five and eight years earlier than other Canadians. Canadians have come to expect the highest-quality medical care as their
national right, but indigenous people routinely suffer from poverty,
violence, sickness, and premature death. Substandard health conditions
are so entrenched that a recent text on the social determinants of health
listed aboriginal status as a key predictive variable in the analysis of
the country's overall health outcomes.[3] The chasm between the health
conditions of First Nations people and mainstream Canadians has
existed for as long as anyone can remember; it too has become part of
who we are as a nation. The primary goal of this study is to identify
the roots of the current health disparity between the indigenous and
mainstream populations in western Canada. Health as a measure of
human experience cannot be considered in isolation from the social
and economic forces that shape it. In Canada, the marginalization of

First Nations people has been the primary factor impeding improved health outcomes for all of its citizens.

Racism among policy makers and members of mainstream society was the key factor in creating the gap in health outcomes as well as maintaining a double standard for acceptable living conditions for the majority of the population and the indigenous minority. In recent years, two important studies have investigated the role of racist attitudes of the dominant society as a cause of declining health conditions of indigenous people in western Canada. In *Medicine that Walks: Disease, Medicine, and Canadian Plains Native People, 1880–1940*, Maureen Lux argued that racism and the government policies that stemmed from it were the central factors in the precipitous decline of health in the reserve population of the prairies.[4] Mary-Ellen Kelm's *Colonizing Bodies: Aboriginal Health and Healing in British Columbia* argued that colonial attitudes toward indigenous people in British Columbia created a self-fulfilling prophecy based on the widespread impression that government action was justified because First Nations were seen to be on the verge of extinction.[5] The construction of a belief in the inherent physical weakness of indigenous people undoubtedly contributed to the physical decline of their communities. The deleterious effects of the Canadian government's draconian policies were rationalized in light of the natural weakness of those suffering from them. The present study acknowledges the importance of racist ideology in the historical relationship between First Nations and the Canadian state. Rather than focusing on the *ideas* that fuelled the marginalization of the reserve population or the worldview of the indigenous groups who were eventually subjugated, this investigation considers the *material conditions,* the result of long-term economic and environmental forces, that ultimately led to such divergent histories of population health in western Canada.

This is not a work of ethnohistory, a comprehensive narrative of each of the First Nations cultures living in western Canada. Instead, it answers the call of Theodore Binnema in *Common and Contested Ground: A Human and Environmental History of the North American Plains* to go beyond what he called the "culturalist preoccupations" of recent scholarship that have focused on the study of individual First Nations.[6] As such, this study presents the Canadian northwest as a whole and considers the ebb and flow of different First Nations in the region from the early 1700s to the end of the nineteenth century. Some groups perished while others greatly increased their territory under the combined influences of epidemic diseases and market economics.

The study does not claim to present an "emic," indigenous perspective on the growing influence of the global economy on health outcomes in western Canada. To a significant extent, this is an investigation of what First Nations people did, where they lived, and what they ate over approximately 160 years as the global economy, described by Immanuel Wallerstein as the "modern world system,"[7] took hold on the Canadian plains. Building on Wallerstein's concept, American geographer Jason W. Moore asserted that economic and environmental changes are inseparable: "the rise of a capitalist world-economy and the rise of a capitalist world-ecology were two moments of the same world historical process."[8] In western Canada, these two "moments" were at the heart of changes in the health of the indigenous population. Ultimately, the shift of the dominant economic paradigm from the fur trade to agriculture and industrial capitalism displaced the indigenous people from their once lucrative position on the periphery of the global economy. It was the alienation of First Nations from a viable economic base in the world system and the imposed environmental constraints of the reserve system that played a key role in the decline of their health in the late nineteenth century.

Prior to being excluded from participating in the agrarian economy that later emerged on the Canadian plains, the First Nations of western Canada had been active participants in the modern world system for at least 200 years.[9] As the commercial fur economy took hold, indigenous people increasingly made choices based on the demands and opportunities presented by market forces. Along with the invisible hand of the marketplace came unseen microbes that brought unprecedented sickness and death to the region.

The singularity of the encounter between the ecosystems of the Old World and the New in the past 500 years is hard to fathom. Never has there been a comparable environmental and human transition. The equivalent exchange of goods, flora, fauna, people, and microbes could only be repeated if there was an exchange of life forms between planets.[10] Alfred Crosby argued that introduced Old World diseases were the fundamental determinants of the demographic history of indigenous Americans for up to 150 years after their initial exposure.[11] In western Canada, the epidemic history to the 1870s corresponds to the Crosby model. Paul Hackett's "A Very Remarkable Sickness": Epidemics in the Petit Nord, 1670–1846 provides an excellent description of the period of introduced infectious disease in the boreal forest region east of the prairies.[12]

The importance of introduced infectious disease cannot be over-stated in the history of indigenous America. In the Canadian northwest, epidemics of introduced contagious diseases swept through the region with regularity from the 1730s to the 1870s. The generational cycle ended when medical intervention curbed their impacts. During that time, *Variola major,* the smallpox virus, and other pathogens were key factors in shaping the historical development of the region.

The secondary goal of this book is to consider the role of disease in shaping the territorial history of the country between the Missouri River and the boreal forest in the years before Canada's acquisition of the west. Differential mortality and survival in epidemics provided the founda-tion for territorial change and the emergence of new ethnic identities under the process known as "ethnogenesis."[13] Disease and death came as unintentional but inexorable parts of the exchange between previously separated ecosystems. As survivors regrouped in the wake of repeated epidemics brought about by the "biological unification" of the planet,[14] they responded to the ever-increasing influence of the global trading network. Expansion of the world economy and its attendant diseases shaped the responses of the surviving communities on the plains to the new economic realities. What brought death to some often translated into economic opportunity for others.

The inseparable forces of trade, epidemic mortality, and reconstitu-tion of survivors provided the context for widespread territorial change among First Nations by the early eighteenth century. In considering what Arthur Ray called "spatial dynamism"[15] on the eastern margins of the plains, this study revisits the debate over the westward migra-tion of the Cree.

Whether or not the Cree were the long-standing inhabitants of the eastern plains is a significant issue. In the academic literature, the view that the Cree expanded west with the fur trade has been around since the publication of David Mandelbaum's *The Plains Cree: An Ethnographic, Historical, and Comparative Study* in 1940.[16] His conclusions were based on interviews with members of Plains Cree communities and secondary literature on the fur trade period. A generation later studies grounded in the Hudson's Bay Company Archives buttressed the interpretation that the Cree and Ojibwa moved west as agents of the global economy.

Arthur Ray's *Indians in the Fur Trade: Their Role as Trappers, Hunters, and Middlemen in the Lands Southwest of Hudson Bay, 1660–1870*[17] and Charles Bishop's *The Northern Ojibwa and the Fur Trade: An Histori-cal and Ecological Study*[18] were effective in arguing that groups that acquired European trade goods, particularly firearms, expanded into areas inhabited by other groups, causing the territorial and cultural dislocation of many aboriginal societies. *Indians in the Fur Trade* was also a pioneering study in its recognition of the role of disease as a significant historical force in western Canada. The economic specialization of groups such as the Cree and Ojibwa (Anishinabe) led scholars to interpret their economic histories in terms of growing dependence on European trade goods and, by extension, the global capitalist system for their well-being. Because of their place on the periphery of the world economy and their eventual marginalization and poverty, First Nations in Canada were seen as analogous to people in the third world. Historical studies dealing with economic change and eventual dispossession became associated with "dependency theory," a Marxist interpretive approach that gained considerable influence after the publication of André Gunder Frank's *Capitalism and Underdevelopment in Latin America* in 1967.[19] Dependency analysis traced the growing imbalance of power and wealth among the core of the world system, the colonial powers that became the developed world, and the periphery of the system, the colonized and impoverished third world.

The goal of materialist histories of First Nations people was to situate their experience and eventual subjugation in a global context. By the 1980s, however, a growing perception that dependency studies stressed weakness and abandonment of cultural traditions of First Nations led to a backlash in the academic and indigenous communities. Studies emphasizing the strength and resiliency of indigenous cultures in the historical period turned the notion of dependency on its head, showing that it was the Europeans who were dependent on local people for their survival. Paul Thistle's *Indian–European Trade Relations in the Lower Saskatchewan River Region to 1840*[20] was among the first monographs to stress the reliance of the newcomers on indigenous people for their day-to-day survival. Eleanor M. Blain addressed the issue head on in her paper "Dependency: Charles Bishop and the Northern Ojibwa," published in 1991.[21] Blain's discussion centred on the agency of the Ojibwa in resisting HBC attempts to manipulate the trade. Others, such as Laura Peer's *The Ojibwa of Western Canada, 1780–1870*,[22] stressed the cultural autonomy of the Ojibwa even as they moved west in response to changing conditions of the monopoly trade period. As studies emphasizing the cultural integrity of First Nations took hold, others argued that the territorial changes described in the works of Ray, Bishop, and others were overblown. The issue of indigenous territorial occupation took on a new importance with the recognition of aboriginal rights in the Constitution Act of 1982. The longer a First Nation inhabited a territory, it was thought, the stronger its claim to the land.

One of the most significant post-Constitution conflicts over land and resource rights was led by the Lubicon Lake Cree Nation in north-central Alberta. They sought recognition of their inherent ownership of their territory, which they saw to be under threat from oil and gas development. James G. E. Smith, an advocate for the Lubicon, wrote "The Western Woods Cree: Anthropological Myth and Historical Reality."[23] Arguing that the westward movement of fur-trading Europeans had created the erroneous historical impression that the Cree too had moved west, Smith asserted that the ancestors of the Lubicon had been in the disputed region for hundreds of years. He concluded his discussion with an acknowledgement of the value of his research to the Cree legal case: "However 'pure' our research, it may have later practical consequences."

By the early 1990s, the view that the Cree were long-standing inhabitants of western Canada was gaining strength. Dale Russell's *Eighteenth Century Western Cree and Their Neighbours*[24] argued that the Cree had not migrated west but been ensconced on the lower Saskatchewan River for several hundred years. Russell also critiqued what he considered to be the misinterpretation of the fur trade record, and that the descriptions of western land showed that not the people but the European reporters were moving west. The study was among the first to focus on the occupation of specific Cree groups on the parklands just east of the plains, including the Pegogamaw, the Cowanitow, and the Basquia, who had inhabited the region before the arrival of traders. Russell's work had such a significant impact on the historical community that at least two contemporary reviewers used variations of the term "demolish" to describe its impact on the literature grounded on geographical change in relation to the fur trade.[25]

Soon after the publication of Russell's work, studies focusing on the territorial shift of the Cree, such as John Milloy's *The Plains Cree: Trade, Diplomacy, and War, 1790 to 1870*,[26] were being damned by reviewers. In a review of *The Plains Cree*, David Smyth asserted that ethnohistorical studies arguing for long-term occupation of the Cree in the west had "virtually destroyed the credibility" of all interpretations of Cree migration into the region and that the debate over migration and economic dependency was "historiographically out of date."[27]

By the mid-1990s, studies based on the economic history of First Nations were increasingly marginalized. In *"As Their Natural Resources Fail": Native Peoples and the Economic History of Northern Manitoba, 1780–1930*, economic historian Frank Tough declared that the "discussion of political economy of the subarctic has essentially been shut down by ethnohistory."[28] Soon postcolonial scholars turned on ethnohistory because its focus on aboriginal agency was thought to diminish the subjugation of indigenous people with the establishment of Canadian hegemony.[29] Ethnohistorians such as Toby Morantz countered that the discourse of colonialism, anchored "in concepts of 'power', 'appropriation', 'territorialization' and 'coercion' creates a powerful appropriation of this early history, leaving little scope for the representations of less violent, dynamic and competitive encounters."[30] Morantz, while admitting that the language of colonial discourse was compelling, nevertheless observed that it "submerged" the particular circumstances of indigenous people "into a more universal style of rhetoric." In a sense, the sheer force of colonial discourse makes it a blunt tool of analysis. As postcolonial studies took on greater sophistication, their methodology became increasingly influential in what was once the exclusive domain of ethnohistory. *"The White Man's Gonna Getcha": The Colonial Challenge to the Crees in Quebec*, by Toby Morantz,[31] and Jeffery Ostler's *The Plains Sioux and U.S. Colonialism from Lewis and Clark to Wounded Knee*[32] are examples of the convergence of ethnohistorical and postcolonial discourse.

In the introduction to the second edition of *Indians in the Fur Trade*, Ray attempted to find common ground with the critics of his earlier approach by positing that the concept of "interdependency" best described the growing relationship between indigenous producers and traders. On the issue of migration, though, Ray stood firm, arguing that "there is overwhelming evidence in the documentary record to support my conclusion that significant population relocations took place before the early nineteenth century." He argued that "new conceptual approaches" and further research were required to go beyond the "simplistic notion that population movement took place in a wave-like fashion."[33] This book presents an interpretation of territorial realignment based on differential outcomes of eighteenth-century epidemics. Any serious consideration of indigenous land tenure in western Canada must consider mortality from epidemic disease as a central determinant in the occupational history of the region.

The first half of this book addresses economic, demographic, and territorial changes among First Nations in the west prior to Canada's acquisition of the territory in 1870. It argues that the spread of foreign diseases among highly susceptible populations comprised a tragic, unforeseen, but largely organic change. Those who place human agency and greed and the expansionism of colonial powers at the centre of the decline of indigenous nations in the western hemisphere are missing half of the story; the role played by biology cannot be ignored. It was a fundamental principle in the history of indigenous America.

Chapter 1 provides a brief description of indigenous societies and their health in the centuries before the arrival of Europeans. As indigenous nations across the eastern half of the continent reeled from a long period of climatic deterioration beginning in the thirteenth century, the northern Great Plains served as a refuge to many whose communities in the woodlands to the east were no longer sustainable. Both long-standing inhabitants and newcomers to the region were large-scale, sophisticated, tribally based societies that managed bison herds in order to maintain semi-sedentary residence patterns, alternating between valley complexes in winter and open plains in summer. Water, a critical resource in the arid plains, was maintained through the purposeful non-exploitation of beaver, whose dams buffered human communities from droughts. With a dependable supply of high-quality food, the regional population probably experienced good health, especially in relation to societies in the east that were undergoing severe hardship in the centuries prior to the arrival of Europeans. While prehistoric North America was far from a disease-free paradise, the burden of disease was minuscule compared with the biological onslaught unleashed with the arrival of Europeans. Because of its effect on hard tissue, we know that tuberculosis was present, though probably rare, in the prehistoric population of the Canadian plains.

Chapter 2 argues that First Nations in western Canada underwent profound demographic and territorial changes in the first half of the eighteenth century. Smallpox and other diseases had already transformed the indigenous landscape west of the Great Lakes. In the 1730s, infection originating in Europe spread as far west as Manitoba and the Arikara villages on the lower Missouri River. Taking hold in "virgin soil," these epidemics brought unprecedented death to groups such as the Sioux, Assiniboine, Anishinabe, and Cree in the boundary waters region and the Winnipeg River, Forks, and Interlake areas of Manitoba. On the eastern plains, disease spread along transportation corridors used by Europeans and the aboriginal trade networks connected to them. Communities along the Rocky Mountains as far north as Alberta were also attacked by smallpox even though they had yet to see their first European. The equestrian trade network controlled by the enigmatic group known as the "Snakes" delivered horses to the northern plains from their source in New Mexico with such efficiency that the disease spread to the war zone on the Red Deer River sometime around 1740.

Before the first European had even laid eyes on Alberta, the local native population had already experienced the greatest demographic shock of its history.

Chapter 3 describes the changes that followed as the middleman trade gave way to the widespread presence of European traders in the region in the 1770s. By then, equestrianism had spread to most First Nations of the prairies. The physical presence of hundreds of newcomers in the region not only undermined the middleman fur trade but also created a burgeoning demand for meat that would prove to be the foundation of the commercial economy of the region for almost a century. The new economic niche created by equestrian hunting drew many from the marginal lands of the boreal forest to the parklands and plains. A continental pandemic of smallpox spread to the boreal forest, killing untold thousands in its path. On the margins of the plains in Saskatchewan, several Cree groups were so depopulated that they ceased to exist as distinct entities in the aftermath of the epidemic.

Chapter 4 investigates changes in the indigenous societies of the region during the "Fur Trade Wars" amid a protracted and escalating struggle among competing fur trade enterprises that spanned the period from 1780 to 1820. Epidemic mortality contributed to the ethnogenesis of new communities as survivors and incoming indigenous groups came together to meet the demands of the commercial economy for beaver pelts and provisions. New regions, particularly in the north, were opened up to the commercial trade. The period when Canadians dominated the Athabasca and Mackenzie Rivers proved to be one of the most repugnant chapters of native–newcomer relations in Canada. To secure their trade, Montreal-based traders relied on alcohol, violence, murder, and the slave traffic of women. Eventually, the local population turned on their tormentors as game depletion and environmental degradation were threatening the stability of groups across the region. Although the bison remained plentiful, the emergence of equestrian dependency among all hunting groups on the plains exposed one and all to severe privations during some of the coldest decades of the climatic period known as the Little Ice Age. In the last and coldest decades of the eighteenth century, horse herds were unsustainable, and intertribal violence increased as a result of raiding. By the 1790s, owing to competition and violence over horses, the Gros Ventre were permanently exiled to below the forty-ninth parallel. By the early decades of the nineteenth century, the people and environment of the northwest were seriously undermined by forty years of unrestrained fur competition. Serious social pathologies, including alcoholism and violence, had taken hold in many communities. Elsewhere, game depletion brought many to the verge of famine and beyond. In the far northwest, disruption of the seasonal cycle that was the foundation of many Athapaskan communities forced many to adopt the harshest measures to survive. The extirpation of furbearers and large game changed the ecology of many regions for decades if not forever. As the struggle for fur trade supremacy reached its climax, a combined epidemic of measles and whooping cough brought sickness and mortality to the region in levels not experienced since the smallpox outbreaks of the 1780s.

Chapter 5 addresses the interaction of economics and health outcomes among First Nations during the five decades that the Hudson's Bay Company controlled Rupert's Land. During the monopoly period, the company tried, with varying degrees of success, to manage the people and environment of its domain. In response to game depletion from overhunting and the debauchery associated with the unrestrained availability of alcohol, the company closed posts, cut its workforce, set limits on fur production, and in some areas imposed a prohibition on liquor. First Nations communities responded to the changes in a variety of ways, ranging from violence to abandonment of fur lands in favour of new opportunities on the margins of the plains. In an attempt to counter what officials feared would be an exodus from the hinterland, missionary groups were allowed into the region to provide material assistance to groups in depleted or unproductive areas. The decision to open the region to the churches was not altruistic. Rather, the HBC sought a cheap alternative to supporting producers in need of help. Indigenous communities in areas that were particularly depleted, such as Red River, underwent the transition to settlement and farming by the 1820s. Among the first to adopt the new life on the margin of the European colony was the Ojibwa band led by Chief Peguis. In a portent of what would become the dominant health trend across the west decades later, the Peguis band was one of the first to manifest clinical tuberculosis.

As more and more communities in the region began to show the physical signs of declining conditions, the HBC introduced a successful and widespread disease prevention program. Vaccination procedures shaped the outcome of a smallpox epidemic in the 1830s and fundamentally changed the occupational history of the Treaty 4 area. Although smallpox could be dealt with through medical intervention, the advancing settlement frontier and changing demographic of the population of Rupert's Land meant that other contagious diseases were striking with increasing frequency. By mid-century, hunting pressure constricted the ranges of the herds, leading to an increasingly tense situation on the plains. Uncertainty over the future of the land grew as the Royal Charter of the HBC came under attack and the east began to view the territory as ripe terrain for the agricultural expansion of Canada.

The annexation of the northwest by the Dominion of Canada in 1870 changed the political, economic, and medical history of the region forever. Although acute contagious disease continued to strike the indigenous population, an epidemic transition took place within a decade of the transfer. Widespread vaccination measures diminished the threat of smallpox, but almost immediately a new pathogen emerged to take its place as the primary cause of sickness and death—tuberculosis. Appearing in tandem with a region-wide famine, tuberculosis exploded and cut down the indigenous population. An epidemic unlike anything the region had ever seen, it swept through the entire newly imposed reserve system. In contrast to smallpox and other infections that had swept through the region like wildfire, to a significant degree the TB outbreak was defined by human rather than simply biological parameters. The most significant factor under human control was the failure of the Canadian government to meet its treaty obligations and its decision to use food as a means to control the Indian population to meet its development agenda rather than as a response to a humanitarian crisis.

The second half of this book deals with the changing health conditions in the west in the context of shifting economic and political realities during the last decades of the nineteenth century. It argues that the TB crisis among First Nations could have been significantly mitigated had the dominion acted in good faith toward its treaty partners. In short, it deals with the politics of famine. The investigation is grounded on the ideas pioneered by Nobel Laureate Amartya Sen, whose *Poverty and Famines: An Essay on Entitlement and Deprivation* stressed that South Asian famines had more to do with the politics of food distribution than the scarcity of foodstuffs.[34] It also draws on studies that have challenged the view that hunger and associated medical problems are not simply the results of environmental crises. In *The Political Ecology of Disease in Tanzania*, by Meredith Thursen, African poverty was portrayed as not "an innate or inherent problem but a product of colonial history, present dependence, and changed social relations of production."[35] Thursen developed a critique of the colonial model of medicine, the concept of the "unnatural history of disease," that centred on the socioeconomic and political roots of ill health. Randall Packard's *White Plague—Black Labor: Tuberculosis and the Political Economy of Health and Disease in South Africa* came to a similar conclusion: tuberculosis was the result of the pathological intersection of political, economic, and biological forces.[36]

In the United States, Gregory Campbell adapted Thursen's concept of the unnatural history of disease in a paper titled "The Changing Dimension of Native American Health: A Critical Understanding of Contemporary Native American Health Issues."[37] In it, he showed that new pathologies such as AIDS, substance abuse, and type II diabetes mellitus emerged from enforced social changes on reservations after 1945. In another article, "Health Patterns and Underdevelopment on the Northern Cheyenne Reservation," Campbell again stressed that the physical decline of the community was the "direct result of the political and economic control held by the Indian office" that deprived the Cheyenne of a viable economic base and the resources needed to maintain their health.[38] In Canada, the second edition of *Aboriginal Health in Canada*, by James Waldram, Ann Herring, and Kue Young, reaffirmed that political economy was the "most appropriate" interpretive tool to balance biology, culture, historical events, and policies with the nature of the Canadian state and society.[39] The present study answers this call with regard to late-nineteenth-century health conditions of the indigenous population of western Canada.

Chapter 6 covers Canada's acquisition of Rupert's Land after the last great western smallpox epidemic in 1869–70. Thirty-five hundred people died in the outbreak, and the misery of survivors was compounded by the decline of the bison and the short-lived but intense period of alcohol smuggling in Alberta known as the "Whoop-Up" trade. Indigenous leaders made repeated requests for treaties to formalize their relationship with the crown, but the dominion ignored their calls, entering into treaty only in areas where development was imminent. First Nations saw the treaties as a bridge between their reliance on the disappearing bison and a new life based on agriculture. The recent experience of the smallpox outbreak led Cree negotiators to request that medical assistance be included in Treaty 6. In addition to assistance in the conversion to agriculture and a "medicine chest," Treaty 6 included a clause that committed the dominion to providing assistance in the case of widespread hunger.[40] But as Chapter 7 reveals, the sudden collapse of bison herds and the immediacy of the ensuing famine caught the dominion government off guard. It was ill prepared to deal with the situation on the ground. In tandem with the famine, clinical tuberculosis was being reported across the west. Because the disease took hold so quickly, the study argues, the population might have already been infected with tuberculosis owing to the role of a hitherto unrecognized pathogen, *Mycobacterium bovis*. Before the widespread sickness of the 1880s, bovine tuberculosis had spread to the human population through ingestion of infected bison and introduced domestic cattle. Hunger then triggered the sudden outbreak of disease across the west. The re-election of the Conservative Party in the fall of 1878 hastened the development agenda for the region. To the hungry indigenous population, this meant that officials quickly turned the food crisis into a means to control them to facilitate construction of the railway and opening of the country to agrarian settlement. Yet not all First Nations endured this transitional period of hunger and sickness. The Dakota, who did not depend on the bison and were not signatories to the treaties, were able to maintain relatively good conditions in their communities. This is evidence that the emerging TB epidemic was not an organic phenomenon but the outcome of prolonged malnutrition and failure of the dominion to meet its treaty commitments.

Chapter 8 deals with the two years preceding the Resistance of 1885. The impending completion of the Canadian Pacific Railway brought the issue of unsettled First Nations to a head. By 1883, only a few hundred people were not yet on reserves and under the control of government officials. Because those on reserves depended on rations supplied by the government, food contracts with the dominion became big business. One company, the firm of I. G. Baker, almost single-handedly controlled the commercial economy of the west in the years before railway completion. Baker used numerous unscrupulous practices to assure its control of the lucrative government trade, undermined its competition, and bought political favours. The company also abused its privileged position by delivering substandard food to reserves, probably with the collusion of government officials. By 1883, reports of tainted food and reserve deaths were common. In addition, government regulations that kept the distribution of provisions on reserves to a minimum required to sustain life exacerbated the TB problem and led to provisions rotting in storehouses even as the reserve population suffered from malnutrition. The level of control over First Nations by this time was such that even low-ranking officials of the Department of Indian Affairs often had the power of life or death over the people whom they were entrusted to oversee. The unsanctioned abuse of departmental authority led to widespread reports of sexual and other forms of exploitation in communities. As might be expected, tension mounted, and violence broke out in the winter of 1885.

Chapter 9 deals with the aftermath of 1885, when the indigenous population of many parts of western Canada declined to its demographic nadir. Completion of the CPR signalled that subjugation of the treaty population was complete. With the infrastructure in place for large-scale settlement and the establishment of agrarian capitalism, the well-being of indigenous people in the west largely disappeared from the public agenda. Bands considered to have been hostile during the insurrection were punished. Their food rations were cut off, and their weapons and horses were confiscated. Reserves became centres of incarceration as the infamous "pass system" was imposed to control movements of the treaty population. While hundreds fled to the United States to avoid retribution, thousands took advantage of a government plan to reduce the financial burden on the Department of Indian Affairs by renouncing their status as Indians and taking Métis scrip. Flight and the adoption of a new legal status reduced the reserve population significantly. The synergy between pre-existing sickness, hunger, and the spread of contagious diseases such as measles along the improved transportation system based on railway travel increased mortality in reserve populations that were bearing a massive disease load. In 1889–90, a global influenza pandemic spread to the region, and the spike in mortality in Saskatchewan reserve communities already weakened by years of hunger and sickness brought them to their low ebb. In Alberta, the population nadir would occur a decade later, largely the result of a lobbying campaign by ranchers to ensure government contracts for their livestock.

By the 1890s, tuberculosis was increasingly seen as a hereditary disease by government officials. Because the problem was perceived to result from the indigenous way of life, officials and the Canadian public could downplay sickness and mortality levels on reserves because, to a significant degree, they viewed the suffering as nature taking its course. Establishment of the residential school system, now widely recognized as a national disgrace, ensconced TB infection, malnutrition, and abuse in an institutional setting that endured for most of the twentieth century. Now, in the twenty-first century, it is for all Canadians to recognize the collective burden imposed on its indigenous population by the state even as it opened the country to our immigrant ancestors to recast the land to suit the needs of the global economy in the late nineteenth century.

INDIGENOUS HEALTH, ENVIRONMENT,
AND DISEASE BEFORE EUROPEANS

I T HAS BEEN ALMOST FIFTY YEARS SINCE AMERICAN SCHOLAR Henry Dobyns shocked the academic community with the proposition that the indigenous population of North America at contact with Europeans might have been 90 million people.[1] Since then, an army of researchers has entered the fray over the true impact of Europeans on the historical trajectory of native America. Defenders of Dobyns, known in the field as "high counters," have argued that populations could have declined as much as 95 percent as previously unseen microbes literally decimated large and vulnerable populations. Proponents of much lower population losses have vilified Dobyns and his adherents, even mocking demographic estimates as "Numbers from Nowhere."[2] Although scholars would probably agree that the severity of population decline and the suffering unleashed on the indigenous people of America were unprecedented, those seeking a precise quantitative resolution to what has been described as an "American Holocaust" on estimates of number of dwellings and number of people within them will probably never come to a satisfactory conclusion. Sadly, the limits of archaeology and the passage of centuries will keep us from ever going beyond informed speculation about the size of the indigenous population on a continental scale and having a full account of the population decline as a consequence of their encounter with Europeans and their microbes.

Although their work has been largely overshadowed by the fight over the magnitude of the horror unleashed by Columbian encounter, researchers have made great strides in the understanding of health and disease in prehistoric North America. Three decades ago Jane Buikstra's edited volume *Prehistoric Tuberculosis in the Americas* showed beyond a doubt that tuberculosis was endemic to the New World, present long before the arrival of Europeans.[3] In addition to TB, prehistoric populations were subject to a host of diseases, including hepatitis, polio, intestinal parasites, encephalitis, arthritis, pinta, Chagas' disease, and American leishmaniasis, a disease of the skin and mucous membranes caused by parasites.[4] We know that North America was not a disease-free paradise before the arrival of Europeans. Advances in both historical climate change and archaeology are contributing to new and perhaps unsettling insights into the changes across much of the continent in the centuries before Columbus.

A stark example can be found in the small community of Crow Creek, South Dakota. Sometime after the turn of the fourteenth century, 500 people, already suffering from malnutrition, were killed and mutilated, their community burned around their bodies and their bones left exposed to scavengers.[5] Soon a new village was built by the invaders on top of the killing grounds.[6] The carnage at Crow Creek was but one manifestation of the hardship experienced across the northern hemisphere resulting from an intense climatic downturn that began in the mid-thirteenth century.[7] Across the eastern half of the continent, from the Arctic to the Mississippi Delta, indigenous societies experienced profound disruption and significant decline in their population as their way of life became unsustainable in the new and unforgiving climate regime. For many societies, the depth and duration of harsh conditions and the resulting social disruptions might have meant that their peak populations did not occur on the eve of the first introduced epidemics but might actually have occurred centuries earlier.

Before the upheaval of the thirteenth century, societies on both sides of the Atlantic had experienced four centuries of growth and development fuelled by favourable climatic conditions equivalent to those of the 1960s. Depending on the geographical region, the period is known variously as the "Climatic Optimum," the "Medieval Warm Period," the "Medieval Climatic Anomaly," or the "Neo-Atlantic Climatic Episode."[8] In North America, 400 years of good weather reshaped both the natural and the human landscapes of the continent. In the far north, the Thule ancestors of the historical Inuit expanded from Alaska to Greenland, hunting whales from large boats in the open water of the Arctic Ocean

Crow Creek bone bed. *Courtesy of the University of South Dakota Archaeology Laboratory.*

and living in villages of stone houses while Norse settlers planted cereal crops in Greenland.[9] For the northern Great Plains and the adjacent forests, archaeologists David Meyer and Scott Hamilton described the climate during this period simply as "benign."[10]

In the halcyon years between 800 and 1200 CE, societies from the Atlantic to the Dakotas revolutionized their food base as they added the horticultural triumvirate of corn, beans, and squash to their diets.[11] Archaeologically, the people who spread the technology, and taste, for corn and its related crops are known as Late Woodland cultures.[12] The heart of the vast cultural and economic network that spread through the eastern half of the continent was the metropolis of Cahokia, a city of as many as 20,000 people in 1100 CE.[13] Its large population, surpassed only by that of Philadelphia at the end of the eighteenth century, and its huge earthen mounds, mark it as the apex of social organization and social stratification in prehistoric North America.[14]

From Cahokia and other centres near the confluence of the Ohio, Mississippi, and Missouri Rivers, farming spread quickly to Iowa, Wisconsin, and Minnesota, where it was adopted by the Siouan-speaking Oneota people.[15] Farther north the addition of corn-based horticulture to hunting and wild rice harvesting propelled the expansion of a people known to archaeologists as Blackduck from the boundary waters region to the interlakes of Manitoba to the shores of Lake Superior, where they lived alongside the Laurel people of the Canadian Shield.[16] Around 1000

CE, a hybrid group, called the Rainy Lake Composite, developed from their Laurel and Blackduck neighbours. The new group might have been the ancestors of the historical Anishinabe or Ojibwa people.[17] To the west, the ancestors of the Siouan-speaking Mandan and Hidatsa were establishing "semi-sedentary" villages in North and South Dakota along the Missouri River, where they added gardening to their traditions of hunting and gathering.[18] The most northerly of these villages was only 200 kilometres south of the forty-ninth parallel.

The horticultural wave that swept across the eastern half of the continent during the Neo-Atlantic Climate Episode stopped abruptly at the Missouri villages, though long-distance trade networks brought corn as far north as the Carrot River near the lower Saskatchewan River and other locations across the boreal forest of central Canada.[19] Archaeologist Dale Walde has shown that climate was not the limiting factor in the westward march of cultivation. Communities that continued to specialize in bison hunting did so because their material needs were more than adequately met.[20] Walde asserted that prehistoric populations on the Canadian plains, rather than small, nomadic, band-level societies, were large, sophisticated, "tribally" organized communities made up of as many as 1,000 individuals working communally to produce "an almost industrial level of resource exploitation."[21] These large groups provided enough labour to drive herds over large distances and then kill and process them, creating large surpluses of food that were traded (often for corn and other crops) or stockpiled for future use. Food surpluses gave communities time to pursue quests for more than just food, developing formal institutions within them based on age, gender, or expertise. Instead of roaming the plains in search of food, these communities were semi-sedentary, remaining in place for as long as six months at a time, alternating between river valley complexes and the open plains.[22] Because these communities were pedestrian, with only dogs as beasts of burden, the distance between winter and summer residences was probably not more than a walk of a few days.

The good conditions of the Neo-Atlantic Climate Episode contributed to the long-term build-up of the biomass of the region, in turn reinforcing the well-being and stability of bison-hunting communities on the northern plains. Before 1000 CE, only two distinct technological traditions were present on the Canadian plains. Archaeologists refer to them as the Besant and Avonlea phases.[23] Besant sites first appeared on the eastern plains of Minnesota about 200 BCE. Makers of Avonlea technology first appeared in the arid southern plains of Alberta and Saskatchewan three centuries later. Avonlea sites are so widespread that Walde cautioned that their makers should not be thought of as a people or single ethnicity; instead, they were probably from a variety of ethnic backgrounds sharing technology—especially the bow and arrow—as a sign of "mutual support," perhaps in the face of Besant encroachment from the east.[24] By the turn of the first millennium, a new tradition called Old Woman's emerged in southern Alberta. The makers of Old Woman's technology are acknowledged to be the ancestors of the historical Niitsitapi or Blackfoot people. Over time, they gradually replaced Avonlea in the region.[25]

The end of the centuries-long period of growth, development, and stability came swiftly and brutally. Hemispheric conditions changed so rapidly that they have been attributed to a single cataclysmic event, a huge volcanic explosion in 1259 CE.[26] Recent scientific scholarship has recognized volcanism as a trigger for abrupt, large-scale climate change and that "LIA (Little Ice Age) summer cold and ice growth began abruptly between 1275 and 1300 AD. ..."[27] Jared Diamond has shown that, when confronted with environmental challenges such as those that came with the deteriorating climate of the late thirteenth century, the choices made by communities were the difference between success and oblivion over the long term. In Greenland, rigid adherence to unsustainable European farming practices marked the beginning of the end for Norse settlement, while their indigenous neighbours shifted their subsistence strategies across the arctic, adapting to the harsh conditions and surviving in the long term.[28] Far to the south, societies that had grown and prospered with the adoption of corn and related crops were especially hard hit. Some, like the horticultural villages of New York State and southern Quebec, came together after several generations of conflict and privation to form the League of the Iroquois, a sophisticated system of governance and diplomacy that continues to function today.[29]

Many others were not so fortunate. The most spectacular failure during this period of climatic decline was the disintegration of Cahokia. By the turn of the fourteenth century, the city was losing its grip on its vast hinterland.[30] Soon, Cahokia itself was abandoned. By the 1450s, portions of the American Bottoms, the heartland of what had been an almost continental system of trade and ideology, were so depopulated that they are referred to in the archaeological literature as the "Vacant Quarter."[31] Violence undoubtedly accompanied the failure of the cities of the region as the masses, including those whose labour had built the massive mound complexes by hand, lost faith in the religious elite, who were unable to maintain control in the face of repeated large-scale crop failure. Outside the crumbling metropolis, once bountiful villages found their new way of life untenable. The abandonment of Woodland villages was so widespread that it triggered a wave of migration from Texas to Minnesota as whole societies turned west in search of refuge. The invasion of Crow Creek was but one tragic episode in a process that must have been repeated hundreds of times as large, sophisticated, and desperate communities overtook smaller and less powerful settlements across the midwest. The exodus of the Siouan-speaking Oneota people from their homeland in Wisconsin, Illinois, and Iowa toward the Great Plains, where they overtook the inhabitants of the Central Plains tradition in western Iowa and Nebraska, has been described as "colonial expansion."[32] Other Siouan communities that abandoned their homes in the Ohio Valley are thought to be the ancestors of several nations west of the Mississippi, including the Ponca, Quawpaw, Osage, and Omaha.[33] In Minnesota near the northern extension of the horticultural revolution, the Mortlach people, the Siouan ancestors of the historical Nakota or Assiniboine, fled the woodlands for the security of the herds in the west. Soon they were ensconced on both sides of the forty-ninth parallel from Manitoba and North Dakota to Saskatchewan and eastern Montana, displacing the local Old Woman's population from their territory.[34] Even in their new home on the plains, they maintained their ties to corn with regular trade with the Missouri villages, a tradition that endured until the nineteenth century.[35]

The Mortlach migration was the most significant intrusion of people into the Canadian plains during this difficult period. Smaller groups, such as the displaced communities of the Scattered Village Complex, almost certainly came north to Canada as refugees from the conflict along the Missouri near the turn of the fifteenth century.[36] Known in Manitoba as the Vickers Focus, they were experts in their craft, intensively planting maize in optimal locations with good growing conditions along the Red River and in the Tiger Hills south of Brandon.[37] In western Manitoba, they persisted for decades until a "sudden, drastic cold spike during the little ice age," probably caused by the cataclysmic explosion of Mount Kuwae in 1453–54, forced them to flee the region.[38] Later Vickers Focus ceramics found in southeastern Saskatchewan were found with "huge amounts of bison bone, suggesting a full adaptation to mass killing of bison."[39] With their move to Saskatchewan, the conversion of Vickers Focus people from horticulturalists to big-game hunters was complete. In doing so, they took on a subsistence strategy shared by all other late-prehistoric societies on the Canadian prairies.

With the exception of a protohistoric group known as One Gun (discussed in the next chapter), Besant, Avonlea, Old Woman's, Mortlach, and Vickers Focus represent all major prehistoric populations of the Canadian plains. All were large-scale, tribally organized societies, either immigrants from the eastern woodlands or profoundly influenced by them.[40] Many characteristics of these large communities survived until well into the historical period. Before the devastating smallpox epidemic of the 1780s, fur trader Alexander Henry described a Nakota–Assiniboine village in the parklands comprised of "about two hundred tents, each containing from two to four families," a community so large that the chief employed a "town crier" to inform the community of his orders and a group he called "soldiers" to enforce them.[41]

These communities used complex strategies to manage the resources available to them on the prairie landscape. Fire was an especially efficient tool in the control of their food supply, flames pushing prey to pounds or jumps where they were killed or drawing herds to areas of new growth in the spring and early summer. A critical factor in the success of pedestrian bison hunting was the need to steer prey to their place of death without significantly disrupting the movement of the greater herd.[42] In practising non-disruptive hunting, the hunters could rely on herd movements and repeatedly use kill sites, thereby giving hunting communities access to their staple food while maintaining a high degree of residential stability.

Although all of the inhabitants of the plains enjoyed a reliable food supply, they shared a vulnerability that continues to limit human occupation of the plains to the present: the need for a dependable supply of water. The large size and limited mobility of prehistoric communities in a drought-prone area undoubtedly made access to water a primary concern. To meet the challenge, the indigenous population developed a water management strategy that buffered them from the effects of even long-term drought. Ecological studies have shown that the Avonlea tradition and the Old Woman's tradition that grew from it purposefully abstained from beaver hunting as a means of managing the amount of available water. Archaeologist Grace Morgan wrote that "bison were the staff of life," though beaver "were at the core of a profound ideological framework which prized the role of the beaver in the stabilization of water resources."[43] The relationship between the species and plains people is so deep that religious practices involving beaver medicine bundles continue to hold deep significance among the Niitsitapi people even in the twenty-first century.[44]

Armed with these key strategies, non-disruptive bison hunting and the preservation of beaver to ensure a reliable supply of food and water, plains bison hunters not only averted the hardship endured by their neighbours in the eastern woodlands but also appear to have flourished in the centuries prior to contact. There is no question that a diet based on a plentiful and reliable supply of bison afforded a high degree of nutrition. Physical anthropologists have described nineteenth-century bison hunters as the "tallest in the world."[45] Members of societies that maintained a continental system of communication and trade without the assistance of horses must have been incredibly fit, since running would have been integral to the maintenance of ties and trade.[46] Buffalo runners were used to reconnoitre the movements of herds, and several strategies, including persistence hunting, were employed in the quest for other game. Largely forgotten during the twentieth century, the latter involves the pursuit of prey, on foot, until the hunter overtakes the animal, which has been immobilized by exhaustion and hyperthermia. This form of chase hunting was common to hunter-gatherers from Africa to Australia to western North America and might have been a factor in the evolution of our species.[47] In Saskatchewan, Samuel Acoose, whose son was a world-famous runner, ran down a deer from Moose Mountain to the Qu'Appelle Valley in the early twentieth century.

Although prehistoric people on the Canadian plains avoided many of the hardships of their woodland neighbours, they were not entirely immune from disease. Because of the occasional effect of tuberculosis on bone, there is evidence of a single case of TB in Saskatchewan from about 1,000 years ago.[48] Because TB is a disease triggered by poverty and malnutrition, those who relied on the herds were less prone to it than their counterparts in the woodlands, who were experiencing severe privation. A discussion of prehistoric TB in North America published in 2003 identified only two individuals from the northern plains with skeletal evidence of TB, in contrast to clusters of infected human remains in the southwest and eastern woodlands.[49] The nature of archaeological discovery precludes a statistical analysis of TB infection rates, but the chronological ordering of all cases found in North America indicates that infection was much more common in the period 1200–1399 CE than in the centuries before and after.[50]

1	Stone Grave	31	Chaco
2	Prehistoric Iroquois	32	Pecos Pueblo
3	Owasco Culture	33	Kechipawan
4	Middle Point Peninsula	34	Hawikku
5	M.T. 17	35	San Cristobal
6	Emmons Cemetery	36	Tonto Basin
7	Chucalissa	37	AZ Q:15:1
8	Crable Site	38	Eldon Pueblo
9	Fairty Ossuary	39	Cowboy Wash
10	Bennett Site	40	Subway Route 2
11	Schild Site	41	Tlatelolco
12	Moundville	42	Los Reyes de la Paz
13	Irene Mound	43	Tecualilla
14	Parkin	44	Chalpa
15	Daw's Island	45	Cuzco
16	Turpin Site	46	El Palito
17	Arnold	47	Hacienda Aqua Salada
18	Averbuch	48	Los Médanos
19	Norris Farms #36	49	Chongos
20	Kane Mounds	50	Montegrande
21	Uxbridge	51	Huayuri
22	Woodlawn Site	52	Caserones
23	Hardin Village	53	Estuquiña
24	Slack Farm	54	Chiribaya Alta,
25	Jamestown Mounds		San Gerónimo,
26	Pueblo Bonito		Yaral
27	Chavez Pass	55	Algodonal
28	AZ J:5:49	56	AZ 71
29	Point of Pines	57	AZ 140, AZ 141, SRI
30	Tocito	58	Marín
		59	La Mesa de Los Santos

● Sites with one case of TB

▲ Sites with 2 or more cases

Map of the Western Hemisphere indicating the location of all sites where human remains with lesions suggestive of tuberculosis cases have been found. Source: Charlotte A. Roberts and Jane E. Buikstra, *The Bioarchaeology of Tuberculosis: A Global View on a Reemerging Disease*, 2003, fig. 4.1, p. 191. *Reprinted with permission of the University Press of Florida.*

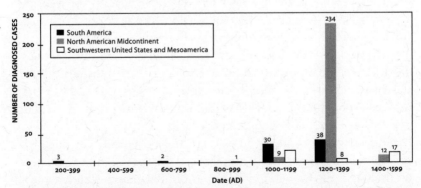

Histogram illustrating distribution of ancient tuberculosis through time. Source: Charlotte A. Roberts and Jane E. Buikstra, *The Bioarchaeology of Tuberculosis: A Global View on a Reemerging Disease*, 2003, fig. 4.2, p. 194. *Reprinted with permission of the University Press of Florida.*

9

The disease we know as TB is caused by a family of germs described in the medical literature as the *Mycobacterium tuberculosis* complex, the two most important of which, *M. tuberculosis* and *M. bovis,* are "indistinguishable" clinically, radiologically, and pathologically in human infections.[51] A significant difference between the human form of the disease (*M. tuberculosis*) and *M. bovis,* whose primary hosts include domestic cattle and bison,[52] is that the latter is as much as ten times more likely to produce symptoms outside the lungs, including lymph glands, organs, and bones.[53] As early as the 1950s, pathological evidence of Pott's disease, tuberculosis of the spine, along with ceramic depictions of individuals with the disease from New York State, Tennessee, Arkansas, and Missouri, among others, led researchers to hypothesize that the illness represented "may be of animal origin from tuberculous buffalo."[54]

In their survey of global tuberculosis, Roberts and Buikstra postulated that, in Pre-Columbian America, "the bovine form of tuberculosis may have been as common as the human type," and other studies have asserted that the intersection of poverty and infection from animals "probably contributed most to its occurrence [TB] in past populations."[55] Veterinary studies from the twentieth century have shown that under conditions of stress bison are extremely susceptible to TB, and the consumption of dried meat from infected animals could easily spread to humans.[56]

Because many infections left no trace on remains that have survived the centuries, we will never see the full picture of disease among the prehistoric peoples of North America. Since lesions resulting from TB infection scarred the bones of its ancient sufferers, we can understand something of its spread through Pre-Columbian communities. For the prehistoric people of the northern Great Plains, the nutrition afforded by reliance on bison as a staple food held TB and probably other diseases triggered by privation at bay. As connection of the region to the modern world system took hold, introduced diseases, the most virulent of which was smallpox, did not discriminate between the healthy and the underfed: all were equally susceptible to sickness and death as infection spread from the Old World to communities in the Canadian west that, in some cases, had never encountered a European in the flesh. The introduction of Old World diseases, the most deadly of which was smallpox, almost completely overshadowed TB as a significant burden of disease on the Canadian prairies until the late nineteenth century, after the former was controlled by medical intervention.[57]

THE EARLY FUR TRADE: TERRITORIAL DISLOCATION AND DISEASE

DESCRIPTIONS OF GAME SCARCITY AND HUMAN LOSSES FROM epidemic diseases have been present since some of the earliest written accounts from western Canada. There is no physical or documentary evidence of a widespread and deadly "disorder" among game animals in the archaeological record, but by the 1760s HBC employees were reporting game shortages along the North Saskatchewan River.[1] The decline in fur bearers might have been the result of commercial hunting. Archaeological studies on the northern Great Plains have uncovered the influence of the fur trade from as early as the 1670s.[2]

Although the fate of the human populations in the region has garnered more interest from researchers, our understanding of the early disease history of the northern Great Plains and adjacent regions remains sketchy at best. Recognizing the arrival and impact of epidemic disease is crucial to understanding the historical experience of indigenous populations. A key concept in understanding the severity of early outbreaks is the phenomenon known as "virgin soil epidemic" or VSE. Described as the single most significant event of a community's demographic history, a VSE occurs when a pathogen infects a population for the first time or when enough time has passed since a previous exposure that even the oldest members of the community have not experienced the disease. In either case, no one has acquired immunity from enduring the sickness, and the entire population can be infected.[3] Mortality from initial infections of smallpox has been estimated to be as high as 70 percent or more. Survivors can be sick and debilitated for long periods. Under these circumstances, food procurement strategies break down since often there is no one with the physical ability to hunt or collect food. Those with the dubious good fortune of living through the initial sickness can slowly die from hunger.

VSEs might have spread through entire regions before Europeans were present to document the horror, so we will never know precisely how bad it was. Yet we know that the mortality was horrific and the impact permanent. Archaeologist Karl Schlesier bluntly stated that epidemic mortality as high as 90 to 95 percent made surviving indigenous communities "poverty cultures when compared with the richness of the past."[4] The reality of the young and strong, the warriors, hunters, collectors, and child bearers, in addition to political and religious leaders and keepers of tribal knowledge (maintained through oral traditions), perishing in a historical instant—in the span of weeks or a few months— surely had a fundamental impact on the social networks, institutions, and collective memories of entire First Nations.

Microbes were the swiftest and most potent force in the environmental process described by Alfred Crosby as the ecological conquest of the New World. Disease came in lockstep as Europeans established beachheads on the eastern seaboard of North America. Some, such as historian and psychiatrist David S. Jones, have argued that the interaction of disease and the influence of the colonial encounter on the social cultural and physical environments of indigenous communities have a greater role in the outcome of epidemics than genetic susceptibility.[5] In some cases, like that of the arrival of the *Mayflower,* celebrated each November by hundreds of millions of Americans, disease preceded the arrival of settlers, clearing the way for what was considered to be a providential feast among the newcomers.[6] Despite their catastrophic impact on indigenous communities, the time and distance required for trans-Atlantic travel actually limited the spread of disease to the New World. During sea voyages lasting six weeks or more, infections aboard ship often ran their natural courses and expired before landfall.

Low population densities in the new colonies coupled with the short life cycle of pathogens prevented most Old World infections, the most dangerous of which was smallpox, from becoming endemic or self-sustaining until the end of the eighteenth century, 150 years or more after their introduction to the continent.[7]

In Canada, the slow pace of French settlement along the St. Lawrence River stalled the spread of epidemic diseases for a generation after initial outbreaks in the English and Dutch colonies on the Atlantic seaboard. With the exception of a few missionaries and traders, few people left the relative safety of the French colony. Instead, the Huron Nation and its allies undertook the exchange of furs for European trade goods as the commercial economy took root. In keeping with long-standing practices, the Huron also produced corn, squash, beans, and tobacco for consumption for both settlers and fur producers in the interior. Their dominance of the early trade with the French, though, proved to be their undoing. As contact increased, the transportation routes that they controlled soon became effective vectors of disease. By the 1630s, imported strains of measles, influenza, and smallpox swept through the First Nations adjacent to the French colony, reducing the indigenous population of the region by half.[8]

Despite unprecedented mortality, the effect of epidemics was to expand the geographical sphere of the trade as new parties on the margins were brought in to make up for losses closer to the source of infection.[9] By the 1650s, war and disease brought defeat and dispersal to a number of indigenous allies of the French, including the Huron, the Neutral, the Petun, and the Nipissing. Their military and economic rivals, members of the League of the Iroquois or Haudenosaunee, took control of the trade and almost immediately brought infections as far north as the James Bay coast.[10] Without indigenous allies, the French headed west themselves, the first "voyageurs" leaving the colony in the spring of 1653.[11] Within a year, traders and missionaries were west of Lake Michigan. As French influence spread toward the centre of the continent, men known as *coureurs de bois* ("wood runners") wintered in the hinterland collecting furs directly from producers. The Haudenosaunee, of course, undermined attempts of the French to expand their influence at every opportunity, but their defeat at the hands of the French in 1666 cut short their opposition to the ever-growing trade.[12] By 1672, an estimated 400 unsanctioned traders were operating beyond the colony, a significant number since the total population of the colony was only a few thousand.[13] As was becoming the norm, trade brought disease. In 1670, smallpox spread to Sault Ste. Marie, hundreds of kilometres west of the settlements of New France.[14]

Unlike earlier outbreaks along the St. Lawrence, the 1670 epidemic was less severe because some communities had developed immunity from previous exposure to the disease. The arrival of the English in the north also tempered the effect of the epidemic. When the *Nonsuch* wintered at the mouth of the Rupert River in 1668–69, many fur producers were drawn north to James Bay, away from their usual rendezvous in the colony and almost certain infection.[15]

The success of Captain Gillam's trading expedition was an important milestone leading to the creation of the Hudson's Bay Company in 1670. In little more than a decade, the company was operating a number of trading posts along the coast and developing a vast network of trade relations with the peoples of the interior. For almost a century, the dominant trading strategy of the HBC was to build posts at the mouths of important waterways (the only significant means of long-distance travel through the subarctic environment) and wait for those with furs to trade to come to them. The economic influence of these scattered outposts was soon felt thousands of kilometres inland, but from a disease perspective the tiny enclaves of Europeans (and their germs) had little impact on the medical history of the region. Indeed, the small number of men who occupied the posts, the length of travel from England (as long as seven weeks in the eighteenth century), and, for the most part, the limited contact during trading sessions served as accidental quarantines, reducing the threat of introduced infections. The traders themselves were probably exposed to many diseases, including smallpox in childhood, and thus were largely immune from infection.

Rather than posing a biological threat to the inhabitants of the northern interior of the continent, HBC employees themselves were at risk in the early years of the trade. Scurvy was a particular problem, especially at York Factory, where fresh fish were often scarce. Tuberculosis, contracted in England, lurked in the crowded living conditions of the posts. Although intimate relations were formally banned between HBC employees and indigenous women, sexually transmitted infections were reported in company records, but the limited nature of interaction with First Nations women served to control the spread of many diseases until the middle of the eighteenth century.[16]

The thinly manned outposts strung along the subarctic coast had little biological impact on the indigenous populations of western Canada, but their presence quickly brought profound changes to the economic orientation of many communities. During the first century of the fur trade in western Canada, the period known to scholars as the "middleman trade," aboriginal groups took on the role of brokers between fur producers thousands of kilometres from the sea and Europeans on the coast. Eventually, some took on regular journeys as long as 3,600 kilometres to exchange furs for trade goods. The Cree and later the Chipewyan Dene pioneered the role, literally taking the modern world system to the interior of western Canada. They quickly expanded their spheres of influence in the historic period and triggered the first waves of significant population movement in the western interior.

The doyen of modern fur trade history, Arthur Ray, argued that these early territorial changes were the result of a peculiar mix of "the coat beaver orientation of the early industry, the socioeconomic organization of subarctic native people, the economic behaviour, and the impacts that disease and warfare had on their population."[17] Coat, or greasy, beaver, as the early product was known, meant furs that had been sewn into clothing and worn—sometimes for several years—until the stiff guard hairs had been worn off, leaving only the soft underwool of the pelt. Each coat was made up of from five to eight skins. Coat beaver pelts were most desired by the Europeans because, until the turn of the eighteenth century, processors lacked the technology to remove the unwanted guard hairs in the production of beaver hats. Ray called the European preference for worn clothing "a godsend to the aboriginal people, by affording them the use and exchange value for their beaver pelts."[18] Good prices paid for cast-off apparel soon drove middlemen beyond their own territories in search of the worn pelts that the Europeans wanted so badly. This was the case with many Cree and Anishinabe (Ojibwa) middlemen, who moved into new territory even before beaver supplies were diminished significantly in their homelands.

The organization of aboriginal societies in the subarctic also served to shape the early fur trade. Low population density in the interior limited trade; the small number of aboriginal hunters, middlemen, and transporters probably influenced the trade more than local availability of beaver did. The boreal forest imposed stern environmental limits on the inhabitants of the region. In the 1760s, a trader wrote that

> Such is the inhospitality of the country over which they wander, that only a single family can live together in the winter season; and this sometimes seeks sustenance in vain, on an area of five hundred square miles. They can stay in one place till they have destroyed all the hares; and when these fail, they have no resource but in the leaves and shoots of trees, or in defect of these, in cannibalism.[19]

Although scarcity and hunger were all too common, the small and dispersed population of the boreal forest limited the spread of disease when it eventually spread to the region.

This was especially the case in winter when family-sized groups often travelled into the forest in search of solitary game animals such as moose. In summer, when plentiful food resources brought hundreds of people together, disease was much more likely to spread. The smallpox outbreak at Sault Ste. Marie in 1670, for example, occurred during a gathering during the annual fishery.[20]

Another factor contributing to territorial realignment in the early years of the trade was the economic behaviour of different populations involved in the system. Middlemen quickly developed specialized economic strategies to maximize benefits. Profits could be great, but they were not achieved without significant risks. Trade journeys were long and arduous, some lasting as long as five months. Drowning and death from exposure were common, and almost all middlemen experienced near starvation.[21] Only the strongest men and women undertook the journey to and from the coast. Children, the old, and the infirm remained in the home territory to rely on dependable summer resources such as the fishery.

Aboriginal traders periodically suffered from the breakdown of the precarious link between Europe and Hudson Bay. When the French controlled Hudson Bay, from 1680 to 1713, they were unable to deliver supplies to the region for four years in succession. The French occupation of the bay posts coincided with a long period of extreme cold that sent temperatures plummeting across the northern hemisphere.[22] On their arrival at the coast, Cree middlemen could find storehouses empty, the traders themselves in need, and be forced to return to their homes empty-handed. Supply lines were scarcely more reliable when the English returned to the bay. When the company supply ship failed to reach York Factory in the spring of 1716, fifty canoes of "Mountain and Askee Cree" were turned away without trade goods.[23] At the coast, they were infected with an illness that led to many deaths, prompting the company to provide special presents in recognition of their hardship on their return the following year.[24] The consequences of failed trading expeditions could be just as dire for those left at home. The absence of able-bodied men and the strongest women left families without hunters and protectors for months at a time every summer, and the permanent loss of the strongest and most productive adults to disease, starvation, and drowning was an ever-present threat to the stability of communities that took on the role of middlemen. Clearly, those that assumed such risks would not have done so had it not been to their advantage.

Another cause of territorial dislocation was military conflict between First Nations over control of access to European goods. Warfare was a major factor in the breakdown of the middleman trade of the Huron and their allies in the mid-seventeenth century. West of Hudson Bay, the advantage gained by proximity of the Cree to English traders and their integration into the trade sparked decades of conflict as they encroached on the land of the Chipewyan Dene in search of furs. Only after the HBC built Fort Prince of Wales at the mouth of the Churchill River in 1717 could the Dene, or northern Indians as they were known to the traders, acquire firearms in sufficient numbers to break the Cree stranglehold on the interior trade.[25]

Disease, of course, played a central part in the territorial change that came with the expansion of commercial trade. Because of their closeness to the source of infection, middleman groups were often exposed to European pathogens earlier than the isolated inland communities. The initial harm brought on by direct contact and infection became a biological advantage to the middlemen since those who survived infections developed immunity from subsequent outbreaks. In the northwest, the epidemic experience of Cree and Dene in the boreal forest was less intense than the experience of the Huron in the early French trade. Because of their position adjacent to New France, disease spread among them in a series of attacks between 1630 and 1650. Under pressure from disease and the military onslaught from Haudenosaunee rivals, Huron society buckled. No such source of regular infection existed in western Canada.

In the second decade of the eighteenth century, political events in Europe brought new momentum to the spread of European influence in western Canada. In 1713, the Treaty of Utrecht ended a quarter-century of war between the French and English. Trading posts on the Hudson Bay coast (and access to the western interior of the continent) held by the French for a generation were returned to the Hudson's Bay Company. With hostilities abated, the French reopened the Great Lakes and Ohio Valley to sanctioned commerce. The re-establishment of their inland networks soon cut into the English trade that depended on the arduous journeys of middlemen for their supply of furs. The reinvigorated French activity in the midwest forced the HBC to look northward for a new supply of furs. Governor James Knight was charged with extending the trade directly to the Dene people on the northern margins of the boreal forest. To succeed, he needed to stabilize relations among the Cree, Chipewyan, and other Dene speakers as far inland as Lake Athabasca who had been at war for decades.[26] In 1715, he sent William Stuart, the Chipewyan woman Thanadelthur, and a party of perhaps 150 Cree men, women, and children inland from York Factory to find the Chipewyan and make peace with them. They returned a year later with a truce.[27] The peace came with a price, however; the expedition had been plagued with sickness, starvation, and violence. The casualties included expedition leader Stuart, who returned a broken man, dying a "lunatic" in 1719. Other inland parties, such as the one sent to the southwestern plains in 1716, simply disappeared, thought to have perished from starvation.[28]

As the British company struggled to augment its fragile trade network, a limited outbreak of smallpox occurred at York Factory in 1720. Sickness did not spread inland, but infection of the local Homeguard Cree marked the first instance of it among them.[29] By the mid-1720s, the tenuous Chipewyan trade was undermined by the resumption of war between them and the Cree.[30] Because the Churchill hinterland was rich in furs, the HBC continued to pursue the difficult but potentially lucrative northern trade.

In 1727, the appointment of Pierre Gaultier, Sieur de la Vérendrye, as commander of the French posts in the western hinterland ushered in a period of unprecedented European expansion. Until then, the limit of direct French occupation was the north shore of Lake Superior.[31] Under his command, the route known as the Grande Portage, a fourteen-kilometre trail around the rapids of the Pigeon River not far from Lake Superior, was developed, laying the foundation for the Canadian-based fur trade for decades to come. Yet Grande Portage opened a passage for the spread of disease well beyond the Great Lakes. By 1731, French traders had built Fort St. Pierre, near the present community of Fort Frances, in far western Ontario.[32] The next year they pushed west again, establishing a post on Lake of the Woods. From there, traders could reach the Winnipeg River and the prairies beyond. Expansion of the French trade to the edge of the Canadian Shield cut even deeper into English trade at the bay. When only sixteen of the usual sixty canoes from Lake Winnipeg arrived at the bay in 1732, Governor Maclish wrote that "the rest went to the French at the first of this summer, not for their being more kindly Used by the French but entirely out of Fear." Wood-runners, "doubtless from Fort St. Pierre," had travelled as far as the territory of the Sturgeon Indians on the lower Saskatchewan River and almost completely diverted trade away from York Factory.[33]

Arrival of the French in the boundary waters had profound implications for the regional balance of power. They supplied their trading partners—the Cree, the Monsoni Anishinabe, and the Assiniboine—with guns, giving them a significant advantage over their enemies, the Dakota and those allied with them. When the chiefs of Lake Winnipeg asked for a formal alliance, French traders accommodated them by building Fort Rouge on the Red River and Fort Maurepas near the south shore of Lake Winnipeg.[34] These new trade and military allies represented a substantial population, their nation being made up of seven villages, some with as many as 900 households and the smallest with no fewer than 100 dwellings. Soon Fort la Reine was built on the Assiniboine River near the modern community of Portage la Prairie, Manitoba.

Arrival of the French in the region, the transportation corridor east to New France, and contact through cooperation and conflict over access to resources created the ecological conditions that sparked the virgin soil epidemic of smallpox along the boundary waters and interlakes of Manitoba. Within a decade, the regional map would be fundamentally and permanently altered in the aftermath of disease. Historical geographer Paul Hackett traced the origins of the epidemic to a ship that unleashed the pathogen in Boston in 1729. From there, it spread through the English colonies, eventually arriving in Montreal, where it killed 900 people.[35] For smallpox to have spread halfway across the continent, certain criteria had to be met. Without large urban centres in the interior, and with vulnerable populations dispersed across a vast region of the eastern and central woodlands, the virus needed speed to remain viable; the human hosts who served as unwitting carriers of the virus must have travelled swiftly. The incubation or prodromal stage of the disease lasts from nine to sixteen days after infection. Those who carry the germ become infectious between thirteen and twenty days after inhalation of the virus, and the disease is spread through the exhalation of infected individuals. According to historian Steadman Upham, "the total infectious period can last a little more than three weeks (a mean of 26.75 days) and terminates with either the patient's recovery or death. It has long been recognized, however, that the smallpox corpse is a potent and continuing source of infection."[36]

Susceptible populations inland continued to feed victims to the epidemic for years. It reached the Anishinabe community of Chequamegon on the western shore of Lake Superior in 1735.[37] Sickness and death continued their unrelenting spread west. In the spring of 1737, La Vérendrye wrote that sixty Barrier Cree from south of Lake Winnipeg died of smallpox. A year later disease broke out as over 1,000 Cree,

Monsoni, and Assiniboine fighters prepared for an attack on the Sioux, killing enough of the gathered warriors to undermine the expedition before it began.[38] By the 1730s, such large-scale military assaults were becoming all too frequent in the region. The spread of disease to armed gatherings or to the large and densely populated villages proved to be catastrophic. Because of their preference for essentially urban living, the Assiniboine were particularly at risk. La Vérendrye wrote that they were numerous, "never staying in any fixed place, but carrying their dwellings [cabannes] with them continually, and always camping together to form a village."[39] The intersection of their patterns of residence and the epidemiology of smallpox forced the rapid constriction of the territory along the Red River and its hinterland that the Assiniboine had occupied for centuries.[40] Before introduced diseases began their decline, the Assiniboine were the most populous and widely dispersed First Nation in western Canada. Recognizing their geographic range, English traders distinguished between the Assiniboine of the plains and those of the woodlands soon after they established their inland trade. Farther west, Assiniboine guides travelled with Englishman Henry Kelsey through south-central Saskatchewan in 1691.[41] Decades later eastern members of the nation guided the French west to Lake of the Woods.[42] La Vérendrye described their territory while at Fort la Reine in 1741:

> The south side of the [Assiniboin] River belongs to the Assiniboin, who also claim the Red River. They are said to number 14 or 15 villages, of which the smallest have 20 to 30 lodges, while several have 100, 200 and 300. They all speak the same Assiniboin language. They occupy about 300 to 400 leagues of country, all of it prairie.[43]

In the wake of smallpox, fatalities among the Assiniboine led to abandonment of their territory east of the Red River. The position of their allies, the Anishinabe-speaking Monsoni, was also undermined by disease.[44] They controlled the country between Rainy Lake and Lake of the Woods and were long-standing participants in the trade, travelling to Montreal during their time as middlemen and witnessing the ceremony marking French annexation of the region in 1671.[45] During the 1730s, as many as 1,000 Monsoni died of smallpox, leaving 500 or 600 survivors to continue their struggle against the Sioux.[46] In the aftermath of disease, the Monsoni sought to replace those lost to sickness with those taken in war. After a successful incursion of the Sioux, so many were captured that the column was well over 200 metres long.[47] Despite the temporary victory, the Monsoni would never return to their pre-epidemic position of power. The arrival of smallpox marked the beginning of the end for the Monsoni as a discrete population. Many of the survivors were integrated into other groups, and post-epidemic descriptions of the Monsoni usually mention them in association with other groups.[48] They disappear from the historical record altogether by the end of the eighteenth century.

The surviving Monsoni joined others in the wake of epidemics in a regional process of ethnic hybridization. In 1805, a Nor'wester described the process as it occurred north of Lake Superior: "Every old man with whom I conversed, and from who[m] I made some enquiry on this subject, told me that his father or his grand father was from either of these two places [Lake Superior—Ojibwa and Hudson Bay—Cree. ... [The people] began to meet one another in the interior and to intermarry by which they, at length, became one people."[49]

As Assiniboine and Monsoni populations plummeted and their territory shrank, other groups, notably other Anishinabe groups, quickly filled the vacuum, taking advantage of immunity conferred from previous exposure in the east. After losing their position as middlemen when the French themselves moved into the western Great Lakes, they found a new niche as trading partners with the Sioux south of the boundary waters.[50] Before the upheaval of the 1730s epidemics, on occasion the Anishinabe raided Cree middlemen heading to James Bay, but their preference for returning to the Sault in summer for the fishery and trade meant that few of them lived year-round north of Lake Superior.[51] In the wake of disease, the Anishinabe increased their territory dramatically, especially north of Lake Superior. A new ethnic group, the Northern Ojibwa, or Bungee, appear in the HBC record as trading partners with the English in the early 1740s, and they later became frequent and valued customers. Cree mortality in the northern forest from Ontario to the Saskatchewan River essentially opened the country for the expansion of Anishinabe territory. Genetic studies support this explanation of Ojibwa expansion: "the apparent restriction of the gene to Ojibwa suggests recent mutation; its geographic distribution suggests population movement by the descendants of a group in which the mutation first occurred. This scenario fits the ethnohistoric model, which states that Ojibwa resided in the northern Lake Huron–eastern Lake Superior region prior to their westward expansion 300 years ago."[52]

Disease undermined the First Nations allied with the French, but it also brought havoc to the Sioux, who had been fighting for control of the boundary waters region since the 1670s when their alliance with the French broke down.[53] As opponents of the French trade, they struck military blows as far to the east as Lake Superior and, before the 1730s, controlled the prized Rainy Lake–Lake of the Woods corridor.[54] Before the epidemic, their pool of an estimated 2,000 warriors was larger than the Cree, Assiniboine, Monsoni, and Anishinabe alliance.[55] In the aftermath of disease and the realignment of tribal politics that went with it, the Sioux could no longer occupy much of their traditional territory. For at least thirty years after their dislocation, most of northwestern Minnesota remained unoccupied.[56]

The spread of disease to the contested region south and east of Lake Winnipeg from the colonies far to the east was but one wave in the storm of disease that swept across North America in the 1730s. Near the Missouri River, other Dakota communities were hit, infection perhaps spreading from the large annual trade gathering known as the Dakota Rendezvous.[57] Pictographic histories of the Dakota, known as winter counts, record the spread of smallpox among them in 1734–35.[58]

To the south, the Arikara, village-dwelling horticulturalists who lived along the Missouri River, began a precipitous demographic decline about this time. Decades later fur trader J. B. Truteau wrote that "In ancient times the Ricara nation was very large; it counted thirty-two populous villages, now depopulated and almost entirely destroyed by the smallpox, which broke out among them at three different times. A few families only, from each of the villages, escaped; these united and formed the two villages now here. ..."[59] The Arikara experience of epidemic mortality, military pressure from Dakota-speaking groups (themselves displaced by disease and war), and decline was common among other plains horticultural people in the eighteenth century.[60] At the confluence of the Missouri and the Mississippi, smallpox attacked the Lower Loup and Pawnee of Nebraska, contributing to the abandonment of their homelands.[61] Other nations, including the Cherokee and the Kansa, were reduced by as much as half in outbreaks around the 1730s.[62]

The American southwest was also increasingly burdened by smallpox in the first half of the eighteenth century. A boundary region of the Spanish world, it was under both the economic and the biological influence of the cities of Mexico. In Texas, the Spanish missions at San Antonio were entirely depopulated in the 1730s by epidemics and the dispersal of the survivors.[63] Sixty-seven deaths were reported at the Santa Fe mission during a two-month period in 1737.[64] A year later the virus hit the Pecos mission, killing twenty-six infants and young children but only a single adult.[65] By this time, smallpox was becoming a childhood disease among the Pueblos, a sign of their long experience with it. Such a dreaded disease being relegated to the status of mere child killer is a testament to the longevity and stability of the Spanish communities at the fringes of its territory and to the speed of travel along the El Camino Real, the highway between Mexico City and its northern hinterland.

The missions of the southwest were truly at the margins of European control. Beyond them lay the burgeoning territory of Comancheria, the Comanche Empire, a hybrid of indigenous political and economic forces literally built on the back of an Old World species, the horse.[66] Horses had been the focus of raids by the Comanche and their Numic-speaking relatives since at least the 1680s, when the overthrow of colonial authorities in New Mexico and the access to equestrian stock started an unprecedented period of indigenous expansion across a vast region of the western United States. Within a generation, the species was being traded along a "continuous band of Shoshone–Comanche speakers [that] stretched from southern Alberta to southern Colorado along the east slope of the Rockies."[67] A century ago anthropologist Clark Wissler argued that Numic equestrianism created "a direct link between the headwaters of the Rio Grande and the Saskatchewan."[68] From their source in the equestrian "hearth" in the southwest, horses were distributed through a system that quickly and efficiently brought them to the Pacific Northwest, the Plateau, and the Shoshone-controlled northwestern plains.[69] By the 1730s, the Snakes, the group that might have included the Shoshone and other Numic speakers, traded horses with the Crow, Nez Percé, Flathead, and Kutenai.[70] Horses revolutionized the indigenous way of life. As historian John Fahey wrote, "Journeys that once took weeks now took days; those of days, hours. ... Caravans with horses might travel thirty miles in one day; mounted men riding hard, almost a hundred."[71]

By the third decade of the eighteenth century, the speed afforded by equestrianism allowed smallpox to spread along the Numic horse distribution network into the western plains of Canada. Because the territory controlled by the Comanche, Ute, Shoshone, and their allies was under indigenous control and beyond the view of Europeans, we will never have a full understanding of indigenous life in this period or the impact of the vse that spread across the western portion of the continent. Oral histories from several First Nations involved in the horse trade in the Plateau region refer to a severe epidemic and territorial changes in its wake. Kutenai tradition maintains that the Kutenai were driven from the western margins of the plains and into the mountains after their infection with smallpox in the 1730s.[72] The persistence of references to an epidemic for more than 200 years led historian Claude Schaeffer to conclude that "within this framework of uncertainty it seems fairly well established that a group of Kutenai survivors made their way westward from smallpox-decimated camps of the bison range in the early decades of the 18th century."[73] Histories of the Pend d'Oreille and Flathead nations also refer to an early outbreak of smallpox. Schaeffer's interpretation is supported by the persistence among many nations inhabiting the Plateau region of bison-hunting expeditions far to the east on the margins of the plains and in the territory of their traditional enemy the Niitsitapi. With the possible exception of the Lemhi or Salmon Eater Shoshone, the groups undertook these difficult and dangerous annual journeys without an apparent need to do so. As one nineteenth-century trader wrote, "Buffalo is the cause of all their misfortunes ... although their lands abound in plenty of other animals; their hereditary attachment to the buffalo is so unconquerable, that it drives them every year to the plains, where they come into contact with the Blackfeet."[74] By maintaining their ties with the staple food of the plains, they retained their connection to a homeland lost, at least in part, to disease.

The same epidemic reached the northern frontier of Snake expansion, the Red Deer River. Two hundred years earlier, the Snake were drawn northward when their ancestral territory experienced a period of desiccation referred to in the scientific literature as a "megadrought."[75] In the eighteenth century, horses propelled the Snake well into the territory of the Niitsitapi or Blackfoot Alliance, pushing the latter as far north as the North Saskatchewan River.[76] In the 1730s, the Snake, mounted on horses of Iberian origin, battled along the Red Deer with the Cree and Niitsitapi equipped with muskets from England. The northerners had never seen horses, and perhaps the southerners had never seen guns.[77] Both were about to undergo their first attack from smallpox.

David Thompson recounted Saukamappee's experience of the epidemic:

> ... [D]eath came over us all, and swept more than half of us by the smallpox, of which we knew nothing until it brought death among us. We caught it from the Snake Indians. ... We attacked the tents, ... but our war whoop instantly stopped; our eyes were appalled with terror; there was no one to fight with but the dead and the dying, each a mass of corruption.
>
> We did not touch them but left the tents, and held a council on what was to be done. We all thought the bad spirit had made

himself master of the camp and destroyed them. It was agreed to take some of the best of the tents, and any other plunder that was clean and good and we did, and also took away the few horses they had and returned to our camp. The second day after this, this dreadful disease broke out in our camp, and spread from one tent to the other as if the bad spirit carried it. We had no belief that one man could give it to another, any more than a wounded man could give his wound to another. We did not suffer so much as those that were near the river, into which they rushed out and died. We had only a little brook, and about one third of us died, but in some of the other camps there were tents in which everyone died. ... Our hearts were low and dejected, and we shall never be again the same people. To hunt for our families was the sole occupation and [to] kill beavers, wolves and foxes to trade [for] our necessaries; and we thought of war no more, and perhaps would have made peace with them [the enemy], for they had suffered dreadfully as well as us, and had left all this fine country of the Bow River to us.[78]

Saukamappee's story is often considered to be a historical benchmark in the region, but his version of events, or rather those of the many editors of his words as interpreted by Thompson, are subject to conflicting interpretations. Some writers, such as Theodore Binnema and David Smyth, make no mention of epidemic disease in the first half of the eighteenth century, while others, such as Dale Russell, attribute the VSE in the region to have occurred "seemingly in the 1730s."[79] Despite the editorial quibble, the epidemic undermined the Kutenai presence on the western plains and contributed to their retreat to the mountains in the face of Niitsitapi expansion. For the Snakes, the epidemic began their long retreat from the Canadian plains, though conflict persisted until the end of the eighteenth century. As Saukamappee told Thompson, many Piikani died during the outbreak.[80]

It would be a generation before the arrival of a European, Anthony Henday, to the region, so many of the events surrounding the battle along the Red Deer River and the spread of disease to the region will remain a mystery. The most vexing questions surround the fortified village known as the Cluny Site on the Bow River on land now part of the Siksika Reserve. The village is truly an anomaly in western Canada, and even today the identity of the people who built and quickly abandoned it is, in the words of the archaeologist who excavated it, "rank speculation."[81] Known archaeologically as "One Gun," the builders of the site occupied a handful of others in southern Alberta between the Oldman and Bow Rivers. Some scholars have posited that they were Missouri village dwellers displaced hundreds of miles west from their territory by conflict and disease, while others suggest that the answer to their identity lies to the south rather than the east. [82] The location of the village was strategic, at an important crossing on the Bow River, the most significant obstacle between the Missouri and the North Saskatchewan. Its construction, including palisades, defensive ditches, and numerous pits, was a considerable undertaking, suggesting that its builders intended to remain for some time, but the site was abandoned within months of completion. Because very few trade goods of European origin were found along with evidence of horses, archaeologist Richard Forbis dated the site to just after 1730, adding that "this date may coincide with the time when smallpox epidemics were sweeping through the Northern Plains."[83] Located on a ford in the Bow River, Cluny was perhaps a day's ride south of the battle field that Saukamappee recounted to Thompson. Although the identity of its inhabitants remains uncertain, the role of Cluny at the northern extremity of the equestrian network that reached over 1,000 kilometres to the south might have been its undoing.

By 1740, disease was the primary factor in the wholesale redistribution of aboriginal populations of western Canada. In the east, the fur trade brought significant epidemic mortality to the Monsoni, Assiniboine, and Dakota, opening a pathway for Anishinabe expansion to the plains. Along the Missouri, the infection of the Arikara and others marked the beginning of the end for the sedentary horticultural villages of the eastern plains. Decades before the arrival of Europeans to the region, germs from distant Mesoamerica travelled along the essentially seamless route to the northwestern fringe of the Great Plains. In southern Alberta, the advantage of equestrianism among the Snakes was overshadowed by the long-term consequences of mortality from infection that spread with the horse trade. As smallpox undermined the Snake occupation of southern Alberta, it provided the Niitsitapi with the means to return to their homeland. By the first half of the eighteenth century, smallpox brought fundamental changes to the demography of First Nations across western Canada.

EARLY COMPETITION AND THE EXTENSION
OF TRADE AND DISEASE, 1740–82

BEFORE THE MID-EIGHTEENTH CENTURY, THE BIOLOGICAL consequences of equestrianism and global trade reverberated on both the east and the west sides of the Canadian prairies. Disease did not spread to the central plains, the region now encompassed by the Province of Saskatchewan, because it was still peripheral to the fur trade making its way from the east and beyond the limit of equestrianism to the southwest. Both factors were about to change. The turnover of Quebec to the English opened the door to a significant expansion of the western fur trade. At the same time, horses spread to almost every community on the northern Great Plains. The demand for food created by the arrival of traders led to the commodification of bison as a commercial source of food. This new economic strategy took hold simultaneously with the decline of the middleman trade in furs. These innovations created the conditions for the spread of pandemic smallpox across North America in the early 1780s.[1]

In the wake of the epidemics of the 1730s, competition for the control of inland fur production continued between European powers despite significant changes to the indigenous societies allied with them. In keeping with its long-standing practice, the Hudson's Bay Company continued to do essentially nothing—remaining at the coast and waiting for furs to be brought there. The French, in contrast, continued their steady march west. In 1738, La Vérendrye accompanied several hundred Assiniboine as they walked to the horticultural villages of the Mandan on the Missouri River. Their destination was both impressive and of considerable longevity, having been established more than 700 years earlier when the technology for the cultivation of corn, beans, and squash spread to the region.[2] Although described as the "high point in plains social organization," the settlements no doubt disappointed the French, who had been told that the Mandan controlled a passage to the western ocean, the holy grail of European exploration.[3] Horses had yet to arrive in the region and across much of the Great Plains as the Apache people maintained tight control over their spread to the Great Plains.[4] This too was about to change. When the French returned five years later, the Mandan had enough horses to sell them some for their journey home. On that trip, the French investigated the country as far west as the Black Hills of South Dakota. Despite the remarkable nature of his travels, La Vérendrye was relieved of his commission in 1744 for pursuing exploration at the expense of trade. French officials were interested in the interior of the continent only as a source of furs.[5] By mid-century, the French had established two trading posts on the Saskatchewan River: one at The Pas, in Manitoba, the other at the forks, east of Prince Albert, Saskatchewan.[6] War between France and England stopped French expansion in its tracks, but even in a moribund condition the few traders in the interior controlled the bulk of fur production in the region. To counter French advances, the HBC shifted from its passive stance on the coast. Over a twenty-year period beginning in 1754, the company sent employees inland on over fifty missions to secure trade. After 1760, the French loss of Quebec even brought a few years of unopposed monopoly to the HBC, but the reprieve would be short lived. Soon the new English-speaking merchant class in Montreal despatched canoes west, initiating a new era of European expansion and heightened competition for the western trade.

In securing food and furs for the newcomers, Cree and Assiniboine middlemen were critical to the success of the expanding trade. Among the most important were the Pegogamaw Cree, who controlled the area around the forks of the Saskatchewan. Several Assiniboine groups across the parklands were also regular visitors to the posts. They had been long-standing residents of the region prior to the arrival of European goods, while the Pegogamaw, who had been middlemen in the early trade, shifted west from their ancestral home on the lower Saskatchewan River in historical times.[7] West of the forks, beyond the line from Saskatoon to the North Saskatchewan River, was the territory of the Archithinue, a catch-all term for all those who were not Cree or Assiniboine.[8] It encompassed the nation known historically as the Water Fall, Fall, or Gros Ventre, or A'aninin, as they refer to themselves today, the members of the Blackfoot or Niitsitapi alliance (Siksika, Piikani, Kainai, and Athapaskan-speaking Tsuu T'ina), along with their southern adversaries, the Snakes among others. Those who lived in the grasslands, known to the traders as the barrens, remained obscure because they remained marginal, if connected at all, to the fur trade. Unlike their parkland relatives, plains Assiniboine communities were not interested in the new economy. Perhaps their disinterest in hunting beaver stemmed from the importance of the species in the preservation of water in the arid grasslands. On his trek to the Missouri in 1738, La Vérendrye was told that the plains Assiniboine understood "nothing of hunting beaver," and it was hoped that the French could "teach them some sense" in this regard.[9] By the 1750s, with fur stocks depleted in the parklands, producers looked to the plains as a new source of supply. An HBC report stated that "there are few Beaver to be had unless the Indians go to the Assinipoets and Archithinue Country" (in the plains).[10] Little more than a decade later, William Pink wrote that the Beaver Cree guides were heading west to war "with the Other Natives Called Ye,artch a thyne a Wock and Kill as Maney as they Can of them." Game depletion in the parklands drove the Cree to war: "Some Yeares a Gow heare was a great maney Beaver in this River [the Saskatchewan], But now Verry few being hunted so often."[11] The victims of this attack were probably the Athapaskan-speaking Dunneza (Beaver) of northern Alberta.[12] Their neighbours, the Tsuu T'ina, were ousted from their territory by the Cree, eventually finding a place on the plains as adopted members of the Niitsitapi alliance.[13] The Cree invasion of northern Alberta was part of a wider conflict between Cree and Dene groups over control of the middleman trade across the north.[14]

The formal handover of Quebec and large portions of the interior to British control in 1763 greatly increased the number of Canadians heading west. By the end of the decade, they had diverted almost the whole of fur production in western Canada toward Montreal and away from the HBC.[15] To boost fur production from its northern hinterland, then still beyond the reach of the Canadians, Samuel Hearne was sent on his epic journey across the tundra to assess the potential of the region. After several false starts, great suffering, hunger, violence, and death among his crew, Hearne returned to Hudson Bay with news of the vast potential of the region far inland known as the Athapuscow.[16] The corporate agenda for Hearne's mission was to gain direct access to fur producers and cut the expense of reliance on middlemen. The HBC's goal to augment trade succeeded, at least in the short term, as hundreds of Cree and Dene delivered the largest return in thirty years to Churchill in the summer of 1772.[17] Even as the furs were being prepared for their journey to England, the proliferation of "French" traders southwest of Hudson Bay forced the company to despatch another servant, Matthew Cocking, to the Saskatchewan region.[18] In addition to securing trade, Cocking was to investigate the possibility that middlemen were taking excessive profits at the expense of the HBC.[19]

The journal kept by Cocking during his time with the Pegogamaw Cree over the winter of 1772–73 provides important insights into indigenous life on the parklands and northern plains as the region entered a period of profound change. As his party left York Factory, contagious disease spread among his guides, turning a journey of three weeks into an ordeal lasting almost seven.[20] Increased interaction with the interior by European and Euro-American traders increased the spread of disease, a far cry from the "accidental quarantine" of the region in the early 1760s when the trade was at its low ebb.[21] Cocking witnessed the shift among indigenous groups from the position of middlemen in the trade to producers trading at inland posts to the consternation of the HBC. He described his encounter with a former middleman, a York Fort leader who "denied having traded with the pedlars; but the Canadian goods that were in their possession contradicted his Assertion."[22] Cocking reported that the Pegogamaw had good relations with their neighbours in the region. While in the Eagle Hills, near Battleford, Saskatchewan, in the fall of 1772, the young Englishman and his guides welcomed the arrival of a highly esteemed equestrian group of Archithinue known to them as the Water Fall Indians after their ancestral home at Nipawin on the Lower Saskatchewan River. The A'aninin, as they are now known, taught the Cree to use the bison pound at their encampment, greatly impressing Cocking: "They appear to me more like Europeans than Americans." After a week of hunting together, the strangers stated that the season was past and rode off to war against the Snakes. By this time, the Pegogamaw and others in the parklands had acquired horses. Cocking and his party had several pack horses with them, though several died during the winter "for want of food; which they say is the case at this season of the year."

To Cocking, the goal of improving the trade must have seemed futile as he travelled by the Canadian posts permeating the lower Saskatchewan. Business was so robust at Finlay's Fort, which was providing "adulterated" rum to fur producers, that Finlay had to close shop because

"He hath no goods left. ..."[23] Adding insult to injury, Cocking's HBC mate, Louis Primo, defected to the Canadians rather than make the arduous trip back to York Factory.[24] As part of the "great invasion" of peddlers in the summer of 1773, a post was built at Playgreen Lake, near the site of what became Norway House, cutting off the trade destined for the shores of Hudson Bay. Later, Canadians built a post between the Saskatchewan and Churchill Rivers, which headed off middlemen from the Athabasca on their way to Churchill. There the Canadian trader secured as many furs as his canoes could carry.[25] With its interior trade evaporating, the HBC again ordered Hearne inland, this time to build a permanent post in the York Factory hinterland to take a stand in the territory that the Canadians increasingly dominated.

The new establishment, Cumberland House, was anything but grandiose, but its location hundreds of kilometres inland, close to the strategic lower Saskatchewan River, marked the beginning of a new era in the west. The company's lack of experience in the interior soon became apparent. Without canoes of their own, or the know-how to build them, Hearne and his men were forced to "hitchhike" aboard those of middlemen to reach their destination.[26] By the time Cumberland House was built, Canadians had been ensconced in the parklands for a decade. As itinerant peddlers, they cared little about documenting their experiences. The HBC, on the other hand, was a large-scale global enterprise with centralized control half a world away from where furs were exchanged for goods. Information from the field was vital to maintenance of the enterprise, so daily records were kept on numerous aspects of life in the hinterland. Centuries later these corporate records provide a detailed account of the people and changing economy of the region.

By moving to the region where furs were harvested, the newcomers rendered the century-old role of fur trade middleman obsolete. The loss of their economic niche and the growing number of traders who were trapping beavers themselves prompted the Cree to withhold their expertise and labour, to set fires that drove game away, and generally to harass their former partners in the long-distance trade.[27] The protests, though, were largely short lived. The Cree soon became key producers in a new economy that developed as a consequence of the growing number of traders and the relative paucity of a dependable food supply in the parklands. The demand for food was largely met by the cornerstone of plains subsistence, the bison. Within years, meat became the principal item of exchange along the Saskatchewan River.

The Canadians dominated the initial period of competition, but securing an adequate supply of food was a struggle for those at the growing number of trading posts in the west. The country around Cumberland House simply could not provide enough food to support the traders who spent most of their first winter subsisting on "two scanty meals per day."[28] Just north of them, Canadians wintering at Frog Portage on the Churchill River were not so fortunate. At least one of them died of starvation that winter, and another was executed for cannibalism. Many were despatched to posts closer to the plains and its dependable supply of bison meat. As soon as they could, the Canadians moved their post south to Amisk (Beaver) Lake, where food supplies were more secure.[29] Food scarcity in the muskrat country of the parkland–boreal forest ecotone led many indigenous communities to move west in search of meat for trade. Basquia Cree hunters, originally from The Pas, were soon hunting near Hudson House on the North Saskatchewan River to supply food to Cumberland.[30]

The advance of Canadians to the rich beaver country of the Athabasca greatly increased the demand for meat produced on the plains. In 1776, Thomas Frobisher built Île-à-la-Crosse on the Upper Churchill River on the Athabasca frontier.[31] As Canadians penetrated the northern interior, they consolidated their control of the parkland meat trade. In January 1776, Alexander Henry visited a camp of about 200 tents of Assiniboines on the Manitoba escarpment.[32] His description of the Assiniboine economy foreshadowed the dominant economic strategy on the plains for the next century. Of the "Osinipoilles," he wrote, "the wild ox alone supplies them with everything which they are accustomed to want." Henry contrasted the Assiniboine economy with that of Cree trappers on the Beaver River: "With them, the principal purchases are of necessaries." [33] The focus on bison became increasingly common among the Assiniboine as they abandoned their journeys to the coast during the 1770s. Soon they were "staking a monopoly in the buffalo trade" along both branches of the Saskatchewan River, feeding the ever-growing demand for provisions among the traders. The establishment of Hudson House in 1778 as a provisioning post for the HBC's northern trade provided the Assiniboine of the lower North Saskatchewan River with a renewed influence over the Europeans who had usurped their traditional role as middlemen.[34]

Rather than a single corporate entity, the Canadians along the Saskatchewan River represented a myriad of small interests competing against each other in addition to the HBC. Quick profits and the chaotic nature of the trade contributed to a saturation of the market, and the number of posts far outweighed the local production of fur.[35] Under this regime, the key to securing trade was a constant and growing stream of alcohol. From the start, traders at Cumberland complained that they could not compete against the Canadians and their liquor. Hearne complained that, even though Canadian prices were twice as high as those of the HBC, "tis nothing but the Brandy or at least the Rum, that makes them part with their goods at such a Deer rate."[36] The growing flow of liquor was accompanied by an increase in sexually transmitted infections. Venereal diseases had been reported among HBC servants as early as the 1680s.[37] Sexual relations between HBC employees and indigenous women were still prohibited by company decree in the 1770s, though such liaisons were "winked at," according to Chief Factor Andrew Graham.[38] At Cumberland House, three servants—Robert Davey, Magnus Sclater, and John Draver—all suffered from venereal disease in 1777. Draver was evacuated to York and deemed unfit for his duties—"[having] been so for some time."[39] The record remains mute on the impact of the disease on their sex partners or among Canadian traders, who did not maintain records of their activities commercial or otherwise. Canadians were at least as likely to spread sexually transmitted infections as their English competitors. Captain Tuite, the Canadian master at Beaver Lake, was reported as "being bad with the Venereal disorder" and was provided with medicine by the HBC in 1778.[40]

By that time, growing competition and diminishing returns along the Saskatchewan led some Canadians to the conclusion that, by pooling their resources, they could extend the trade into the largely untapped Athabasca country.[41] Peter Pond, later implicated in the murders of at least two associates, was the first trader to cross Methy portage, a twenty-kilometre trail between the Churchill and Clearwater Rivers. His expedition passed Cumberland House in May 1778: "going to penetrate the A tho pus cow country as far as he can possibly go and there to stay this next winter." He returned a year later, almost starved, with half of his canoes destroyed but with proof that the Athabasca country was extremely rich in furs. Pond had to leave most of the 6,000 kilograms of furs behind since his remaining canoes simply could not handle the full cargo.[42] In addition to the windfall in furs, Pond's success in crossing from the Hudson Bay watershed to the Mackenzie watershed had profound implications for decades to come. In completing the eight-day portage, the Canadians were beyond the territory recognized in the HBC charter, so a vast territory was open to anyone who could exploit it. The arrival of Canadians in the Athabasca quickly derailed the middleman trade to Churchill, leaving both the Dene and their trading partners at the bay in a precarious situation.[43] To fully capitalize on their advantage over the English, Canadians headed to the new territory had to overcome another significant obstacle: Athabasca contained some of the richest fur territory on the continent, but it could not produce enough food to sustain trade in the region. Bison meat, the staple of a region far to the south, would have to be imported to the boreal forest for the trade to operate. Pemmican soon became the staple for travellers in the north and would dominate commerce on the plains for a century. Among the indigenous communities across the west, it would involve a region-wide reorientation toward the seemingly limitless bison herds, not just for food but also for profit. The emergence of the ethnic identity known as the Plains Cree was a result of the shift from forest toward prairie.[44]

Within years of their arrival, the unrestrained nature of the fur trade along the Saskatchewan brought hardship and violence to many indigenous communities. Canadians' abuse of producers often led to retribution and bloodshed.[45] Within months of the completion of Hudson House in 1778, Robert Longmore wrote that Canadians were using "guns and hangers, tobacco and 10 gallons of rum to give away to the Indians to draw them from me, and if not to take them by force." The trader described the tactics of his Canadian rivals: "when the Indians came to where the French guard was, they made them drink, and Seized on all their Horses and goods, and guarded them in and Locked them up within their Stockades."[46] Not surprisingly, those who were abused by the traders retaliated when they could. In 1776, four Canadians were killed along the Assiniboine River, and supplies on the Swan River were plundered.[47] A year later three Canadians were killed on the North Saskatchewan.[48] By the end of the decade, competition among Canadians and the violence surrounding it were out of control and heightening tensions across the northwest. In March 1779, Tomison wrote from the relative calm of Cumberland House that "the present proceedings of the Canadian Traders striving against each other, not only will but have already drove the Indians into a state of Debauch and Indolence, it is a great Pity such a body of natives should be destroyed by a parcel of wild fellows."[49] HBC servants arriving from Hudson House later that spring reported "that an open War has broken out between the Natives and the Canadians at the Upper Settlement," forcing the HBC men and the Canadians to retreat downstream to safety. At least two Canadians and two indigenous people were killed. Violence prompted the HBC to relocate Hudson House in 1779 downstream from where the fighting had taken place. Still the killing continued. In November, Captain Tuite and his men abruptly left their post after the death of an aboriginal producer while drinking there.[50] Amid the growing violence between the indigenous population and Canadian traders, the latter sought to undermine the resolve of the few HBC men in the west through misinformation. In December 1779, Tomison was told that Cumberland House had been destroyed, but the trader dismissed the news, adding that "there has been many false reports made by them to the Natives concerning Us; Sometimes telling the Indians that your Honour's Ships is cast away, and at other times that, we are all dying of the small Pox."[51] By the end of the year, the plains were too dangerous for travel even by employees of the HBC, who had better relations with plains groups than their Canadian rivals. Servants wintering on the plains were recalled to Hudson House for their safety. Their master, Tomison, reported that "its dangerous to send our men with the Natives at present, as several of them is of a very savage nature." Recognizing the danger, Canadian traders began shipping furs at night so "that the Natives shall not see them."[52]

Tension and fear were exacerbated by widespread hunger. In the fall of 1780, provisioners lit prairie fires to keep the herds away from the upper settlements to protect their source of income. The destruction of grass coupled with the late arrival of snow led to widespread hunger across the northern plains. Many ate their dogs and beaver skins to survive on their way to traders. Compounding hunger was an outbreak of "white flux," which according to Robert Longmore was affecting the "whole of the Indians."[53] By mid-December, the food situation at Hudson House was so serious that a dozen servants were sent to spend the winter on the plains with indigenous families. Those who remained at the post assisted indigenous hunters who were "starved and unable to walk to the house." Some, such as two emaciated hunters who arrived at Hudson House in mid-winter with furs to exchange for food, the trader wrote, "are in such a miserable Condition, that at night they are afraid to lay down, for fear of being killed and Eat[en] before day." Soon even the men sent away from the house returned since they were starving. Food shortages were also reported to the east at Cumberland House, where provisions were given to starving Indians. Hundreds of kilometres west the Beaver River Cree ate their horses and dogs, "and part of them died after for want." The A'aninin, who occupied the land between the forks of the Saskatchewan, also complained of widespread hunger.[54] By spring, frustration and hunger boiled over, and there was an armed standoff over what few provisions remained at the post, though the situation was diffused without bloodshed. The arrival of meat in the spring allowed the resumption of full rations, though months of malnutrition had taken their toll. Longmore was reported as being "very bad with the Bloody flux." For some, relief from the famine was slow in coming, at the end of April 1781; many aboriginal people were still lacking food.[55]

On witnessing numerous fires on their way back to Hudson House in the fall of 1781, the HBC contingent prepared themselves for a tough winter.[56] They could scarcely imagine the misery that was about to befall not only the North Saskatchewan but also the western portion of the continent. On 20 October, news came from the south that smallpox had spread from the Snakes and was now widespread among the different tribes that traded along the river.[57] As had been the case decades earlier, disease spread along the indigenous trade network that funnelled horses to the northern plains.[58] Although the source of infection has been traced back to Mexico City, the outbreak of disease was part of a greater continental epidemic that affected the outcome of the revolutionary war in the United States.[59]

For the indigenous nations of western North America, the consequences of the epidemic were no less profound. Mortality from disease unleashed an unprecedented period of territorial and demographic change. In Canada, disease among the Snakes undermined their centuries-long occupation of southwestern Alberta.[60] Saukamappee told David Thompson that they were so reduced they were pushed back to the Missouri River and beyond.[61] Within years, the once dreaded Snakes had retreated into the mountains, where they were attacked almost at will by their northern adversaries.[62]

While Niitsitapi territory grew in the wake of the epidemic, one in three members of Saukamappee's Piikani community died in the outbreak, and other groups suffered even higher death rates.[63] In March 1782, fourteen Niitsitapi men, "all recover'd of the smallpox," were reported to be on their way to trade with the Canadians. Although still high, the lower relative proportion of deaths among the Piikani might be evidence of their previous exposure to the disease. Groups to the north and east with no experience of the disease suffered horrific losses.

Along the North Saskatchewan, the Assiniboine were particularly hard hit. According to an HBC trader, "they are very few, if any left alive, ... the Indians lying dead about the Barren Ground like rotten sheep, their tents left standing and the Wild Beasts devouring them." The Assiniboine from the Touchwood Hills were also badly hit. Of twenty tents, only five men and "a few women and children" reportedly recovered from the disease. William Walker of the HBC wrote of them, "I neither see nor hear of any being alive, The most part of them that has recover'd is Women and Children."[64] A year later the arrival of a group of Touchwood Hills survivors comprised of "17 stout men" surprised the traders at Hudson House. Tomison wrote that they had "squandered far off into the Barren Grounds, and have been at no settlements for these twelve months past; indeed I was informed by William Walker, that the whole gang was dead." For the Assiniboine, the epidemic contributed to the process of population loss and territorial constriction that began four decades earlier. They would never fully recover from their losses. Anthropologist Dale Russell observed that the Assiniboine, "the most numerous group on the north-eastern plains and parklands in the eighteenth century," are largely absent from discussions after the 1780s.[65]

At Cumberland House, the disease was first reported on 8 December 1781. By February, the death toll was "upwards of Thirty, for which number there is only two recovered and they are but children." Tomison added that "The U'Basqui'au Indians is all dead and ten tents of Pegogamy and Cowinetow Indians that was pitching towards this place all dead, as to all those that went up the Sturgeon River, I have neither seen nor heard from them since they had Debt last Autumn."[66] The epidemic largely depopulated the lower Saskatchewan valley. The Basquia Cree, who controlled the region, ceased to exist as a distinct cultural entity by the turn of the nineteenth century.[67] Their demise opened the lower Saskatchewan to immigrant groups closely attached to the fur trade, in particular the Muskego Cree and Anishinabe.[68] The latter also occupied the upper Assiniboine region in the wake of population losses among the Assiniboine. Along the Red River in Manitoba, Assiniboine losses in the community that came to be known as Dead River led to an invitation of Anishinabe to occupy the region north of the forks.[69]

The Pegogamaw Cree were hit in their land near the branches of the Saskatchewan. They suffered horribly from the outbreak, leading Tomison to report that between the Pegogamaw and Assiniboine of the Saskatchewan River "not one in fifty have survived."[70] Like their Basquia relatives to the east, the Pegogamaw disappeared from the historical record soon after 1782.

Equestrianism spread the disease quickly through the open country of the plains and parklands, but in the boreal forest the contagion lingered for as long as two years.[71] From its proximal source at the posts in the hinterland, infection spread east and north along fur trade routes across the subarctic. From York Factory, Matthew Cocking reported that, among the various tribes, "almost all of them died on their return, what few reached their own Country communicated the disorder to their Friends and it spread through the whole country." Infection arrived at York Factory in July 1782, carried by a group of Bungee trappers. Among some of the Bungee, mortality was reportedly close to 100 percent.[72]

Cocking did his best to maintain a quarantine, but his efforts were undermined by an attack by the French Navy. Disease spread through much of northern Ontario, significantly depopulating the Rainy River corridor and travelling the length of Albany River to James Bay.[73]

Sickness and death also spread northwest from the plains into the Athabasca. The Beaver Cree, living between the North Saskatchewan and Churchill Rivers, were reported to be the only group in the region to have survived intact; their relative isolation and caution in keeping contact with the Churchill traders brief and infrequent probably saved them from cultural extinction.[74] Although they fared better than others in the region, they too lost territory after the epidemic. In the 1790s, Peter Fidler reported that the Beaver River was by then the home of Anishinabe trappers.[75]

North of the Beaver Cree, the Athapuscow Cree, who controlled the middleman trade on the upper portion of the Churchill River north to Lake Athabasca, might have been wiped out. Their virtual disappearance brought an end to aggression in the Athapaskan-speaking Beaver country around Lesser Slave Lake.[76] At the close of the decade, Alexander Mackenzie found only forty Cree families on the lower Beaver, upper Churchill, and lower Athabasca Rivers. They were so severely weakened that the designation "Athabasca Indian" shifted from them to their former subordinates, the Chipewyan-speaking Beaver Indians.[77]

The outbreak might have been even more damaging to the neighbouring Chipewyan Dene communities. The disease spread north to the Chipewyan from Peter Pond's post at Lac la Ronge. The Missinippi Cree, who probably infected the Chipewyan at La Ronge, were, according to David Thompson, reduced by 50 percent. Their losses led to their retreat from their northern boundary at Reindeer Lake.[78] In 1795, Samuel Hearne wrote that "The Northern Indians, by annually visiting their Southern friends, the Athapuscow Indians, have contracted the smallpox, which has carried off nine-tenths of them, and particularly those people who composed the trade at Churchill Factory. The few survivors follow the example of their Southern neighbours, and all trade with the Canadians, who are settled in the Athapuscow country."[79] Beyond the human tragedy, Hearne lamented the loss of trade from the Chipewyan and Athapuscow Cree, as theirs "for more than ten years past, [provided] at least 7/8 of the whole trade." Trade relations were not re-established between the HBC and the Chipewyan from Athabasca until at least 1787, though incursions into the country by Canadians made the trade tenuous at best.[80] As terrible as it was, the epidemic did not descend the length of the Mackenzie River. Low population density and isolation from trading posts buffered the effect of disease. Even before the outbreak, small northern Dene groups avoided middlemen because of harsh treatment by them.[81] At the end of the decade, Alexander Mackenzie found no evidence of the epidemic among the Athapaskan groups whom he met as he travelled down the river that eventually bore his name.[82]

Indigenous mortality was so significant that the sick were often abandoned for the welfare of those not yet infected. Traders such as William Walker were shocked at the practice: "These Natives are such a Dastardly kind of people, that if any of their relations should be bad with this disorder, they think they need not look for any Recovery, they just throw them away, and so the poor soul perishes, they never [did] any thing of this kind before."[83] Walker might be excused for what he perceived to be a lack of compassion, but abandonment of sick individuals was probably the most logical response for group survival. Documents from the HBC indicate that company servants did what little they could to comfort the sick and dying at their posts, but as Walker wrote from Hudson House "it does not lay in our Power to help them."[84]

The English and most of the Canadians in the west had been exposed to smallpox, chicken pox, or cowpox in childhood and were generally immune to the virus that proved so deadly to their aboriginal suppliers.[85] The traders did not understand the reason for their survival while so many around them perished, though many recognized their good fortune in the face of catastrophe. Surrounded by the dead and dying, Tomison wrote, "There is something very malignant that we are not sensible of, either in the constitution of the Natives, or in the disorder, those that die before the smallpox breaks out tormented with great pains and many of them die within 48 hours."[86]

Even at the height of the epidemic, traders did what they could to secure furs. Throughout the winter, HBC men from Cumberland House were sent to camps to secure debt still owed to the company.[87] Furs that cloaked the dead were taken, and corpses were wrapped in company duffle. Rather than illustrating the pure mercenary nature of the trade, the missions to the tents of the dead and dying indicate the value of the resource to the Europeans. Although they themselves were not susceptible to the virus, the traders, particularly those inland, were engaged in a dangerous business. Starvation and even murder were never distant threats. The sheer number of dead instilled a sense of fatalism among the traders. On Christmas Day 1781, William Tomison at Cumberland House reported on a group of infected southern (Cree) Indians: "In the Evening Traded with the Indians & made them presents as Usual, but never expect to see them again." In March 1782, the trader at Hudson House remarked that his hunters were infected: "One of the men intend to send a hunting to morrow; When these die, I have nobody to kill a Beast for Us." A month later all of the post's fourteen hunters were dead.[88] The company's view of the epidemic was probably best summarized by Matthew Cocking in his report from York Factory in August 1782:

> I believe never a Letter in Hudson's Bay conveyed more doleful Tidings than this. Much of the greatest part of the Indians whose Furrs have formerly & hitherto brought to this place are now no more, having been carried off by that cruel disorder the Small Pox. The trade at this place is 6761 3/10 Made Beaver, including 154 ½ After Package last year. This great fall is owing to our loss of Indians but what is worse, several of the Indians who brought the little we have got are since dead.[89]

By the end of the 1780s, the indigenous occupation of western Canada had undergone profound changes as a result of the spread of smallpox. Entire cultural entities, such as the Basquia and Pegogamaw Cree, ceased to exist. In time, survivors came together into new communities in a process known in the academic literature as "ethnogenesis." In the wake of the epidemic, many indigenous newcomers, including the Muskego Cree and the Anishinabe along with the Ottawa and Iroquois, came west as part of the ever-intensifying fur trade, which continued to grow despite the turmoil brought on by the loss of such a large portion of the indigenous workforce.

CHAPTER 4

DESPAIR AND DEATH DURING THE FUR TRADE WARS, 1783–1821

THE SMALLPOX EPIDEMIC OF THE EARLY 1780S UNLEASHED A series of events that fundamentally and permanently changed the ethnic composition of western Canada. The death toll from the epidemic was unprecedented. The Basquia, Pegogamaw, and Cowanitow Cree simply ceased to exist as distinct groups. Differential mortality altered the balance of power between rivals, leading to a succession of territorial realignments across the west. In the north, high mortality among the Cree, a consequence of their close relationship with traders, forced their retreat from land that they had long dominated in their role as fur trade middlemen. In Athabasca, the Dunneza (Beaver) people regained control of the region, and the Chipewyan Dene pushed the Cree south to the Churchill River. Muskego Cree trappers came west from the boreal forest of central Canada to exploit fur resources, as did several groups from the woodlands of the Great Lakes, including the Anishinabe, Ottawa, and Iroquois.[1] After the epidemic, new community identities evolved as newcomers and local survivors merged in a process of "ethnogenesis," including the Plains Cree and western Ojibwa or Saulteaux and the development of Plains Métis culture.[2]

The redrawing of the indigenous map was fuelled by decades of often frenzied competition for control of the region between the Hudson's Bay Company and a succession of Canadian ventures. In the years after the epidemic, the overwhelming majority of trade continued to be in Canadian hands. Until 1810, the HBC had no more than one-seventh of the entire fur trade. The rivalry among Canadian traders ushered in some repugnant chapters in the history of native–newcomer relations in the region that included widespread violence and substance abuse. During the fur trade war, social pathologies undermined many communities, leading to as much misery and death as biological pathogens.

Decades of cutthroat competition and the need for immediate returns by a myriad of small-scale peddlers nurtured an ethos that every pelt was to be taken from the region without consideration for the sustainability of the harvest. As newcomers inherited or took by force portions of the northern plains, they quickly denuded the region of game. The beaver were gone a generation after traders set up shop along the Saskatchewan River. Extirpation of the species and adoption of equestrianism marked the end of an ecological relationship between humans and their environment that was thousands of years old. By the turn of the nineteenth century, the increasingly desperate trade prompted one trader on the Saskatchewan to write that the country is "entirely ruined."[3] Nature itself added to the misery of many in the region. The period 1780–1820 was marked by extreme climatic variability and harsh weather conditions that further reduced game populations and threatened the humans who relied on them.[4] As winter temperatures plummeted, equestrian communities saw their herds perish. By then, horses were a necessity for hunting and security, and efforts to replenish them triggered a cycle of horse raiding and intertribal violence that continued until the 1870s. During the last decade of the century, the western plains experienced the longest and most severe drought of the past 500 years, and reduced water levels across the region spawned water-borne illnesses that hit human and game populations alike. Two deadly epidemics of introduced disease spread from Red River to the Mackenzie Delta, adding to the hardship. Under the weight of these combined factors, many groups were pushed to the brink of disaster.

The epidemic of 1781–82 had immediate implications for the Euro-Americans spread across the region. In the short term, it literally dealt a deathblow to aboriginal plans to mount an armed resistance to them.[5] Canadian peddlers were granted further reprieve by the French Navy, which briefly occupied HBC forts along the coast in 1782.[6] The Canadians were quick to capitalize on their advantage. Soon after the epidemic subsided, several Montreal enterprises banded together under the auspices of the North West Company.[7] Competition and violence continued between the NWC and its main rival, known as the New Concern, until the two merged and began to monopolize the Athabasca trade until the end of the century.[8] Fort Chipewyan, the trading centre built beside Lake Athabasca in 1788, provided the Canadians with access to the Peace River in the west, the Mackenzie River to the north, and the barren grounds to the northeast. To maintain the trade among Lake Athabasca, its fur supply beyond it, and its destination in Montreal, a reliable food supply was critical. As transportation networks expanded, so did demand for bison meat from herds increasingly far south. Three locations emerged as key pemmican supply centres for the brigades: Red River, Cumberland House, and Île-à-la-Crosse. Feeding the northern trade was a lucrative economic pursuit and a major factor in the ethnogenesis of the Plains Cree lifestyle.[9]

Cree communities had been migrating up the Saskatchewan since the return of Montreal traders in the 1760s. Before the epidemic, so many Basquia Cree were hunting near Hudson House that the HBC could find none of them to work in their homeland near Cumberland House, hundreds of kilometres to the east.[10] After 1782, many Cree-speaking newcomers came west, subsuming local Cree survivors into their communities.[11] Although they shared a language and many cultural traits, the Plains Cree that emerged were not the same people as those who had inhabited the region prior to the epidemic. Ethnohistorian Charles Bishop warned that blanket terms such as "Cree" and "Ojibwa" have "created a false impression of cultural homogeneity that ignores regional ecological differences."[12]

The ancestors of the Cree, known archaeologically as the Selkirk people, occupied the lower Saskatchewan valley for hundreds of years prior to the arrival of Europeans. Cree groups such as the Pegogamaw were well ensconced at the margins of the plains in the early eighteenth century as participants in the middleman trade.[13] They guided HBC servants such as Anthony Henday and Matthew Cocking on their reconnaissance missions to the west prior to the establishment of Cumberland House. Good relations between the Cree and their Archithinue neighbours to the west, the members of the Niitsitapi confederacy, and the A'aninin (Gros Ventre) have been interpreted as evidence of a formal alliance between the nations of the Canadian plains.[14]

Perhaps the starkest evidence of transformation in the region can be found in the breakdown of relations between the Cree and the A'aninin. Before the epidemic, Cocking's Pegogamaw guides held the A'aninin in high esteem and were taught pound hunting by them. Others, such as the Sturgeon River Cree, were also unfamiliar with pounding, a key hunting strategy on the plains, evidence of their status as new arrivals there.[15] As the epidemic subsided in the fall of 1782, a party of A'aninin and Cree came to Hudson House together.[16] The demise of the Pegoga-maw and other frontier Cree groups in the epidemic ushered in what have been called "the most tragic years" in A'aninin history.[17] By all ac-counts, the A'aninin and other "Yachathinues" fared better than many of their neighbours during the epidemic. One camp stayed 100 miles from Hudson House, earning the scorn of trader William Tomison but wisely maintaining a safe distance from a known source of infection.[18]

The A'aninin were never more than marginal participants in the trade with Europeans. Their first documented visit to a trading post occurred only in the fall of 1779.[19] On their few visits to the European enclaves along the North Saskatchewan, they brought only wolf pelts and other low-value furs even though their country abounded in bea-vers. A common explanation for their alienation from traders, which erupted into bloodshed in the 1790s, was the devaluation of wolf pelts, their principal item of trade.[20] Not widely recognized is that the A'aninin refusal to commercially exploit beaver, the prime item of exchange at the posts, was a vestige of the centuries-old proscription on hunting the species that was a cornerstone of successful adaptation to life on the arid grasslands.

As Cree newcomers moved up the Saskatchewan in the 1780s, they capitalized on the advantage conferred by firearms acquired from traders and usurped A'aninin territory, at the frontier between the Niitsitapi and the territory controlled by the Cree and Assiniboine.[21] Another reason for territorial expansion was the differential in equestrian stock between the well-supplied A'aninin and the horse-poor Cree. By the 1780s, horses were a necessity for life on the plains. Equestrianism was nearly universal among plains hunters by the 1770s and greatly facilitated hunting to meet the growing demand among traders for bison meat. Yet, in the final decades of the eighteenth century, temperatures plum-meted, killing horses across the region and especially on the eastern plains, the territory controlled by the Cree and Assiniboine. Because horses were both a military and a subsistence necessity, those who lost stock to the elements turned to theft to recoup their losses. Raiding became essential to maintain herds above the Missouri River. Horse raids evolved into an outright invasion by the Cree in the spring of 1788 when a war party from the South Saskatchewan attacked a camp of A'aninin near the Battle River, robbing them and mutilating the body of their leader. After the incident, so many of the attackers retreated to the safety of the east that the Canadian trader, Montour, followed them to Nipawin on the lower Saskatchewan to retain their business. Despite fears of recrimination, the A'aninin did not counterattack; instead, they headed south and were not seen for two years.[22]

Five years later, in the summer of 1793, a party of South Branch and Swan River Cree reinforced by a number of Assiniboine attacked another A'aninin community, killing all but a few children, who were taken captive. Again the aggressors retreated eastward, wintering at Red Deer Lake in Manitoba.[23] Once more the A'aninin did not seek vengeance since they were vastly outgunned. Rather, they and their Siksika allies took revenge on the traders who had armed the aggressors at their posts along the North Saskatchewan. The violence at Manchester House was clearly a protest against the incursion of the trade into their homeland. After forcing the retreat of the traders, they scattered meat and flour around the yard and, significantly, "staved the brandy at the gate," a sign of their contempt for the use of liquor in the trade.[24] Tomison and other traders were shocked by the incident. The trader at South Branch House recognized that, for the A'aninin, described as "the most rational and inoffensive in this part of the country," their situation had changed; "should they come here we are prepared to receive them, and hope we have it in our powers to give them a repulse."[25] Yet the post was not prepared for the events of the coming summer, when 150 A'aninin and Siksika attacked the post and killed three HBC servants. The nearby Canadian post, reinforced with a number of Cree, repelled the assault.[26] To protect themselves from further bloodshed, traders quickly abandoned their posts and headed downriver. The Cree continued their offensive through the winter of 1794–95, forcing the beleaguered A'aninin to retreat to the Missouri River, where the Mandan provided them with sanctuary.[27]

Alcohol was increasingly perceived as a problem within First Nations communities. The Canadian advantage in the trade was a steady flow of alcohol from Montreal. The ceremonial consumption of spirits was a feature of trade protocol, but the volume of alcohol brought to the northwest led to addiction and violence.[28] Edward Umfreville, a trader along the North Saskatchewan in the 1780s, witnessed the growing pathology associated with alcohol: "intoxication, bordering on madness, for two or three days," and "fifty to one but someone is killed before the morning."[29] Officers of the HBC implored officials in London to curtail the flow of Canadian liquor.[30] Rather than altruism, though, HBC indignation was grounded in Montreal's colonial status, which allowed the trade of "double distilled" alcohol, literally twice as potent as that imported from England. The HBC, unable to dependably supply the product demanded in the interior, was at a significant disadvantage until 1791, when a distillery was built at York Factory. Without alcohol, traders simply could not find business. Alcohol might have been seen by those who pursued the new bison economy as a luxury item, a sign of their newfound affluence, but the amount of liquor used in trading soon led to a myriad of social pathologies. For many, alcohol became the raison d'être for their participation in the trade.

Competition became increasingly ruthless after 1795 when the so-called XY, or New North West Company, was formed following the breakdown of the main Canadian company's negotiations for a renewal of its charter. For a decade, unchecked competition among Canadian enterprises had brought social pathologies, particularly alcoholism and violence, to their peak. In the spring of 1796, Tomison complained that his trade had dwindled to nothing since his XY rival had "sent out a number of men with rum to meet the Indians and debauch them from paying my credits."[31] At Pembina, rum was a part of every transaction, if not every encounter, with aboriginal producers.[32] Alexander Henry despaired of the deleterious effects of alcohol and acknowledged the role of competition in undermining Saulteux society.[33] The stress of interethnic warfare, pressure from competing traders, and alcohol simply might have been too much for some individuals to bear. Suicide, according to John Tanner, was frequent.[34]

The insatiable desire for rum turned many from sellers of furs to buyers of liquor.[35] Even before the distillery was operational at York Factory in the early 1790s, the value of rum rose four times in relation to its value in furs. A decade later, at the height of the battle between the XY and North West Companies, the amount of double-strength rum imported from Canada swelled to over 20,000 gallons per year. Traders soon learned to use it to their advantage. After amalgamation of the rival Canadian companies in 1804, Henry reported that Canadian double-distilled spirits were diluted according to levels that the traders could get away with. For the Niitsitapi, he wrote on 15 September 1809,

> We do not mix our liquor so strong as we do for tribes who are more accustomed to use it. To make a nine-gallon keg of liquor we generally put in four or five quarts of high wine and fill them up with water. For the Crees and Assiniboines we put in six quarts of high wine, and for the Saulteurs eight or nine quarts.[36]

In the aftermath of the epidemic, new groups came west to fill the growing demand for furs. The most numerous of those who moved west to trap were the Anishinabe. With their long connection to the trade and their home territory in the east depleted of fur bearers, they were quick to take advantage of the new opportunity. By the 1790s, they had emerged as an identifiable new group, the Western Ojibwa or Saulteaux.[37] Armed with new steel traps and using castoreum as bait, they soon distinguished themselves as valuable commercial harvesters across the west.[38] Like Canadian traders, they used their increasingly important position in the trade to maximize their returns, often by playing competing traders against each other. In doing so, they earned the reputation as "rascals" along the Assiniboine River.

As the Anishinabe expanded their trapping grounds, they displaced local groups, often with a combination of psychological and physical intimidation. Even their allies were intimidated by them.[39] Along the Beaver River in western Saskatchewan, Peter Fidler could not secure the services of the local population since "all of the Indians of this quarter are frightened of the Bungees [Anishinabe]."[40] Anishinabe trappers brought their powerful religious customs with them from the east, leaving evidence of their power for all to see. At the portage between the Beaver River and Lac la Biche, the "intruders ... set up this image in the Beaver River for what protection it might give them."[41] Occasionally, as along the Peace River, Canadian traders encouraged the violent expansion of the Anishinabe into new territory to augment the production of fur.[42]

Expansion brought the Anishinabe into conflict with others on the eastern plains. Their occupation of southern Manitoba brought them into renewed conflict with the Dakota, with whom they had fought intermittently since the 1730s.[43] During the 1790s, the area along the Red River was largely unoccupied and essentially a war zone. Even the confluence of the Assiniboine and Red Rivers, known as the Forks, was recognized as a dangerous location by traders.[44] The Assiniboine, who once lived along the Red, "requested ... a person to summer with them, as they did not like to go to the Saulteur fort [Pembina]."[45] When the Cree entered the Selkirk Treaty in 1817, they were only too willing to cede the land east of Portage la Prairie to the Saulteaux.[46]

As the Anishinabe secured their hold on Red River, the trade in provisions escalated to support the ever-increasing number of Europeans in the interior. Most of the food supplied to Canadian traders was brought to the mouth of the Winnipeg River from as far away as the Qu'Appelle Valley up the Assiniboine River. Several factors contributed to the spiralling competition in the country west of Red River in the mid-1790s. HBC expansion seriously interfered with the NWC's trade routes and strategies, which depended heavily on the supply of pemmican.[47] Complicating matters along the Assiniboine was the "invasion" of independent traders led by Peter and David Grant, known as the "South Men" because of their exploits in what later became American territory. The region came under more pressure when Grande Portage was ceded to the Americans under Jay's Treaty in 1794,[48] thus cutting into NWC routes and trading territory. The result was an explosion in the number of trading establishments along the Assiniboine, which grew from nine to twenty-nine between 1793 and 1795.[49]

Although not as numerous as the Saulteaux, the Iroquois (Haudenosaunee) became important fur harvesters in the years after the smallpox epidemic. In 1801, over 300 Iroquois hunters came west in the employ of competing Canadian interests.[50] They became the largest part of the North West Company's workforce north of Methy Portage.[51] Although many newcomers were unpopular with resident populations, the single-minded practices of Iroquois trappers made them notorious. As commercial trappers, they were highly mobile, prepared to go anywhere to get beavers and move on when they were depleted.[52] As Tomison put it, they "leave nothing wherever they come."[53] Overtrapping by the newcomers was encouraged by the avarice of traders rather than ignorance of the impact on the beaver population.

Resentment over unsustainable harvesting by the Iroquois occasionally exploded into violence. In 1802, a dozen Iroquois trappers were killed in the Cypress Hills by A'aninin defending their last bastion on Canadian soil. Losses from a localized smallpox outbreak the following year forced the A'aninin to retreat to American territory, where they remain to the present.[54] The Iroquois continued to make enemies over the continental divide. Trader Daniel Harmon mentioned the killing of an Iroquois family by members of the Carrier nation in Oregon.[55]

The Iroquois, almost exclusively in the employ of Canadian firms, were loathed by the HBC. Angus Shaw, an experienced HBC trader, compared them to the locusts of Egypt, bringing with them devastation and ruin wherever they wintered.[56] The English view of the Iroquois probably changed in 1818 when large numbers of them defected to the HBC, an important factor in the collapse of the North West Company.[57]

Fur bearers, already threatened by overhunting, were pushed to the brink of extinction in many areas by disease. At Edmonton House in 1796, George Sutherland noted that fur returns were down because of "a great distemper among the beaver."[58] A few years later John Tanner described a similar outbreak in Manitoba.[59] The sudden drop in beaver stocks was so severe that one producer along the Swan River was convinced that the plague had been sent by the creator as a punishment for overhunting.[60] The disease might still have been active, at least in some places, as late as 1820, when Peter Fidler observed it.[61]

The disease was clearly zoonotic: that is, it affected human beings as well as animals. The sickness spread to Tanner's Anishinabe community, killing many; the pain drove Tanner to madness and the brink of suicide.[62] The disease has been tentatively identified as a typhoidal variety of tularaemia,[63] caused by the bacterium *Franciscella tularensis*, a creature well adapted to stagnant water and mud and infectious to humans as well as fur bearers.[64] Low water levels resulting from a plains drought between 1792 and 1804 provided the perfect conditions for tularaemia to thrive. Tanner's observation that the animals in "ponds and stagnant water" died while those in "large rivers and running water" suffered less fits the diagnosis of tularaemia bacteria breeding in shallow water in drought conditions.

Over the fall and winter of 1800–01, Henry reported that "most of the people" were sick with symptoms that included an "ugly cough," sore limbs, and convulsions that occurred "twice or thrice a day." In January, his guide, Charlo, died of the illness. Charlo's wife, two daughters, and two sons all died of it within five months.[65] Pulmonary consumption (tuberculosis) was among "the most common fatal diseases" in Henry's community,[66] and it is possible that Charlo and his family perished from TB.

Along the Albany River, "a great and Uncommon Mortality" afflicted the Cree in the spring of 1795, and the disease was unknown to the surgeon at Albany.[67] The western posts of the HBC were afflicted by an outbreak of another disease over the winter of 1795–96. This disease, characterized by "rheumatic pains" and coming with increasing frequency, struck down traders and Indians alike and underscored the weakness of the HBC supply network since medical supplies were woefully inadequate.[68]

Before the turn of the nineteenth century, sexually transmitted diseases were spreading among plains communities, and according to Edward Umfreville they were "very common" among the natives of Hudson Bay.[69] Alexander Mackenzie identified syphilis as "a common complaint" that could be cured "by the application of simples [medicinal plants]."[70] Among the Fort Vermilion Cree, venereal disease seemed to be the principal cause of death.[71] The Assiniboines also suffered from venereal disease and apparently had no remedy for it. At the western edge of the plains, Daniel Harmon reported that, while "The Indians in general are subject to few diseases, the venereal complaint is common to all tribes in the north."[72] It was also present among the people of the Missouri River, as Lewis and Clark noted.[73] The trading strategy known as *en derouine,* in which fur company employees travelled to Indian communities to exchange goods, was no doubt another means by which sexually transmitted diseases spread, but the practice of sending servants to winter with aboriginal groups to lessen the pressure on provisions at trading locations undoubtedly eased the spread.[74]

Canadian traders, generally the worst purveyors of spirits, also abused their aboriginal clients and employees.[75] The cycle of abuse began within years of the arrival of Montreal traders in the area. In 1786, a Canadian trader recorded the beating of a Chipewyan with the flat of a sword: "Mr. Pond told him that the Country and the Indians belonged to him & he would do with them as he pleased & no other person should meddle with them."[76] Some groups, such as the Chipewyan Dene, resisted the use of alcohol, and when chemical dependency was insufficient to get what they wanted Canadian traders turned to assault, murder, and kidnapping. The Chipewyan were reluctant to enter the fur trade wholeheartedly because doing so jeopardized their traditional subsistence cycle in a precarious environment. As historian Kerry Abel summarized, "the costs were simply too high."[77]

Canadian traders soon found ways to overcome the Chipewyan aversion to commercial trapping. By the early 1790s, they routinely took women from their families to ensure payment of debts and sold them to company employees for between 500 and 2,000 livres. "If the father or Husband or any of them resist the only satisfaction they get is a beating and they are frequently not satisfied with taking the Woman but their Gun and Tent likewise," wrote scandalized HBC surveyor Philip Turnor.[78] Canadian trade practices, unfettered by legality or morality, initially met with great success. By 1795, Canadian posts were established on the Mackenzie River. The chief Canadian trader along the Mackenzie, Duncan Livingstone, was highly regarded by his peers. "Under his management these people were modelled anew and brought under an implicit obedience to the White's authority," NWC post master Willard Wentzel wrote to Roderick Mackenzie.[79] That "authority" in the Athabasca included a slave traffic in women.[80]

Trade descended into "profligate" competition following entry of the XY Company into the region in 1799 and arrival of the HBC in 1802.[81] Between 1800 and 1806, when the Canadian rivals merged, fur returns from the north plummeted. Liquor imports increased from an average of 9,600 gallons in the 1790s to over 21,000 gallons in 1803.[82] Wentzel concluded that the decline in trade was the result of competition between the two Canadian concerns and, "partly, by the death of many Natives." He added that, by 1807, trade had "almost totally abolishe[d] every humane sentiment in both Christian and Indian breast."[83]

Aboriginal populations responded as best they could to the frenzy of competition and violence. The Chipewyan quit the trade in large numbers from 1799 to 1806, turning to the quest for food instead of fur. The Dunneza in the Peace River country resisted the increasingly coercive nature of the trade and barred XY Company traders from their territory for three years. The competition ignited several intertribal wars. The Dunneza attacked not only Saulteaux trappers in the Peace River region but also continued northward down the Mackenzie River into the territory of smaller Athapaskan-speaking nations. As the frenzy for furs extended to marginal production areas in the north, local populations were not only threatened by both European and aboriginal aggression but also displaced from their seasonal subsistence cycles, suffering from terrible malnutrition and succumbing to pathogens that spread along trade routes.[84]

In 1802, the year that the HBC established posts in the district, ten Dunneza died of sickness near Lake Athabasca. Survivors fled southward to Île-à-la-Crosse. The following winter was so severe, and game was in such short supply, that the HBC abandoned its outpost along the Peace River after an outbreak of disease exhausted the company's meagre food reserves.[85] Adding to the turmoil, Iroquois continued to overtrap along the river, eventually displacing the Dunneza from the region, forcing them north into the territory of less powerful groups.[86]

The combination of "severe and even homicidal rivalry" for the trade,[87] food shortages, and the spread of infectious disease was not confined to the Peace River. In 1803, thirty-seven Chipewyan from Lake Athabasca died. Fidler worried that survivors might abandon the trade.[88] The increased incidence of disease might have been related to greater population density around Fort Chipewyan. In the early years of the century, James Macdonnell reported over 400 people at the post.[89]

In the far north, Nor'westers threatened local fur producers with death if they traded their goods with the HBC. Company servants at Chiswick House beside Great Slave Lake were reduced to eating what few parchment skins they had over the winter of 1803–04 as a result of such tactics.[90]

As the trade descended into a cycle of violence and despair, rival traders turned on each other with increasing frequency. In one case, the "North West bully James King" was killed trying to take furs belonging to a young XY clerk.[91] King's murder forced a response from the colonial authorities. The Canada Jurisdiction Act, though a flawed piece of legislation, was the first attempt to impose legal authority in the far northwest.[92] Passage of the act was an acknowledgement by British authorities that the trade had gotten out of control. Aboriginal inhabitants in the interior had, by this time, come to the same conclusion. In the summer of 1804, the Chipewyan, long considered docile in their dealings with traders, killed at least ten Canadians in two incidents near Fort Chipewyan before abandoning the Canadian trade completely for two years. The combination of imperial law and Indian reprisal prompted the Canadian rivals to come to an arrangement in the trade. In November 1804, a formal merger took effect, creating a unified Canadian enterprise.[93]

By 1805, the entire western fur trade was in crisis. Aboriginal hostility toward traders was manifest in conflicts throughout the country. Beside the Assiniboine, Daniel Harmon reported that the post at Montagne à la Basse had closed its gates when surrounded by "about eighty lodges of Crees and Assiniboine ..., who threatened to kill all the White People who were in it."[94]

If there was any respite for the people of the northwest from amalgamation of the Canadian trade, it was short lived. Posts belonging to the HBC, considered little more than nuisances during the murderous competition among the Canadians, soon became targets of the united Canadian enterprise. In 1806, the HBC was pushed out of the Peace River district. The same year Canadians destroyed the HBC post at Green Lake between the Saskatchewan and Churchill Rivers.[95] Intimidation of HBC employees continued for at least a decade after the merger, severely curtailing English fur returns from the Athabasca.[96] The pattern of violence shifted, but the cycle of illness continued as it had prior to the merger. In the far north, outbreaks occurred yearly from 1804 to 1807 and resulted in numerous deaths.[97]

In addition, a macabre practice appeared among the smaller Athapaskan nations dislocated by the turmoil of the trade—the killing of female infants. The first reference to the practice in European journals occurred in 1807 when Willard Wentzel attributed the relative scarcity of women among the Dene tha (Slavey) along the Mackenzie River to "the custom they have of often destroying the female children when just born."[98] The practice continued well into the nineteenth century and led to significant disparities between numbers of men and women in the far north.[99]

The Dene tha were under terrible pressure at this time. In addition to years of unrelenting disease among humans, there was disease among animals, and the Dene tha were dislocated by the Chipewyan who moved into their beaver-trapping territory.[100] The Dunneza, ousted earlier from the Peace River by Cree and Iroquois agents of the North West Company, expanded their territory, pushing the Nahanne out of their country along the upper Liard River.[101] In one confrontation, the Dunneza killed twenty-two of the Nahanne. Disease spread as intertribal violence raged.[102] The sickness in the north during 1806–07 might have been the northern manifestation of a whooping cough epidemic that had spread from the Red to the Columbia Rivers.

Hunger was a constant threat to all inhabitants of the far north. In the spring of 1809, Daniel Harmon reported that a number of Canadians at Great Bear Lake starved to death, and among those who pulled through the ordeal "some ... ate their dead companions."[103] Two years later failure of the rabbit population during an intensely cold winter led to widespread starvation across the region.[104] Periodic starvation resulting from the cyclical decline of the rabbit population in the north underlined the poverty of the environment for human subsistence.

The winter of 1810–11 was particularly horrible. At the Mackenzie River Post, three "of four Christians" died of starvation. People were reduced to drastic measures to survive. Instances of cannibalism were reported across the north; nine were confirmed in the Nelson River district of northern Manitoba between 1811 and 1815.[105] Continuing scarcity of rabbits and fish reduced fur returns to a trickle since traders "have much ado to make sufficiency of provisions for the winter."[106] When war broke out between the United States and England, it further reduced the already precarious supply of trade goods to the Canadians, leaving them in an "almost unsupportable situation."[107]

During the winter of 1812, indigenous producers along the Liard River turned on the traders, killing five of them and their families.[108] In January 1814, Canadian trader George Keith reported that "Athabasca itself is dwindling down to nothing."[109] Under the auspices of the Canadians, the Iroquois had trapped the region out, and the local indigenous population could take no more. Canadian traders prepared as reports of planned attacks on all Europeans in the region circulated.[110] In the spring of 1815, Canadians retreated from the region "with great hazard to our lives ... [since the Indians] had formed the design of destroying us on our way out."[111] Years of overhunting and abuse ruined the country that had been opened only decades before.

Far to the south on the plains, the tide was also turning against the Canadians, who had long dominated the region. Near Red River, supplies of pemmican crucial to the support of canoe brigades were commandeered by official decree and used as rations for the settlers in the newly established Selkirk Colony.[112] The colony was part of a plan by the HBC to develop an agricultural settlement to revitalize its flaccid trade and buttress its hold on the royal charter that it had been granted a century and a half earlier. Reorganization of the English trade proved to be successful in the long term, but the emphasis on economy and efficiency led to a serious, if temporary, labour crisis. At Brandon House, company servants mutinied.[113] The HBC gained further momentum by the defection of NWC officers, who became key players in the battle to control the trade.[114]

By 1814, the HBC was ready to take up arms against the Canadians. The London Committee, the company's executive, authorized the use of force and committed itself to the invasion of Athabasca, the "decisive issue" in the war for the trade.[115] In 1815, the HBC sent a force of over 100 men in fourteen large canoes to counter the Canadians at Fort Chipewyan, a significant achievement for the English company.[116]

Meanwhile, a new catastrophe for traders and aboriginal peoples was about to strike. Half a world away the massive volcanic eruption of Mount Tambora in April 1815 filled the earth's atmosphere with so much ash that sunlight was greatly reduced. Weather patterns around the globe changed. 1816, "the year without a summer," was one of the worst weather years in the historical record,[117] characterized by intense cold and absence of sunlight. It brought widespread starvation and death to the subarctic. In Athabasca, almost one-fifth of the HBC contingent that had "invaded" the district died of hunger in the winter of 1815–16.[118] Survivors were forced to abandon their new depot, Fort Wedderburn, and a number of outposts in an attempt to ward off starvation. Daniel Harmon estimated that the HBC lost, "in fight and by starvation," sixty-eight men in the aftermath of the Indonesian eruption.[119] Included in his estimate were those killed in the confrontation at Seven Oaks. Although the connection between the eruption of Mount Tambora and the violence at Red River in the spring of 1816 has yet to be integrated into mainstream accounts of the event, scholars such as Tim Ball have argued that the climatic crisis might well have sparked the confrontation.

The weather, already unstable since the late 1780s, remained highly volatile until after 1820. On the plains, a three-year drought and record low temperatures seriously affected food and fur resources by forcing changes in bison and other large game animal migration patterns and subsequent starvation among hunting groups.[120] Competition for unreliable resources triggered several violent outbreaks among First Nations. In 1813, a Sioux war party attacked a group of Bungees (Anishinabe) and French Canadians. In December 1815, as the first effects of the Tambora eruption were felt, the Sioux descended on a group of thirty-four Bungees south of Red River, killing all but three of them. The following spring they set on a party of Assiniboines near Brandon.[121]

A number of military campaigns carried out by the Plains Cree also coincided with the environmental crisis. By 1817, they were at war with their former allies, the Mandan. At Carlton, hostilities between Cree and Niitsitapi continued as they had since 1811, coming to an abrupt end only in 1819 when a simultaneous outbreak of measles and whooping cough attacked the combatants.[122]

As war and disease raged on the plains, scarce resources in the north led to numerous confrontations. North of Great Slave Lake, Dogribs killed a dozen Hare people in 1815. In the Peace River and Lesser Slave Lake regions, armed hostilities between Dunneza and Cree escalated. In September 1817, Daniel Harmon reported an armed standoff at Fort Chipewyan involving about 100 Chipewyan.[123]

In spite of harsh climate, scarce resources, and starvation, the HBC mounted an assault on the NWC post at Athabasca, assisted by a company of Chipewyan fighters, in 1817.[124] The North West Company rallied by re-establishing posts along the Mackenzie, but by this time the damage had been done. Aboriginal producers in the far north abandoned their Canadian tormentors in large numbers, preferring the "less tyrannical" trade practices of the HBC.[125] The shift of Athabasca communities to the English was an important factor in the outcome of the fur trade war. Before the merger of rivals in 1821, the entire northwest was rocked by new and catastrophic disease episodes.

In 1818–19, a simultaneous outbreak of whooping cough and measles across the northwest brought such high levels of mortality that they rivalled those of smallpox in the 1780s.[126] The measles infection was particularly lethal to aboriginal populations. Because it had not been seen inland for seventy years, it acted as a virgin soil epidemic, and all ages were equally susceptible. The harsh effects of the disease were exacerbated in populations suffering from malnutrition. The years of environmental and military turmoil in the early years of the nineteenth century, made worse by Tambora's pollution of the atmosphere, served to increase both morbidity and mortality from the disease.

Fur producers in the boreal forest were hit hard by disease in 1819–20. Wentzel reported that "one fifth of the population of the country is said to have been destroyed all the way from Lac la Pluie to Athabasca."[127] The southern region too endured the force of the combined measles and whooping cough epidemic. It has been estimated that almost one-third of the Niitsitapi trading at Fort Edmonton and approximately one-fifth of the Plains Cree died. The spike in mortality forced a temporary truce among the Niitsitapi and their enemies, the Cree and Assiniboine.[128] Mortality among plains people ranged from 40 to 65 percent. Twenty-four hundred Assiniboine died in the Brandon district alone.[129] Possibly one in four of all Assiniboine people died.[130]

Smallpox also appeared again, moving north from the Missouri River to the plains communities.[131] The disease first manifested in the summer of 1818 and might have spread northwest along two pathways.[132] By the nineteenth century, it was common for Canadian canoe brigades passing through Lake Superior and west to Red River and the plains to carry microbes in the bodies of one or two sick canoemen. The second vector for the epidemic was the Missouri River, where many communities were still recovering from a limited smallpox epidemic in 1816. It probably reached the Mandan on the Missouri early in 1819. By spring, it had reached Brandon House and moved downstream by June to the struggling colony at Red River.[133]

By fall, the epidemics had reached the Athabasca, leading Wentzel to conclude that the newly arrived German settlers at Red River had spread it. Fidler of the HBC blamed the Nor'westers for the outbreak.[134] In keeping with the acrimony surrounding the dying days of the fur trade war, Canadian traders started a rumour that the HBC had deliberately infected people at Lac la Biche and Lesser Slave Lake and caused forty deaths there.[135]

Hunger worsened the direct effects of the pathogens. Some groups, such as the Muskego Cree at Cumberland House, were "totally incapacitated from hunting by sickness."[136] At Île-à-la-Crosse, survivors of the epidemic starved because hunters were too sick to procure game.[137] Along the Peace River, HBC surgeon William Todd reported that those who were not debilitated were frustrated in the search for food by their symptoms, "the whole of their caution in approaching an animal being rendered abortive by a single cough."[138] Others quit hunting according to customary law that prohibited hunting during mourning. At Fort Resolution, the fishery failed in December 1819, worsening the effects of measles and diminishing what returns remained. Although some survived on "bits of skin and offal," others were not so fortunate. Dr. John Richardson, a member of the ill-fated first Franklin overland expedition to the Arctic coast, reported that one woman was "reduced to feed upon the bodies of her own family to prevent actual starvation," while another "had been the principal agent in the destruction of several persons, amongst the number her husband and nearest relatives, in order to support her life."[139]

George Simpson reported that, among the Athabasca Chipewyan, the diseases "carried away whole bands, and they are now dispersing in all directions, hoping that a change of residence may arrest the progress of the contagion."[140] Dispersals also occurred among Dene groups to the east. At Reindeer Lake, Hugh Leslie, in charge of the HBC post, recorded the avoidance strategy of a group hunting near the Cree territory to the south.[141] The Dunneza people along Peace River suffered "great mortality" for two consecutive years.[142] Wentzel's report from Great Slave Lake in the spring of 1820 put the turmoil in context, saying that "the fur trade is ruined for some years to come."[143]

By 1821, the Canadian northwest was in social, demographic, and environmental crisis. Harsh climatic conditions compounded by the eruption of Mount Tambora, along with catastrophic disease episodes, created severe conditions for the physical environment and people of the northwest. Even as disease, starvation, fur trade company rivalry, and interethnic hostilities did their damage, negotiations to end at least one of the irritants, fur trade competition, were under way in London.[144] With the merger of the two companies in 1821, the reorganized HBC began downsizing, a move only partially designed for the benefit of the new monopoly. The company, and the British Colonial Office, recognized that the inhabitants of the interior and their environment had to be pulled back from the brink of disaster.

CHAPTER 5

EXPANSION OF SETTLEMENT AND EROSION OF HEALTH DURING THE HBC MONOPOLY, 1821–69

THE END OF THE FUR TRADE WARS IN 1821 USHERED IN A NEW era for the people of the Canadian northwest. For half a century, the Hudson's Bay Company was the de facto government of Rupert's Land and tried, with varying degrees of success, to control the people and economy of the region. George Simpson, the London clerk who came to be known as the "Little Emperor," was governor of the HBC through most of the monopoly period. The guiding principle of his tenure was maximum returns with minimum investments.[1] Simpson closed many of the competing posts that had littered the landscape during the decades of desperate harvesting.[2] The combined total of sixty-eight HBC posts and fifty-seven Canadian posts prior to the union was slashed to slightly over fifty after the merger.[3] The result of the downsizing was a region-wide labour crisis as the majority of fur trade workers found themselves without employment. [4] The company curtailed, and eventually prohibited, the flow of alcohol to large portions of the interior.[5] The HBC also worked to prevent contagious diseases, especially smallpox, with the widespread distribution of vaccine. For the first time, the people and environment of the northwest came under the management of a single corporate entity. Company policies met with different levels of success but had profound impacts on the development of First Nations in the northwest.

During the monopoly period, the growth of the agricultural community at Red River, part of the wider phenomenon of westward expansion of European settlement, led to fundamental changes in the demography and economy of the northwest. The burgeoning demand from the colony for meat eventually strained the viability of bison herds, a resource once thought to be almost limitless. With diminished supply and increased demand, conflict grew. The growing human population served as an ever-increasing repository of infection that threatened the indigenous communities of the west. Improved transportation networks delivered pathogens to the susceptible with greater speed. By the mid-nineteenth century, the heightened disease load signalled "a change in status in which the region moved from the periphery of several urban disease pools to being within the immediate hinterland of the eastern pool."[6] Relentless microbial attacks brought some indigenous communities to the brink of collapse. Others were spared by medical intervention that came with their commercial relationships with British traders, equipped with medicines that made the difference between life and death. During the HBC monopoly, differential demographic outcomes of disease episodes among plains groups shaped the pattern of territorial occupancy that largely remains to this day. The unstoppable movement of the settlement frontier, particularly in the United States, also increased pressures on game populations to unsustainable levels. Climatic instability through most of the mid-nineteenth century contributed to the increasingly desperate competition for reliable food supplies.[7] On the plains, precipitation patterns oscillated between inundation and severe drought, undermining the predictability of bison movements. By the 1820s, the ascendancy of equestrian chase hunting over less disruptive harvesting practices such as pounding also undermined predictability.[8]

While plains populations were still reeling from the measles and whooping cough, word spread from the south that smallpox was raging along the Missouri River and that many of the Assiniboine had perished from the dreaded disease. In US territory, the Sioux, A'aninin, and Flathead in the plateau, along with other groups in the south, suffered terrible losses during the 1820s. West of the continental divide disease reportedly killed four-fifths of the population along the Columbia River.[9] Fortunately, smallpox did not become widespread in British territory. At Red River, the HBC vaccinated large numbers of people, halting spread of the disease[10] and providing the community with some immunity against the even more serious smallpox outbreak of 1837.

As inhabitants of the plains coped with epidemics and renewed warfare in the 1820s, the agricultural colony at Red River took root. The eventual success of the settlement was not achieved without great effort and considerable frustration. During the first decade of the HBC monopoly, the settlers endured a series of environmental setbacks that included shortages of bison meat, prairie fires, poor crops, a major flood, and in 1827 another epidemic of whooping cough.[11] The worst was the flood of 1826, which led many European settlers to abandon the struggling colony.[12]

Although settlers had established themselves less than a decade before, the country surrounding Red River had been under severe hunting pressure for decades before the 1820s. Since the re-establishment of the Montreal trade in the 1760s, the land between the forks of the Red and Assiniboine Rivers and Lake Winnipeg served as the hunting ground for both Canadian and English traders in addition to the aboriginal population of the area.

The Anishinabe, who migrated to the Red River area in the last decades of the eighteenth century, experienced severe depletion of game in the region even before establishment of the colony. By the time the Selkirk colonists arrived, the country along the Red was all but hunted out. The depletion of large game, along with mortality from epidemic disease and military conflict, contributed to territorial abandonment, which opened the region for settlement by the Anishinabe. Miles Macdonell, who oversaw establishment of the new community, said that the Anishinabe were eager for the settlers to arrive. Their long relationship with European traders had made them "quite dependent, their country being stripped of its most valuable furs." He added that "The Saulteaux are now quite afraid of being altogether abandoned by the traders & are pleased to see people of steady habits arrived who are to make permanent residence; acting toward them on fair and just principles and administering to their wants."[13] The Anglican missionary John West, touring his parish in 1820, recorded the hardship of the aboriginal population who had settled near the colony. During the winter of 1822–23, the scarcity of game and severity of the weather drove the Saulteaux chief Peguis and his people to eat their dogs and the remains of a horse that had succumbed to the cold.[14] The Saulteaux under Peguis were experienced farmers, but their expertise was probably no match for the harsh conditions of the early nineteenth century.

The situation among the Saulteaux foreshadowed the region-wide TB epidemic that came with the extermination of bison and the failure of agriculture half a century later. The strategic location of Red River, along the route from Canada to the northwest, spread tuberculosis as sick members of Canadian canoe brigades on tight schedules passed by communities along the waterway.[15] A recent scientific study asserted that a genetic lineage of tuberculosis traced to Quebec was spread by French Canadians during the fur trade period and persists in TB among isolated indigenous communities into the twenty-first century.[16]

Despite the hardships, the population of the Red River settlement continued to grow through the 1820s. Part of the increase was the result of corporate downsizing after the merger. The unemployed drifted to the colony, supplementing the trickle of agricultural immigrants from the east and Europe. Agrarian missions, such as St. Peter's under the tutelage of West in the early 1820s, were established to help displaced aboriginal employees become self-sufficient. Officials who sought to create an island of European settlement along the Red River saw the number of country-born people moving to the colony as a problem. By the mid-1820s, the HBC stopped granting its retirees land in the colony to control what it considered the wrong kind of growth—those who depended on corporate assistance or would not commit themselves fully to an agrarian lifestyle. By 1834, the company required its retirees to purchase a minimum of fifty acres to settle in the colony. A decade later it banned them from the settlement entirely.[17]

Because the HBC in monopoly served as the de facto government of the northwest, changes to corporate strategies had important consequences for the people of the region. Recognizing that the free flow of alcohol had created serious social problems during the decades of unrestrained competition, the company imposed what was essentially a prohibition on alcohol in some of its domain. In 1822, the Northern Department Council directed that the flow of alcohol to the interior be reduced by 50 percent. In isolated areas, it imposed a complete ban. In 1826, it prohibited the trade in alcohol in the districts of Athabasca, Mackenzie, and English River, eliminating the sanctioned flow of alcohol to fur producers and company employees beyond Cumberland House.[18] The policy was unpopular with fur producers: in 1824–25, Chief Factor James Leith at Cumberland House attributed the decline in his returns to restrictions on the trade in alcohol.[19] Along the southern and western boundaries of HBC territory, the official liquor trade continued as free traders and others undermined the jurisdictional realities of the charter. The illicit sale of alcohol by American traders on the southern margin of the country prompted many producers to shift their trade away from the HBC, which held the titular monopoly in the region.[20]

Game conservation was another issue that the company took on, imposing limits and even banning the harvest of certain species in depleted regions. In Athabasca, beaver had largely been extirpated by Iroquois trappers working for the North West Company, and by the 1820s large game such as moose, caribou, and bison were also rare.[21] On his inspection tour in 1823, George Simpson was "appalled" at the condition of the Nelson and lower Churchill districts since "he did not see a solitary vestige of beaver and he could see no remedy save to forbid beaver-hunting there entirely for the next five years." His first policy directives banned any trade in summer beaver, prohibited the use of steel traps and castoreum, and put in place strategies to rehabilitate the Athabasca as a major source of low-value muskrat fur.[22]

Only where fur production could be realistically curtailed and the monopoly secured were controls placed on the depleted resource.[23] In the relatively isolated but game-depleted country surrounding Lesser Slave Lake, producers were coerced into leaving as traders "threw out [the] visiting Beaver without even the common courtesy of providing them with a gift of tobacco."[24] The closure of posts was intended to nurture game, but the result was often hardship for the local indigenous population. Simpson himself acknowledged that the closing of Fort St. John "reduced the whole population of the upper Peace to the utmost distress" and led to the deaths of many from famine.[25]

In areas where the monopoly rang hollow, such as the plains and parklands, the company was faced with competition from free traders and American interests. Aboriginal producers were encouraged to trap areas out, leaving a fur-denuded buffer along the margins of HBC territory.[26] When a country-wide quota system on beaver was introduced in 1826, border areas such as the Rainy, Red, and Saskatchewan Rivers were exempted from the plan.[27] On the southwestern margin of HBC influence, Peter Skene Ogden's expedition to the Snake River was ordered "to hunt as bare as possible all the Country South of the Columbia and West of the Mountains."[28]

Aboriginal producers responded in a number of ways to the strictures. Some, such as the Dunneza of the Peace River area, protested the closure of their fort by turning on the traders. In the fall of 1823, five were killed.[29] Elsewhere in Athabasca, Anishinabe commercial trappers who had invaded the area a generation earlier abandoned the country around Lesser Slave Lake and shifted to the mixed economy of the parklands in the south. Other Anishinabe groups, such as those in the Cumberland House district, responded to the unpredictability of the muskrat trade by abandoning the region and becoming bison hunters.[30] As they withdrew from fur production and focused their attention on the plains, the Anishinabe increasingly became important participants in the cycle of warfare as allies of the Cree in opposition to the Niitsitapi and the Mandan along the Missouri.[31]

The Plains Cree recovered from their losses during the 1820s largely by migrating from the woodlands to the prairie and bison.[32] In shifting their focus west, the Cree (along with the Anishinabe) continued a pattern of migration that had endured for 500 years. The withdrawal, or at least retreat, of many groups from the diminished possibilities of the monopoly fur trade helped them to maintain their independence during what was considered the despotic rule of the HBC.[33] Rather than withdrawing from the economic relationship with Europeans altogether, those who moved from the forest responded to new market opportunities afforded by free trade and the bison hunt.

Fur producers isolated from the borders of HBC territory, particularly inhabitants of the boreal forest and the marginal lands at the edge of the tundra, did not fare so well. The company's new policy mandated that trappers trade at only one post, with authorization required from corporate officials for a transfer to a different region.[34] HBC censuses were part of a strategy to set production quotas appropriate to the sizes of post populations.[35] Corporate authorities strongly opposed the migration of displaced aboriginal producers from areas of restricted trade to other areas, including Red River. By the 1820s, the depletion of large game forced northern hunters to make wholesale changes in their subsistence strategies. For many, fish and hares became necessary, if precarious, food staples. To keep the aboriginal population in the game-depleted hinterland, the HBC used a number of measures, including the distribution of gratuities and the extension of credit.[36] Seasonal employment on York boat brigades was an inducement for those who chose to stay and trap during the winter in the overhunted fur country north of Norway House.[37] In the York district, bonuses were paid to trappers who did not hunt depleted species.[38]

In areas where conservation measures were imposed and local harvesters accepted them, producers who "trespassed" from other districts often hunted game illegally.[39] To circumvent differential prices decreed by the company, Chipewyan and Inuit groups exchanged furs before trading with Europeans at Churchill to maximize their returns.[40] Around Cumberland House, the Cree simply ignored appeals for conservation.[41] Their refusal to comply was undoubtedly related to the presence of free traders who had congregated along the lower Saskatchewan River after the merger. To counter the threat to its monopoly, the HBC attempted to bar freemen from the hinterland.[42]

The growth of Red River led to significant changes in both the economy and the epidemiology of Rupert's Land. The colony served as a pool of seasonal labour for the vast transportation network of the monopoly organization. With a surplus of native-born workers at its inland entrepôt and elsewhere in its territory, the HBC no longer had to import workers from the British Isles. Increasingly, the workforce was of mixed heritage. By 1830, 20 percent were country born. Thirty years later half of HBC employees were born in the northwest. Officers, many of them still from Great Britain, found them unmanageable.[43]

By the mid-1850s, the population of the colony was estimated to be 8,000.[44] The ever-increasing demand for meat was met by a burgeoning Métis-controlled hunting economy that had first developed during the competition era to supply the North West Company brigades. As other aboriginal societies focused on the herds, interethnic conflict grew. For a time, Anishinabe fought Métis hunters, though the two groups later cooperated in the context of wider competition for the resource. Sioux antagonism toward the Red River hunters festered until "a state of war" erupted in the 1840s.[45] As the herds declined, tensions grew between the colony's meat suppliers and the Plains Cree, escalating into open violence by the 1850s.[46] Alexander Ross said of the bison at mid-century that "They are now like a ball between two players."[47]

Demand for hides in the global market outstripped the expanding but essentially local market for meat. By 1865, 200,000 hides were being delivered annually to St. Louis. The hides ended up as "gun belts for British soldiers in India, drive belts for industrial machinery in Liverpool, and luxury furniture in Manhattan townhouses."[48] Meeting the world demand destroyed the provisioning economy, leaving Red River short of meat. As herds at the eastern margin of the plains were hunted to extinction in the 1850s, Métis supply lines became too long for hunters to return to Red River after the chase. They set up winter camps, known as *hivernants,* farther and farther west.[49] The HBC also had to move its pemmican-gathering stations west as herds declined. In 1829, Fort Pitt was built between Carlton and Edmonton to secure meat for the trade.[50] In 1830, Fort Ellice succeeded Brandon House as the chief source of supply. Within twenty years, even Fort Ellice was too far east, and the company opened outposts closer to the shrinking herds.[51]

The shift from a European to a largely indigenous workforce after the merger also brought significant changes to the disease ecology of the northwest. Most Europeans in the region had immunity from diseases that were endemic in their countries of origin but often deadly to the country born who had not been exposed to them. With increasing frequency, contagious diseases spread along the transportation routes of the interior. The burgeoning population of Red River served to maintain infections for extended periods, often ensuring the spread of pathogens as brigades left for the hinterland every spring.[52]

Increasingly, the west came under the economic and microbial influence of eastern North America. Completion of the Erie Canal in the mid-1820s turned a trickle of immigrants to the American midwest into a flood. In 1826, as many as 1,200 people a day passed through Buffalo on their way west.[53] As in the northwest decades later, large-scale economic development brought hardship and the inevitable emergence of tuberculosis among indigenous populations of upstate New York.[54] The introduction of steam-powered vessels during the period served to bring greater numbers of people and their germs with increased speed to the frontier.[55]

Along the Missouri, expanding American trade and the flow of pathogens that came with it contributed to the destruction of the sedentary horticultural societies south of the forty-ninth parallel. By 1830, the American Fur Company had established a number of "strong forts" along the waterway. Trade was invigorated by the participation of First Nations moving south in response to corporate downsizing in Rupert's Land. The new American establishments siphoned off a significant portion of beaver returns from HBC territory. Almost immediately, American traders along the Missouri displaced the Mandan, who had long controlled the aboriginal trade on the northern US plains. Soon the Mandan were isolated, with only the Hidatsa and Crow as their allies, and under attack by Cree, Saulteaux, and Assiniboine from the north and Sioux from the east.[56] By the mid-1830s, military and economic pressure, following decades of unpredictable harvests during particularly variable weather,[57] contributed to the emergence of tuberculosis among the besieged population of the Missouri villages. Whooping cough and cholera outbreaks during the early 1830s also damaged the health of Missouri villagers.[58] In a survey of pulmonary consumption (tuberculosis) published in 1837, Samuel Morton stated that the disease "occasions a large share of the mortality which annually occurs among the Mandans of the Upper Missouri."[59]

In 1831, smallpox swept across the central American plains, killing half of the Pawnee nation.[60] In response to a lobbying campaign led by Reverend John McCoy, the US government implemented a smallpox prevention program that conferred immunity to over 3,000 inhabit-

Combat between Blackfoot, Cree, and Assiniboine people, Fort Mckenzie, Montana, 1833. *Glenbow Archives, NA-2347-1.*

ants of the lower Missouri River. Unfortunately for the communities upstream, the physicians could not complete their work during the summer of 1832. They asked to be sent to the unvaccinated region the following year but were refused. Mandan, Hidatsa, Arikara, Assiniboine, Cree, and Niitsitapi in US territory were not vaccinated.

Those nations were severely debilitated when smallpox broke out along the Missouri in 1837. The partial success of the vaccination campaign shaped the differential outcomes of that epidemic, which in turn had important consequences for the development of the American plains for decades. Most Sioux bands, through vaccination or avoidance, were spared the mortality endured by their neighbours, and their better health facilitated their subsequent territorial expansion.[61]

The epidemic of 1837–38 killed an estimated 17,000 people and turned the region into "one great graveyard."[62] The outbreak spread up the Missouri from a steamboat, the *St. Peters,* whose crew carried the infection. For the Mandan, the death blow came less than two years later. Weakened by mortality estimated as high as 90 percent,[63] the villages were overrun by the Sioux in January 1839.

The disease ravaged the Assiniboine and Niitsitapi, whose territories straddled the forty-ninth parallel. The epidemic spread to the former when they ignored the warnings of American traders to stay away from Fort Union.[64] At Edmonton, John Rowand estimated mortality among the two groups as high as 75 percent.[65] Evidence of the carnage was still visible a decade later. In 1848, Paul Kane saw "[t]he bones of a whole camp of Indians, who were carried off by that fatal scourge of their race, the small-pox, ... bleaching on the plains."[66]

The epidemic did not sweep through HBC territory unchecked, for the company delivered medical and other types of assistance to its producers in viable areas of its domain. Governor Simpson described each post as "an Indian Hospital, where those who are unable to follow the Chase during the Winter months, are fed, clothed, and maintained."[67] The company was motivated by more than a sense of altruism; traders offered assistance to women, the sick, and the elderly so that able-bodied men could continue the commercial hunt.

In the Swan River district, Dr. William Todd, known as 'Picotte' because of his own disfigurement from smallpox, was largely responsible for stopping the epidemic in its tracks through extensive vaccination.[68] His work had important consequences for the demographic future of indigenous peoples on the Canadian plains. Ethnic boundaries were blurred as Cree, Saulteaux, and Assiniboine survivors joined together.[69] One effect of differential outcomes of the outbreak was the ascendancy of the Anishinabe or Saulteaux in the territory that they shared with the Cree and Assiniboine, especially south of the Assiniboine River.[70] Most of those who could obtain HBC vaccine did so; many groups travelled to Todd's post to request the procedure. A few, such as a band of Qu'Appelle Cree, agreed to vaccination after talking to Todd.[71]

Communities protected from the contagion augmented their territory in the aftermath of the outbreak. The Plains Cree and Saulteaux, vaccinated in large numbers, expanded their territory after 1837–38.[72] The opposite was true for the Assiniboine and Niitsitapi, who did not have the opportunity to be vaccinated and suffered high mortality rates.[73] Because of the high death toll among members of the Niitsitapi, as many as 6,000 individuals, groups such as the Siksika retreated from their northern frontier along the Battle River to what became their reserve at Blackfoot Crossing on the Bow River.[74] In 1841, Simpson reported that the Siksika "have been reduced by one half of late years by Small Pox and other causes." The Tsuu T'ina (Sarcee) were particularly hard hit. Simpson estimated that they were reduced from a population of 1,800 to a mere 250.[75]

Tribal historians have noted the role of the epidemic in the decline of the Assiniboine, once ubiquitous in the northwest. According to Chief Dan Kennedy, the group was "literally wiped out."[76] Even early chroniclers of the west recognized that the Assiniboine, whose bands tended to have larger population aggregates than their neighbours, were especially vulnerable to smallpox. In 1860, Dr. James Hector wrote that the disease "seemed to single them out for more severe visitation than any of the other tribes, till at length they were almost extirpated, the northern part of their country being occupied by the less mischievous Crees."[77]

Chief Kennedy believed that the surviving Assiniboine fled westward through enemy territory to the foothills of the Rockies, where their descendants today occupy the reserve at Morley, Alberta.[78] The idea that Assiniboine survivors took refuge among the Stoney is plausible but not likely; linguistic evidence indicates that the two groups have been discrete for so long that Stoney is "on the verge of becoming a separate language" from other Sioux dialects, including Assiniboine.[79] Although losses from disease undoubtedly played a hand in displacement of the Stoney to the foothills, they had occupied the region since at least the late eighteenth century and traded with the HBC at Edmonton and Rocky Mountain House.[80] Whatever the losses among the Assiniboine in the 1837 outbreak, mortality from smallpox was a key factor in their precipitous decline over the nineteenth century. Their position was also undermined by their inability to maintain sufficient horse herds to compete in the bison hunt. By the mid-nineteenth century, they were described as "impoverished," with few horses.[81] The handful of reserves that they occupy today provide but a faint reminder of the influence they once held across the west.

In addition to the protection afforded by vaccination, numerous groups used the time-tested strategy of heading into the bush or onto the plains to diminish the chances of contagion. At Pelly, Dr. Todd reported that at least two bands, one along the Red Deer River (in Manitoba) and the other in the Beaver Hills, refused to come to the post for fear of infection. Both groups endured privation by subsisting on rabbits rather than risk infection on the plains, where bison were numerous.[82]

Vaccinations performed by Dr. Todd, other HBC servants, and even First Nations people instructed in the procedure were the most significant example of the HBC's medical assistance to aboriginal groups in the monopoly period. Todd sent one group of aboriginal producers to the "Strong Woods" with a lancet and medicine to counter any infection that they might find there, and he "took many pains in instructing them how to use it in vaccinating others."[83] Although smallpox was the most virulent pathogen at the time, prevention through the use of cowpox vaccine was relatively simple. Lewis and Clark took vaccine with them on their expedition.[84] In Rupert's Land, the value of immunization was recognized early on. In 1811, before the arrival of the first settlers, Lord Selkirk suggested a vaccination campaign for the aboriginal inhabitants of Red River. Two years later the procedure was performed at York Factory with serum supplied by the HBC. During the measles and whooping cough outbreaks of 1820, the company vaccinated the population of Red River in response to rumours spreading northward. In the mid-1820s, the procedure was performed at Cumberland House, Norway House, and along the Albany River. What can truly be called a comprehensive vaccination program, however, was not implemented by the company until after the smallpox outbreak of 1837.[85]

Orders sent to HBC posts to conduct a vaccination program six months prior to the outbreak along the Missouri were never implemented.[86] When the crisis was over, the company conducted a territory-wide vaccination program, the first large-scale public health campaign undertaken in the northwest.[87] Vaccine was distributed as far northwest as the Mackenzie River. A sad irony, however, is that, as the HBC sought to end the most virulent disease of the time with some success, its employees infected communities with influenza and other diseases, which kept mortality rates high.

The HBC worked in other ways to prevent disease. Within years of the merger, the London Committee urged George Simpson to implement sanitation regulations at York Factory to combat chronic health problems there.[88] The company posted surgeons to a number of locations, and by 1830 at least two doctors were practising at Red River.[89] Quarantine techniques were also used to halt the spread of pathogens. In 1844, isolation measures perhaps stopped the spread of scarlet fever from Red River to the population north of Lake Winnipeg.[90] The company's interest in public health in its domain was prompted by humanitarian concerns as well as protection of its enterprise in the face of an increasingly complicated environment of disease and trade.[91]

Beyond the epidemiological situation, or perhaps because of it, the 1840s saw the introduction of the first large-scale missionary work outside the Red River settlement. Simpson had no affection for missionaries, but deteriorating conditions in the 1830s led him to accept their increasing presence. His change of heart was due to exhausted fur lands, the uncontrolled migration of displaced or unemployed Indians, and the slump in the beaver trade resulting from the growing popularity of silk hats in Europe.[92] Cutbacks in the trade resulted in increased hardship and dependence of aboriginal producers on the company's stores. Missionaries, whatever their faith, provided the HBC with a cheap way to deliver assistance. The missions also served to anchor communities to territories that otherwise would have been abandoned. By the early 1830s, the number of Muskego Cree heading south to Red River was straining the supplies of St. Peter's mission.

Anchoring surplus suppliers to HBC territory was also the rationale for establishment of the Roman Catholic mission at Île-à-la-Crosse in 1846. Father Thibault was invited to the district to stop the movement of Cree hunters south to the plains bison hunt. The Lac Caribou mission on Reindeer Lake was built to draw the Denesuliné (Caribou Eater Chipewyan) south from their independent life on the barrens.[93] The presence of missions, particularly the agrarian settlements established by Protestants, aided the material well-being of many, though the arrival of Christian groups in the north proved to be a mixed blessing.

As Fathers Taché and Laflêche were on their way to their postings in the interior in the summer of 1846, they held a mass at Frog Portage, where the routes north to Reindeer Lake and west to Île-à-la-Crosse intersect. The service had deadly consequences. It spread a fatal epidemic of measles to those who had congregated, and as many as eighteen people died from the infection caught at the mass.[94] Later twenty-nine converts at the newly established Anglican mission at Lac la Ronge also succumbed to measles.[95] Many of the inhabitants of the bush blamed missionaries for the spread of infection and death. The murders of the Roman Catholic missionary and his assistant at The Pas in June 1844 were in retribution for their perceived role in the spread of a scarlet fever epidemic the previous winter. The rapid acceptance of Catholic missionaries among the struggling populations in isolated regions of the north was in sharp contrast to the resistance of plains people to the efforts of Christians among them.[96]

A major factor in this increasing complexity was the growth of the agricultural colony at Red River, stimulated by its growing trade with the Minnesota Territory. In the 1840s, American traders such as Norman Kittson conducted a lucrative though illegal trade with the colony.[97] Métis free traders who, by the mid-1840s, were agitating for the legal right to an open trade further developed the link between Red River and the American frontier. Opponents of HBC rule in England quickly took up a petition attacking the monopoly, signed by almost 1,000 residents of the colony.[98]

The most vocal English critic was actually a native of the northwest with experience in the fur trade. Alexander Kennedy Isbister submitted his critique of the HBC monopoly to an inquiry in the British House of Commons in February 1847.[99] He attacked the monopoly charter on a number of points. The first was that the HBC had "to the utter impoverishment, if not ruin, of the natives" acquired "a princely revenue" through its monopoly. The second charged that the company had undermined aboriginal societies through the trade in liquor, a "deadly and demoralizing poison." The third dealt directly with the connection between the fur trade and hunger among "the larger part" of producers. His submission also lashed out against the trading monopoly imposed by the HBC, which he described as "gross aggressions on the rights and liberties of the natives."[100] Central to Isbister's critique was the connection between the fur trade and difficulty in securing food. The unpredictable climate of the 1840s undermined the Athapaskan societies of the western subarctic.[101] In the mid-1840s, the ships *Erebus* and *Terror,* part of the ill-fated Franklin Expedition, were frozen in the ice, and their crews perished from starvation and exposure. The description of the famine among the Dene by English explorer Henry Lefroy ignited a controversy over the HBC's role in the far north.[102] Isbister's criticism of the HBC was eloquent and probably just, but it failed to persuade Parliament to revoke the charter until the late 1850s, when the reality of the northwest's integration into the world economy was too strong to ignore.

By the 1840s, pathogens delivered overland from the expanding American frontier increasingly threatened the inhabitants of Rupert's Land. The opening of the Oregon Territory to settlers in 1846 had serious medical consequences, even for populations as distant as York Factory. That year an entire English regiment, comprised of almost 400 men,[103] travelled from York Factory to Red River. The force was sent to protect the colony against the threat of Americans, the result of the escalating conflict over the Oregon Territory.[104] Because the soldiers could not be maintained by the HBC at Hudson Bay, the company abandoned its usual quarantine protocol and moved them from the coast to the colony, where they could be sustained. Yet the hasty transfer of troops spread infection throughout the region. York boat crews dispatched from Red River to assist in the movement of troops were infected with measles, which greatly exacerbated the compound epidemics of influenza, measles, and dysentery. 1846 proved to be one of the most calamitous years in the history of Red River.[105] Aboriginal mortality in northern Manitoba was so severe that traditional mourning practices were abandoned.[106]

Another source of infection was the little-used route from the lakehead to Red River. Influenza spread from northern Ontario, where Charles Mackenzie reported that as many as 100 people had gathered at Lac Seul. The post, according to the trader, was "more a hospital than a kitchen."[107] Disease extended as far northwest as the Yukon.[108] As influenza blanketed the country, measles infected populations west from the eastern seaboard, possibly along the Oregon Trail and then north into HBC territory.[109] Dysentery was added to the deadly mix during the summer of 1846. At Red River, George Simpson estimated that, in a span of four weeks, 300 out of a population of 5,000 inhabitants died. He likened the mortality to the devastating cholera pandemic that had spread through Europe and eastern North America during the early 1830s. Simpson, who had seen the misery of the combined epidemics of 1819–20, reported that the outbreaks of 1846 "led to a greater mortality than at any former period within my recollection."[110] Alexander Ross, the first historian of Red River, described the suffering as a "pest" that spread "terror" in the colony: "From the 18th of June to the 2nd of August, the deaths averaged seven a day, or 321 in all; being one out of sixteen of our population. Of these one-sixth were Indians, two-thirds half-breeds, and the remainder whites. On one occasion, thirteen burials were proceeding at once."[111]

In the late 1840s, political and economic developments further undermined the monopoly of the HBC and the relative isolation of the inhabitants of Rupert's Land. The settlement of the Oregon question and the subsequent partition of the west coast between American and British interests led to the first large-scale influx of agricultural immigrants overland to the Pacific Northwest. The intensified interaction between Europeans and the indigenous population of the American west led to almost yearly epidemics of one sort or another.[112] Resolution of the Sayer trial in 1848 both opened trade with Minnesota and provided judicial acknowledgement that the HBC had a monopoly in title only. Before the end of the decade, gold was found in California. In 1849, 25,000 emigrants travelled through the plains at the height of the California Gold Rush, infecting the Sioux population along the route with smallpox, measles, and cholera.[113] Amid the gold fever, the HBC was forced to allow many of its employees leaves of absence for up to six months to prevent the wholesale desertion of its workforce.[114]

By 1850, the company's hold on the country was eroding at an ever-quickening pace. From within, labour strife threatened its complex, if precarious, transportation system as native boatmen "began to flex their collective muscle."[115] Agricultural settlers, "mostly Orkney halfbreeds," left Red River and headed west, adding to the largely unsanctioned mixed economy in the Qu'Appelle Valley that had begun a generation earlier.[116] By mid-century, the shift westward of mixed bloods was matched by corporate restructuring as provision posts were moved farther onto the plains to tap into the ever-decreasing bison herds.[117]

South of the forty-ninth parallel, the ill-fated Turtle Mountain Treaty between the American government and the Ojibwa, negotiated in 1851 but never ratified, sparked a land rush along the border. The derailed treaty process dispossessed the Turtle Mountain Ojibwa.

Across the plains, tension increased as bison herds dwindled and European settlement loomed. In addition to an escalation of interethnic violence, aboriginal groups began to resist the encroachment of European interlopers. The Anishinabe of Lake of the Woods refused to cooperate with the Hind Expedition in 1857.[118] As Hind surveyed the eastern plains for agricultural potential, Chief Peguis petitioned the Aborigines Protection Society in London for assistance in completing a treaty since his people feared the hardships that would follow the imminent European invasion.[119] Hind met with a council of Plains Cree, led by the highly esteemed chief Mis-tick-oos. The council was firm in its resolve to resist the encroachment of both Europeans and Métis bison hunters.[120] The explorer was told that leaders of the Plains Cree had earlier agreed that, because so many promises had been broken in the past, "They wished to establish some sort of toll of tobacco and tea for permission to pass through their country, threatening that if it were not given they would ... stop us by force."[121] The council blamed Europeans and their weapons for the declining herds and the pathogens that had accompanied the traders and settlers for the loss of human life. Europeans were no longer seen as allies and neighbours but as "others" who, like the Métis, were threats to the Cree. James Hector, the physician with the Palliser Expedition, estimated the population of Plains Cree at 12,500; "They are, however, rapidly on the decrease, as the small pox and other disease annually sweep them off in great numbers."[122]

Diseases continued to attack plains populations through the 1850s. Early in the decade, influenza spread across the interior from York Factory, the sixth such outbreak in twenty years.[123] The onset of winter mitigated the outbreak somewhat, but it still appeared as far west as Fort Vermilion, where, it was reported, "as many as 50 souls including 24 of our best hunters hav[e] been carried off by influenza." In 1856–57, smallpox again spread sickness and death along the Missouri hinterland[124] and northward, where "again the Qu'Appelle Crees were smitten, so that, added to their incessant strife with the Blackfeet for possession of the buffalo hunting grounds and for horses, the tribe was nearly wiped out."[125] Two years later "hundreds" of people in the Qu'Appelle Valley were reported to have died from scarlet fever.[126] As with earlier outbreaks, vaccinations at Red River prevented the spread of sickness to the colony.[127]

Scarlet fever swept across the aboriginal no man's land at the elbow of the South Saskatchewan to the Niitsitapi.[128] Dr. Hector spent a week in the Kainai (Blood) camp, and in that time between twenty and thirty people died from the disease, a sign, according to him, of their inevitable extermination.[129] Scarlet fever, a disease related to the streptococcus bacterium, might have been spread through interpersonal contact, perhaps by Hind's expedition. The typhoidal symptoms, resulting from salmonella bacteria spread through contaminated food and water, might have been exacerbated by the protracted drought in the southwestern plains that began in the mid-1850s (and lasted until the late 1860s).[130] For the Niitsitapi, the threat of water contamination from drought might have been made worse by their recent abandonment of the centuries-old practice of maintaining fresh water supplies by conserving beaver stocks within their territory.[131]

The already tense situation on the plains was further complicated during the summer of 1858 when gold was discovered on the Fraser River, prompting large numbers of Americans and eastern Canadians to cross Rupert's Land on their way west.[132] In addition to straining the food supply at Edmonton, miners virtually ignored the authority that the HBC had grown accustomed to over the years. By the end of the decade, the company had been stripped of even its titular monopoly.[133]

Over the mountains, the tide of gold seekers flooding into Vancouver Island and the mainland prompted imperial authorities to grant the district colonial status to deal with the myriad problems arising from the arrival of as many as 30,000 people.[134] The invasion of so many of what Governor James Douglas termed "rowdies" was no less than a catastrophe for many aboriginal populations in British Columbia. Among the disasters resulting from the gold rush were the massacre of an unarmed band near Okanagan Lake by miners and other "indiscriminate killings" and starvation resulting from the destruction of fish habitat. In 1862–63, a smallpox outbreak killed a significant portion of the aboriginal population. Among the dead were "no fewer than 500" Tsimshian at Fort Simpson.[135] In the Caribou, the British adventurer Walter Cheadle reported that 300 people had died.[136]

On the eastern plains, the shift from the fur trade to agriculture became inevitable.[137] Minnesota was granted statehood in 1858, and with it came a population explosion, railway development, and, as was so often the case in the American context, an "Indian war." The violence that erupted in the new state led to the deaths of 500 settlers, the subjugation of the Dakota nation, and the arrival of 450 Sioux refugees at Red River in 1862.[138] The Dakota also had a reputation for violence arising from their incessant struggles with the Anishinabe and later the Métis. By the spring of 1863, the presence of 2,000 Dakota was causing panic in the colony.

For a time, the violence in Minnesota slowed the pace of settlement and the looming changes that it meant for Red River. Although the first steamboat arrived at the colony before 1860, catching the inhabitants and especially the HBC off guard, it was a decade before the connection had a major effect on both the economy and the disease ecology of Canadian territory. The unsanctioned and unregulated flow of alcohol to the Indians in the colony was a serious problem, and calls were made for authorities to deal with it.[139] By 1862, the bison herds had disappeared from Red River altogether, and hunters had to travel farther west onto the plains to find them.[140] There were still herds near the elbow of the South Saskatchewan River, though hunting there was fraught with the risk of armed conflict. The HBC, which had used pemmican as a staple of its supply network for decades, contemplated "the immediate establishment of extensive farms in the Saskatchewan district."[141] Some aboriginal groups began cultivation on their own to supplement their hunts.[142] Even on the western plains, the bison were becoming scarce, increasing the demand on the limited crops grown in the territory. Throughout the decade, food shortages were common in the colony and on the plains.[143] In 1863, the sale of the Hudson's Bay Company itself to the International Financial Society sealed the fate of the northwest as a bastion of the fur trade.[144] A year later the Canadian government announced that the plains could sustain a large agrarian population.[145]

The stability of the fur trade was further eroded by the discovery of placer gold deposits near Fort Edmonton in the early 1860s. The gold strike proved to be unproductive, but the number of gold seekers, perhaps as many as 100, doubled the European population of what became the province of Alberta. William Gladstone, the errant HBC servant, noted that both Governor McTavish and the aboriginal inhabitants of the plains opposed the development of the gold fields.[146] Americans from Montana came north in ever-increasing numbers to work the gold fields in British territory. Among them were unemployed fur traders, and according to Gladstone at least seventy-five miners who were ordered out of Fort Benton. Before the end of the Civil War, gold discoveries in Montana contributed to its being granted territorial status in the fall of 1864. By the end of the war, Benton had a population of 1,500, including the infamous James brothers. Gladstone described the community as "hell on earth for a time."[147] Adding to the turmoil, hostilities flared between the Niitsitapi and the Cree–Assiniboine alliance.[148] Horse raiding and the shortage of food fuelled intertribal conflict. In their winter count, the Piikani (Peigan) described 1861 as the year "when they ate dogs" because of the scarcity of game.[149]

As was so often the case, disease and food scarcity created a synergy of hardship. Scarlet fever killed 1,100 members of the Niitsitapi Confederacy over the winter and spring of 1864–65.[150] The epidemic spread as far north as the Mackenzie district, where up to 800 people died of scarlet fever and measles in less than a month in 1865.[151] Tensions flared as diseases spread. At Rocky Mountain House, the trader there requested "assistance in men and arms" because Indians were blaming whites for the sickness and threatening to kill them. Along the Missouri, the Niitsitapi killed eleven American miners. In June 1865, they killed almost thirty Cree or Assiniboine, "principally women and children."[152]

As the death toll from disease and violence mounted throughout the northwest, the inhabitants of Red River faced a more immediate problem by the summer of 1868. Crops were destroyed by insects for four years in succession.[153] Starvation loomed as drought and grasshoppers turned crops into "a complete failure—even seeds having to be imported."[154] Governor McTavish estimated that as many as 2,346 people were in immediate need of assistance.[155] By mid-summer, the Council of Assiniboia allocated all of the funds available to it to relief. An international campaign was launched to assist those afflicted by the crisis.[156] The Canadian government pledged financial assistance for the colony, but no money was sent to Red River. Instead, the dominion concentrated its relief effort on construction of the road linking the community with Lake Superior. Canada's response to the agricultural crisis served as the pretext for its annexation of Rupert's Land.

As the era of monopoly came to an end, plains communities were on the precipice of a new economic and social order. George Simpson, the "Little Emperor," who ruled the entire northwest as a despot, had died in 1860. Chief Peguis, among the most influential aboriginal leaders of the early nineteenth century, and signatory to the Selkirk Treaty, had died four years later. On the eastern plains, the bison economy had run its course. The new Dominion of Canada was about to annex the west and make the plains its own agricultural hinterland. The shift in economic paradigms after Canada's dominion over the west would bring unparalleled changes to the aboriginal inhabitants of the plains.

CANADA, THE NORTHWEST, AND THE TREATY PERIOD, 1869–76

ACQUISITION OF THE WEST BY THE DOMINION OF CANADA IN December 1869 brought unprecedented changes to inhabitants of the plains. Within a decade, the bison would be gone, and the people who had depended on them would be marginalized by a new political and economic reality. Shrinking herds, coupled with imminent settlement of the plains by European immigrants, forced the original inhabitants of the region into an increasingly desperate situation. The numbered treaties between the First Nations of the west and the crown, negotiated between 1871 and 1877, attempted to reconcile the clash between two mutually exclusive economic systems in that fateful decade. The treaties were not monolithic; each took place under specific geographic and social conditions in the context of the dominion's short-term agenda for development. From the perspective of the dominion, treaties were a means to facilitate regional economic and political development. To Canada, they were a legal imperative, an obstacle to be overcome before settlement could proceed in earnest. From the perspective of the plains communities, the bison economy, which had sustained them for so long, was on the wane, and the arrival of large numbers of agrarian settlers was inevitable. To First Nations, the treaties were a means to secure their well-being in the face of an unsure future.

Before completion of the first post-Confederation treaties, the expansion of Canada into the fur trade society centred at Red River brought the two populations into armed conflict. The insurrection in Manitoba was but the first manifestation of discord between the expanding society of the east and the aboriginal one that had developed in the west. More than a century later many of the issues that sparked the trouble in Manitoba over the winter of 1869–70 remain unresolved.

As events were unfolding in the communities along the Red River, the end of the Hudson's Bay Company's stewardship of Rupert's Land created a jurisdictional vacuum on the plains. The void was filled by an invasion of essentially lawless bison and wolf hide traders who operated from Fort Benton on the Missouri River. In addition to the rampant alcohol use and violence of the terrible, and fortunately brief, "Whoop-Up" trade, they might have brought the last large-scale smallpox outbreak to the plains. The epidemic killed over 3,500 people, mostly Niitsitapi, Cree, and Métis.[1] As a result of the epidemic, Plains Cree along the North Saskatchewan River insisted on a Treaty 6 clause requiring the dominion government to provide a "medicine chest" for the reserve population. The true meaning of that amendment remains disputed.

As had been the case with all major outbreaks of smallpox over the previous century and a half, the disease spread northward from the major transportation artery of the American northwest, the Missouri River. An increasingly large fleet of steamers and construction of the Union Pacific Railroad in 1869 added to the tension in the Montana territory. As early as 1863, some Niitsitapi were engaged in a sporadic guerrilla war against the American population in Whoop-Up country. By the late 1860s, the country north of the Missouri River was "one of the most lawless areas on the frontier, a rendezvous for tough and lawless men from every part of North America and Europe."[2]

The Niitsitapi met the expanding and essentially anarchic incursions of the whisky traders with increasingly violent resistance. In 1869, fifty-six Europeans were reported to have been killed by Indians, and more than 1,000 horses had been stolen. The killing of Malcolm Clark, a Helena-area rancher, led to an attack in January 1870 by the American Army under the command of Colonel Eugene Baker on a group of friendly Piikani who were sick with smallpox on the Marias River, just south of the international boundary.[3] The raid, intended to strike the band of Mountain Chief, who were suspected of Clark's murder, was mistakenly directed against a peaceful band led by Heavy Runner and resulted in 173 deaths, including many women and children.[4] The massacre and its cover-up led to an uproar in the eastern press and seriously undermined President Grant's Indian peace policy. The killings also had the effect of immediately pacifying the Niitsitapi in American territory.[5]

The first report of smallpox among the Niitsitapi was in the spring of 1869.[6] Distrust between them and the newcomers was so high that they blamed the epidemic on

> the evil genius of an American trader who swore revenge for the loss of his horses to a raiding party. He allegedly purchased several bales of infected blankets in St. Louis and placed them on the banks of the Missouri River where innocent Indians filched them. Indians always denounced the reappearance of disease as a deliberate act of wicked white men.[7]

William Butler, who investigated the effects of the epidemic in Canada, accepted the belief that the disease had been spread by Missouri traders "with a view to the accumulation of robes."[8] Belief that the disease was spread purposefully was common during the early settlement period. One suspect was John H. Evans, the notorious American whisky trader and right-hand man to the infamous Thomas Hardwick. Both were members of the so-called Spitzee Cavalry, wolfers responsible not only for the Cypress Hills massacre of 1873 but also for the lesser-known Sweet Grass Hills massacre of 1872. Even recent works on the whisky trade attribute at least partial blame for the epidemic to the actions of a vengeful trader. Margaret Kennedy concluded that "One band of Blackfeet were thought to have contracted the pox from a man who set out to revenge himself for some grievance the former had caused on him. Infected himself, he collected all the scabs from his body, rubbed his shirt in them and left the shirt on a trail used by the Peigan (Piikani) on the Highwood Creek."[9] Hugh Dempsey has shown that the legend of the smallpox blanket is apocryphal, in fact "pure fiction," while acknowledging that the story of the intentional spread of disease as a tool of genocide "has gained a life of its own and will continue to be told and retold as historical fact."[10]

Although the outbreak in Montana was probably part of a larger epidemic that swept across the American plains,[11] Kennedy attributed the source of the infection along the Missouri to an outbreak aboard the steamboat *Utah*.[12] Within a year, 750 of 1,900 A'aninin died from it. The outbreak was catastrophic to the Niitsitapi and other First Nations on the Canadian plains. According to the report of the Board of Health appointed by dominion authorities to deal with the epidemic in their new territory, the death toll was horrendous (see the following table).

GROUP		DEATH TOLL OF INDIVIDUALS
Blackfeet		675
Bloods		630
Peigans		1,080
Sarcees		200
Crees	Ft. Pitt	100
	Edmonton	30
	Victoria	55
	Whitefish L.	15
	St. Paul's	150
	Carlton	78
Métis	St. Albert's	335
	St. Ann's	40
Mountain Stoneys		123
Total		**3,512**

Mortality from the smallpox epidemic of 1869–70 by ethnic group.
Source: Nix, *Mission among the Buffalo*, 67.

Among the Niitsitapi, the epidemic did more than kill a significant segment of the population. The high death toll among chiefs and elders from the disease and the famine that ensued shook the leadership of the alliance. The Fish Eaters, a Kainai band eventually led by Red Crow, lost two chiefs.[13] Many other leaders and elders also died.[14] Mortality among the Tsuu T'ina might have been much greater than the official report indicated; from an estimated pre-epidemic population of several thousand, only 300 to 400 remained alive.[15]

The terrible toll among the Niitsitapi—2,500 dead—was not the only disaster that they faced in the early 1870s. Their military power was broken by the American Army after the Marias River massacre. The unrestrained flow of alcohol from Fort Benton caused near anarchy. Within months of their victory over the Cree-led alliance at Belly River, the Blackfoot were suffering terribly at the hands of American traders. An anonymous but "close observer" who spent two months in the vicinity over Christmas 1870 wrote that "no language can describe these drunken orgies; more than sixty Blackfeet have been murdered; and if there can be a transcript of hell on earth, it is here exhibited."[16] In 1872, Colonel Patrick Robertson-Ross of the Canadian Militia was sent to assess the situation on the southern plains. He reported that, of the 221 deaths among the Niitsitapi the previous year, only 133 had been from disease.[17] He attributed the remaining fatalities to the Montana liquor trade.[18] Emboldened by their profitable if unscrupulous trade, six whisky merchants went as far north as Edmonton. When advised by Richard Hardisty of the HBC that they were breaking the law, "they coolly told him they knew it very well, but he had no force to prevent it, so they would do just as they liked."[19] During the winter of 1873–74, Methodist missionary John McDougall reported that over forty able-bodied northern Blackfoot men died, "all slain in drunken rows. Some terrible scenes occurred," he continued, "when the whole camp went on a spree, as was frequently the case, shooting, stabbing, killing, freezing. Thus these atrocious debauches were continuing all that winter not far from us. Mothers lost their children. These were frozen to death or devoured by the myriad of dogs of the camp."[20] Rhetorical flourish aside, conditions in southern Alberta must have been terrible. Predations against First Nations are well documented in the years before the arrival of Canadian law in the west in 1874. The grisly murder of Kainai chief Calf Shirt,[21] and the massacres of Assiniboines at the Sweet Grass and Cypress Hills, are bloody examples. Occasionally, First Nations turned on their neighbours in the increasingly desperate and hostile environment of the northern plains.

The decline of the Niitsitapi at the hands of the whisky traders was precipitous, but the group experienced a single and important victory in their ongoing and increasingly desperate war with the Cree-led alliance. In the fall of 1870, while camped on the banks of the Belly (Oldman) River near the present site of Lethbridge, they repelled an attack of 600 to 800 Cree, Saulteaux, and Assiniboine warriors in what has been called the "Last Great Indian Battle" on the Canadian plains.[22] The Cree alliance chose to attack precisely because of the high death toll suffered by their enemies during the epidemic.[23] Although the attackers were routed, both sides recognized that the days of intertribal war were at an end. A peace treaty was concluded between the long-time antagonists in 1872.[24]

The loss of between 200 and 300 warriors among the northern alliance at Belly River, though an important military defeat, paled in comparison to another outcome of their long-standing conflict with the Niitsitapi. During one of the many raids on Blackfoot camps in the spring of 1870, the Cree contracted smallpox.[25] Over the next few months, more than 1,000 perished. The coincidence of the outbreak with a political crisis in Red River undermined the HBC's ability to counter

Bodies of Crow people killed by Blackfoot, near the Sweet Grass Hills, 1874. *Glenbow Archives, NA-249-75.*

the spread of the disease. The chief officer in the infected country, W. J. Christie, requested the immediate delivery of vaccine in August 1869.[26] None came until April 1870.[27] Communication lines across the prairies were so tenuous that even the turmoil at Red River remained only a rumour until travel was facilitated with the spring breakup.[28]

Although the company's efforts to counter the spread of the virus were frustrated for at least eight months, some groups were successfully vaccinated. Isolated successes played a decisive role in limiting the spread of the epidemic to the east. Isaac Cowie's memoir recounts the "providential visit" of the Métis leader Pascal Bréland and his newly vaccinated grandchild to Fort Qu'Appelle in the fall of 1869.[29] Cowie, whose father was a physician in Scotland,

> secured, on bits of window glass, enough vaccine to protect everyone requiring it in the fort, from whom the supply was increased sufficiently to vaccinate all the people about the lakes and the Indians visiting them that fall. ... [T]hose who had been vaccinated at the fort took it out to the plains and spread it so thoroughly there among the Qu'Appelle and Touchwood Hills Indians that not a single case of smallpox was ever heard among them.[30]

His work probably prevented the spread of the epidemic to the urban population at Red River.

To the north of Cowie and his vaccinated clients along the Qu'Appelle River, immunity was conferred to some of the inhabitants of the lower North Saskatchewan River. At the Prince Albert mission, Reverend James Nisbet used his own supply of serum to vaccinate over 150 people.[31] The success of the procedure, and the order to abandon the mission and disperse into small groups, halted the spread of the disease east of the forks of the Saskatchewan.[32] A vaccination campaign conducted later by Dr. McKay of the HBC's Mackenzie River Department with the assistance of Anglican clerics over the winter of 1870–71 shielded inhabitants along the Churchill River from the dreaded outbreak.[33]

The communities of the disputed territory west of the forks of the Saskatchewan suffered the full brunt of the epidemic. Hostilities on the western plains and the months-long breakdown in communications between the west and Red River prevented vaccine from reaching the sufferers.[34] Along the North Saskatchewan, famine, disease, and inter-ethnic violence contributed to an ever-deepening crisis.[35]

As already mentioned, the infection spread to the northwestern plains by a Cree horse-raiding party who ransacked an infected camp of Blackfoot in April 1870. All seventeen raiders were infected, and only two survived. From them, the virus spread to a Cree encampment "assembled together from different directions in large numbers." By summer, sickness extended across the entire country from Rocky Mountain House to Fort Carlton.[36]

Malaise over the future of the west under Canadian rule quickly turned into hostility and even violence toward Europeans with the outbreak of the epidemic. The Methodist mission at Victoria on the North Saskatchewan River was attacked by a group of desperate and infected Niitsitapi; of eleven in their war party, ten died.[37] Relations were no better between Europeans and Cree attached to the mission. According to Reverend McDougall's son John, they were "at times very insolent; they went about armed to the teeth, and were ready for any excuse to commit violence. This was a white man's disease, and they hated the whites."[38] At Edmonton, Chief Factor Christie echoed the McDougalls' views on aboriginal hostility toward Europeans for their role in the spread of the disease. He reported that a party of Indians travelled to Fort Pitt with the specific intention of murdering traders Watt and Traill in retaliation for spreading the disease among them.[39]

As smallpox spread, aboriginal hostility toward traders, who were largely immune to the disease,[40] was manifest in the most grisly of manners. At Fort Pitt, where the epidemic broke out in early summer, the situation descended into anarchy. Although a supply of vaccine was sent up the Saskatchewan in April 1870,[41] trader James Sinclair soon ran out of supplies for the two camps of infected Cree who came to the post for help.[42] They believed that only Europeans could cure the disease that they had introduced to the country and that their own medicine men were powerless in confronting the plague. According to Butler, the Cree then turned to more potentially fatal measures:

[T]hey appear to have endeavoured to convey the infection into the fort. ... The dead bodies were left unburied close to the stockades, and frequently Indians in the worst stage of the disease might be seen trying to force an entrance into the houses, or rubbing portions of the infectious matter from their persons against the door-handles and window-frames of the dwellings.[43]

The Cree persisted in their "macabre picketing" until only weeks before Butler's arrival at Fort Pitt in mid-November. Butler reported that over 100 people had died near the stockade.[44] The scene was horrific even at a distance: "The unburied laid for days by the road-side, till the wolves ... approached and fought over the decaying bodies."[45] Amid the chaos, the chief factor at Edmonton requested eighty armed men to reinforce the company's tenuous hold on its posts along the North Saskatchewan.

The epidemic also struck hard at Fort Carlton. Two of the company's servants were infected. Clerk Donald McDonald died in August, and Peter Ballandine, the mixed-blood postmaster, recovered only after a long convalescence.[46] William Traill, who had recently transferred to

Carlton, was forced "to act as officer in Charge, Clerk, Interpreter, Doctor, Nurse and Sexton"[47] when the disease debilitated the entire post staff. Despite his heroic efforts, thirty-two of the seventy residents of the post were infected, and twenty-eight died.[48] Carlton's strategic location in the overland trade served to spread the disease to smaller posts in the interior. Of the cart brigade sent to the post from Lac la Biche, eight of fourteen drivers died on their return or soon after their arrival in the northern community.[49]

Traill was not completely alone during the epidemic. For a time, the Roman Catholic bishop of Lac la Biche, Vital Grandin, assisted him in caring for the sick and dying. At Fort Carlton, he walked from tent to tent

> doing what he could to make the sick more comfortable. He had no medicine to fight the disease. It simply had to run its terrible and often deadly course. He heard confessions of those who were dying, putting his head close to theirs to hear the final weak whispers of sorrow and repentance. Many asked him to baptize them before they died.[50]

The bishop counselled one of the infected servants, even though he was a Protestant, because "his Minister has not come."[51] The Protestant minister was James Nisbet, who did not travel to the infected fort for fear that he would take the disease back to Prince Albert. He was said to have been "deeply grieved that he could not visit his friends at Fort Carlton when they were in danger."[52]

Grandin's actions while at Carlton and Nisbet's refusal to travel there illustrate the different strategies adopted by Catholic and Protestant missionaries in dealing with the epidemic. The differences are critical to understanding the wide variances in infection and mortality in the communities ministered by the two groups. The Cree, largely cared for by Methodists and Anglicans, suffered terrible casualties, but the disease was much worse in areas under the ministry of Catholics. At the Protestant missions, orders to disperse were often given as soon as word of the epidemic arrived.[53] Henry Steinhauer, the missionary at Whitefish Lake, led his people north into the bush "and became so isolated that nothing was heard from them for a long time."[54] To avoid contagion, many of the Cree travelled as far north as the Peace River. In other districts, territory was probably abandoned temporarily to avoid the dreaded illness. While travelling through the Touchwood Hills, Butler reported that "all is silent and deserted—the Indian and the buffalo gone."[55] At Pomass Lake, not far from the Touchwood

Hills, oral histories indicate that as many as 100 Saulteaux died during the epidemic.[56]

Catholics, in contrast, dealt with the suffering by bringing their communities together. Métis communities, which had developed around the Catholic missions in Alberta, suffered extremely high mortality rates in the summer of 1870.[57] Very few cases were reported inside Fort Edmonton because of quick and effective measures taken by HBC authorities.[58] Outside the palisades, the outcome could not have been more different. At St. Albert, a Métis community only eight miles from Edmonton, two-thirds of a total population of 900 were infected. Of those, 320 died.[59] McDougall, whose mission at Victoria suffered over fifty deaths and whose survivors were ordered to disperse, vehemently denounced the role of Catholics during the epidemic.[60] His son John, who contracted the disease himself,[61] contrasted the measures taken by the competing churches. Catholics saw the isolation measures taken by Protestants as a sign of cowardice, but he noted the results of the Catholic approach: "many of the Indians and half-breeds gathered together, and died like rotten sheep."[62] The high death toll among people under the care of Catholics might have been the result of more than a simple failure to disperse. Some Catholics vaccinated their people, but according to Butler the serum bought at Fort Benton and dispensed at the height of the epidemic at St. Albert was "of a spurious description."[63]

The epidemic brought suffering and death west to the foothills of the Rockies. Father Leduc travelled to Jasper to minister to fifteen infected families and "dispense among them the consolations of religion."[64] A Stoney witness described Banff as "a graveyard."[65] Northeast of Edmonton and the infected Catholic missions, the disease depopulated the small trading post community of Moose Lake at the headwaters of Beaver River. Cree historian Joseph Dion wrote that the "whole settlement was carried off, leaving as sole survivor a little boy among the unburied dead, who scampered in the bush, and with great difficulty was caught and saved."[66] Near Sounding Lake, Dr. A. E. Porter, attached to the treaty party that travelled through the "Ghost Woods" on their way to meet Big Bear in 1878, reported that "many of the tent poles were still standing and the bones of many victims lay bleaching in the sun."[67]

The response of dominion authorities to the epidemic was a stark and fatal contrast to the measures taken by the HBC against the outbreak a generation earlier. Government officials did not have a clue about the magnitude of the suffering or, in the short term, how to organize medical assistance over such a vast region. The HBC, the de facto government for the previous half-century, used its own supplies and transportation network to check the epidemic in its establishments.[68] That the dominion was unprepared for the scale of the crisis is an understatement. Only in October 1870, when the epidemic had all but run its course, was a Board of Health appointed to manage the situation.[69] The jurisdictional vacuum of the plains was such that the legislation empowering the board, the Temporary Government Act (1870), was described by one writer as "extralegal."[70] Because his papers had yet to arrive from the east, Lieutenant Governor Archibald responded to the epidemic without the benefit of consulting the documents that empowered him to govern the plains. He appointed the board without the permission of the dominion government almost a week before his papers arrived at Red River. To his horror, his appointment of the board was beyond his authority, but he rationalized the action because "the validity of these (actions) is taken for granted."[71]

Two weeks earlier Archibald had ordered William Butler, a young British officer attached to the Red River Expeditionary Force, to undertake a reconnaissance of the plains to determine the extent of the epidemic.[72] Because a physician could not be found to travel west,[73] Butler was provided with medicine to relieve the stricken country. Unfortunately for those infected or still at risk, his cargo was not properly prepared for the rigours of an early winter trip across the plains, and much of it was destroyed. At Fort Carlton, Butler salvaged what medicine he could, enough, according to the young officer, "to poison a very large extent of the territory."[74]

Another measure taken by dominion authorities was the establishment of a cordon sanitaire to protect Red River from the epidemic. Reverend E. R. Young reported that "Not a single cart or traveller was permitted to go on the trail. This meant a good deal of suffering and many privations for the isolated Missionaries and traders. ..."[75] Supplies of local food stocks, usually procured by the infected Métis, also stopped during the epidemic. The chief factor at Edmonton reported that, with no trade and no provisions, "the prospect of the coming winter is dark in the extreme. ... [O]ur sole dependence will be on our Fisheries and Crops."[76] The harvest proved bountiful, but the fishery was reduced by two-thirds, the result of forty deaths at Ste. Anne and bad weather, and "entail[ed] an amount of starvation to many."[77] Famine followed the epidemic at Victoria, where George McDougall wrote that "multitudes who recovered from the disease have perished from destitution."[78] The situation was no better on the eastern plains. Isaac Cowie recorded that near the forks of the Saskatchewan the epidemic led to the failure of the provision trade, "a great loss, which we will feel all throughout the

(Saskatchewan) District."[79] It was in the chaos of disease and famine that the ill-fated attack at Belly River took place.

In the waning days of 1870, the authorities in Winnipeg were finally able to secure the services of a medical doctor to supplement Butler's hobbled effort on the plains. Captain McDonald of the Ontario Volunteers, who "had great experience in the treatment of Small pox," arrived at Edmonton on 29 December,[80] but he did not live up to the expectations of those who had lobbied for his services, interested more in drinking liquor than in healing people.[81]

As McDonald drank his way across the plains, and as Butler distributed his pamphlets, HBC physician McKay made an extensive and successful vaccination tour from the Mackenzie through parts of the Athabasca, English River, and Saskatchewan districts.[82] The Mackenzie watershed was further protected by a vaccination campaign undertaken by Catholic missionaries Pettitot and Seguin that conferred immunity on 1,700 people.[83]

The most significant response of the authorities to the crisis was the prohibition of fur exports from the northwest. Even pelts from the far north were quarantined as they passed through the infected depot at Fort Carlton on their way to Red River.[84] Orders were sent to traders on the plains "to trade nothing" that might infect the isolated populations to the north.[85] At Edmonton, Chief Factor W. J. Christie reported to the officers of the Northern Department that "I need hardly say that there will be no Returns from the Saskatchewan this Year, and it has yet to be decided whether it would be *politic* to send out the few furs we have."[86]

The question of what to do with furs from infected areas, often from destitute producers, remained until the spring of 1871.[87] On 24 April, the Board of Health convened at Edmonton House and passed a resolution prohibiting the export of furs from the Saskatchewan district for the rest of the season.[88] Christie commented that enforcement of the quarantine was one of the most difficult responsibilities of the board.[89] He was referring to the control of native movements during the epidemic even though the company worked to get furs to Red River in breach of the quarantine. Cowie admitted in his memoir to having done so. When his furs were confiscated and placed in storage by a provincial constable, he travelled to Winnipeg to "clear the foul aspersions against our cargo." On his way up the Assiniboine to gather affidavits from Fort Ellice to support his claim, Cowie was told that the confiscated furs had almost produced a riot since "people were so alarmed that they had been hardly restrained from burning the building in which the robes were stored."[90] It appears that his cargo eventually passed through the quarantine without further mishap. In his report, Butler noted that the location of the cordon, at Rat Creek near Portage la Prairie, was too close to the populated part of the country to be an effective barrier to the disease.[91]

Butler submitted his report in March 1871, when people were still worried that the epidemic might spread to Manitoba. He recommended the establishment of a new quarantine station at Fort Ellice, the only settlement between Fort Carlton and Portage la Prairie, and advocated compulsory vaccination of the halfbreed population.

His fears of the epidemic reigniting with the coming of spring did not materialize. By June 1871, the disease was reported to have "entirely disappeared" from the Saskatchewan district. Within a month, trade was back on track, with several hundred bags of pemmican traded at Fort Carlton. In August, the flow of buffalo robes to Montreal via St. Paul resumed.[92]

Deep resentment remained among plains communities toward Europeans for the introduction of disease and the general turmoil in the wake of the transfer of Rupert's Land to Canadian control. According to John McDougall, there was even talk among the Indians of "a war of extermination among the whites. They laid the blame of all their calamity upon these."[93] There was, of course, no race war, but authorities recognized the bitter feelings among the Indians and Métis.[94]

There was growing anxiety among the aboriginal population over the future of their land under Canadian sovereignty. Before the transfer of Rupert's Land in 1869, McDougall petitioned dominion authorities on behalf of First Nations for the prompt completion of a treaty to formalize relations between the crown and inhabitants of the west.[95] Many of those who entered treaties with the crown during the 1870s had sophisticated knowledge of, and occasionally participated in, American treaties prior to the transfer.[96] Although the crisis brought on by the epidemic temporarily overshadowed the longer-term question of treaties, the Butler report stressed the need for a judicious settlement of the issue.[97] In January 1871, the Cree circulated a petition requesting government action to resolve uncertainty in the west. Sweet Grass, the Cree chief who converted to Catholicism during the outbreak, requested a treaty in April.[98] Through William Christie, the chief emphasized Cree ownership of the territory.[99] Christie's report on the meeting with Sweet Grass and the other Cree chiefs was unambiguous:

> The object of their visit was to ascertain whether their lands had been sold or not, and what was the intention of the Canadian Government in relation to them. They referred to the epidemic

Sweet Grass, head chief of the Cree, in St. Boniface, Manitoba, 1872. *Glenbow Archives, NA-1677-10.*

that had raged throughout the past summer, and the subsequent starvation, the poverty of their country, the visible diminution of the buffalo, their sole support, ending requesting certain presents *at once,* and that I should lay their case before Her Majesty's representative at Fort Garry.[100]

A common theme of recent writing regarding the early treaty-making process is the forcefulness of First Nations' claims to ownership of their territories.[101] Even before the first of the numbered treaties, First Nations demanded recognition of their ownership of the land, and dominion officials recognized the need for treaties on the prairies. Indian Commissioner Wemyss Simpson wrote to Joseph Howe on this issue on 3 November 1871. He stated that the negotiation of, or at least the promise of, a treaty in the Saskatchewan district was "essential to the peace, if not the actual retention[,] of the country."[102]

Concern among aboriginal communities was justified. By the spring of 1871, the flood of Ontario immigrants overwhelmed provincial authorities in Manitoba: "An embarrassed provincial government found itself without immigrant sheds, without a Commissioner of Lands and with no surrendered lands for the emigrants to settle on."[103] The arrival of so many immigrants forced the completion of Treaty 1 in Manitoba. The government was only willing to negotiate treaties according to its own timetable based on external and often short-term needs rather than concern for the long-term well-being of the Indians.[104]

With no immediate development agenda pressing the need for a treaty west of Red River, dominion authorities did not act. In March 1872, Adams Archibald, the Lieutenant Governor of Manitoba told Joseph Howe, secretary of state for the provinces, that "when the time comes they will be fairly dealt with."[105] In June, the prime minister was informed of increasing tensions on the plains between Crees and settlers resulting from government inaction on treaties.[106]

The threat of European immigration was not the only issue fuelling First Nations' demands for treaties. The early 1870s saw significant changes to the fur trade economy that for decades had been dominated by the HBC. Having sold its charter, the company no longer felt responsible for the physical well-being of its suppliers. In 1872, a reorganization of the company trade eliminated all credit to Indian suppliers in order to cut costs.[107] The withdrawal of credit signalled a fundamental shift in the relationship between the HBC and aboriginal producers after two centuries in which the social safety net provided by the company included "liberal credit to the able-bodied and aid to the elderly, sick, and destitute."[108] The introduction of steamboats on Lake Winnipeg and the Saskatchewan River severely curtailed wage employment for seasonal fur procurers who could not subsist on trapping alone. On the plains, the scarcity of bison and the vagaries of weather contributed to the hardships of the winter of 1872–73. In January, rain made travel impossible. Many deaths resulted from a combination of hunger and sickness.[109]

The end of the old economy was underscored in the summer of 1872 when the railway expedition led by Sir Sanford Fleming arrived in the west. George M. Grant, who chronicled the journey, saw their mission as the "dawning of a new industrial economy" on the plains.[110] The downside of the new era, according to Grant, would be extirpation of the indigenous population.[111] The main cause would be not only "scrofula and epidemics" but also the invasion of southern traders, whose chief commodity was "rum in name, but in reality a compound of tobacco, vitriol, bluestone and water."[112] His fatalistic assertions regarding the future of the plains Indians were based on the erosion of Niitsitapi society at the hands of American traders. Grant's gruesome prediction might well have come true were it not for the arrival of the North-West Mounted Police in the southwest in the fall of 1874.[113]

As anxiety grew over the uncertain future on the plains, some officials downplayed the situation. Gilbert McMicken, the dominion land agent in Manitoba, wrote to the prime minister in April 1873 remarking that "there has been a gross exaggeration in regard to Indian trouble. [I] am perfectly satisfied if a Treaty is made with the Crees this summer and small holdings of lands granted the Sioux there will be no difficulty."[114] Fleming dismissed the concerns of Mennonite leaders regarding the safety of the plains by telling the elders of the immigrant community that on his journey across the west he had kept nothing but a cork screw for protection—and that he had rarely had the opportunity to use it.[115]

The western Indians received no treaty, and hostilities grew. When the International Boundary Commission began its survey of the forty-ninth parallel in 1872, Alexander Morris recognized the perceived threat posed to First Nations of uniformed Canadians and Americans working together. In October 1873, Robert Bell of the Geological Survey of Canada reported to Lieutenant Governor Morris that the indigenous people of southern Saskatchewan were increasingly anxious about "the intentions of the 'English' and Canadians towards them. ... On several occasions these Indians threaten[ed] to steal our horses and outfit and even to kill us all and finally ordered us to turn back—saying at the same time that we might thank God if we got home safely."[116] Bell also noted that mistrust of the "English" was so high among the Indians of the area that they believed the massacre at Cypress Hills a few months earlier "was committed by people belonging to the English side" and that the Assiniboines "were bent on revenging it upon any English people" in the country.[117] East of Fort Qu'Appelle, the Saulteaux at Fort Ellice petitioned Morris to halt the survey being conducted by A. H. Whitcher until their land issues were dealt with.[118] Morris asked his superiors to reconsider a treaty to facilitate immigration to the west.[119] The situation was resolved by late summer 1874 with arrival of the police and conclusion of the Qu'Appelle Treaty in September.[120] At the ceremony, dominion officials were lambasted for allowing surveys to be conducted without the surrender of aboriginal title.[121] Chief Pasqua articulated the frustration of the Indians succinctly. Pointing to the HBC's McDonald, the chief was reported to have said that "You told me you had sold the land for so much money—£300,000. We want that money."[122] A sign of the acrimony surrounding completion of the treaty was that the pipe ceremony, symbolizing mutual respect, was not performed at the Fort Qu'Appelle meeting.

Hunger played a role in the completion of Treaty 4, an event witnessed by 3,000 people who converged at Fort Qu'Appelle.[123] Joseph Reader, the Anglican missionary who had arrived in the Touchwood Hills a year earlier, reported that starving people had eaten one of his dogs.[124] Dominion officials advocated agriculture as "the best means to break them of their roving habits, to elevate and assure their position."[125] Yet even communities that had already begun the conversion to agriculture underwent severe hardships. In Manitoba, the band at St. Peter's, which had 2,000 acres under cultivation, suffered a crop failure in the summer of 1875.[126] Compounding the situation was a decline in the fall fishery that placed the entire Treaty 1 population in jeopardy. Indian Commissioner J. A. N. Provencher reported that "only the assistance of the Government prevented great sufferings at St. Peter's, the Portage and Roseau River."[127]

The shortage of food among the Saulteaux contributed to the severity of a measles outbreak that "embraced the whole population" at Fort Alexander in 1875.[128] The disease, which initially affected the children and then spread to "a greater number than usual of adult Indians," confounded both the Indian commissioner and the doctors sent to investigate the outbreak. Within weeks, the epidemic subsided. The main factors in its termination were "their adoption of a few rational practices in the method of diet and nursing." [129] The use of food to mitigate the outbreak and the isolation of the disease to communities of Treaty 1 experiencing malnutrition underscore the connection of the epidemic with food scarcity.

The hardships in Manitoba and the eastern parklands were not isolated occurrences. In fact, the plains experienced widespread hunger throughout 1874. In February, the HBC post at Battle River reported little trade because of the lack of bison.[130] At Fort Carlton, the meat trade declined to the point where the HBC abandoned its Cree producers in favour of the Métis. Charles Napier Bell wrote to David Laird, the Liberal minister of the interior, about the impending food crisis:

> The Crees are very troublesome at Carleton, Pitt, Victoria and Edmonton. I saw some at Victoria, last spring, who came in from the plains starving, and demanded provisions from the settler & the H.B. Co. There were no buffalo on the plains all winter, and they suffered frightfully. They told us that many Indians had eaten their horses, dogs, buffalo skins and in some cases their snowshoe laces & moccasins and then died. How much worse will it be in a year hence?[131]

Bell warned that there would be trouble the coming summer without at least the promise of a treaty. Even non-Indians advocated the quick resolution of treaties in the west. The residents of Prince Albert, "principally English Halfbreeds," requested resolution of the issue, or "there must always be danger."[132] Presents were distributed by the newly arrived police force at Fort Carlton to facilitate construction of a telegraph line in 1874. The next year Crees stopped construction of the line because they objected to the presence of workers without their consultation. Again presents were distributed to those who would accept them.[133] By October 1875, the temporary measures taken over the previous two summers to smooth development in the Saskatchewan country were no longer sufficient.

George McDougall stressed the general consensus of the chiefs with regard to a treaty, though he acknowledged that there were dissenters. Big Bear was adamant in his opposition: "We want none of the Queen's presents; ... let your Chiefs come like men and talk to us."[134] Even bands sympathetic to the idea of a treaty with the crown were wary of its implications. Peter Erasmus reported on the anxiety among Seenum's Cree band at Whitefish Lake,[135] and Mistawassis, the Cree chief who later became a main proponent of Treaty 6, was ambivalent about the process.[136]

It was in an atmosphere increasingly marked by privation, resignation, and dread that the dominion treaty party met with the First Nations of the northern plains in the late summer of 1876. By then, the Cree along the North Saskatchewan River knew that the bison economy was all but over, and they recognized that conversion to a new economic paradigm based on agriculture would be extremely difficult.[137] Another factor that shaped the negotiations was the relative power of the Plains Cree in 1876. Five years earlier Butler had noted that they were exceptional, "perhaps the only tribe of prairie Indians who have yet suffered no injustice at the hands of the white man."[138] The Plains Cree still posed a serious military threat to the small number of Europeans who had ventured onto the western prairie. A recent study of Treaty 6 acknowledged that the threat of armed conflict and pressure for economic development were the main motivations for dominion negotiators.[139] The fear of violence was heightened by the military victory of the Sioux under Sitting Bull over the American Army at the battle of Little Big Horn only two months before negotiations began at Fort Carlton.

The possibility of bloodshed was real, but most of the Cree who attended the treaty talks recognized the futility of armed resistance to dominion authority. Mistawassis stressed this point to Poundmaker and The Badger, two opponents of the treaty: "We are few in numbers compared to former times, by wars and the terrible ravages of smallpox. ... Even if it were possible to gather all the tribes together, to throw away the hand that is offered to help us, we would be too weak to make our demands heard."[140] Chief Ahtahkakoop echoed the sentiments of

Treaty Six negotiations with the Saskatchewan Cree, 1876. *Glenbow Archives, NA-1315-19.*

Mistawassis: "We are weak and my brother Mista-wa-sis I think is right that the buffalo will be gone before many snows. What then will be left us with which to bargain?"[141]

To the bulk of the Cree leadership, the successful negotiation of a treaty represented their best hope for survival in the new economic order on the plains.[142] Hunger contributed to the urgency of the treaty. Sweet Grass's priority was to protect his people from starvation.[143] To Morris, a guarantee of food aid during the transitional period was too extravagant and would result in idleness among the adherents to the treaty.[144] Difficulties arising from "hard winters or the hardships of single bands"[145] would not be covered by the treaty, yet Morris told Chief Beardy, a holdout at Fort Carlton, that, "In a national famine or general sickness, not what happens in everyday life, but if a great blow comes on the Indians, they would not be allowed to die like dogs."[146] The Cree stressed that they sought not a steady supply of free food from the dominion but assistance in times of hardship. Morris described the goodwill of the dominion in assisting Manitoba bands during the crop failure and the measles epidemic, "although it was not promised in the treaty." On the fourth day of negotiations, Tee-Tee-Quay-Say requested "That we be supplied with medicines free of cost." Morris later responded that "A medicine chest will be kept at the house of each Indian Agent, in case of sickness amongst you."[147]

The Cree successfully negotiated three innovations in Treaty 6: extra assistance in their conversion to agriculture, protection from famine and pestilence, and inclusion of the "medicine chest."[148] The concessions strove to maintain "two-hundred-years-old traditions of Native–White relations as established by the HBC. Having obtained these crucial concessions, the chiefs signed the treaty."[149] The Cree accepted agriculture as a solution to the decline of the bison economy; they negotiated assistance during the years of transition to farming; and, given their experience of the smallpox epidemic a few years earlier, and their recognition that the imminent flood of Europeans would increase sickness among them, they pushed for a promise of medical assistance. Yet the Cree leaders who signed Treaty 6 failed to plan for miserly interpretation of the terms of the treaty in the years following extirpation of the bison and marginalization from the new agricultural economy on the plains.

TREATIES, FAMINE, AND EPIDEMIC TRANSITION ON THE PLAINS, 1877–82

WITH COMPLETION OF THE NUMBERED TREATIES, THE BLUE-print was set for conversion of the indigenous population to agriculture and settlement of the prairies with European farmers. With few exceptions, agreements between the crown and First Nations were reached from positions of mutual strength. Before the end of the decade, however, the balance between indigenous and newcomer populations would be irrevocably altered. The key factor in the changing relationship was the single greatest environmental catastrophe to strike human populations on the plains: disappearance of bison in the wild. Without the herds, indigenous communities could not maintain their freedom. Clauses providing greater assistance in the conversion to settled life, especially those added to Treaty 6, indicate that Cree negotiators were aware of such an eventuality.[1] As Chief Ah-tahkakoop declared during treaty negotiations, the bison "will be gone forever before many snows."[2] Lieutenant Governor Alexander Morris, though reluctant to accept what he considered extravagant demands for regular food assistance, agreed that the dominion government should provide relief in case of a "national famine."[3] Neither side was prepared for the suddenness and finality of the collapse of herds in the late 1870s. The region-wide famine that ensued and the inability of authorities to provide adequate food relief sparked the widespread emergence of tuberculosis among immune-compromised communities. By the turn of the 1880s, dominion officials tailored their response to the famine to further their own agenda of development in the west by subjugating the malnourished and increasingly sick indigenous population.

By the early 1880s, tuberculosis, relatively infrequent on the plains prior to the treaty period, was reported to be the main killer of reserve populations.[4] It had been present in American populations long before the arrival of Columbus,[5] but its emergence as the primary disease within aboriginal communities is widely acknowledged to be the result of the upheaval of the early reserve period.[6] The bacterium itself is a necessary, but not exclusive, precondition for the illness.[7] During the fur trade era, Euro-Americans with tuberculosis who often were not sick but highly infectious spread the germ to people in the west by coughing, sharing pipes during tobacco-smoking ceremonies and other forms of close contact.[8] The proliferation of trade and increased interaction between the contagious and the susceptible probably reintroduced tuberculosis to much of the northwest. Still, the vast majority of those infected did not become ill. The critical factor in the time lag between their infection and the widespread manifestation of illness in the final decades of the nineteenth century was the high level of nutrition afforded by bison predation. Studies of skeletons have shown that, in the mid-nineteenth century, peoples on the plains were perhaps the tallest and best-nourished population in the world.[9] By the early 1880s, the nutritional advantage provided by the herds would be gone for good.

Because overcrowding and malnutrition are primary environmental factors in the development of tuberculosis, it "was not the major cause of death until after they [plains peoples] settled on reserves in the 1880s."[10] Dr. R. G. Ferguson, a pioneer in the battle against TB in Canada, described the sudden appearance of the disease among them:

> With few exceptions all these plains Indians were reported to be free of anything that would even approach an epidemic up to at least 1882. Between 1882 and 1885 for some reason there was a tremendous increase in the frequency of the disease, and at a later date, on practically all the reserves on the plains, the disease had taken the proportions of an epidemic.[11]

Years of hunger and despair that coincided with extermination of the bison and relocation of groups to reserves, exacerbated by inadequate food aid from the dominion government, created ecological conditions in which the disease exploded.[12] Half-hearted relief measures during the famine of 1878–80 and after, which kept plains people in a constant state of hunger, not only undermined the government's half-baked self-sufficiency initiative but also illustrated the moral and legal failures of the crown's treaty commitment to provide assistance in the case of a widespread famine on the plains.

Observers were stunned by the collapse of the Canadian bison hunt in 1878,[13] but the end of the bison economy had been predicted for years, if not decades, prior to the actual disappearance of the species. By the 1870s, periodic bouts of hunger were all too frequent as dwindling bison populations were hunted for food and their hides for the industries of the urbanized east.[14]

Over the winter of 1873–74, Crees at the Victoria mission near the present Alberta–Saskatchewan border were reduced to eating "their horses, dogs, buffalo robes and in some cases their snow shoes and moccasins and then died."[15] The situation was similar in the parklands of the Touchwood Hills.[16] By the early 1870s, the link between privation and disease among the indigenous peoples of the plains was widely recognized. As the North-West Mounted Police made their way west in 1874, Dr. John Kittson made the connection after encountering a small group of Teton Dakota near Old Wives Lake in south-central Saskatchewan.[17] Although George M. Grant encountered few aboriginal people on his reconnaissance of the Yellowhead route in 1872, he assumed that "almost all of the Indians of the North-West are scrofulous."[18] A popular medical text of the day, *The People's Common Sense Medical Adviser,* described scrofula, glandular tuberculosis, as "the consequence of insufficient nourishment, resulting from subsisting upon poor food, or too exclusively a vegetable diet, with little or no animal food."[19]

Government officials had recognized the precipitous decline of the bison and its potential impact on the inhabitants of the west even before completion of the western treaties. In the spring of 1874, the deputy minister of the interior reported that "The buffaloes have in the last few years been rapidly diminishing in numbers, and there seems every reason to expect ... they will within the next decade of years be entirely exterminated. To the Indians extermination of the buffalo means starvation and death."[20] Indian Commissioner J. A. N. Provencher was also aware of the problem.[21] During his tenure as minister of the interior, David Mills was optimistic about the inevitable conversion to farming among plains peoples, but in his report for 1875–76 he acknowledged growing anxiety over the shrinking herds and advocated that "prompt measures be taken in the meantime to prevent the catastrophe."[22] In the spring of 1876, Father Lacombe reportedly "pleaded" with dominion officials for a law to protect the dwindling herds.[23]

As bureaucrats pondered their jurisdictional authority over remaining stocks, the bison still in Canadian territory came under increased pressure. In 1876, the "great annihilation" of the species in the northern United States began when the Northern Pacific Railroad reached Bismarck, North Dakota.[24] North of the border, hunting pressure intensified with the arrival of between 6,000 and 8,000 Sioux refugees in the spring of 1877.[25]

Moreover, in the final years of the bison herds, the spread of cattle ranching brought intense competition for forage and introduced diseases to the already endangered bison population.[26] The ecological significance of the introduction of cattle cannot be overstated. From the end of the American Civil War to the turn of the twentieth century, between 6 and 10 million cattle and 1 million horses were driven north from Texas in what has been described as the "largest short-term geographical shift of domestic herd animals in the world."[27] With them came diseases such as anthrax, Texas tick fever, brucellosis, and, significantly, bovine tuberculosis. According to one study, "Historical evidence indicates that the disease did not occur in bison prior to contact with infected cattle."[28] While bovine TB was present before the arrival of Europeans, the relocation of huge numbers of domesticated animals into the harsh environment of the northern plains certainly increased the magnitude of the threat posed by the disease.

Infection brought by Texas longhorn cattle threatened not only the bison but also the human population that consumed them after the bison disappeared. One characteristic of *M. bovis* posed a particular threat to the aboriginal populations that preyed on infected herds. The bacterium can be transmitted by the ingestion of infected meat.[29] Traditional patterns of consumption, which included the eating of organs and entrails and some cuts of flesh raw, and the practice of sun-drying meat provided the ideal medium for spread of the disease.[30] Beef supplied as emergency rations unwittingly exposed reserve populations to a new threat to their health in the form of bovine tuberculosis. Texas longhorns, driven hundreds of miles north from what was essentially an Iberian climate, quickly sickened with tuberculosis and other diseases under the harsh conditions of the northern plains.[31] During the first years of the ranching industry in Canada, large proportions of cattle herds perished every winter. Rather than being a panacea for the hungry, domestic cattle almost certainly spread bovine tuberculosis through the hungry and immune-compromised population.[32] Cattle with latent

This is the real thing
painted the winter of 1886
at the OH ranch
C M Russell

This picture is Chas.
Russell's reply to my
inquiry as to the
condition of my cattle
in 1886. L E Kaufman

Watercolour by C. M. Russell depicting the effect of harsh winters on cattle. This specific image reflects the decline of stocks over the winter of 1886. *Used with permission from the Montana Stockgrowers Association, Helena, Montana.*

tuberculosis displayed no symptoms but posed a serious threat to those who ate their flesh, a factor recognized by Dr. Fred Treon among his Sioux patients: "Supposing that only one of a thousand cattle received be affected with tuberculosis or actinomycosis, from the manner of dividing the beef it is possible, and probable, that one hundred persons may become inoculated by a single animal."[33] As cattle replaced bison as the dominant ruminant in the west, aboriginal people across the region were exposed to a new and as yet unrecognized source of tuberculosis.[34] Infection that came with the introduction of cattle eaten by so many might explain the sudden and widespread explosion of clinical TB in the late 1870s.

In the dying days of the bison in the wild, even climate seemed to turn against them. Consecutive years of very strong El Niño activity in 1877 and 1878[35] brought unseasonably warm winter weather, pushing the remaining bison population to the brink of collapse. Because there was no snow accumulation, 1877–78 was known as the "black winter."[36] Prairie fires resulting from the winter drought spread over much of the western plains in what became Alberta and Saskatchewan and destroyed large tracts of pasture. As would be the case with the human population on reserves, hunger triggered sickness in both wild and domestic animals in the region. Conditions were bad enough for tuberculosis to spread to secondary host species such as horses.[37] A disease identified as mange broke out among Indian horses and bison populations on the Canadian plains. The brother of Chief Star Blanket lost all of his ten horses to the disease during the winter of 1877–78. Reverend John Hines reported that "Indians take their ponies, dying from the effects of the mange, kill them and boil their bones in order to get a little fat, with which to grease the wheat, when roasting, in order to make it more digestible."[38] The consumption of sick animals or those that had died of disease spread zoonotic diseases to the reserve population already weakened by malnutrition.

The fires resulting from the black winter forced remaining herds to winter between the branches of the Saskatchewan River, where hunting by the Blackfoot, Cree, Assiniboine, and newly arrived Sioux placed the constrained bison under "tremendous pressure." During the spring of 1878, herds broke through the "ever tightening circle" of hunters and headed southwest to Montana.[39] Combined pressure from the US military,[40] American Indians, and increasingly desperate Canadian aboriginal hunters drove the few remaining bison south of the border until their final extermination in the early 1880s.

As the scarcity of food grew to a crisis, First Nations north of the Province of Manitoba experienced another consequence of large-scale European settlement. In 1876, 1,000 Icelandic immigrants arrived on the shores of Lake Winnipeg.[41] As they settled on land either requested by or already occupied by Treaty 5 Indians,[42] smallpox broke out among them. Between 100 and 200 colonists succumbed to the disease during the epidemic that raged through the fall and early winter.[43] Hundreds of Saulteaux and Cree also perished during the outbreak.[44]

The epidemic was contained to the vicinity of Lake Winnipeg and was largely exhausted by the spring of 1877. The official response to the medical emergency in the largely unorganized territory of Keewatin was mired in controversy over the financial responsibility of the relief effort.[45] As the disease spread along the shore of Lake Winnipeg, Morris was refused dominion money to establish a quarantine to protect the population of Red River. In a coded message, the Prime Minister's Office sent a terse order to Morris: "People themselves must avoid contagion—decline expenditure for that quarantine."[46] Historian Jim Mochoruk characterized the move as an attempt by the dominion "to off-load financial responsibility for the quarantine on to a government it knew to be on the brink of economic disaster."[47] As lieutenant governor of Keewatin, Morris was ultimately responsible for the medical response to the crisis and paid the political price for his unsanctioned actions during the outbreak. He soon fell from grace with the Liberal government and returned to the east. His political downfall came "because he had allowed his conscience, rather than financial concerns, to dictate his actions during the epidemic."[48]

The end of his career in the west was part of a political bloodletting that came in the wake of the epidemic. There was at least one positive outcome of the Liberal purge of the frontier civil service. In response to the threat of smallpox, Minister of the Interior David Mills hired his crony from London, Dr. Daniel Hagarty, as medical superintendent of the North-West Territories. Between 1877 and the spring of 1880, when Hagarty was dismissed because the rejuvenated Conservative government deemed his services "no longer necessary," the vaccination campaign undertaken by Hagarty and physicians attached to the North-West Mounted Police in the southwestern prairies[49] virtually eliminated smallpox as a major cause of mortality among First Nations. Sadly, the medical victory over smallpox was a solitary one. Hagarty's dismissal reflects the cynicism of Indian administration while Macdonald served as both prime minister and minister of Indian affairs. The Department of Indian Affairs dispensed with its own physician in favour of medical services performed by police doctors and local practitioners since doing so was "best for the Indians and the most economical for the government."[50] The abandonment of a successful medical policy precisely when the Indian population of the west was most in need because of the famine stands as a testament to dominion indifference. Within a year of the Carlton Treaty, the seeds of a large-scale famine were taking root. In 1877, the critical shortage of bison prompted almost 3,600 treaty Indians to move to Cypress Hills, the last refuge of the species in Canadian territory.[51] Many others who had yet to enter into treaty had also converged in the hills,[52] and to all them were added, in the spring of 1877, Sitting Bull and 5,000 followers from south of the border in search of both sanctuary and sustenance.[53]

Treaty 7 was hurriedly negotiated during the summer of 1877 to defuse the increasingly tense situation in southern Alberta caused by armed conflict just south of the border.[54] Confusion persists over the precise meaning of the treaty, which, according to a witness, included David Laird's cryptic promise to the Niitsitapi: "the Queen wishes to offer you the same as was accepted by the Crees. I do not mean exactly the same terms, but equivalent terms, that will cost the Queen the same amount of money."[55] In what must have been one of the most hollow

The Blackfoot Treaty (Treaty 7), 1877, Crowfoot speaking. *Glenbow Archives, NA-40-1.*

government guarantees of the treaty period, the Blackfoot were assured that the bison would survive for another ten years.[56] There was reason for the hasty formalization of relations between the dominion and the inhabitants of southern Alberta. That spring the US Army began its campaign against the Nez Percé. Rumours circulated about the possibility of Chief Joseph and his people joining forces with Sitting Bull and his people at Cypress Hills.[57] Fear of a race war spread through the interior of British Columbia. The military nature of the Canadian presence on the southwestern plains was underscored by the fact that, until after 1879, the Mounted Police were responsible for the day-to-day administration of Indian affairs in the Treaty 7 region.[58]

Anxiety over the possibility of bloodshed in Canadian territory was high in 1877, but the Niitsitapi had yet to undergo a decline in health due to depletion of bison herds. Early in the year, police surgeon R. B. Nevitt reported from Fort Macleod that TB was not that prevalent among the Indians whom he saw.[59] In 1876, Father Constantine Scollen reported to Morris that, though they were in "awful dread of the future," the Niitsitapi had rebounded since the dark days of the Whoop-Up trade.[60] Hunger was not a factor in the negotiations at Blackfoot Crossing. Crowfoot refused government food until his concerns with the treaty were addressed.[61]

The mild conditions through the black winter of 1877–78 changed subsistence conditions in the southwest. The drought made the grass-

Destitute family of Cree, Cypress Hills, 1878. *Glenbow Archives, NA-1101-1.*

lands a tinderbox, and the fires that ensued contributed to a food crisis among plains hunters. The winter hunt in the foothills was a complete failure. Bands were forced to travel as far as 100 miles to find game on the plains. Those who stayed in their traditional winter hunting grounds faced starvation conditions. In April 1878, Indian Agent M. G. Dickieson reported that, over the winter, "the Indians were very poorly off, starving in fact." He estimated the entire Indian and Métis population of the northwest to be about 26,500. He then calculated that to "provide food for this number of people would require at least 132,500 lbs of meat, or about 350 animals daily, over 10,000 annually."[62]

In May 1878, Lieutenant Governor Laird warned Minister of the Interior Mills that the government had three choices in its response to the famine: help the Indians to farm and raise stock, feed them, or fight them.[63] Laird was frustrated with Ottawa's parsimony,[64] but the purse strings had been loosened somewhat. A month earlier, in April, Dickieson was sent to Montana on the first of what would become regular missions to secure cattle for the starving population.[65]

By spring 1878, bison were scarce even in the Cypress Hills. Norbert Welsh, a Métis trader who travelled through the region, "didn't see a buffalo, an Indian, or anything. Everything was bare."[66] The Niitsitapi, and their former Dakota adversaries under Sitting Bull, joined together in the Great Sand Hills, north of the Cypress Hills.[67] Big Bear and other Cree leaders led their people north to discuss the crisis and to confer with dominion officials in what might have been the last large-scale summer gathering of the Cree, who were still self-sufficient in their quest for food. Those who had entered into treaty received their annuity payments, and Big Bear again discussed the possibility of adhering to Treaty 6 with Canadian officials, including Dr. Hagarty, who later wrote that "I think a good deal of Big Bear. ... I would like every Chief to think and act like Big Bear."[68]

As Big Bear tried in vain to improve the terms of the treaty, the hungry gathered at European settlements seeking respite. Failure of the hunt at Carlton and other provision posts forced the newly arrived Sioux to proceed to Prince Albert, where, by November, eighty-nine tents of them were reportedly "begging from door to door."[69] At Battleford, the Indian department office was under daily pressure from the hungry, some of whom "had been forced to eat their dogs to keep them from starving."[70] Officials responded to the increasing demand for food in the territorial capital by increasing security rather than the flow of food. A stockade was built "for fear that starving Natives might attack the fort where supplies were held."[71] In a sad irony, labourers were paid with food to build the fortification intended to keep the hungry away from the dominion ration house.[72] By the end of the year, suffering at Battleford was so pervasive that it became banal. Under the heading "Lost and Found," the Saskatchewan Herald ran the following item on 16 December 1878: "FOUND Where the Indians starved to death, about the 1st of October, a white mare. The owner can have the same by proving property and paying expenses. Apply to Antoine Morin, Battleford."[73]

As if famine and an outbreak of scarlet fever[74] were not enough of a burden for the aboriginal population of the plains, the return of John A. Macdonald and his Conservatives to power under the platform of the National Policy brought a new approach to Indian policy. Management of the increasingly serious food situation and Indian affairs generally shifted from a position of "relative ignorance" under the Liberals to one of outright malevolence during the Macdonald regime.[75] "Pacification" of the plains Indians was an integral, if not always explicit, component of the Tory government's program of development.[76] To ensure that the west would be ready for the Canadian Pacific Railway and settlement,

Macdonald himself became superintendent general of Indian affairs.[77] In light of the trouble that was to plague Indian affairs management for decades, if not generations, Agent Dickieson's statement to his new political superiors, written a month after the Tories took office, was prophetic: "When the Government has to spend $1,000.00 to perform what $10.00 would at present, they may wake up to the fact that they have been sleeping on a volcano."[78]

The winter of 1878–79 was a difficult one. When Laird met with the chief of the Eagle Hills Cree during the first week of February, the *Saskatchewan Herald* reported that the Indians "say that they have never been so near starvation. Their tone is peaceful but resolute. ..."[79] By spring, the situation had deteriorated to the point of crisis. On 2 April, Father Scollen told Major Irvine of the police that some Indians had been reduced to eating poisoned wolf carcasses.[80] "In my opinion," the priest added, "give us another winter like the past and we are done for."[81]

At Calgary, a delegation of Niitsitapi chiefs petitioned Cecil Denny of the North-West Mounted Police for help.[82] On his arrival in the west, Edgar Dewdney, the newly appointed Indian commissioner, provided many of the hungry Niitsitapi with enough rations to take them south of the border, a move that saved the dominion at least $100,000 over 1879 and 1880.[83] Even so, expenditures on Indian affairs more than doubled between 1879 and 1881, and provisions took on an ever-increasing percentage of the departmental budget.[84] Most Indians headed south in a desperate attempt to find the remaining herds, but some Cree travelled as far to the north as Peace River, where competition between the new arrivals and the resident Dunneza population depleted game and nearly ignited a war over access to wild food.[85]

By the beginning of May 1879, 200 destitute Cree had converged on the territorial capital of Battleford. Three weeks later their number had swelled to almost 750, and "all were hungry."[86] Between January and June, 75,000 pounds of flour were shipped to the settlement.[87] On 19 May, the *Saskatchewan Herald* stated that the settlement had "no bacon, no beef, no pemmican, no fish, no game, no potatoes, and until Monday (May) 12th, no flour to be had."[88] Dickieson requisitioned at least 20,000 pounds of bacon, 300,000 pounds of flour, and 100,000 pounds of beef to mitigate the famine.[89]

In July, Laird reported that there had been no game in the vicinity for the past two months and that, because supplies were running out, the police post at Battleford should be reinforced in case of trouble.[90] James McKay, the Anglican cleric and interpreter of the Treaty 6 negotiations, chronicled the deteriorating situation at Battleford. On 31

May, he wrote that "We of course have constant applications for food … ," and by August the Niitsitapi had largely headed south toward the United States, while the Cree and Assiniboine remained near town, "staying for govt. relief."[91]

Earlier the Niitsitapi had travelled to Battleford for help since "many of them were dying because they could not subsist on a diet of roots."[92] Dickieson, acting Indian superintendent, gave them food on the promise that they would return to their territory and resume the hunt for the elusive herds to the south. Even the unsympathetic editor of the *Saskatchewan Herald*, P. G. Laurie, was moved by the plight of the hungry: "the condition of these Indians is deplorable in the extreme. Accustomed all their lives to a diet consisting largely of animal food, the rations of flour and tea they receive here leave them but one remove from starvation."[93] Laurie wrote that Dickieson, Laird's temporary replacement, "has to deal single-handed with a thousand starving Indians," with no meat or any means of requisitioning it from his superiors.[94] Dickieson, a Liberal appointee, left the frontier service in September. On his departure, Bobtail, a spokesman for the Cree, expressed sorrow, for Dickieson had always done "the best he could to keep them from starving."[95]

The despair at Battleford was only one episode in the terrible summer of 1879. The *Saskatchewan Herald* recounted the hardship experienced by the family of Koo-qua-a-witt, who arrived at the Victoria mission with his starving children. One son, unconscious, died five days after the family's arrival. Another, whose bleeding nose could not be stopped, perished nine days after his younger brother. The distraught father, described as "skin & bones from caring for his sick children," then left for the plains, where he too was reported to have succumbed to hunger.[96]

At Edmonton, Indian Agent James Stewart reported on the crisis:

> … I have never seen anything like it since my long residence in this country. It was not only the want of buffalo, but everything else seemed to have deserted the country; even fish were scarce. … [T]he poor people were naked, and the cold was intense, and remained so during the whole winter; under these circumstances they behaved well, and no raids were made on anything here. They ate many of their horses, and all the dogs were destroyed for food. …[97]

To the south, at Blackfoot Crossing, Dewdney "found about 1,300 Indians … on the verge of starvation."[98] In his diary, he described "strong

Rattler, a Niitsitapi healer treating a young man with a fatal case of tuberculosis. The treatment may have provided spiritual comfort to the victim in the last stages of his illness. *Source: The Walter McClintock Papers, Yale Collection of Western Americana, Beinecke Rare Book and Manuscript Library. Reproduced with permission.*

young men ... now so weak that some of them could hardly walk."[99] While most relied on charity, many wealthy Niitsitapi were reduced to exchanging their horses for a few cups of flour. At Calgary, where the Blackfoot, Stoney, and Métis "were starving and even resorting to eating grass, Inspector Denny took it upon himself to purchase and issue beef at the rate of 2,000 pounds a day."[100] Dominion botanist John Macoun described his encounter with a group of Niitsitapi women near the Hand Hills who offered to wash the crew's dishes. The astonished scientist remarked that, "before they washed the plates, they actually licked them clean." Apparently oblivious to the suffering around him, Macoun was berated by Father "Scallen": "Do you know that the people here are dying of starvation? ... There are two lying dead in their tents now who have just died of starvation."[101]

Amid the desperation, Indian Commissioner Dewdney maintained his focus on fiscal restraint. After a long and heated argument on the situation with Colonel Macleod, Dewdney remarked that "I arranged with the Col. that he should do as had been done heretofore—food be issued when it was found that the Indians were really starving, to those who would work & to the sick & infirm who had no friends & who could not work."[102]

In December 1879, the *Saskatchewan Herald* reported that more than twenty-five Blackfoot "had died of actual starvation."[103] By the end of the year, the malnourished were showing signs of clinical tuberculosis. Surgeon George F. Kennedy's medical report for Fort Macleod noted that women were especially vulnerable: "phthisis and chest infections were found to be especially common among the females, and it was rare to find a woman over thirty years old with sound lungs."[104] Despite their efforts, practitioners of traditional medicine could do little other than comfort their patients who were succumbing to the new disease.[105]

Making a desperate situation worse in the southwest was a disease called mountain fever.[106] It attacked everyone in the region, including the police. During the winter of 1878–79, nine Métis and "some Sioux" succumbed to the fever at Wood Mountain. The disease is caused by contact with infected ticks, though accounts of the outbreak attributed the infection to the rotting carcasses of cattle and bison that polluted the streams used for drinking water.[107]

The food situation was no less distressing on the eastern plains. In April 1879, Archibald McDonald wrote from Fort Ellice that most of the cattle supplied to reserves as draft animals had been eaten during the winter. He predicted the failure of the new administration's Indian policy: "But as the wise men at Ottawa know more of Indians and Indian matters than those who have passed a lifetime among them, it is of little use saying anything on the subject. Master Indian is going to cost the country a trifle more than they fancy."[108]

Reports of starvation also came from Fort Qu'Appelle, Touchwood Hills, Fort Ellice, and Moose Mountain.[109] At Moose Mountain, Dickieson noted that "the Indians were in a deplorable condition, and it is reported that several died from exposure and want of food." At Fort Qu'Appelle, he reported that "Very little provisions have been given out in Treaty No. 4. This led to a demand, accompanied by a show of force, being made on the Hudson's Bay Company at Qu'Appelle."[110] In August 1879, Dr. Hagarty blamed the decline of White Bear's band on inadequate provisions: "The Indians at this place are very much emaciated. Hunger has shown its terrible effects on them and scrofula and other kindred diseases are becoming deeply rooted." At Touchwood Hills, he noted "about the same condition of things ... disease, hunger and lassitude."[111] At the Yellow Quill Reserve, two oxen and some flour were stolen three days before the band was to be provided with rations. The chief, who refused to participate in the theft, was given extra provisions by Hagarty, who "complimented him on his devotedness to the laws of the Great White Mother, for which he thanked me, expressed his attachment to the Queen and was very proud of his conduct."[112] Near Fort Qu'Appelle, where Poorman's Band had broken into the storehouse in June,[113] the physician was shocked to find another aspect of the worsening situation on the plains, the outbreak of venereal disease. On his return to Portage la Prairie, he found venereal disease emerging there.[114]

Hagarty's report described the growing tension between the hungry on reserves and officials of the Indian department. The incident at the Yellow Quill Reserve, and other cases of trouble over Indian access to government supplies, underscore the fact that, while the Indians were starving, in many cases to death, the authorities withheld food that was available. The famine on the plains was more than the simple Malthusian equation of too many people and too few bison.[115] Episodes of starvation, studied in a global context by Nobel Laureate Amartya Sen, do not arise solely from an absence of food: "Starvation is the characteristic of some people not *having* enough food to eat. It is not the characteristic of there *being* not enough food to eat. While the latter can be the cause of the former, it is but one of many causes."[116]

The dominion government established its own set of entitlement relations to deal with the famine in the waning months of 1879. As First Nations people starved, in many cases to death, the cattle industry was being established on the land that had served as pasture for bison only a short time before. The historical literature is replete with accounts of tensions flaring over Indian predation, or rumours of it, of newly established cattle stock on the western plains.[117] The purported rise in cattle theft by the famine-stricken Indians in the southwest led the *Saskatchewan Herald* to conclude that "A collision between the ranchmen and the Indians may be expected at any moment."[118] Although isolated incidents of poaching cattle were reported, Colonel Macleod explained that, "under the circumstances, I think it a matter of congratulation that the Indians throughout the country have behaved so well."[119] The increase in arrests of Indians was correlated to the starvation of 1879–80.[120] The number of stolen livestock was limited, though. Official reports of the Department of Indian Affairs recognized that most of the starving and malnourished Indians behaved well. Most of the hungry did what they could to secure food within the law, and most were grateful for what meagre assistance they could secure.

Some appealed for help on the basis of their treaty right to assistance in times of crisis. Chief Beardy of the Willow Cree demanded that the government fulfill its promise of aid negotiated at Carlton in 1876. Within a year of the treaty, Beardy organized what the police called an "indignation meeting held at Duck Lake ... condemning the government for their treatment of the Indians and Halfbreeds in the country."[121] Beardy refused his annuity payment for 1878 because he was dissatisfied with the dominion's delivery of its treaty promises.[122] During the winter of 1879, the chief was involved in a standoff after he threatened to pillage the local warehouse. He claimed that the goods were owed to the people as part of the dominion's treaty obligations.[123] Beardy's refusal to accept government neglect, and the perceived threat from American Dakota who had recently come to Prince Albert, led to the formation of a local militia.[124] In 1880, Beardy was temporarily deposed as chief on the questionable charge that he was a cattle thief.[125] Stephen Sliwa asserted that the adversity the band endured in the early years of treaty "galvanized the community, uniting them together with a sense of purpose."[126] Many long-time residents of the west saw the protests of the Carlton Cree as reasonable. Early in 1880, Lawrence Clarke, an HBC oldtimer, described the increasingly bleak situation among them: "Those Reserve Indians are in a deplorable state of destitution, they receive from the Indian Department just enough food to keep soul and body together, they are all but naked, many of them barefooted. ... Should sickness break out among them in their present weakly state, the fatality will be dreadful."[127]

After 1880, Indian protests against ill treatment by government officials became increasingly frequent.[128] Chief Thunderchild threatened that he would "retain a first-class lawyer" to secure what he considered Indian money paid to the HBC at the time of transfer. In a comment that would remain relevant for over a century, the *Saskatchewan Herald* reported on the chief's threat of legal action: "They [the lawyers] will make a pretty good thing out of it, as he will give half the amount to any one recovering it; and it will be singular if they do not secure a good share of the other half—there are so many expenses with the law with which the Indians are unacquainted."[129]

Instead of supplying rations to famine-stricken populations "in a national famine," as Morris had promised, rations were used as a means of coercing Indians into submitting to treaty.[130] Malcolm D. Cameron, a Liberal MP, accused the Indian department of being driven by "a policy of submission shaped by a policy of starvation."[131] In 1879, a number of bands traded their independence for food. In the Battleford Agency, Mosquito, Moosomin, Thunderchild, and Little Pine all accepted treaty in exchange for rations.[132] Once on reserve, First Nations people were at the mercy of officials with little patience for protest. When Strike Him on the Back refused to accept a survey of his reserve, Dewdney simply "took his cattle for the Sioux."[133] He also turned down an offer from ranchers who, fearing predation of their herds by hungry Indians, were prepared "to sell their own animals at cost, and wait until conditions were more favourable."[134] His indifference to the gesture might well have stemmed from his financial association with the Montana-based firm of I. G. Baker and Company, by far the largest meat contractor to the dominion government. Dewdney profited by getting Canadian contracts and favours for the Baker firm.[135]

In the Speech from the Throne on 1 May 1879, the Conservatives admitted that they were "bewildered" by news of a famine in the west. In August, the prime minister set up a council to assess the extent of the food crisis and the threat posed by thousands of First Nations people to the tiny population at Battleford.[136] Macdonald set out instructions to the council: "the one to supply food to the Indians and the other the increasing of the means of defence amongst the settlers."[137] Two weeks before the council met the prime minister was told that a large herd of bison "had gone north [and] had in fact outflanked Gen. Miles and his army. This will afford relief to a very considerable body of Indians."[138] With the local crisis temporarily averted, Macdonald was advised to focus on getting troops to "remote settlements such as Prince Albert."[139]

As the dominion was arming its settlers against the threat of an Indian uprising, thousands of hungry people were abandoning the country. An estimated 3,533 people were already in US territory, another 2,770 were in the Cypress Hills, and 700 alone were at Fort Walsh, searching for the few remaining herds.[140] Crowfoot and other Niitsitapi leaders took their people to Montana, giving Canadian authorities a temporary reprieve.[141] Big Bear, who also headed south to hunt, lost almost half of his followers to Lucky Man and Thunderchild when the Cree were told that only treaty Indians were eligible for assistance. Some of those who accepted treaty in return for food sought new strategies to maintain at least partial autonomy. Piapot, Little Pine, and Big Bear hoped to establish a concentration of reserves in the Cypress Hills in 1880–81.[142]

The Home Farm program, "hastily contrived" during the fall and winter of 1878–79, was as close as the government came to developing a legitimate plan for the economic reorientation of reserves.[143] Described as an "abysmal failure,"[144] the program was concocted when 5,000 people, probably 20 percent of the total First Nations population of the plains, were out of the country searching for food in American territory. The scheme was doomed from its inception.[145] Not only was the plan incapable of dealing with the magnitude of the famine, but also its specifics were sketchy at best.[146] When farm instructors finally took up their positions in August 1879, many were either incapable or

Cree camp, Cypress Hills, 1879. *Glenbow Archives, NA-98-35.*

incompetent in the face of the monumental task.[147] The prime minister himself had misgivings about the feasibility of reserve agriculture, but in the absence of an alternative he "found it expedient to promote the plan in parliament."[148]

The Conservatives suspended the work-for-rations policy introduced during the Liberal administration, at least temporarily, after the famine conference at Battleford. A secret agenda was in place, however, as the report of Deputy Superintendent of Indian Affairs Lawrence Vankoughnet makes clear:

> Strict instructions have been given to the agents to require labor from able-bodied Indians for supplies given them. This principle was laid down for the sake of the moral effect that it would have on the Indians in shewing that they must give something in return for what they receive, and also for the purpose of preventing them from hereafter expecting gratuitous assistance from the Government.[149]

Although Dewdney enforced the policy, he recognized that, "Until the Indians were settled on reserves, there was, in effect, no work that they could do. In the meantime, the starving condition of the Indians rendered the operation of such a proviso impossible." Minister of Finance Sir Leonard Tilley proposed the use of Indian labour as a means to offset the high cost of aid to the northwest, but remarkably no concerted attempt was made by the authorities to provide the plains Indians with gainful employment other than the cutting of firewood.[150] The Indian commissioner noted that the Indians "showed, on the whole, a good disposition to work at anything that could be found for them to do."[151] By the new year of 1880, Dewdney worried that so many were willing to work for rations "that we will not be in a position to keep them all going."[152]

Rations kept many from starving, but the government had few other contingencies. No provision was made to assist the destitute with clothing, which, because of the paucity of animals, was as scarce as food.[153] Dewdney recognized that the lack of clothing and a "winter [that] was the severest that has been felt for many years" prevented many along the Saskatchewan River from undertaking winter hunting.[154] Vankoughnet, perhaps pandering to Dewdney, acknowledged the need for clothing among the destitute: "they cannot be expected to work unless they are properly clad."[155]

The farm instructor at Touchwood Hills had to provide his labourers "with a few blankets and moose skins" without departmental authorization.[156] During the winter of 1879–80, the Willow Cree were described as "all but naked, many of them barefooted."[157] At Fort Walsh, the Indian agent reported that the 2,500 Niitsitapi drawing rations were "almost without clothing of any description."[158] Hundreds of kilometres to the east, in January 1881, Chief White Bear requested "something to cover their women and children." The agent informed him that supplies would be issued to the absolutely destitute, but "those who had blankets and clothing must expect nothing."[159] Inspector Denny requested that Treaty 7 women be given clothing "and bales of common print ... to make dresses, it would help them greatly as the women suffer most, literally in rags. The women fight over old cotton flour sacks, of which they make dresses."[160] At the same time, meat contractors were keeping the hides, heads, and entrails of "government" cattle to make private deals with those who could afford the extra cost.[161]

Official reports stressed that the condition of the people near Fort Qu'Appelle was "not so severe ... as their brethren in the south west,"[162] yet twenty members of the Okanese band starved to death over the bitterly cold Christmas of 1879.[163] By spring 1880, hunger among the Dakota at Wood Mountain forced many to eat horses that had died of "scurvy" the previous fall and winter. Major Walsh was moved by the fate of those who endured the famine:

> Following this want of food and the eating of diseased horses, an epidemic appeared, which marked its results by the many graves now seen in Wood Mountain. The conduct of those starving and destitute people, their patient endurance, their sympathy, and the extent to which they assisted each other, their strict observance of law and order, would reflect upon the most civilized community.[164]

In the Cypress Hills, the police struggled to deliver food to the hungry. Superintendent Crozier saw the rations as essential, "otherwise hundreds certainly would have starved to death."[165] In September, Dr. Kennedy reported that a large number of Assiniboine were "prostrated" from sickness near Fort Walsh. Diarrhea and dysentery broke out among an "entire" camp of 1,500 Cree, "and quite a number, principally children, died. As an instance of how common it was, I [Dr. Kennedy] may mention that I visited and treated one hundred and fifty cases in one day."[166] To the west, at Fort Macleod, Dr. Kittson reported to his superior that there was simply not enough game east of the Rockies, and he stressed that the people under his care were receiving less than half the ration provided to state prisoners in Siberia.[167]

Dewdney admitted that dominion rations were inadequate.[168] In addition, many questioned their quality. In January 1880, farm instructor Scott described the Indian department pork that he distributed at Touchwood Hills as "both *musty* and *rusty* and totally unfit for use—although we are giving it out to the Indians, in the absence of anything better, but we *cannot use it ourselves*."[169] The *Saskatchewan Herald* reported on the "soup kitchen" established by Mr. Loucks for the Sioux at Prince Albert: "It is claimed for him that he has discovered the secret of feeding fifty Indians on two pounds of pork a day."[170] Even supplies in good condition had harmful effects on the malnourished population. When Mosquito's band took up their reserve in the Eagle Hills in the spring of 1880, "they had been subsisting on bulrushes, roots and grass; and when the [salt] pork and flour were distributed, many who ate it were so weak that they became seriously ill in consequence of the sudden change."[171]

During the summer of 1880, food shortages sparked a number of violent incidents. At Fort Walsh, a riot broke out when officials tried to withhold food from the hungry and sick Cree who had gathered at

Assiniboine council near Fort Walsh, n.d. *Glenbow Archives, NA-936-34.*

the post. The actions of the Cree contributed to the disbursal of many bands from their chosen refuge in the Cypress Hills.[172] Some groups responded to the poverty by returning to traditional means of acquiring wealth.[173] Dewdney reported that "Almost every tribe have had what they call war parties out, which means horse stealing expeditions."[174] When Chief Pasqua was refused rations, he organized such a party.[175] His theft of a small number of horses in American territory precipitated a retaliatory attack on Ocean Man's Assiniboine band by American Indians.[176] With their horses stolen, Ocean Man's people had to abandon their possessions and walk three weeks to the sanctuary of Fort Ellice. At least four people died from exposure and want during the miserable journey.[177] Conditions in the southeast deteriorated to the point that moose were denuded from the "mountain" that bore the name of the species.[178]

As hunger spread across the plains, so did disease. In March 1880, Lawrence Clarke warned that the desperate condition of the Willow Cree made them particularly susceptible.[179] The threat of disease among people of the eastern plains was exacerbated by the termination of Dr. Hagarty's position that spring.[180] While Hagarty was employed by the Indian department, his vaccination campaign in Saskatchewan and western Manitoba had achieved the goal of protecting the Indians from infection "from the large immigration that will pour into there during the coming spring and summer." Those who submitted to the procedure, according to the doctor, "could now with impunity sleep with a smallpox corpse." His dismissal at the height of the famine underscores the lack of dominion concern for treaty partners.[181]

As the people eked out what living they could from rations, measles and other diseases broke out in the southwest. The effects of sickness were worsened by malnutrition. Scarlet fever "of a very virulent type" erupted among the 2,500 destitute who had gathered at Fort Walsh, killing as many as thirty people in September 1880.[182] In October, simultaneous outbreaks of scarlet fever and measles occurred among large numbers of Siksika, Piikani, and Cree south of the international boundary. In one camp, over 100 people died.[183] Disease prevailed to the spring of 1881 as starving and infected bands of Niitsitapi made the desperate journey back to Canadian territory on foot.[184] Measles spread as far northeast as Fort à la Corne, where at least nine members of the James Smith band perished.[185]

The crisis deepened as the hungry straggled back to their reserves in southern Alberta through 1881. Dewdney reported that over 5,000 Treaty 7 people were added to the rations list; otherwise, "they will die of hunger, there being no game on the Plains."[186] Dominion relief was limited. On their return to Canada, Crowfoot's people were issued a pound of beef and half a pound of flour a day, both of dubious quality. Intended as a nutritional supplement by those who could still afford it, entrails, usually consumed raw, undoubtedly hastened the spread of disease.

When Crowfoot requested additional aid for his people in the fall of 1881, he was branded a troublemaker and reprimanded by Agent Macleod. Rumours circulated that the government was intentionally starving the Niitsitapi to death. On 2 January 1882, a side deal over a beef head and some offal turned sour and led to an armed standoff known as the Bull Elk Affair. The event signalled the end of almost a decade of good relations between the Niitsitapi and the police.[187]

Blackfoot people unloading beef at a ration house, circa 1883-84. *Glenbow Archives, NA-1033-4.*

Elsewhere, the cycle of hunger and disease continued to spiral almost out of control. At Fort Qu'Appelle, smallpox broke out in January 1881.[188] The disease was checked by prompt measures undertaken by a Board of Health. By this time, witnesses to the conditions on reserves realized that infections were acting synergistically. In its story about the smallpox outbreak, the *Saskatchewan Herald* observed that "There is a strong scrofulous taint amongst many bands of Plain[s] Indians, and where the disease broke out in this case, the afflicted ones had been eating the flesh of horses that had died of the scab or mange, and it is almost impossible that they could do so without taking into their systems the germs of the disease."[189] Although it was yet to be recognized as a scientific certainty, P. G. Laurie recognized the link between the consumption of diseased meat and the onset of scrofula, cervical lymphadenitis, a key indicator of sickness with bovine tuberculosis.[190]

The inhabitants of the plains were forced to adopt an "impure" diet out of sheer desperation. At Fort Ellice, on a daily ration of twelve ounces of flour and four ounces of bacon, three people starved to death in January 1881.[191] The *Saskatchewan Herald* commented on four deaths at Strike Him on the Back Reserve in April: "Thus the Red Man is surely and steadily passing away."[192] A month later the Dakota of Moose Woods were "destitute of clothing and provisions; some three or four died actually skeletons."[193] In July, a dead horse was taken from the street in Battleford and eaten. Laurie's description of the event is evidence of the callousness of settlers to the misery of the indigenous population:

> The natives of this land are fully up to the buzzards of the south. Few deceased animals escape their rapacious maws. A horse died a few nights ago on the street opposite to our office, and at early dawn we beheld a posse of native beauties cutting up the dead animal a la buffalo mode of past days, and conveying it to camp, where a grand gorge was being prepared.[194]

Later the paper reported that a disease that had killed large numbers of horses had spread to the weakened reserve population.[195]

The dominion did not increase its expenditures to counter the growing crisis. In fact, the government responded to Liberal criticism that aid to the Indians was a waste of public money by making even more stringent cuts in its famine relief.[196] Sir Leonard Tilley, the finance minister, stated the policy directive succinctly: "They must work or starve."[197] During the winter of 1881, Dewdney, who had no real interest in Indian administration,[198] passed on the management of Indian affairs in the west to Hayter Reed, a brigade major and adjutant of the Canadian military. Reed was told "to use his discretion with regard to the issue of rations to the hungry" while being "as economical as possible."[199] He balanced the two pieces of advice in favour of economy.[200]

Food was to be provided only to people on their reserves, a move intended to undermine the growing resistance of the treaty population. Farm instructor D. L. Clink, who applied the work-for-rations policy "with unmitigated zeal,"[201] was threatened with a knife during a dispute with members of the Thunderchild and Moosomin bands.[202] Dewdney responded to the increased tension with a temporary softening of the rule restricting assistance to treaty Indians only.[203] In July 1881, the Indian department imposed a new measure intended to manage its available food supply for the hungry treaty population. An order in council was passed to forbid the inhabitants of reserves from "selling, bartering, exchanging or giving any person or persons whatsoever, any grain, or root crops, or any other produce grown on any Indian Reserve in the Northwest territories."[204] The move was intended to preserve locally grown food for the communities that produced it, but it also had the effect of barring reserve farmers from participating in the commercial economy of the northwest.

By the summer of 1881, dominion refusal to assist Sitting Bull led to his return to the United States. By then, officials on both sides of the border could command bands to move to places that best suited their management as essentially subjugated peoples. The most significant relocation was the forced removal of communities from their chosen reserves in the Cypress Hills after the decision to build the Canadian Pacific Railway along the southern prairies. On New Year's Day 1882, Chief Poundmaker of the Cree stated that the advancing railway sealed their fate: "Next summer, or latest next fall, the railway will be close to us, the whites will fill our country and they will dictate to us as they please."[205] Within months, Poundmaker's prediction became government policy. On 24 March 1882, the prime minister announced to Parliament that all Indians in the territory of Assiniboia would be removed, by force if necessary, from the land south of the proposed railway.[206] Within a year, 5,000 people were expelled from the Cypress Hills. In doing so, the Canadian government accomplished the ethnic cleansing of southwestern Saskatchewan of its indigenous population.[207] With its usual cynical tone, the *Saskatchewan Herald* described the removals as "Marching Northward toward the Government Grubpile."[208] Officials were merciless in their use of food to control the First Nations population after the decision to use the southern route for the CPR. The prime minister described the government's position on relief: "We cannot allow them to die for want of food. ... [W]e are doing all we can, by refusing food until the Indians are on the verge of starvation, to reduce the expense."[209]

Bands were driven from their chosen reserves in the high country of the Cypress Hills to meet the related goals of opening the country close to the railway for European settlement and to minimize the potential threat of a concentrated Indian population to the planned establishment of an agricultural economy. By the end of 1882, Big Bear, the most prominent of Cree dissidents, adhered to Treaty 6 in exchange for food for his starving band. For almost a year after their return from the United States in 1881, his people had endured terrible hardship in the Cypress Hills. In the fall of 1882, police physician Augustus Jukes reported to Dewdney that "it would indeed be difficult to exaggerate their extreme wretchedness and need." Rations were deliberately withheld until the chief capitulated on 8 December 1882.[210]

Big Bear was among the last holdouts. By then, almost all of the Cree, with the exception of the small band under Foremost Man, had taken up their reserves. By January 1883, the construction crews of the CPR were approaching the Cypress Hills. Later in the year, the railway reached Medicine Hat, opening eastern markets to ranchers of the west. The success of the relocation scheme was ensured by the closure of Fort Walsh, which, until the arrival of the railway, had served as the seat of Canadian authority and the primary point for the distribution of relief during the famine in the southwest. With the exception of the brief armed resistance during the spring of 1885, the First Nations of the plains were pacified, if not subjugated, by the beginning of 1883. Reed continued to curb the flow of food and other types of assistance to the reserve populations of the plains.

By the early 1880s, tuberculosis was the primary cause of morbidity and mortality within the indigenous population of the plains. For years, the people suffered from malnutrition if not outright starvation. The resulting immune suppression triggered latent infection with *m. tuberculosis*, exogamous infection of *m. bovis*, or probably both into a full-blown epidemic. At the Carlton negotiations, the Cree knew that disappearance of the bison would have profound implications for their health. Cree negotiators succeeded with the inclusion of famine relief in the text of Treaty 6. Canadian officials, who accepted their responsibility to feed the hungry in times of crisis, either ignored their commitment or used food to suppress the population who, less than a decade earlier, had controlled the plains. Dominion management of the famine resulted in more than simply subjugating the people of the plains. The inadequate Canadian response to the humanitarian crisis was to provide TB with an immune-suppressed population across the region.

There was, however, a single and important exception to the post-treaty cycle of poverty, famine, and epidemic tuberculosis during this period. It illustrates that the region-wide outbreak was more than simply an organic event, as had largely been the case with smallpox in previous generations. Unlike acute contagious diseases that spread sickness like a blanket or wave, tuberculosis can occur in local outbreaks depending on site-specific conditions.[211] While the overwhelming majority of treaty Indians endured economic dislocation, famine, and TB in the early 1880s, the Canadian Dakota did not suffer the same terrible decline. The Dakota should rightly be thought of as a "borderlands" people, with a long history north of the forty-ninth parallel,[212] but in the nineteenth century they were considered to be immigrants or refugees from American territory. As such, they were not bound by the same regulations as other Indian groups who underwent the treaty-making process. The Dakota were granted reserve status for their communities in Manitoba and eastern Saskatchewan by dominion authorities; however, "when the expansion of settlement halted in the early 1870s, the government promptly forgot about the Dakota."[213] Many of the exiles from Minnesota, such as the Sisseton led by Chief Standing Buffalo, underwent severe privation, hunger, and sickness with tuberculosis before their flight from the United States in the early 1860s.[214] The Dakota who came to Canada had been farming since the early nineteenth century. They did not require much assistance from dominion authorities and were largely economically autonomous.[215]

In 1879, as the treaty population across the plains was starving, Dr. Hagarty was frustrated because large numbers of Dakota between Portage la Prairie and Fort Qu'Appelle could not spare the time to be vaccinated because they were away working or out hunting.[216] Most of the adults on Ewack's (Enoch's) reserve were away working for settlers, and their gardens were doing well.[217] In his discussion of Dakota communities in western Manitoba, Elias commented that "they probably did as well on the frontier as many of their distant white neighbours did."[218]

Although the Canadian Dakota population endured hardship and were not immune from acute contagious diseases, their economic and medical history diverged sharply from the steep decline in conditions experienced by most treaty Indians during the 1880s. As their treaty neighbours endured hunger and humiliation, the Sisseton Dakota at Standing Buffalo by the end of the 1880s were "completely independent of government aid, a position they were able to maintain for the better part of a generation."[219] Several reasons account for the positive deviance[220] of the Dakota in relation to the precipitous decline of the treaty population.

The Sisseton had been farming in Minnesota since the early years of the nineteenth century. Their experience with agriculture gave them an advantage not shared by groups that subsisted on bison herds until their demise in the late 1870s. Because they did not depend on the bison as a primary food, the community at Standing Buffalo did not require government rations when the herds disappeared. They were skilled farm workers whose labour was in demand in the nascent communities of the North-West Territories. Most important to their success were the facts that they could live their lives and undertake economic strategies outside the systemic constraints imposed on those who entered into treaties with the crown. Communities that entered into treaties assumed that the state would protect them from famine and socioeconomic catastrophe, yet in less than a decade the "protections" afforded by treaties became the means by which the state subjugated the treaty Indian population. One measure of the dominion's oppression of the indigenous population of the prairies was the explosion of tuberculosis. The Dakota, however, did not succumb to the epidemic in the early 1880s because they were relatively free from the oppressive management of the Department of Indian Affairs and could participate in the commercial economy of the region; in other words, they were free from treaty.

DOMINION ADMINISTRATION
OF RELIEF, 1883–85

B Y 1883, HEALTH CONDITIONS AMONG THE TREATY POPULATION were being shaped by the new economic and political reality developing in the west. With the exception of a few holdouts, settlement on reserves was "virtually complete."[1] The government was unapologetic for its use of starvation to complete the occupation of reserves, and the police, who resisted the closure of Fort Walsh in the fall of 1882 because of fears that it would contribute to the famine, were brought under tighter control of the Conservative administration. Lawrence Vankoughnet, the senior DIA bureaucrat in Ottawa, suggested to the prime minister that the police were following their own agenda.[2] The police argued that the fort was necessary to protect railway crews and for defence in case of an uprising, but "the important consideration of keeping good faith with the Indians" was also a major factor in their attempt to keep the post open.[3] In October 1884, the force was brought under the mandate of the Department of Indian Affairs.[4] The administrative change marked a turning point in the relationship between the North-West Mounted Police and the aboriginal population of the northwest. Once regarded as the saviours of the indigenous population of the west, the police became the ambivalent agents of their subjugation.

Macdonald's plan to starve uncooperative Indians onto reserves and into submission might have been cruel, but it certainly was effective. With the exception of a few brief confrontations, construction of the Canadian Pacific Railway west of Swift Current continued almost unabated. By August 1883, the first train reached Calgary, linking the western plains to eastern Canada and the world. It would take another two years for completion of the all-Canadian route across the nation, but travellers could venture from the Atlantic to within sight of the Rockies without ever leaving the comfort of a rail car. The railhead at Calgary marked completion of the infrastructure required for full-scale settlement of the prairies. It was, however, only the most sophisticated in a series of major transportation innovations introduced to the region since 1870.

Soon after the transfer of Rupert's Land in 1870, the Hudson's Bay Company introduced steam-powered vessels along the major waterways of the west. The steamers delivered an unprecedented amount of imported goods to the region and quickly rendered the centuries-old trade route through Hudson Bay obsolete. Impressive though it was, the HBC steamer fleet was no match for the American trade network that eventually extended to the Canadian plains. South of the forty-ninth parallel, traders integrated the long-running steamer system on the Missouri River with rail connections to the east. The western terminus of navigation—Fort Benton, Montana—grew rapidly from its origins in the Whoop-Up trade. The extermination of the bison provided Fort Benton merchants with commercial opportunities far greater than whisky trading.[5] On both sides of the international boundary, the delivery of food and other supplies to the reserve populations and their government overseers became big business. In Canada, appropriations for food relief alone to treaty populations shot from $157,572 in 1880 to $607,235 two years later.[6] From 1882 to 1885, DIA expenditures in Manitoba and the North-West Territories exceeded $1 million annually. Before the establishment of agrarian capitalism, dominion contracts drove the commercial economy of the west. Millions of dollars were spent, and tons of food and other goods were stockpiled in government warehouses. Yet the suffering continued among the malnourished and increasingly sick populations on reserves.

In the decade between arrival of the NWMP and completion of the CPR, a single company rose to dominate the contract economy of western Canada: I. G. Baker and Company, based in Fort Benton.[7] The company was quick to adapt to the new realities of the west as the Whoop-Up trade evaporated. In 1874, brothers William and Charles Conrad bought the company from its founder, Isaac Baker. In less than a decade, the business acumen of the Conrads turned Fort Benton from a whisky post

I. G. Baker and Company's store, Fort Macleod, Alberta. 1879. *Glenbow Archives, NA-98-24.*

to a "business metropolis," the heart of a network that stretched from Great Slave Lake to New Orleans, New York, London, and St. Petersburg. The key to the astonishing growth of the Baker company was not the growing demand of the settler population for goods on the frontier of settlement. Incredibly, the growth of the enterprise into what was essentially a transnational corporation dominating commerce in western Canada took place before there was any significant level of immigration. Baker was an important supplier to the American government, but its stranglehold on dominion contracts made the Conrad brothers and their company rich.

The relationship between Baker and the dominion government began precisely when the whisky trade ended. When the police trekked across the plains in the summer of 1874 to shut down the illicit sale of liquor, Baker employees supplied them with the necessities for the establishment of law and order. Baker stores shadowed police posts and often provided the materials for their construction. One-third of total dominion expenditure on the force was paid to Baker.[8] Completion of Treaty 7 provided the company with $40,000 in contracts for supplies.[9] Until 1882, annuity payments in southern Alberta were made in American currency.[10] Disappearance of the bison provided the firm with an unprecedented economic opportunity. By 1878, the first year of widespread hunger, Baker shipped $2.5 million worth of goods through Fort Benton. To secure its economic power, the company "exercised political influence stretching through Helena to Washington and from Regina to Ottawa."[11]

Baker's move into Canada quickly made the Hudson's Bay Company an anachronism in the territory that had once been its domain. The HBC simply could not compete with Baker for supply contracts. After 1880, Baker opened stores across the Canadian plains, competing with the HBC head on. The venerable but humbled company was often forced to buy supplies from its nemesis.[12] Shrewd management was the key to the American firm's success. Baker functioned as a transnational company, avoiding high import tariffs by purchasing most of its supplies in Montreal and shipping them to the North-West Territories through Duluth, Bismarck, and its own steamers to Fort Benton.[13] The shipping of "bonded cargoes," the strategy that began soon after imposition of a tariff on imported goods in 1876, allowed Fort Benton merchants to undersell the HBC across western Canada.[14] It is difficult to overstate Baker's grip on the commercial economy in the post-treaty period. In addition to securing government contracts, the Conrads were major suppliers to the ranching industry in Alberta.[15] Despite personal lobbying in Ottawa, provision of copies of Baker's successful tenders, and assurance of the prime minister that he wished to "shut out Baker altogether," the old company could not secure any significant contracts in the west before completion of the CPR.[16]

Several factors undermined HBC attempts to compete with Baker's frontier capitalism in the burgeoning marketplace of the North-West Territories. The HBC was still controlled by its governor and committee, who were unwilling to risk the capital needed to fill dominion contracts.[17] Its supply system had met the demands of the fur trade economy for 200 years, but it simply could not deliver the quantity of goods required by the dominion in the west.[18] The steamer fleet was quickly overcome by the growth of commerce and the unpredictability of the Saskatchewan River. The shipment of HBC goods remained hostage to open water, and often the river was too shallow and turbulent even for vessels with limited draft. Major investments were required to clear obstructions for large watercraft.[19] West of Cumberland House, changing water conditions in the early 1880s led to the opening of a new channel on the lower Saskatchewan, forcing steamers to inch their way through uncharted water. Five hundred tons of freight destined for western settlements and the Indian department remained at Cumberland House over the winter of 1882–83. Much of the detained cargo was perishable. In May 1883, the *Northcote* delivered 3,600 bags of flour that had been stored for the winter at Cumberland House to DIA officials at Battleford and Fort Pitt.[20] During the navigation seasons of 1883 and 1884, cold temperatures diminished snow melt in the mountains, yielding exceedingly low water levels along the river. On 29 August 1883, the steamer *Lily* ran aground in three feet of water downstream from Medicine Hat.[21] The cargo included fifty tons of bacon destined for the North Saskatchewan. Official reports stated that forty sacks of bacon suffered water damage from the accident. More important, though, was the time that it took for the salvaged pork to reach its destination.[22] In mid-October, almost two months after the *Lily* ran aground, the *Saskatchewan Herald* reported the arrival of 200 carts for the Indian department at Battleford "with goods intended to come by steamer."[23] Low water levels continued to undermine the HBC trade. In the fall of 1883, the Saskatchewan River ran dry for fifty miles.[24] The following spring cold temperatures again reduced mountain runoff. At Cumberland House, a steamer captain reported that he had never seen the river so low. When the steamer *North West* arrived at Edmonton in mid-July 1884, the *Edmonton Bulletin* reported that it had taken three years for some of its cargo to arrive from Winnipeg.[25] Clearly, the HBC could not reliably transport goods using steamers. This was particularly the case with food, severely undermining the company's reputation on the plains through the 1880s. For the hard-pressed reserve populations, delays might have proven deadly as the malnourished consumed rations that had often languished for long periods during shipment.

In contrast to the HBC, Baker freighted its goods overland from Fort Benton to Alberta. The company's slow but dependable bull trains hauled large quantities for relatively little cost. In the early days of the famine, the demand for food was so great that it taxed even Baker's ability to meet it. Before the notorious Bull Elk Affair on the Blackfoot (Siksika) Reserve, supplies from Baker were exhausted twice during November 1881.[26] Indian Agent Cecil Denny promised that he would maintain "an adequate supply" of beef and flour to allay fears that the government was purposefully starving the Indians. Hunger persisted on reserves even though the dominion made large purchases from Baker not anticipated in the original contracts.[27] Supplemental contracts were particularly profitable because premiums were paid for quick delivery.

Malnutrition, sickness, and death continued among the reserve population, but by 1882 it was not because of a shortage of food in the west. Rather, the growing stockpiles of food and the inability of the hungry to secure them greatly increased frustration toward dominion

I. G. Baker and Company's bull team in front of Murphy, Neel and Company's store, Fort Benton, Montana, circa 1870s. *Glenbow Archives, NA-98-23.*

authorities. Several factors contributed to widespread malnutrition while food was withheld until it spoiled in dominion storehouses. In 1880, the Macdonald government acknowledged the "absolute failure of the usual food supply of the Indians in the North-West" and prepared Parliament for "the necessity of a large expenditure in order to save them from absolute starvation."[28] To counter Liberal criticism, the Tories stressed that strict regulations be placed on the distribution of food, such as the work-for-rations policy. The Macdonald administration avoided the political backlash from a region-wide mortality of the indigenous population from famine, yet the quantity of rations was often the absolute minimum to sustain life. Those who oversaw the ration policy overlooked or ignored the inevitable health consequences of widespread and protracted malnutrition. The trail leading from malnutrition to immune suppression, sickness, and death might have been too obscure to captivate the voting public in the east. The goal of Indian self-sufficiency through farming was probably articulated partly to assuage voters in the east.

Reserve farming was beginning to reap rewards, a factor emphasized in government reports of the early 1880s.[29] By 1882, agricultural production from reserves was deemed sufficient to warrant a review of the Home Farm program. Because reserve farms were meeting the immediate needs of the population, home farms were severely curtailed.[30] By 1884, the sale of surplus reserve produce had become "routine."[31] The dominion was quick to respond to the progress on some reserves by reducing assistance, though even bands that had made gains were still not self-sufficient. The shortage of milling equipment, required to turn grain into palatable food, was a chronic problem. In November 1883, the *Saskatchewan Herald* described the predicament of reserve farmers who could not consume their crops because of the lack of milling equipment: "So long as the Indians are confined to the growth of coarse grain, they will be a burden on the Department for flour. ... [W]hile the raising of barley and oats may serve to keep them from idleness, it will do nothing towards making them self-supporting."[32] The number of acres under cultivation, the measure of progress used by the Indian department, might not have been a true indicator of food produced on reserves. Dewdney admitted to Macdonald that the large number of acres carelessly planted often did not "pan out" in the fall and that "half the area properly cultivated would probably give better yield."[33] Hunting and fishing supplemented nutrition on some reserves. The practice was encouraged by the DIA even though it required the temporary abandonment of reserve agriculture, the focus of dominion policy.

To Canadian officials, the widespread occupation of reserves had another benefit: it greatly facilitated their control of the treaty population. In the early years of the famine, distribution of food was fuelled by a joint sense of "obligation and fear."[34] Once the Indians were settled on reserves (and dependent on rations), the government could counter protests by withholding food.[35] Official correspondence and contemporary scholarship on First Nations history have focused on the small number of bands that resisted dominion pressure to take up reserves. By the end of 1883, however, only a few hundred people at most had not settled on their appointed lands. Demographically, the holdout bands represented but a fraction of the total indigenous population in the west that was experiencing chronic malnutrition and hunger-related disease on government-controlled reserves.

Political pressure from the opposition Liberals was an important factor in constraining government expenditures on the Indian population: "The most serious charge laid against the Indian administration prior to the rebellion of 1885 was that of spending too much on feeding the Indians." As he announced relief appropriations in 1880, the prime minister pre-empted criticism by promising to keep the hungry from dying but assuring the House that his government would be "rigid, even stingy," in the distribution of food. Later, in refuting charges that spending on food was too high, Macdonald stressed that food was refused "until the Indians were on the verge of starvation, to reduce the expense."[36] This was certainly the case for thousands of people on reserves. By the end of 1882, the Indian commissioner was being pressured to further reduce the cost of Indian assistance. For decades, historians have attributed the cuts in Indian department appropriations to the economic downturn in the east and the fiscal crisis over construction of the CPR that began in 1883, but cuts in spending began almost a full year before that. Government appropriations for food peaked at $607,235 in 1882.[37] The following year dominion expenditures for food were slashed by more than $76,000, to $530,982.

Within the DIA, the man responsible for cost cutting was Lawrence Vankoughnet, a clerk with family connections to the prime minister who rose through the ranks of the department to become its chief civil servant.[38] He was never a significant player in the power politics of the Ottawa bureaucracy, dismissed as an "imbecile" by the Liberal press and some of his superiors. His focus on reducing departmental expenditures was central to the further deterioration of conditions on western reserves.[39] Vankoughnet was a fastidious keeper of DIA accounts, but he had little direct knowledge of conditions in the northwest. His only experience there was a brief tour made only weeks after rail service began to Calgary. He refused to travel to the reserves of Treaty 7 and only grudgingly met with chiefs in the agency office at Fort Macleod before leaving the region.[40] In Battleford, Vankoughnet announced a radical change in dominion policy: Indians would be given assistance only "if they showed a disposition to help themselves." Gift giving, a long-standing practice symbolizing respect between parties, was discontinued, and measures were introduced to stop bands from demanding food. So long as the treaty population expected to be fed, "so long will they be helpless as a people, a bill of expense to the country, and a nuisance to their neighbours." As deputy superintendent, Vankoughnet micromanaged his department, and when he was absent little or nothing was accomplished. His zeal for fiscal restraint might have been fuelled by his three-and-a-half-month absence earlier in the year because of a medical condition diagnosed as "a disordered nervous system."[41]

The man charged with implementing Vankoughnet's fiscal regime was the newly appointed assistant Indian commissioner for the North-West Territories, Hayter Reed.[42] A contemporary observer described Reed's systematic approach to his new duties:

[Reed] had calculated to a nicety how much work a yoke of oxen and a plow were capable of performing in a given time and the Indian fell a good deal short of this. He had figured out how little food it was possible to get along with and the Indian was always hungry. The Indian was lazy and therefore he must have short rations, if he felt sick, there was a doctor who could give him pills but no food.[43]

Officials such as Vankoughnet and Reed adopted what they considered a rational approach to maintenance of the reserve population, but even sympathetic accounts have described the reduction of food quotas as extreme.[44] For reserve communities, the departmental reduction of already inadequate food supplies in the fall and winter of 1883–84 could not have come at a worse time.

The thin margin of survival calculated by dominion authorities had no contingencies for the unexpected disruption that shook the budding agricultural economy of the west in the fall of 1883. On 27 August, the Indonesian island of Krakatoa exploded with such force that global temperatures suddenly dropped by at least one degree Fahrenheit.[45] Ash and gases from the eruption blocked sunlight for so long that the global climate was affected for several years.[46] In Canada, temperatures plummeted within weeks of the eruption. In early September, frost destroyed ripening crops from the prairies to the Maritimes.[47] In Manitoba, the diminished harvest fuelled discontent among settlers and contributed to the collapse of the real estate market in Winnipeg. The annual report of the Bell Farm, a massive industrial farm at Indian Head, Saskatchewan, explained that "On the 7th of September frost fell over a vast belt from the Atlantic Ocean to the Rocky Mountains, and from latitude 40 to the desolate Arctic. No unripened grain or fruit, or the delicate vegetables escaped where at all exposed."[48] The frost was the death blow for the massive Bell Farm at Indian Head. Crop failure brought other communities to the brink of disaster. In Saskatoon, hunger during the winter of 1883–84 required some people to make a desperate journey to Batoche to procure flour and stave off famine.[49] Food shortages and even famine were reported in the woodlands from Lake Athabasca to James Bay.[50] On the Carrot River, the HBC supplied rations, mostly potatoes, to the needy at Pas Mountain and other communities between 1883 and 1885.[51] From The Pas, Anglican cleric James Settee lamented that "The times is getting worse the people running in all directions hunting for food."[52] Hunger, according to Settee, was the main reason for increased sickness in the region. Reserve populations, already bearing the burden of long-term malnutrition, must have experienced even greater hardship than inhabitants of the bush.

On the prairies, cold temperatures undermined commercial agriculture and contributed to the financial crisis in the east. Official reports of the DIA did not report a drop in reserve crop production even though many Treaty 4 farms were only miles from the Bell Farm. Accounts of agricultural progress on reserves presented in the *Sessional Papers* might have deliberate falsifications. Only ten days after the killing frost, Macdonald wrote to Dewdney ordering "a full & favourable report on the progress of Indians sett. on the reserves—amt. of crops raised and the prospect of diminished expenditure." The prime minister worried about debate over the DIA file in the upcoming session of Parliament, scheduled to open in January 1884. Macdonald stressed that the report was the "most pressing matter" of the new session.[53] To Dewdney, the political well-being of his mentor and the Conservative Party in Ottawa was paramount. If his patron and party required a positive report on affairs in the northwest, then Dewdney would provide it, despite the large death toll on many reserves resulting from disease and malnutrition.[54] The annual report of the DIA, dated 1 January 1884, clearly reflects Macdonald's letter to Dewdney, for "the progress of the Indians is generally very satisfactory … and … the Department has been able to reduce considerably the rations of flour issued to them on several of the Reserves. …"[55]

Dewdney was a loyal and capable servant of his political master in Ottawa; however, because he knew the level of suffering of the reserve population, he resisted the most egregious aspects of the new policy, and conflict soon erupted. In a letter to the prime minister, Dewdney called Vankoughnet's plan "most unwise and impracticable, if we wished our work to be done satisfactorily."[56] As the dominion's chief official in the northwest, Dewdney responded quickly to the order to curtail expenses. Macdonald praised him for doing so on 17 November 1883.[57] Two days later Vankoughnet told Dewdney that "the Country" expected a lowering of expenditures; otherwise, "serious reproach will be cast on the Department and its officers."[58] Dewdney was particularly galled that Vankoughnet had ordered cuts without consulting him.[59] The government was well aware of the delicate balance between its policy of starving holdouts into submission and onto reserves and the risk of scandal from widespread death from hunger. Before the final withdrawal from Fort Walsh, Vankoughnet articulated the political predicament for the government: "In the interests of humanity, I think that we should take every precaution to prevent any disastrous consequences from want of sufficient shelter for those poor creatures and if we do not, we will certainly incur a great deal of opprobrium at the hands of the public."[60]

Parliament controlled the level of spending on Indian administration, but within the DIA there were questions about how money was being spent. In his dual role as lieutenant governor and Indian commissioner, Dewdney had considerable influence in the management of dominion affairs throughout the region. His power was tempered by Vankoughnet, who controlled departmental accounts, and his focus on fiscal restraint and the concentration of decision making in Ottawa soon led to a power struggle with Dewdney. On his return from the west in the fall of 1883, Vankoughnet unilaterally slashed $140,000 destined for the region.[61] He reported that, in addition to excessive spending by field staff, Indian administration in the west was rife with corruption, and he recommended the termination of several employees.[62] Discretionary powers of DIA officials, including those of Commissioner Dewdney, were severely curtailed as administration was centralized in Ottawa.[63] The prime minister, troubled by the irregularities described in Vankoughnet's report and the poor quality of goods delivered by I. G. Baker, told Dewdney that "If there has been any connivance by any of our agents—or carelessness in receiving inferior articles, they should be dismissed without mercy."[64]

Dewdney was furious that the changes had been made without his input, but he followed his orders. He warned that some of the cuts would result in hardship for both the reserve population and DIA employees.[65] He tempered his anger when responding to Macdonald but asserted that Vankoughnet had come to "hasty conclusions."[66] Vankoughnet's report had been prepared without Dewdney's input and focused on the "belief that there was manipulation and connivance between Indian Agents and the I. G. Baker Co."[67]

The Montana firm was by far the most important contract supplier for the dominion in the northwest, billing the government for supplies for the destitute of Treaty 7 more than $327,000 in 1883 alone.[68] Baker's dishonest business practices were known to Macdonald as early as 1881 when the firm paid competitors thousands of dollars to withdraw their lower tenders on dominion contracts.[69] Senior HBC officials were assured that the dominion wanted Baker removed as its chief supplier in the west. Despite promises to the contrary, their contracts with Baker were renewed, prompting C. J. Brydges to comment that "I fear there is a strong desire in some quarters to deal with them, for reasons which may be imagined."[70] The HBC land commissioner hinted that Dewdney, the most powerful Canadian official in the northwest, was financially tied to the Montana firm. That the HBC complained that its chief rival used dishonest business practices is not surprising. Yet criticism of Baker's undue influence came from other sources. Assistant Commissioner Irvine of the NWMP complained that "a large amount of money has been expended, in return for which there is little or nothing to show, our money is merely adding to build up the town of Benton, U.S.A."[71]

Historian Paul Sharp outlined the political influence of Benton firms in both Washington and Ottawa fifty years ago in his study of the Alberta and Montana frontiers. In the United States, the chief lobbyist in Congress for Benton firms was Major Martin Maginnis. In exchange for financial and political support from Benton businesses, Maginnis secured the support of the US government that "frequently went so far as to call [for] the shifting of army troops or the redrawing of Indian reservation boundaries to satisfy the desires of the merchant princes of the northern plains."[72] Baker secured its economic position in Canada through its relationship with Dewdney, who was paid in shares of a Benton bank that received hundreds of thousands of dollars in Canadian government accounts. His attempts to enrich himself through involvement in financial ventures beyond his official capacity have been well documented. There were few rules governing conflict of interest during his tenure, but his "self-serving opportunism" led to "growing indignation at what were clearly corrupt practices."[73] His effort to locate what became the capital of Saskatchewan on his land is part of local lore in Regina. Before that, he tried to have the capital placed near the Bell Farm at Indian Head. He was a stockholder in the venture and, using a front man to counter suspicion by the CPR, invested in land surrounding the enterprise.[74] Because the prime minister's son Hugh was an investor along with Dewdney and "Eden" in the scheme, Macdonald probably knew of it. Dewdney's financial relationship with Baker probably began when Dewdney spent a week at Fort Benton meeting with Baker officials while preparing in 1879 to take up his new duties as Indian commissioner.[75] Four years later his dismissal of the Vankoughnet report might well have been motivated by his financial interest in the Montana company rather than the substance of the charges.[76]

Questions about tendering processes and the quality of hardware supplied by Baker were soon overshadowed by far more serious allegations. On 6 November 1883, Dr. F. X. Girard, the medical officer for Treaty 7, reported that flour supplied by the company was "unfit for food" and had been responsible for many deaths. The situation was especially bad

Blackfoot people receiving rations, circa 1883-84. *Glenbow Archives, NA-1033-3.*

at the Blood (Kainai) Reserve, where at least twenty people died over a six-week period in September and October.[77] Oral accounts from the area reflect strongly held beliefs that the flour had been tampered with and even that the poisonings were deliberate.[78] Given the high mortality and tension on reserves, the notion that government food was poisoned is not illogical to the descendants of those who died. For the flour identified in the Girard report, this was probably not the case. As the scandal escalated, the government was forced to undertake an independent scientific investigation. The analysis of I. G. Baker flour in Ottawa from Treaty 7 reserves might have been the only independent investigation of dominion food in this period. The results were damaging to both Baker and the dominion government.[79] Documents submitted to Parliament indicate that Baker was paid for "flour ... equal in quality to No. 1 superfine" throughout the northwest, including the reserves where the substandard samples had been procured. An agent of A. W. Ogilvy and Company, the milling firm that provided the flour to Baker, inspected the product at several reserves in the northwest and affirmed that it was all right except for some damage due to storage in unsuitable warehouses.[80] In the end, a reduction of about $7,800 in the Baker contract was recommended, but the firm settled the matter with a reduction of only $2,500.

For the dominion, this was yet another in a series of allegations of corruption in its frontier civil service. Liberals accused William Pocklington, the Indian agent who had accepted the flour, of being either corrupt or incapable of fulfilling his duties. Dr. Girard, the whistle blower and the only dominion employee who had acknowledged a problem with the flour, spent the rest of his tenure with the DIA being hounded by Commissioner Dewdney for his reported inefficiency.[81] Charges of collusion between DIA field staff and Baker were frequently laid. In 1881, Edwin Allen, the Indian agent at Fort Walsh, was fired for mismanaging the delivery of rations in the Cypress Hills. Because Allen "had issued certificates for nearly twice the quantity of beef received," Dewdney was ordered to investigate the relationship between Baker and "Allen's friends."[82] Allen was sacked for double-billing dominion accounts, but the practice continued, at least sporadically, for years. "Lying Allen" as he was known, later joined a group known as the "Calgary Syndicate" who were involved in numerous shady deals including the fixing of athletic events for their own benefit.[83] Vouchers for beef submitted to the House of Commons show that Baker billed the dominion for thousands of pounds of meat twice, on the same day, for the population at Blackfoot Crossing in 1883 and 1884.[84] For the Blood Reserve, the dominion was billed $48,744 for beef to feed at most 2,200 people during the last five months of 1883. Liberals castigated the government for its failure to establish a means of checking these large vouchers that were often authorized by low-level employees such as farm instructors. M. C. Cameron, the most vocal critic of Conservative Indian policy, stressed that, "If the Indians are getting inferior supplies, a poorer quality flour or bacon than the contract requires, that is a fraud on the Indians as well as on the Government; and the middlemen who furnish the government with supplies must have been guilty of the very grossest misconduct during the last three or four years." The prime minister admitted that there were "occasional frauds" by contractors but emphasized that "It cannot be considered a fraud on the Indians because they were living on Dominion charity ... and, as the old adage says, beggars should not be choosers." Macdonald then shifted to the culpability of reserve populations in acquiring more than the dominion deemed sufficient. He quoted a report that found that the number of rations doled out exceeded the official count of the reserve population.[85] Dr. C. F. Ferguson, a Conservative MP and land speculator, who witnessed the deaths at the Blood Reserve, stressed that rations had not been the cause; rather, the unsanitary habits of the Kainai had made them susceptible to "autumn fever or mountain fever."[86] He added that chronic stomach ailments in their community were "a result of too much food and not enough exercise."[87]

By the end of 1883, problems were appearing throughout the dominion's food distribution system. Perhaps buoyed by Vankoughnet's increased influence in the department, T. P. Wadsworth, inspector of Indian agencies, reported to Dewdney that large quantities of bacon at Farm 17 near Edmonton were deteriorating.[88] Indian Agent Anderson was praised for his initiative in dealing with the problem of spoiled salt pork by re-curing it and distributing it along with flour that was "a little musty."[89]

Questions regarding the government's choice of food were also being raised. Officials steadfastly maintained their dependence on bacon as a staple despite almost continual criticism of it as expensive and difficult to digest (even when it was in good condition).[90] When spoiled, however, bacon was deadly. The worst incident resulting from consumption of rancid salted pork occurred among the Assiniboine bands near Indian Head in the fall of 1883. The experience of the Cree chief Piapot, leader of the victims of the tragedy in dealing with dominion authorities, was marked by hardship and frustration. In 1882, Piapot and his people were forced from the Cypress Hills to their reserve east of Regina, enduring a journey on foot of over 350 miles with a daily ration of "one half pound of flour and a small amount of pemmican per person."[91] The agent at Indian Head acknowledged their "discontent and expression of unwillingness to go to their reserve," but he assured them that both treaty terms and other promises made at Fort Walsh would be honoured.[92] On his arrival in the agency, the chief was "incensed" by the starvation among those who had taken to their reserves near Qu'Appelle. Within months, Piapot, Long Lodge, Cree leaders Lucky Man, Big Bear, and Little Pine, along with over 2,000 followers, abandoned their reserves, returning to the Cypress Hills to take their chances in the high country near Fort Walsh.[93] Because the authorities did not sanction these departures, they received no help.[94] Once in the hills, the holdouts were fed but at minimum levels. Agent MacDonald explained to Dewdney that they "were not getting enough flour but I like to punish them a little."[95]

When Fort Walsh was finally closed by direct order from Ottawa in the spring of 1883, Piapot and the other holdouts again headed to their reserves in the east and north.[96] Those journeys were fraught with difficulty. Little Pine's band was reduced to trading their horses for food. Piapot was provided with passage east, though several of his people were injured when their train derailed.[97] In August, Piapot's

Piapot, Cree chief, circa 1880s. *Glenbow Archives, NA-532-1.*

plan to hold a council of Treaty 4 chiefs to discuss their conditions was thwarted by the Indian department's refusal to supply the gathering with rations.[98] His band then took up their reserve near Indian Head. The *Regina Leader* assured its readers that the move, and the rations that came with it, would mean no more trouble: "The Government is bound to feed the Indians, so as they are fed, the poor creatures are no more likely to give trouble than a kennel of dogs fed at regular intervals. ..."[99] As winter approached, the newspaper reported that all was quiet on the reserves east of Regina.[100] The Indian Head reserves during the fall and winter of 1883–84 were anything but the picture of serenity presented by the *Regina Leader*, whose explicit editorial policy was to gloss over anything that might detract from settlement of the country.[101]

Assiniboine historian Abel Watetch wrote that members of Piapot's band who had been cutting cordwood were given rancid bacon for their work.[102] W. W. Gibson, a settler whose land was adjacent to the Piapot Reserve, stated that 130 people died.[103] Piapot placed blame for the tragedy squarely on the dominion officials who had pressured him to take up his reserve on the promise of fresh meat for his people. Before the deaths, Long Lodge complained that his people could not eat the bacon, to which Dewdney replied, "the Indians should eat the bacon or die, and be d____d to them."[104] In Parliament, M. C. Cameron accused Dewdney of taking a firm stand on the issue of the bacon because "his friend the contractor, who happened to be in a land syndicate with him, had 90,000 pounds of bacon to dispose of." Watson, another Liberal, went further, stating that Long Lodge was fed rotten meat "bought in Chicago for 1 ½ cents a lb, and sold to this government for 19 cents; also that the Governor shared in the profits of this contract."[105] Predictably, the prime minister dismissed charges that there was a connection between Dewdney, the consumption of spoiled bacon, and the sudden spike in deaths on the Indian Head reserves.[106] Still, Dewdney's position on the Board of Directors of the Bell Farm, his relationship with I. G. Baker, supplier of the deadly pork, and his penchant for self-enrichment cast shadows over his involvement in the affair.

Soon after the deaths, Dewdney was granted a two-month leave of absence in February 1884.[107] His departure further complicated matters on reserves as Vankoughnet took control of Indian affairs in the west. His fiscal restraint soon led to confrontation and heightened tension on reserves at the breaking point. For survivors of the Indian Head tragedy, still suffering from malnutrition and high levels of tuberculosis infection, assistance was slow to come. On 7 February 1884, Dr. O. C. Edwards reported that "the mortality of these Indians has been very great and

A political cartoon regarding starvation that appeared in *Grip* in 1888. *Source:* Grip, *Vol. 30, No. 775, April 14, 1888.*

... the death rate was accelerated if death was not immediately caused [by the] scant Supply of food served out to the Indians."[108] Although "prompt remedial measures" were called for, there was no response for six weeks on account of Dewdney's absence. Then the DIA suggested that "a moderate quantity of beef might be sent to the Indian Head reserves occasionally for the sick, as well as tea and sugar."[109] Although the Conservative *Regina Leader* did not comment on the event, the *Moose Jaws News* called the Indian Head deaths a "burning shame to us [and] a lasting reproach to our government."[110]

By the end of May, the situation for Piapot and Long Lodge had become unbearable. The fresh meat and clothing promised months earlier had still not been delivered. Hayter Reed and Commissioner A. G. Irvine of the NWMP met with the exasperated chiefs to keep them on their reserves. Long Lodge told the officials that there was no game or potable water on his reserve and that "his people were all dying, and that if they continued to remain there they would all die." Among the many grievances of Piapot was that he "could not endure the stench that emanated from the dead bodies of unburied Indians then lying on the ground."[111]

A week before the chiefs met with Reed and Irvine, Dr. Edwards described the worsening situation on the Assiniboine reserves. Among "Jack's people ... suppurating and enlarged glands on the neck [have] now spread generally ... and [a]ffects men, women and children alike. In February, I saw no cases among Piapot's people, now I find it very general. ... [B]ronchial trouble[s] are numerous ending as many of these cases do in spitting of blood, quick consumption and death."[112] Long Lodge refused the physician's offer of medicine, pointing to the real source of their misery: "I want no Government Medicine. What I want is medicine that walks. Send 3 oxen to be killed and give fresh meat to my people and they will get better."[113] Neither Long Lodge nor anyone else in the northwest was aware that fresh beef was contributing to the growing TB epidemic.

Government officials saw abandonment of reserves as a security threat. Commissioner Irvine intercepted Piapot's band with more than half of the total police contingent from the depot at Regina and an artillery piece.[114] Arrival of the force caused panic among the band, who thought they were going to be attacked.[115] Bloodshed was averted as the police commissioner negotiated their temporary return to Indian Head. By the end of the summer, the band took up their new home in the Qu'Appelle Valley, where fresh water and game were available. Long Lodge, who led his band south to the United States, was dead by the end of the year.

The dispute between Piapot and the authorities ended without violence, but resentment escalated as Vankoughnet's cuts took effect. The One Arrow Reserve near Fort Carlton experienced an astounding death rate of 141 per 1,000 during the winter of 1883–84.[116] At File Hills, seven children in a single family died of hunger in a two-month period. It was reported that the sick there were allowed to die.[117]

The most significant confrontation during Vankoughnet's brief time in charge of the DIA occurred on the Sakimay (also known as the Yellow Calf) Reserve in the Qu'Appelle Valley. A feature of his austerity plan was the dismissal of low-level employees during the winter because Vankoughnet considered their retention a waste of money.[118] In the Treaty 4 area, Indian Agent MacDonald managed to keep his position despite Vankoughnet's attempt to have him sacked for what he considered excessive spending.[119] MacDonald's farming instructor at Crooked Lake, James Setter, was not so lucky. He was dismissed to cut costs and for his apparent laxity in the distribution of food.[120] Setter's dismissal, and his replacement with the inexperienced Hilton Keith, led directly to the armed standoff known as the Yellow Calf Incident. The new man followed Vankoughnet's orders to the letter. His adherence to the new departmental policy almost led to a bloodbath.

On 6 January 1884, MacDonald reported that the storehouse on the reserve contained 12,400 pounds of bacon and 5,100 pounds of flour. Keith arrived on the reserve six days later. After personally inspecting the community, Assistant Commissioner Reed gave Keith strict orders regarding the rationing procedure. The entire band under Sakimay, "with two or three exceptions," was to be cut from the ration list. Trouble erupted five weeks later. Driven by hunger and frustration, Chief Sakimay and a number of armed men forced their way into the agency storehouse on 18 February. Sixty bags of flour and twelve containers of bacon were taken. Reed later admitted that at least some of the people were starving, that Keith had refused them food acting under the new regulations, and that the hungry believed that the stored food was theirs: "If ... the provisions were not intended to be eaten by the Indians why were they stored on their reserve?"[121]

Four representatives of the group, including Sakimay, stood trial for larceny. The charges against him were dropped, and the others were discharged after pleading guilty. Reed acknowledged that "justice has been tempered with mercy" as Sakimay "had acted in the interests of humanity, from first, to last."[122] Similar events were reported from the nearby File Hills reserves as tension mounted across the west over what was described by the *Saskatchewan Herald* as "cast iron regulations" of the DIA.[123] In Ottawa, Vankoughnet expected trouble and warned the police that "efforts will be made to seize unprotected stores" near Indian Head, Broadview, and Battleford.[124]

When Dewdney returned to duty in April 1884, he was confronted with the seething anger resulting from Vankoughnet's new order. He quickly undertook an inspection tour of reserves, including Sakimay's, where he ordered the immediate purchase of new farm equipment to diffuse tension.[125] He agreed that salted foods were contributing to the high rates of sickness and stressed the need for a more liberal supply of food. By summer, the prime minister acknowledged the short-sightedness of Vankoughnet's move to centralize control of Indian matters in the Ottawa office, and he authorized Dewdney to repair the damage done during the previous months.[126]

Dewdney's management skills were certainly required during the summer of 1884. The Niitsitapi of Treaty 7 demanded fresh meat instead of the government bacon that had killed so many the year before.[127] Assistant Commissioner Reed knew that there was a problem with the food distributed by the department and admitted to the prime minister that rations were both inadequate and probably indigestible.[128] Between 1883 and 1887, Treaty 7 people received 50–70 percent of departmental expenditures for supplies and rations even though their population never exceeded 35 percent of the total Indian population of the northwest. The Niitsitapi were spared the worst of the cuts to Indian appropriations to avert trouble until the railway was complete and the ranching industry was well established. Still, their ration during the summer of 1884 was less than five ounces of flour per day.[129]

Tension among the Cree of Treaty 6 seemed ready to explode. At Battleford, where the northern plains reserves were concentrated, farm instructor Craig's refusal to provide food in the spring of 1884 precipitated a confrontation between a large body of police, local volunteers, and over 2,000 Cree at the Poundmaker Reserve. As had been the case at the Sakimay Reserve, sacks of grain withheld from the hungry were used to fortify the police positions during the standoff.[130] Before the incident, the *Saskatchewan Herald* pointed to a growing rift between the DIA and the judiciary over food because the Cree "think that the formal appearance before a magistrate will be an easy way of procuring a large increase in their rations."[131] The newspaper assured readers that "The noble red men may try to intimidate an odd storehouse keeper, and in an emergency capture a bag of flour or a side of bacon; but as for a general uprising, he has strong reasons for letting that job out."[132] Although what has been called the Cree Rebellion of 1884[133] was diffused

Photo entitled, "Cree Indian, Maple Creek, Saskatchewan, 1884." *Reproduced with the permission of Natural Resources Canada 2012, courtesy of the Geological Survey of Canada (Photo 615 by T. C. Weston).*

without bloodshed, conditions at the Battleford reserves had deteriorated over the previous years to the breaking point. During the winter
of 1883–84, Father Cochin described the condition of the children at
the mission school:

> After the disappearance of the buffalo, the bacon and the cakes
> made with some bad flour did not satisfy the appetite of the In-
> dians. I saw the gaunt children dying of hunger, coming to my
> place to be instructed. Although it was thirty to forty degrees
> below zero their bodies were scarcely covered with torn rags.
> These poor children came to catechism and to school. It was a
> pity to see them. The hope of having a little morsel of dry cake[134]
> was the incentive which drove them to this cruel exposure each
> day, more, no doubt, than the desire of educating themselves.
> The privation made many die.[135]

Robert Jefferson, a teacher on one of the Battleford reserves, questioned
the motives of the dominion's reserve agricultural policy. He wrote
that the reserve population earnestly took up farming because "they
had borne hunger, disease and want for several years and they were no
nearer their goal. It looked as [if] they might die off before they reached
it—that is, if it existed." Jefferson elaborated on the cynicism within
the DIA: "Craig had a fixed idea that it was not intended that the Indian
should become self-supporting. He was only to be kept quiet till the
country filled up when his ill will could be ignored."[136]

Before 1885, the dominion's agricultural policy was a failure. Only six
treaty bands in the entire northwest were not dependent on government
assistance.[137] According to Aidan McQuillan, "The best claim that the
Department of Indian Affairs could make in 1884 was that only 770 of
a total of 20,230 Indians in the Territories were not reliant on government relief supplies."[138] The Indian department further undermined
commercial farming by discouraging the use of machinery.[139] At the
Stoney (Nakota) Reserve west of Calgary, progress under the tutelage
of Reverend John McDougall led to major reductions in aid to the
community in 1884. The short-sightedness of the cuts meant that there
was no margin of safety during hard times. An early history observed
that "The result of this action was that the winter of 1885 saw droves of
starving Stonies wandering through the hills, from below Pincher Creek
to the main line of the CPR, begging food from the ranchers, picking
the flesh from the bones of dead horses and cattle, even eating coyotes
when they could get them."[140]

Even bands with good crops went hungry under DIA supervision. In March 1884, John Hines, the missionary at Assissippi, told his superior that "I am certain our Indians would have been better off to-day if the government had not taken them under their charge."[141] Despite having threshed 2,000 bushels of grain, "There is a great deal of sickness among the Indians just now, brought on we believe principally by starvation." Farmers from the community had to travel more than 100 miles each way to have their grain milled in Prince Albert, "leaving nothing behind for their families but unground wheat."[142] Officials knew that the scarcity of equipment undermined the work of reserve farmers: "Nothing prevents all of our Indians from being settled on their reserves, except for our incapacity to furnish enough material for agriculture."[143]

Bad weather continued through 1884, bringing the entire northwest to the verge of famine. James Settee reported that "we had frost early in the summer in Saskatchewan, consequently all the farms are lost, which is a very severe trial to the immigrants and to the natives."[144] He proposed the resettlement of "Plains Indians who will perish from hunger" to the shores of Lake Winnipeg, where fish could still be found in large numbers.[145] The government, then nurturing the commercial fishery in Manitoba, rejected the offer.[146]

Settee's plan failed because the large-scale shift to fish as a subsistence base for the indigenous population would have undermined commercial fishing by newcomers. Fish populations in western Canada were under severe pressure from both subsistence and commercial harvesting. In the Carlton Agency, Macrae reported "the wholesale destruction of fish during the spawning season. Two remedies are suggested: declaring a closed season or preserving certain waters for the exclusive use of Indians."[147] North of Fort Pitt, fish were "failing fast, owing to outside parties fishing on a very large scale, and robbing the Indians of every fish they catch."[148] Agent Anderson wrote that decline of the fishery of Lac Ste. Anne and other lakes in Alberta would "be a serious loss to the native and white population which is so rapidly filling up the country."[149] Jackfish Lake, near Battleford, continued to be a reliable source of food. Inspector Wadsworth reported that a number of treaty holdouts were living there in relative affluence: "if Big Bear and his followers will not work, they can subsist by devoting their whole time to hunting and fishing."[150] Later, aboriginal harvesters were blamed for the scarcity of fish; in June 1887, the *Saskatchewan Herald* commented that, "if the strong arm of the law is not laid on them soon, they will have our lakes as destitute of life as the prairies. ..."[151]

By the summer of 1884, the treaty population was in crisis. A bad climate, the depletion of fish and small game, and departmental indifference to the miserable conditions on reserves compelled Cree leaders to renew their demands for better treatment. They met with government officials at Duck Lake and Carlton. Dewdney and Reed "shared concerns about Vankoughnet's new hard-line approach to Indian rationing," but they did not yield to the demands of the united chiefs. Instead, the Indian commissioner pursued a policy of "sheer compulsion" to counter Cree resistance to dominion authority.[152] In a letter to the prime minister, Dewdney dismissed Cree grievances as "the same old story—more cattle, more implements, more grub, more clothing & fact more everything," and he discounted accounts of starvation among children,[153] yet protracted malnutrition had been a factor in their deaths.

Although Dewdney took a hard line against political agitation on reserves, his efforts to mitigate the crisis spawned by Vankoughnet's cuts brought some respite to the hunger of the reserve population. Allocations for food were increased by almost $17,000 in 1884 from the previous year.[154] Because most of the additional spending went to I. G. Baker, Fred White, comptroller of the NWMP, warned Dewdney that he should prepare for the "coming onslaught" of criticism in Parliament. Especially troubling to White was the perception that Dewdney had a "pecuniary interest in everything ... over which you have control."[155]

Things appeared quiet on reserves at the beginning of 1885, but tension seethed beneath the surface. Just days before the outbreak of violence in the spring of 1885, the *Saskatchewan Herald* castigated the government for its misguided ration policy and its role in making the indigenous population sick: "Everyone here knows that almost all of the Indians in the district suffer from scrofula and dyspepsia. ... Their policy seems to be comprised in these six words: feed one day, starve the next."[156] The newspaper also criticized the DIA for not giving Indian agents, responsible for the daily management of reserves, discretionary power in the distribution of rations. In addition, they had no control over the appointment or removal of their subordinates, the farm instructors. Political appointments to the bureaucracy and dominion indifference to the success of its own agricultural initiative made the position of farm instructor attractive to the worst candidates. Because the DIA controlled almost every aspect of daily life on reserves, even the lowest-ranking employees had considerable power, and many took advantage of their positions. According to Lawrence Clarke, farm instructors were "universally known to be brutal wretches."[157]

Historians Stonechild and Waiser argue that the violence committed by the Cree in the spring of 1885 was not an open rebellion but a series of "isolated and sporadic" events.[158] Revenge was directed against instructors and agents who had taken particular zeal in carrying out the parsimonious directives of their superiors. The DIA employees who were killed had acted beyond the authority granted by the dominion. The unsanctioned abuse of departmental power was a key factor in the events leading to the deaths of ten Europeans at Frog Lake on 2 April 1885.[159] Confrontations between the hungry and frustrated on reserves and officials over access to food were common. What was different about Frog Lake was that the Métis had begun their armed insurrection in the country to the east and against the cruelty of the Indian sub-agent, a Dakota mixed-blood named Thomas Quinn. The killings were sparked by his refusal to provide the hungry Cree with food. The daughter of one of the killers later remarked that "all he ... had to do was consent to move away to the Main Camp and let my people help themselves."[160] In their discussion of the incident, Stonechild and Waiser described Quinn as "a mean spirited, petty little man completely lacking in compassion."[161] In the fall of 1884, Little Poplar told him that his reputation for intransigence was widespread: "I heard of you away over the other side of the Missouri River. I started to come this way and the farther I came the more I heard. *You're* the man the government sent up here to say *"No!"* to everything the Indians asked you!"[162] Resentment against Quinn stemmed from more than his carrying out departmental directives to the letter. Numerous accounts indicate that his parsimony was matched by his brutality. His summoning of the people to the ration house, a call that essentially began a stampede among the emaciated population, only to inform them that it was an April Fool's Day prank and they would get nothing, is well documented.[163] With understatement, the mother of Cree historian Joseph Dion noted that "we made a great laugh for the whites; but we failed to see the humour in it."[164] Quinn's sadism would certainly have contributed to the tension at the settlement, but his murder, and those of the others once the violence began,[165] might well have been precipitated by other events.

Twenty-six years after the killings, fur trader-turned-missionary Jack Matheson provided a more sinister motive for the violence in the *Toronto Saturday Night:* "An Indian girl more or less didn't matter; and I've seen rations held back six months till girls of thirteen were handed across as wives for that Sioux brute."[166] One of the killers at Frog Lake, Wandering Spirit, had spent eighteen months in prison for assaulting another DIA employee, John Delaney. While he was incarcerated,

Delaney "took his girl wife. Do you wonder that Indian became a rebel? Do you wonder when the discontent seethed up to rebellion, that it was Wandering Spirit who poured the blackguard full of shot?"[167] Maureen Lux characterized Delaney as being "roundly hated for his relationships with very young women of the reserve, and for his casual humiliations of the hungry people."[168] A survivor of the incident, William Cameron, also pointed to sexual predations as contributing factors in the killings.[169] The sexual improprieties of the DIA employees at Frog Lake might have contributed to the ambivalence of Quinn's own widow. A decade after the killing of her husband, Owl Sitting refused to identify Imases and Lucky Man as participants in the killings. Indian Commissioner A. E. Forget, present at the interview, expressed his astonishment: "By Gad! ... I might have known. These are her people and it was only her husband that they murdered."[170]

Persistent allegations of sexual predation against both DIA employees at Frog Lake indicate that it was not a solitary occurrence. Archbishop Taché stated that the dominion's wards were "left a prey to the seductions of men revoltingly immoral."[171] In Parliament, M. C. Cameron charged that the sexual exploitation of Indian women was so pervasive that 45 percent of "one class of officials" in the northwest had sexually transmitted diseases, "an extraordinary showing for a class of men paid by the people of this country to control, manage and set an example to the Indians of the North-West Territories."[172] Cameron charged that girls as young as thirteen were being sold to white men in the west, some for as little as ten dollars. Government member Hector Langevin refused to accept that this constituted trafficking in young girls by asserting that to Indians "marriage is simply a bargain and sale that the parents of a young woman are always on the alert to find a buyer for her."[173] If there was any truth in his rebuttal, traditional "bride price" practices would have been severely strained by the horrendous conditions on reserves.

By the 1880s, the inadequate rations provided by the DIA had probably driven many women to prostitution simply to feed their families. In 1883, prostitution was considered a problem on reserves near Calgary.[174] That year the Cree chiefs at Edmonton petitioned the prime minister that "their young women were now reduced by starvation and prostitution, a thing unheard of among their people before." When the missionary Samuel Trivett exposed the sale of young Blood women by their desperate parents to male settlers in Fort Macleod, the *Macleod Gazette* defended the involvement of its readers in the practice: "there are scores of Indians on the reserve, on which he is a missionary, who practice the revolting and unnatural crime of peddling their women around the towns and settlements."[175]

Contrary to S. W. Horrall's assertion that prostitution came to the North-West Territories as sex workers moved west with the railway,[176] prostitution among aboriginal women was a survival strategy resulting from the poverty experienced in their reserve communities after disappearance of the bison. Increased sexual contact between members of reserve communities and newcomers soon resulted in a jump in reports of sexually transmitted diseases. In 1882, the police surgeon at Fort Walsh, Augustus Jukes, requested an assistant to cope with the problem.[177] Such diseases soon became a growing problem among members of the force themselves. Cases of venereal disease soared from twenty-two in 1882 to 132 in 1884, when the total compliment of the NWMP was 557 men.[178] Senior officers, such as Inspector Deane, considered the growing rate of infection among his men to be a lack of discipline. In 1883, he advocated charging infected members for their medical care and confinement to barracks on their release from hospital.[179]

By 1886, the Indian Act was amended to make First Nations prostitutes subject to prosecution, "but there existed within the department a long standing view that Indian women were unwilling partners in this activity."[180] The new laws were applied in response to "a national scandal" over the traffic of Indian women involving DIA employees.[181] John Norrish, the farm instructor at the Blackfoot Reserve, was fired for trading food for sex in 1882.[182] During his abuse, the daughter of Calf-Woman was given a bogus ration card providing her with an extra three rations for her family of four. While Norrish was buying sex with flour, the farm instructor at the Stoney Reserve in Morley reportedly kept two "wives" while he was in the community.[183] Sexual contact between DIA officials and First Nations women was probably not limited to the lower levels of the service. Assistant Commissioner Reed, who advanced an ordinance in the Territorial Council in the fall of 1886 "to compel men to support their illegitimate offspring," was himself accused of sexual misconduct.[184] William Donovan, a settler in Prince Albert, charged that Reed had a "girl ... from Touchwood Hills, she was his mistress at Regina, and has a child she says is his."[185] Donovan also claimed that Reed "debauched Mrs. Quinn, (another indigenous woman). ... [H]e is a libertine and has not respect for the virtue of women."[186] Not surprisingly, the accusations against Reed were never pursued, and in 1888 he was promoted to the rank of Indian commissioner when Dewdney was elected to Parliament and entered cabinet as minister of the interior and superintendent general of Indian affairs.

In 1885, many killings were the settling of personal scores. Europeans such as William Cameron, the HBC trader at Frog Lake, and police officers at Fort Pitt were spared in recognition of their humanity.[187] Farm instructors who merely followed orders, such as Craig and McKay, safely passed through groups of rebels during their flight to Battleford.[188] McKay was even assisted in crossing the Battle River by a group of Nakota. Barney Tremont, the Battleford man killed by Man without Blood, had been an Indian fighter in the United States.[189] Beal and Macleod remarked that Tremont "hated Indians and would threaten them whenever they came near his ranch."[190] Walter Hildebrandt said that he was killed for refusing to help a Cree boy during a blizzard.[191]

Another victim at Battleford, farm instructor James Payne, was considered to be particularly cruel, and several motives have been posited for his murder. Stonechild and Waiser stated that Itka killed him in retribution for the beating death of his daughter, who had tuberculosis.[192] At his trial, the accused testified that he had killed Payne in a fight over rations that had been withheld for ten days.[193] Hildebrandt provided another reason for the murder:

He [Payne] had a common-law wife and several children. Returning one night from Battleford under the influence of liquor, he drove his wife and children out of doors during a snow storm. Before they succeeded in reaching an Indian shelter, the poor woman, who had used her own garments to protect the children from biting frost, had both her breasts frozen and never quite recovered from the effects of that dreadful night. When the rebellion broke out, her Indian relatives sought revenge against the Farm Instructor and shot him to death.[194]

In his obituary, the *Saskatchewan Herald* noted that Payne had married the daughter of Chief Grizzly Bear's Head the previous summer and that his widow gave birth to a son the day after his death.[195] Two weeks later the newspaper mentioned that Payne had not been alone at the time of his death. The murder scene had included "[t]he body of a woman apparently about twenty years of age, shot through the cheek, and of a one year old child with a fractured skull, ... found near Mr. Payne's body."[196] The newspaper made no further reference to the unnamed mother and child or to the fate of their bodies.

Although the killing of Europeans was widely publicized in the contemporary press, and remains a fixation of historians of the 1885 uprising,[197] the murders of indigenous people during the conflict have received scant attention. In June, the *Saskatchewan Herald* reported that "a sepulchral teepee was found in the Eagle Hills in which there were nine dead Stonies, and nearby was another resting in a tree. All had died of gun shot wounds, but whether they proved fatal on the battlefield or on the reserves is not known; nor is it material."[198]

The newspaper's solitary reference to the murder of Payne's companion and child, and its dismissal of the shootings of the nine people as irrelevant, suggest that other murders might have gone unreported during the uprising. Fear of retribution might have driven many to abandon the country altogether. Before the mass execution at Battleford, many left the Stoney reserves. Chief Grizzly Bear's Head, sixty of his followers, and another "forty dissidents from other bands" fled to the United States, where they spent years of hardship, "managing to escape American authorities, who wished to send them back to Canada."[199] The decision of the Stoney and other bands to abandon their reserves could not have been taken lightly. Official retribution would be meted out later to the large number of bands deemed disloyal, but the fear of personal attack was widespread.

During the conflict, some of those hunted by dominion authorities took their own lives rather than allow themselves to become prisoners. Near Loon Lake, trooper Lewis Redman Ord, among those pursuing Big Bear, came upon a woman who had recently hanged herself; "she had been left behind and hearing of our approach had committed suicide in preference to falling into our hands."[200] The woman's fear of capture might have been nurtured earlier when, at Frenchman's Butte, a Cree fighter attempting to surrender was blown to pieces while waving a white flag.[201]

The Cree bands who, according to one trooper, were "hunted to death and starving,"[202] were punished severely after their surrender. The judge at the Battleford trials, C. B. Rouleau, who had expressed sympathy for the plight of the Cree in 1884, turned against them after the destruction of his home during the insurrection.[203] The trials at Battleford were very informal; the accused were provided with little if any legal counsel. The executions there, the largest number in Canadian history, were designed to ensure swift retribution for those who had taken European lives and to intimidate the reserve population.

Dewdney wanted the hangings to be "a public spectacle."[204] Reed recommended that the local Indian population be brought to witness the executions "to cause them to meditate for many a day" on the "sound thrashing" meted out by the dominion.[205] The prime minister acknowledged the political importance of the executions, which "ought

Poundmaker and men who were later hanged. Photograph taken at Battleford, 1885. *Glenbow Archives, NA-363-62.*

to convince the Red Man that the White Man governs."[206] To reinforce the point, a large number of the surrounding reserve population, including students of the Battleford Industrial School, were brought to witness the hangings.[207] Those present must have had the dominion's intended message driven home. The executed were not cut down from the gallows for fifteen minutes. Robert Jefferson wrote that the bodies were cut from their ropes, falling into their caskets, which were then hauled to the bank of the river and buried in the sand.[208]

The executions marked the end of Cree resistance to the increasingly draconian measures instituted by the dominion government. Deprived of their leaders and their freedom, subjugation of the Cree was complete.[209] Even before the uprising, DIA officials controlled almost every aspect of their lives. The many abuses committed by dominion employees were evidence of their power over the reserve population. Mismanagement of official policy and disregard of official misconduct led to accusations that the dominion government was "culpably negligent" in its handling of the treaty population in the west.[210] Although debate over the issue in Parliament was acrimonious, the Tories would govern for another decade. Completion of the transcontinental railway signalled transition of the prairies to a new economic paradigm from which the overwhelming majority of treaty people were excluded. In the wake of these changes, the aboriginal population would decline to its nadir.

THE NADIR OF INDIGENOUS HEALTH, 1886–91

D OMINION RECRIMINATION AGAINST THE RECALCITRANT treaty population did not end with the Battleford executions in the fall of 1885. Indians were charged and imprisoned in much larger numbers than Métis. Of the eighty-one treaty people charged, forty-four were imprisoned. Only forty-six Métis were charged and only seven incarcerated. First Nations participation in the trouble was far from universal, but the Department of Indian Affairs consolidated its control over the entire reserve population.[1] In his report for 1886, Edgar Dewdney described the dominion's initiatives as a "Policy of Reward and Punishment." Under the plan, bands deemed "loyal" were provided with livestock and other forms of assistance for good conduct. Cattle were sent to reserves to replenish herds depleted during the chaos of the previous year. In contrast, "rebel" bands were punished: their annuities were withheld, and horses and firearms were confiscated. Recognizing that withholding rations on reserves was a source of conflict prior to the rebellion, some food and clothing were provided even to communities considered to have been disloyal.[2] The pass system would be enforced throughout the region, making reserves essentially places of incarceration. Big Bear's band, considered the most rebellious of the treaty population, was broken up.[3]

After 1885, the government initiated a serious bureaucratic assault on what it called the "tribal system": the traditional forms of governance practised by the treaty population. The focus of the attack was the subdivision of reserves, a policy known as "severality" in the immediate aftermath of the fighting.[4] Reserve lands would be subdivided and worked by individuals rather than collectively. DIA permits were required for all transactions between reserves and the outside world. Produce grown on reserves could not be sold legally without the permission of a DIA official. The move was intended to increase the consumption of locally produced food on reserves, but it weakened the ability of reserve farmers to participate in the growing commercial economy. Self-sufficiency became imperative as the dominion cut assistance to First Nations generally. Subsistence or "peasant" farming in reserve communities diminished economic competition with newcomers.[5] A few reserve farmers, such as the non-treaty Dakota, fared well on their forty-acre plots, but the general result of severality was the widespread emergence of subsistence farming, which kept those who toiled in their fields both poor and alienated from the mainstream economy.[6] Eventually, even the Dakota were brought under tighter control by the DIA.[7] The bureaucratic obstacles put in place by Hayter Reed after he became Indian commissioner in 1888 served to marginalize reserve populations and contributed to the failure of agriculture as a practical alternative to the bison hunt.

The state-sponsored attack on the tribal system was not the only threat to reserve communities after 1885. The leaders of the various groups fared little better than the hundreds of their people who were dying of malnutrition and related diseases. The loss of political and moral direction during this critical period of hardship and enforced change only augmented the misery. Long Lodge, whose band had suffered terrible mortality alongside Piapot's band at the Indian Head reserves, died in the United States on Christmas Eve 1884.[8] Little Pine, who endured bouts of blindness prior to the outbreak of hostilities, died of disease in the spring of 1885. Red Pheasant, another Cree chief from Battleford, was dead.[9] Eagle Tail, the head chief of the Piikani, succumbed to lingering illness in early 1886.[10] Many of the leaders imprisoned at Stony Mountain Penitentiary were released early because of their failing health. In May 1886, four sick chiefs were set free from the institution.

One Arrow was so sick that he had to be lifted onto a wagon transporting him from the prison, only to die in Winnipeg at the home of Archbishop Taché within days of his release.[11] The deaths of so many

North-West Resistance prisoners at Stony Mountain Penitentiary, Manitoba, 1886. *Glenbow Archives, NA-20-2.*

chiefs and elders in the aftermath of 1885 were a severe blow to the treaty population. Big Bear and Poundmaker, voices of restraint during the fighting, were imprisoned, and both would soon die. Poundmaker would succumb to tuberculosis in July 1886.[12] Commenting on his passing, the *Saskatchewan Herald* surmised that "His death practically settles the Indian question in the north on the side of peace, there being no one clever or influential enough to take up the banner he has just left down."[13] The shortage of experienced leaders was compounded by the actions of the DIA in deposing chiefs whom it considered rebellious and unsuitable in light of the new regime that it was imposing on the treaty population. Some bands had no chief at all for years after 1885.

Punishment meted out by the authorities was swift and effective. To check the possibility of further trouble, horses and guns were confiscated and thus hobbled efforts to acquire wild game.[14] The pass system, "perhaps the most onerous regulation placed on the Indians after the rebellion,"[15] was implemented to limit the mobility of treaty Indians, keeping them on their reserves and away from European communities. Of course, the system further undermined access to game and crippled the economic prospects of reserve communities.[16] Dewdney knew that imposition of the pass system was on shaky legal ground, informing the prime minister that "To compel the Indians to live wholly on their

Big Bear and Poundmaker, Cree chiefs, 1886. *Glenbow Archives, NA-1315-18.*

Reserves our Treaty must be altered."[17] The police protested that the legislation was a breach of trust,[18] but they carried out their orders. By 1886, all Indians encountered off reserve were questioned by the police.[19] Father André of the Calgary mission questioned the initiative: "sending them back to the Reserve" will not "help those poor Indians—there the agents will refuse to feed them as they have done already."[20]

The dominion's hard line on Indian administration had a profound impact on the people of the west. Tuberculosis, rare in the 1870s, was soon ravaging the treaty population. In 1884, the reserve population peaked, but over the next ten years it would decline precipitously due to malnutrition, overcrowding, exposure, poor sanitation, and oppressive government policies.[21] Within a decade, the population at Crooked Lake declined by 41 percent, that at File Hills by 46 percent. Between 1885 and 1889, a third of the inhabitants of the Edmonton reserves either left, renounced their Indian status, or died. By 1889, less than half of the pre-rebellion population of the Battleford reserves remained.

Not all of the depopulation was the result of disease. Hundreds of people, including as many as 100 members of the Battleford Stoney bands[22] and the followers of the Cree chief Little Bear, fled to the United States.[23] Little Poplar also took refuge south of the border, where his band endured terrible hardship until 1887, when American authorities agreed to provide help.[24] By that time, their chief was dead.[25] A decade later, when an amnesty was offered by the dominion, 500 people returned from Montana.[26] But many of those who fled Canada perished in exile. Some of the worst suffering occurred among the Turtle Mountain

Ojibwa, whose reservation was just south of the international boundary. Many refugees from the insurrection had joined the band, and, though the American government initially provided them with assistance, none came in 1887. That year 151 people died of starvation.[27]

Abandonment of reserves was only one aspect of the startling decline of the dominion's official count of the Indian population. In the summer of 1886, new regulations for the "Half-Breed" Scrip Commission allowed treaty Indians with white ancestry to apply for scrip; many did, if only to free themselves from the oppressive measures of the Indian Act. The new policy was seen as an easy means of reducing the size of the reserve population and the financial burden to maintain it.[28] If shrinking the treaty population was the government's goal, then it was swiftly achieved. Those who could opted to use the new departmental measures to renounce their legal status as Indians. More than half of the 1,159 certificates granted during 1886 in western Saskatchewan and Alberta were for people opting out of treaty.[29] In the Edmonton Agency, 150 took scrip, leaving an official population of 843. At Lac la Biche, as many as 470 people withdrew from treaty in 1886.[30] By spring 1888, the *Saskatchewan Herald* reported that three-quarters of the population of Slave Lake were "half-breeds."[31] On the lower Saskatchewan River, the Indian population declined by a third during 1886.[32] The population of the newly established Onion Lake Agency declined by more than half.[33] In the Battleford Agency, more than 10 percent of the reserve population withdrew from treaty in 1887.[34] In the File Hills Agency, 117 individuals participated in what economist Carl Beal called a "voluntary exodus," which resulted in a 15 percent decline of the reserve population of the area.[35] Although free from the institutional restrictions imposed by treaty, many of those who acquired new legal status as Métis became itinerant farmers often reliant on the charity of neighbours or the police for their survival. One such group in the Prince Albert area was known as "the Cumberland breeds." After years of uncertain weather and failed crops, police Inspecting Superintendent John Cotton reported, "now they are without means of obtaining a livelihood, except by manual labour. They have little or no stock either horses or cattle and consequently are in a helpless condition."[36]

That so many chose to flee the country or abandon their status as Indians is not surprising given that dominion authorities routinely slashed food rations, particularly to those deemed disloyal. In 1885, when most reserve farms were in disarray because of the conflict, dominion appropriations for food were cut by more than $40,000.[37] In the aftermath of the violence, the DIA severely curtailed ration allotments and cut off rebellious bands altogether. The prime minister acknowledged that the cuts would cause "genuine suffering" but "prevent imposition on the treasury."[38]

Mortality rates for bands deemed rebellious for the two years after 1885 are striking. Maureen Lux estimated that the Cree at Thunderchild incurred a mortality rate of 233.5 per 1,000 people and at Sweet Grass 185.0 per 1,000.[39] Deaths in the Battleford Agency exceeded births by a ratio of 4:1. So many died among the Sharphead Stoney group in central Alberta that they ceased to exist as a distinct population.[40] While tuberculosis was the primary cause of death for Indians in the 1880s, two other serious epidemics of acute infectious disease near the decade's end contributed to the death toll.

Even bands that did not suffer the wrath of dominion revenge for disloyalty underwent enormous hardship and loss. A photograph of Crowfoot and his children, taken in 1884, presented in his biography by Hugh Dempsey, illustrates the depth of suffering in a single family. All eight of the children in the photo died within two years.[41]

Crowfoot himself perished from "congestion of the lungs" in the spring of 1890.[42] Although loyal bands were not supposed to be punished, many underwent severe privation in the aftermath of the fighting. At Assissippi, Reverend John Hines reported during the summer of 1885 that people were "literally starving" since all the DIA officials were "off to Regina in connection with the trials & appear to have forgotten about food for the loyal Indians."[43] As many endured famine, rations imported for the militia lay "piled up and spoiling."[44]

Just as the TB-prone reserve population was slipping deeper into a cycle of destitution, it was dealt yet another blow. Recent completion of the Canadian Pacific Railway not only marked the beginning of large-scale agrarian settlement but also brought a host of new infectious diseases to the indigenous population of the northwest. For many on reserves, the railway proved to be a fatal disease vector. In short order, mortality from the synergy of chronic tuberculosis and other infectious diseases, especially measles and influenza, brought the indigenous population of the Canadian plains to its demographic nadir.

In 1886, measles and whooping cough spread via transportation corridors to the malnourished and immune-suppressed aboriginal population. Measles, first reported that August in eastern Alberta, had spread by September to the entire population in the Edmonton region.[45] Not surprisingly, the impact was most severe on reserves. Indian Agent Anderson reported that "a good many deaths this year" occurred from the effects of "a bad type of measles; in many cases,

Chief Crowfoot and his family, 1884. *Glenbow Archives, NA-1104-1.*

they caught a cold in their lungs. I saw that they had good medical attendance, which saved many of them."[46] To the south, the Niitsitapi suffered many deaths, especially among the young.[47] By this time, the connection between hunger and increased severity of measles was a growing concern on reserves, but the link was discounted by officials such as Magnus Begg, who stated that cuts in rations had "nothing to do with children having measles, but the Indians do not look at it in that light."[48] Despite such denials, the relationship between malnutrition and severity of measles is well documented. With measles, infection among the malnourished can lead to mortality rates 400 percent higher than in well-fed populations.[49]

In northern Alberta, where the Hudson's Bay Company was making significant improvements to its transportation system, the disease spread easily. Game depletion and a killing famine exacerbated the medical crisis.[50] The migration of many Cree northward into the territory of the Dunneza undoubtedly contributed greatly to the problem. Although the population suffered from "Consumption, rheumatism and Scrofula, as well as the scarcity of food," the changing demography of the Peace River region was the result of the Dunneza "dying out fast, but the Crees, who are coming in from Lesser Slave Lake and Edmonton, are increasing."[51] At Lac la Biche, twenty-seven died of the outbreak in October 1886. By spring, 160 people would be dead.[52] In Athabasca, where measles and whooping cough lingered, 150 people perished at Slave Lake.[53] Writing from Assissippi mission, Hines stated that the epidemic "attacked my Indians at Stony Lake, and about one fourth of them died of the effects, and its victims were mostly men."[54] The mission itself was spared the brunt of the epidemics, but its mortality rose dramatically through 1886 and 1887.[55] Although causes of death were not reported for the Anglican mission at Lac la Ronge, mortality was more than five times higher than normal in 1887.[56] The spike in deaths from measles in northern Saskatchewan is evidence of the otherwise good health of the population there. Other than mortality from the measles epidemic, northern populations underwent no significant changes to their health conditions through the second half of the nineteenth century. Able to feed themselves and maintain their traditional economies, and not bound by the harsh reserve system, northern communities in Saskatchewan did not succumb to epidemic tuberculosis in the way that their brethren to the south had.[57] Within a decade of the treaties, divergent health outcomes between relatively healthy northerners and suffering southern communities were well ensconced. As was becoming the norm, those with the least contact with the Indian department were the healthiest.[58]

In southern Alberta during the winter of 1886–87, measles claimed 10 percent of the Stoney (Nakota) population.[59] Indian Agent William de Balinhard commented that "the Stonies have always seemed to have less power of resistance to attacks of sickness of every kind ... although no satisfactory explanation of this unfortunate peculiarity has been discovered." Among Chapoostiquan's people, deaths were reported in almost every family.[60] In October 1886, sickness broke out in Sharphead's Stoney band, and within a year a third of them would be dead.[61] The community never recovered, and the survivors were amalgamated into the band led by Ironhead. By the end of the decade, the disease claimed twenty-nine lives at Onion Lake.[62]

By 1889–90, mortality associated with the measles epidemic was overshadowed by a more deadly outbreak of acute contagious disease. Influenza spread to the malnourished and reserve populations suffering widespread sickness from TB; the attendant mortality resulted in a population nadir. The influenza that led to this low point was part of the first truly global pandemic for which records are available. Called the Russian flu because of its origin east of the Caucasus Mountains in 1889, the disease spread around the world within a year.[63] The pandemic, "the first to move with the speed of trains and steamships," killed as many as a million people globally.[64] Dewdney described its effects on the indigenous population of the dominion:

The epidemic of influenza, popularly known as *la grippe,* prevailed very generally among the Indians last winter and spring. Almost every band from the Atlantic to the Pacific, and as far north as the Department has had reports from, was attacked ...; and in the case of many old persons, and those who were suffering from diseases of a pulmonary or other chronic character, or who were otherwise of a delicate constitution, the end was precipitated owing to the complications caused by catarrhal infection. A decrease in the population of many Bands, even in the older Provinces, has resulted from the fatality, which in so many instances followed from attacks of the disease.[65]

In his report, Reed noted that "the tendency to pulmonary complaints among the Indians" made sickness with influenza much more severe than it did among the mainstream population.[66] Mortality from influenza itself, and impacts of the infection on those already ill with TB, were widely recognized in DIA annual reports. At Touchwood, Indian Agent Keith noted that influenza "carried off many of the consumptive people." At Muscowpetung, J. B. Lash remarked that it killed "a number of people suffering from lung complaints." At Birtle, Manitoba, J. A. Markle reported that "a number afflicted with scrofula ... suffered with the prevailing complaints of last winter 'la grippe.' A number died from these two complaints, and a number yet feel their effects." At Clandeboyne, Manitoba, the agent reported that "I am sure that five hundred people were laid up with it, and in many cases have not yet recovered. ... I notice an increase in consumption and scrofula as a result."[67]

In some cases, severe whooping cough (pertussis) preceded influenza. In January 1889, whooping cough had spread to "nearly every house in town" in Battleford.[68] The community, hit by simultaneous outbreaks of disease, led the *Saskatchewan Herald* to decry that, "whether the plague be scarlet fever, small pox, or any other contagious disease, it is serious enough to call for prompt action on the part of the authorities." By February, sickness spread to the Dene community at Cold Lake, where thirty people died. The newspaper, seeing infection take hold among the relatively affluent Denesuliné (Chipewyan), knew that the disease would be far more dangerous for the poor and hungry reserve population of the plains, where "it would not fail to be fatal to an appalling extent." The newspaper described the symptoms of the disease: "All the muscles of the neck swell, accompanied with much pain in the swollen parts and a soreness in the throat; and ... there is a general feeling of sickness. The only food they can take is boiled rice and other soft articles of diet."[69]

Without doubt, the paltry rations provided by the DIA contributed to mortality. Piapot, who lost twenty-six people to influenza, petitioned Dewdney for "beef for my sick." Near Edmonton, farm instructor O'Donnell was criticized in January 1890 for exceeding the allotted daily ration issue to alleviate suffering among the infected population. In March, rations were withheld from members of the Thunderchild and Sweet Grass Reserves when they refused to send their children to school.[70] Despite the sickness, the DIA continued to make widespread cuts to its ration program.[71]

Other initiatives of the Indian department only deepened the crisis. During the epidemic, the DIA instituted its now infamous "peasant farming policy" to accommodate white farmers by limiting market competition from reserves and to minimize the cost of maintaining the reserve population;[72] "so daft a plan," the policy forced Indian farmers to "step aside and function in isolation from the rest of western Canadian society."[73] Agricultural progress for all peoples across the plains was undermined by a protracted drought cycle from 1887 to 1896.[74] Poor crops contributed to a growing concern among settlers of unfair competition from Indian farms, leading to further restrictions.[75] In Dakota, crop failure brought an estimated 20,000 settler families to the verge of starvation.[76] It was so dry that settlers burned weeds for fuel. Permission was later granted to settlers to harvest wood from reservations. In northern Alberta, low water levels contributed to the deaths of thousands of beavers, seriously eroding the already precarious economy of the region.[77] The beavers were reported to have died from "diseased" hearts, the result of water contamination, similar to the beaver die-off from the tularaemia epidemic of the 1790s.

The convergence of harsh weather, tuberculosis, and influenza deprived a number of reserves of their leaders. The death of Chief Beardy was one of several fatalities in his community during the epidemic.[78] The Stoney chief Mosquito died in February 1890.[79] Crowfoot, head chief of the Niitsitapi, was another casualty: "By the winter of 1887–88 [he] ... was almost continuously sick, and even though he continued to work for his people's rights, he knew he was losing the battle for his own life." Bedridden for almost a year, he suffered from declining vision and near the end slipped into a coma. After his death, the position

Cree Thirst Dance, Edmonton, Alberta, circa 1883-84. *Glenbow Archives, NA-4489-4.*

of chief passed to a succession of his relatives, "but none was able to replace him in effective leadership."[80]

Communities did what they could to cope with the increasing onslaught of disease and death in their midst.[81] Many turned to religion. A resurgence of Ojibwa spirituality occurred at Lake Winnipeg, and *midewiwin*, or grand medicine ceremonies, were reported as far west as Onion Lake during this period.[82] Other religious ceremonies spread during the late 1880s. At the Ahtahkakoop Reserve, a number of ceremonies, including the Sun Dance and the Give Away Dance (*matahitowin*), "a sacred dance held for pahkahkos, the spirit of famine, were conducted."[83] A Sun Dance was held at Fort Macleod in 1889, prompting an official to remark that "it makes them unsettled and anxious to emulate the deeds of their forefathers."[84] Health concerns were the primary motivation for Sun Dances. Persistence of the ceremony "stemmed from the fact that its ideology of world and personal renewal and regeneration continued to have relevance."[85]

The most widespread indigenous revitalization movement of the influenza period was by far the Ghost Dance. It swept through the western United States from its origin among the Paiute people of Nevada.[86] The founder of the movement, Wovoka, obtained his vision on the day of a solar eclipse, when he "was very ill with a fever."[87] He stressed peace and right living, based on the notion that "dead Indians would return to life and prosperous aboriginal conditions if the Ghost Dance rituals were performed."[88] By completing the ceremony, adherents would be "forever free from death, disease and misery." The movement took numerous forms, but James Mooney noted that all shared the belief "that devout attendance on the dance conduces to ward off disease and restore the sick to health. ..."[89]

The most tragic manifestation of the Ghost Dance occurred among the Lakota of the Standing Rock Agency in 1890. Mooney described the conditions that led to the spread of the dance among the Lakota:

> In 1888 their cattle had been diminished by disease. In 1889 their crops were a failure. ... Then followed epidemics of measles, grippe and whooping cough, in rapid succession and with terrible results. ... The people said their children were all dying from the face of the earth, and they might as well all be killed at once. ... Then came another entire failure of crops in 1890, and an unexpected reduction of rations, and the Indians were brought face to face with starvation.[90]

Between 1886 and 1888, rations for the approximately 10,000 Lakota Sioux at Pine Ridge and Standing Rock Reservations were cut by more than 50 percent. When further cuts were ordered during the summer of 1890, the Indians "made their first actual demonstration by refusing to accept the deficient issue and making threats against the agent." Unable to remedy the situation, Agent Gallagher resigned.[91]

The Lakota Ghost Dance was akin to a prayer for annihilation of the white man and the return of Indian supremacy. Lakota militancy might have been anathema to the original pacifist intent of the dance, but the combined pressure of American policy, drought, and influenza, along with the myriad of other diseases associated with malnutrition, created conditions for a millenarian expression of Wovoka's teaching. Fear of the Lakota was such that Sitting Bull, the leader of Standing Rock, was killed in a botched arrest attempt on 15 December 1890.[92] Two weeks later an attempt by the army to disarm a large group of Lakota at Wounded Knee resulted in the killing of over 200 men, women, and children.[93] Mooney's interpretation of events leading to the killings is generally sympathetic to the army, but his account acknowledges that atrocities were committed: "There can be no question that the pursuit was simply a massacre, where fleeing women, with infants on their arms, were shot down after resistance had ceased and when almost every warrior was stretched dead or dying on the ground."[94] The killings at Wounded Knee are widely acknowledged to be the low ebb of Indian conditions in the American context. In considering the demographic aspects of the Ghost Dance phenomenon, Russell Thornton noted that the movement "coincided almost exactly with the total American Indian population nadir."[95]

During the turmoil of 1890, border patrols were increased north of the 49th parallel, and Indian purchases of ammunition were closely monitored.[96] Police officers were ordered to "disarm all American Indians coming in and collect duty on their ponies, or turn them back."[97] In November, Superintendent Antrobus wrote that the Battleford reserves were effectively sealed off; the people "seldom leave their reserves, unless on pass. Their success is in great measure, if not altogether, due to the ability of the Indian Agents and Farm Instructors, whose exertions are highly commendable."[98] Just days before violence erupted at Standing Rock, Inspector G. E. Sander reported that over 20,000 people were "on the large Sioux Reservation in southern Montana where the trouble was most likely to be," and he warned of trouble spreading north.[99] A week before the bloodshed "Indians travelling in armed bodies towards the reserves west of Qu'Appelle were apprehended and brought under escort to Indian Head."[100] When reports circulated that war dances were taking place at Turtle Mountain, North Dakota, in January 1891, police were despatched to the border to stop the Ghost Dance, and any trouble, from coming to Canada.[101] Farther west, news of runners meeting with the Kainai in anticipation of an uprising south of the border was an "excuse for panic" among dominion authorities.[102]

The violence at Standing Rock reverberated across the continent. Dewdney's opening statement of his report as superintendent general of Indian affairs for 1891 acknowledged the significance of what he called the "Messiah Craze" and that there was "sufficient cause for believing that runners or messengers were sent from the disaffected Indians of the United States to some of our Indians, in the hope that they might be induced to lend their aid to the movement, but their overtures were rejected and met with no purpose."[103] Yet, while the radical form of the Ghost Dance did not spread north of the border,[104] anxiety over growing unrest among the reserve population motivated authorities to suppress other indigenous religious practices.[105] In fact, since 1885, popular opinion of First Nations people had become increasingly hostile. Once considered merely "nuisances," "vagrants," and "members of a dying race," by the 1890s they were increasingly perceived as "a threat to the property and lives of White settlers."[106] Until 1895, strict enforcement of the pass system served to curtail broad participation in indigenous religious ceremonies. That year the dominion attacked religious practices directly by extending Section 14 of the Indian Act to prohibit most religious ceremonies.[107] Strict enforcement of the pass system had a dual purpose: it was also a response to the protests of ranchers who claimed that Indians were killing their cattle. A Calgary newspaper admonished the DIA for issuing too many passes to Indians to hunt given that "the only surviving game was cattle."[108] Another motivation for ranchers in pressing for enforcement of the pass system was renewal of government beef contracts that had been severely curtailed.[109] By 1892, the police had serious doubts about the legality of the system.[110] Undeterred, the dominion imposed even more strictures on the Indian population and passed legislation to ban trade between reserves and white communities without the consent of departmental officials.

Despite the dominion's repressive measures, there was no uprising on Canadian reserves as there had been in the United States. Cultural differences between American and Canadian Indians limited the spread of the Ghost Dance to all but a few Canadian Dakota communities with relatives south of the border. Canadian Indians came to rely on their own spiritual practices, such as the Sun Dance, for strength. With Indian populations on both sides of the border suffering high death rates from tuberculosis and influenza, they reached their demographic low points at the same time. But Canadian Indians never came close to acting out against the situation in the same radical fashion as their American cousins in the 1890s.[111]

Because official records are clouded by abandonment, exile, and the relinquishment of Indian status, we will never know the precise number of indigenous plains people who died of disease in the years after 1885. However, we cannot deny that the suffering on reserves in the 1880s and 1890s was horrendous. As Beal observes, "It is a shameful episode of Canadian History that such a devastating destruction of the population—a third disappearing over six years—should have been justified as a necessary cost of civilizing influence."[112] In the collective experience of subjugation, hunger, sickness, and death is the origin of the chasm that exists even today between health conditions of mainstream Canadians and western Canada's First Nations population.

By the mid-1890s, the populations of many reserves began to stabilize.[113] But the period of large-scale immigration to the west had begun. Soon the approximately 15,000 people who remained on prairie reserves were swamped by a sea of immigrants dedicated to recasting the region as an agricultural bastion of the British Empire. The health of reserves became such a marginal issue that it largely disappeared from the popular consciousness of the new society taking root in the west. Newcomers rarely understood the nature of the problem, and their governments, both local and federal, tended to react slowly or not at all to the crisis on reserves. The abject poverty and the high mortality rates merely served to reinforce the notion that they were reservoirs of disease that threatened the health of the wider community. Rarely was the focus placed where it truly belonged—on the need for the redirection of resources to alleviate the suffering of the reserve population.

In 1895, Hayter Reed ordered DIA physicians to report on the changes in health conditions on reserves in the previous five years.[114] In general, conditions on the eastern plains reserves that had born the brunt of the suffering through most of the 1880s because of the cuts to government rations were said to be improving somewhat.[115] However, DIA reports acknowledged that the reserves in southern Alberta were in need of more assistance because of the threat that the hungry posed to private cattle stocks in the region. In the words of Edgar Dewdney, "Were any persistent effort made to stop the rations of these Indians, it is more than probable that they would commit depredations upon stock belonging to the ranches. ..."[116] A more plausible argument is that ranchers maintained pressure on authorities to feed the reserve population because they profited directly from the dominion's acquisition of their cattle.[117] Their lobbying can be interpreted as a means of maintaining their position as suppliers of beef to the captive reserve population.

But private contracts or not, cuts to food rations saw Alberta's Niitsitapi lose their nutritional protection against disease. By the mid-1890s, the whole of the Treaty 7 population was in declining health. Dr. F. X. Girard, the long-time physician to the Kainai and Piikani, described consumption as "quite unknown in old time [but] is now prevailing. Consumption and scrofula ... at the present date are the two worst enemies to the health of the Indians; the last undermining slowly but surely their constitution and the former appearing at the last period of the struggle to fight down their prey."[118] Scrofula, according to Girard, was an environmental disease, originating with bad food, inadequate ventilation and light, and lack of hygiene among those afflicted. Although it was yet to be recognized, it was also a symptom of bovine tuberculosis infection.

In southern Alberta, the peak in mortality resulted from the synergy of a severe measles epidemic and rampant tuberculosis. Among the Niitsitapi, the nadir of the population did not occur until after the turn of the century, a full decade after that of the reserve population in Saskatchewan.[119] In 1902, Indian Agent J. A. Markle described the rise in mortality on the reserves of southern Alberta:

[W]hile measles may truthfully be assigned as the direct cause, there is in my opinion an indirect reason for many of the fatalities. Scrofula is lurking in the system of nearly every adult member of the band, and when parents are afflicted with this insidious disease, it goes without saying that the constitution of the children is weakened, and if attacked by almost any of the ailments that children are heir to, the results are more likely to be fatal than with children of strong constitutions.[120]

Aside from the declining health of the Treaty 7 population, even small improvements to living conditions had health benefits on reserves by the mid-1890s. A simple yet significant step was recognition that adequate ventilation in homes was critical to control the airborne spread of diseases, especially tuberculosis. Woodstoves, the main source of heat after the transition from tents to wooden structures, were identified as important factors in disease transmission. In Manitoba, Ebenezer McColl described the effect of woodstoves on the air of reserve houses as "absolutely stifling, ... probably generating more pulmonary and other fatal diseases than all other agencies combined."[121] The chief advocate for improved ventilation and the replacement of stoves with open fireplaces was Dr. George Orton, who worked tirelessly for improved health conditions on reserves through the 1890s.[122] Another departmental "innovation" was acknowledgement that tent living was healthy if not conducive to the dominion policy of "advancement" for the reserve population through the adoption of wooden homes. J. J. Campbell, the Indian agent at Moose Mountain, noted that "During the summer they all live in tents; and although this tends to keep them from making as rapid advances in civilized in-door customs, the gain in health more than offsets that drawback."[123] Before antibiotics, providing fresh air was an important part of the treatment of tuberculosis.

During the early 1890s, some progress was made in the construction of hospital facilities near reserves for the treatment of Indian patients.[124] Surgical advances perhaps increased survival rates for patients with TB infections of the glands (scrofula) or bones. Orton was an innovator in both surgical and postoperative care of the sick. In 1895, he reported on a particularly difficult case:

One rare and most difficult operation—excision of the whole joint and removal of the diseased portions of the pelvic bones, was successfully performed by me, in the St. Boniface Hospital upon Peter Smith, a young man from St. Peter's who was sent

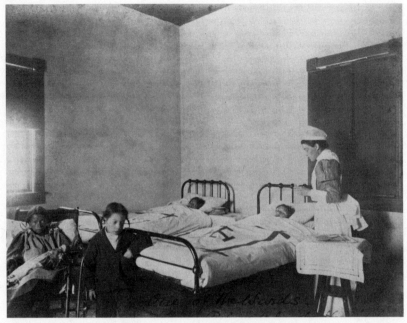

Ward in first native hospital, Gleichen, Alberta, before 1900. *Glenbow Archives, NA-1773-14.*

home from the Elkhorn school in a most deplorable state, with running sores in every direction, from these diseased bones. My specially devised bed and splint for which I asked the department to pay ... was most valuable in facilitating the dressing and lessening the suffering and pain after treatment which necessitated months of rest, in one position. Unless a bad cough which he has should develop into consumption or fresh disease arise, his final recovery is now assured, four months having elapsed since the operation.[125]

What Orton failed to recognize was that infection of the young man's bones indicated that Smith was probably sick with bovine tuberculosis, perhaps from drinking the raw milk of an infected cow at the Elkhorn School. Milk continued to be a vector for the spread of TB to children at schools for decades after the pasteurization eliminated the threat in the commercial milk supply in western Canada in the early 20th century.

Despite improvements to the physical and sanitary conditions of reserves reported in the departmental circular, Hayter Reed confided to Assistant Indian Commissioner A. E. Forget that "the spread of consumption and other tubercular diseases is on the increase."[126] By that time, poverty and sickness—especially tuberculosis—were entrenched characteristics of the reserve population of western Canada. As Dr. Patrick stated in his 1895 report from Yorkton, "Tuberculosis is practically the only constitutional disease affecting the Indians of this Agency."[127]

While reserve conditions were deplorable, the long-term ill health of the indigenous population became increasingly defined by the growing Indian residential school system.[128] For decades, overcrowding, poor nutrition, and neglect contributed to systemic TB infection among children who attended the institutions. Once infected with the disease, they died much sooner than adults.[129] Responses to Reed's 1895 circular show that physicians were aware of the relationship between overcrowding and TB in the schools. Dr. Seymour's report could not have been more pointed: "One of the first things to do towards lessening the amount of Tuberculosis is to relieve the over-crowded condition of the School. Additional sleeping and class room accommodation should be immediately provided."[130] The death toll at the schools was enormous. Three years before Seymour's report Father Hugonnard at the Qu'Appelle Industrial School, with fewer than 170 students, had noted that "the general health of the children has been good. ... We had to record five deaths."[131] Included in the principal's report was a list of the fifty-two children who had died since founding of the school in 1884.

Hugonnard saw his work as successful even though almost 20 percent of the children at the school died while under his care between 1884 and 1905.[132] On the twelve deaths at the school in 1893, the principal remarked that consumption was "hereditary in the families of the deceased and the germs were brought from home."[133] Hugonnard was not the first official to comment on the hereditary nature of Indians and tuberculosis. In 1886, Dewdney stated that increased mortality on reserves was "directly due to hereditary disease, which had its origin at a time prior to that which our responsibility began," and improved reporting of sickness, "which, in former times, would have gone unnoticed."[134]

By the late 1890s, heredity was increasingly cited as a source of tuberculosis.[135] In the case of high rates among Indian children, it was generally assumed that the contagion was part of their heritage. In documenting the inadequate facilities at Indian schools, Dr. Martin Benson wrote that "without adequate provision for the admission of fresh air ... it is scarcely any wonder that our Indian pupils have an hereditary tendency to phthisis ... [and] develop alarming symptoms after a short residence in our schools."[136] By 1900, healthy bands, such as the Red Earth Cree at The Pas Mountain, were described as being "almost entirely free of any hereditary diseases."[137]

By the beginning of the First World War, physicians who opposed the interpretation of tuberculosis as hereditary were in the minority. Dr. P. H. Bryce emphatically opposed the notion of heredity with regard to the disease in 1914.[138] Despite the force of his assertions, belief in the hereditary nature of the disease prevailed. In a 1922 report to the Saskatchewan government by the Anti-Tuberculosis Commission, the authors stated as their first principle that "Tuberculosis is now to be considered hereditary."[139]

One of the authors of the report, Dr. R. G. Ferguson, became the authority on the treatment of tuberculosis among Canadian Indians.[140] Using mortality data gathered from annuity lists,[141] he estimated that the death rate on the Qu'Appelle reserves rose from 40 per 1,000 in 1881 to 127 per 1,000 in 1886, an increase of 87 per 1,000 in only five years.[142] The rise in the general death rate was attributed "almost entirely to the increase in the tuberculosis death rate." He noted the relative absence of the disease prior to the reserve period. Because he was unable to find comparable death rates in European populations,[143] he concluded that "This study of the prolonged tuberculosis epidemic among the Indians of the Qu'Appelle Valley from 1874 to 1926 demonstrates the difference in the level of susceptibility between primitive recently exposed and the white race exposed for centuries."[144] This erroneous conclusion might well have stemmed from the fact that his discussion was based on work published before 1930. If his estimates of the peak mortality on the Qu'Appelle reserves are correct, a European population would not experience a comparable rate until 1942—among the Jewish population of the Warsaw ghetto.[145] In 1929, Ferguson reported that the Indians of Qu'Appelle were "universally tuberculized" and that mortality from the disease was twenty times greater than that among the surrounding white population.[146] The sheer magnitude of infection led him to the misguided conclusion that indigenous people were inherently susceptible to disease.

With the construction of this belief, their marginalization from Canadian society was complete. In 1920, when establishment of the first federal Department of Health was debated in the wake of the influenza pandemic of 1919, Arthur Meighen, who would soon be prime minister, stated that jurisdiction over the health of Indians was purposefully left out of the act creating the new administration.[147] Because their race was more important to the Canadian government than their need for medical attention, the official ultimately responsible for the health of First Nations people until 1945 was the minister of mines and resources. Control of the TB epidemic among Indians was the result not of im-

Charcoal, or "Bad Young Man." A staged portrait, with a Mountie's Stetson covering handcuffs, conceals the extreme ill health of the prisoner. *Saskatchewan Archives Board, R-23918.*

provements in their economic conditions but of antibiotic drugs after the Second World War.

Recent studies have shown that the rise in Indian tuberculosis was not a genetic weakness but "the result of enforced changes in ecological factors rather than exposure to a new, introduced infectious disease."[148] Another significant study on indigenous health concluded that the belief in innate resistance to disease overlooked "the important ecological and environmental factors influencing transmission and immunity."[149] There is no dispute that the end of the bison hunt led to unprecedented

Charcoal, barely able to walk, escorted in leg irons, Fort Macleod, Alberta, 1896. *Glenbow Archives, NA-4035-70.*

ecological changes that adversely affected the whole indigenous population of the North American plains. The explosion of tuberculosis along with the rapid demographic decline resulting from the synergy of the disease with other acute infections to its lowest point in history is evidence of its magnitude. The inequity in health outcomes between the indigenous and mainstream populations in Canada continues to the present.

A fitting metaphor for the plight facing the plains Indians is that of the Kainai man Charcoal, who "became the most wanted man on Canada's western frontier" for killing his wife's lover and a police officer who tried to arrest him.[150] Although ill with tuberculosis, Charcoal eluded the authorities for a year before his capture. When his death sentence was carried out, he was on the verge of expiring. Hugh Dempsey described his execution: "Unable to walk, the Indian was loaded onto a wagon, driven to the scaffold, and carried up the last few steps to eternity. His body, having no will of its own, was not even capable of standing, so a chair was placed over the trapdoor, a white cloth draped over his head, and the noose placed around his neck."[151] With the execution of a man so sick that he had to be carried to the gallows, Canadian justice was done.

The notion that the treaty population endured severe hardship under the increasingly harsh measures imposed by the Canadian government after the uprising of 1885 is widely accepted. The population, rife with tuberculosis after a decade of malnutrition, suffered a terrible burden of infectious disease that led to their demographic nadir in the aftermath of the influenza epidemic of 1889–90. The confluence of coercive dominion policies that abetted the rise of disease meant that Indians were not only punished after the rebellion; in many cases, they were punished to death.

CONCLUSION

THIS BOOK HAS EXAMINED THE ECOLOGICAL, ECONOMIC, AND political forces that shaped the medical histories of First Nations people in western Canada. In doing so, it has outlined the origin of the health inequity between Indigenous and mainstream Canadians in western Canada that persists into the twenty-first century. In considering the history of indigenous health, two distinct phases emerged.

The first was the period of introduced acute contagious diseases that swept through otherwise healthy populations, bringing unprecedented mortality to the communities affected by them. The terrible epidemics were the result of extension of the global economic system to western Canada. Microbes cannot be isolated from commerce; there is no way to envision the expansion of trade between the Old World and the New World without considering the impact of disease. Disease eventually reached every community in the region, but the effects of early outbreaks were by no means monolithic. Differential outcomes were shaped by factors such as population density, geographical location and mobility, frequency of contact with outsiders, and access to imported goods. These factors created ecological conditions that determined the geographical extent of epidemics and the severity of outbreaks within communities.

Every First Nations community in the west was fundamentally shaped by acute infectious disease.

In general, groups with eastern origins fared better than those with western origins because of their longer experience with diseases that provided them with increased immunity. The Anishinabe, some of the first to be integrated into the global trade, experienced epidemic sickness early on. By 1670, smallpox reached Sault Ste. Marie, the heart of their ancestral homeland. Over the next century, their relationship with traders and game depletion drove them to migrate toward the plains. Although fuelled by market forces, the move was predicated on biology. Their early experience with disease was an advantage in subsequent outbreaks, allowing them to expand their territory in the late eighteenth century.

The Anishinabe inherited much of southern Manitoba from the Assiniboine people, who had dominated the region for 500 years before arrival of the first epidemics. The Assiniboine were among the most widespread and populous First Nations on the eastern plains when trade with Europeans was first established. The size and complexity of their communities, a sign of their success, proved to be their downfall in the new disease ecology that came with trade. The population density of the Assiniboine communities described by La Vérendrye in the 1730s greatly increased the death toll when sickness struck. Under the weight of epidemic mortality, the Assiniboine abandoned the Red River valley and intensified their occupation of the parklands in Manitoba and eastern Saskatchewan. Later, in the nineteenth century, their location between the territories of English and American traders meant that they suffered the full brunt of the smallpox epidemic in the 1830s while their Cree and Anishinabe (who came to be known in the west as Saulteaux) neighbours to the north were largely spared through the medical intervention of the Hudson's Bay Company. Today the Assiniboine people, once the dominant nation of the region, are relegated to a handful of reserve communities across the plains. The decline of agricultural villages along the Missouri River occupied by the Arikara and Mandan was also defined by high mortality resulting from disease spreading through densely packed communities.

The complex interaction of the global economy and the spread of disease is illustrated by the virgin soil outbreak of smallpox among the Niitsitapi of southern Alberta prior to 1750. Disease spread to the region decades before the arrival of Europeans. *Variola* was delivered to the western plains along an equestrian trade network that unwittingly served as a disease vector between the Pueblos of the American southwest and Alberta. The speed of equestrian travel changed the disease ecology for those who adopted the new species.

The Cree people of the Saskatchewan parklands did not experience their virgin soil outbreak of smallpox until the 1780s. So many died that the existing band structure of the region buckled. Survivors were integrated into bands of Cree speakers, probably with previous exposure to the disease, who came west to meet the demand for labour in the post-epidemic period. In some cases, they moved west at the explicit request of fur traders. The reconstitution of the population and their adaptation to the market conditions of the post-epidemic period contributed to the ethnogenesis of the Plains Cree, who dominated the eastern plains for the next century. A part of Plains Cree ascendancy was the ouster of the A'aninin people from their homeland between the branches of the Saskatchewan River that they had occupied for centuries prior to the arrival of the fur trade to the region.

By the time of Canada's acquisition of the territory, the indigenous people of western Canada had already undergone profound changes to their territory and economic orientation. In many cases, the First Nations that entered into treaties with the crown were inheritors of the plains rather than inhabitants since prehistoric times. The relationship between First Nations and the Dominion of Canada signalled the beginning of the second phase of health and disease considered in this study.

The numbered treaties were pivotal to establishment of the new economic and social paradigm in the west. To the Canadian government, completion of the treaties was an essential legal precondition to development of the region. First Nations leaders saw treaties first and foremost as a bridge to a future without bison. In exchange for relinquishing their claim on all but a small percentage of land in the region, First Nations sought renewal of the social safety net that they had grown accustomed to during the fur trade and assistance in the conversion to agriculture. In addition to securing greater agricultural support than in previous agreements, Cree negotiators in Treaty 6 astutely negotiated for medical aid and famine relief. After days of negotiations, Alexander Morris, the queen's representative at Fort Carlton, accepted the new terms of the treaty on behalf of the Dominion of Canada, assuring the Cree that "they would not be allowed to die like dogs."[1]

Within two years of that promise, the bison were gone. Their disappearance ended a way of life that had endured for 10,000 years. While extermination of the herds was the greatest environmental catastrophe ever on the grasslands, it also brought a fundamental change in the power dynamic between First Nations and the Canadian state. With loss of the bison, indigenous people lost their independence and power. The Cree at Fort Carlton knew that the bison hunt was nearing its end and that conversion to farming would be so difficult that famine was a genuine threat. Unfortunately, they were right. With Canada's acceptance of the famine clause, the state took on the legal responsibility for the food crisis that would soon explode across the west. It is safe to say that no one foresaw the suddenness or magnitude of the famine that hit the region in the spring of 1878. Other than the North-West Mounted Police, the Canadian presence in the west at the time was minuscule. When the hunger began, Canada simply did not have the people or infrastructure to meet the demand for food. The police did what they could to counter the famine that swept across the region. Their physicians toiled to assist the malnourished and increasingly sick people who gathered at police posts to seek respite from the food shortage. Physicians' reports from these besieged posts provide the first documentary evidence of the sudden emergence of tuberculosis in the region.

Within months, large quantities of food were being shipped north from Fort Benton, Montana, the shipping terminus of the Missouri River. The value of dominion ration contracts soared as the government scrambled to feed the thousands of people desperately in need of assistance. One firm, I. G. Baker and Company, seized the opportunity and quickly secured most of these lucrative contracts. Management of the famine took on a more sinister character after the election of the Conservative Party in the fall of 1878. The cornerstone of the party's platform, the National Policy, was the swift construction of a railway to the Pacific Ocean. Faced with a pressing agenda of development and saddled with thousands of starving people across the prairies, the government used food as a means to control the indigenous population. The strategy was cruel but effective. By 1883, only a few hundred desperate holdouts were still not on reserves and under the control of the Department of Indian Affairs.

Between 15,000 and 20,000 people were on reserves, and the overwhelming majority relied on the government as their sole source of provisions. As the chief supplier of food to the region, I. G. Baker abused its privileged position, supplying inferior or contaminated food to the hungry to maximize its profit, often with the complicity of government officials. Canada's chief official in the west, Edgar Dewdney, was almost certainly on the Baker payroll. Because so many people were off the land and under the thumb of the DIA on reserves, the government took new and draconian action with regard to the delivery of food. In addition to the work-for-rations policy, food that had been delivered to reserves was withheld as a means to cut expenditures. Food rotted in storehouses on reserves as the malnourished population succumbed in increasing numbers to tuberculosis and other diseases. Because there was no alternative source of food for many living on reserves, their dependence on rations made many vulnerable to the predations of officials who abused their authority. Women were especially vulnerable to sexual abuse by those who controlled the flow of food. For others, prostitution became the only means to feed their families. The sheer number of dominion officials who contracted sexually transmitted diseases in the early 1880s is astonishing, a sign of the pervasive nature of such contact. When violence erupted in the spring of 1885, many of those killed had been personally implicated in the physical or sexual abuse of the treaty population.

The severity of Canada's response to the uprising of 1885 worsened the already desperate situation of reserves. Implementation of the pass system and further cuts to DIA spending increased the misery on reserves while confining the population to them. Completion of the Canadian Pacific Railway brought a new wave of infectious disease to the malnourished and largely tubercularized people now confined to their reserves. Fatal epidemics of measles, whooping cough, and influenza brought the reserve population of Saskatchewan to its demographic low point by the early 1890s. Officials began to interpret the chronic bad health of the indigenous population as a condition of their race, claiming that tuberculosis was largely hereditary. By the early twentieth century, the notion that indigenous people were biologically more susceptible to disease than the mainstream population was medically and politically orthodox.

With construction of the belief in the inherent vulnerability of aboriginal people to disease, their marginalization from Canadian society was complete. Canadians could accept TB rates on reserves as high as twenty times those in neighbouring settler communities because it was believed that Indians were just prone to sickness. The TB epidemic on the reserves of western Canada was not brought under control by significant improvements to the living conditions that had been so central to its spread. Rather, the widespread availability of antibiotic drugs after the Second World War was something of a silver bullet in treatment of the disease. The resurgence of antibiotic-resistant tuberculosis in recent years indicates that pharmaceutical victory over the disease might have been only temporary. Without significant improvements to living conditions on reserves, new "unnatural" pathologies such as AIDS, diabetes, and suicide have emerged under physical and social constraints experienced by aboriginal communities.[2]

In their conclusion to the second edition of *Aboriginal Health in Canada,* authors Waldram, Herring, and Young stated that, "most importantly, there remains a need for an overall general improvement in the socio-economic status of Aboriginal Canadians."[3] This study has shown that the decline of First Nations health was the direct result of economic and cultural suppression. The effects of the state-sponsored attack on indigenous communities that began in the 1880s haunt us as a nation still. The Cree negotiators at Treaty 6 recognized the need for their people to adapt to the new economic paradigm taking shape in the west. They acknowledged that the conversion would be difficult. What they failed to plan for was the active intervention of the Canadian government in preventing them from doing so. Tuberculosis and pathologies that have emerged in aboriginal communities in recent decades are the physical manifestations of their poverty and marginalization from mainstream Canadian life.

The gap between the health, living conditions, and other social determinants of health of First Nations people and mainstream Canadians continues as it has since the end of the nineteenth century. While Canadians see themselves as world leaders in social welfare, health care, and economic development, most reserves in Canada are economic backwaters with little prospect of material advancement and more in common with the third world than the rest of Canada. Even basics such as clean drinking water remain elusive for some communities. Identification of the forces that have held indigenous communities back might provide insights into what is required to bridge the gap between First Nations communities and the rest of Canada today.

MAPS

The maps on the following pages depict geographic features, locations, and trade routes discussed in this book.

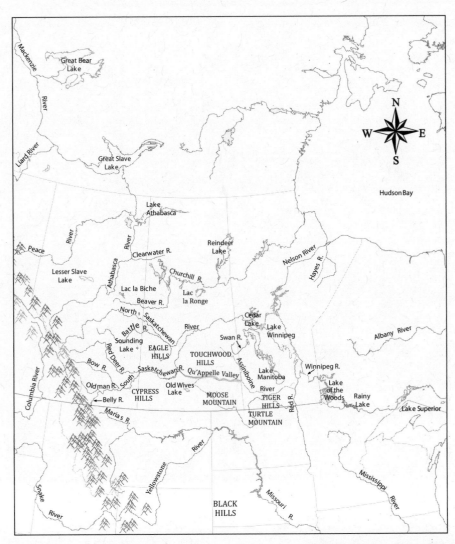

GEOGRAPHICAL FEATURES

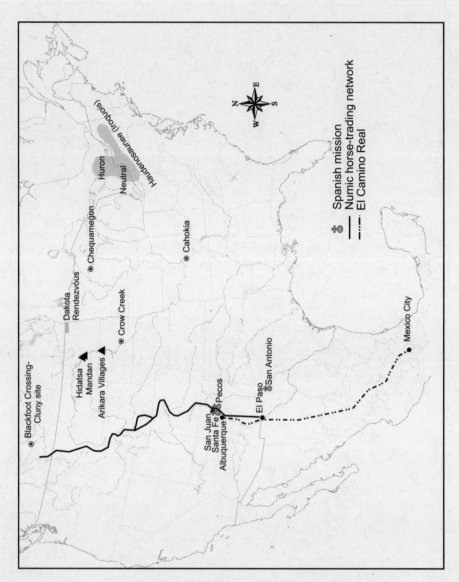

EARLY INDIGENOUS AND SPANISH COLONIAL LOCATIONS

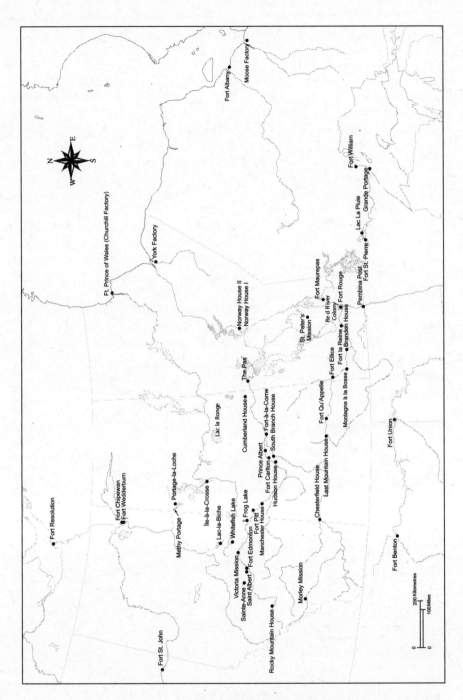

FUR TRADING POSTS AND CHRISTIAN MISSIONS

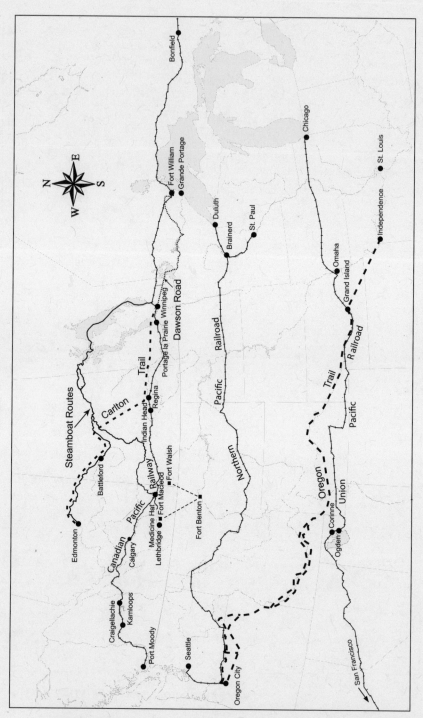

SETTLEMENT PERIOD LOCATIONS AND TRANSPORTATION ROUTES

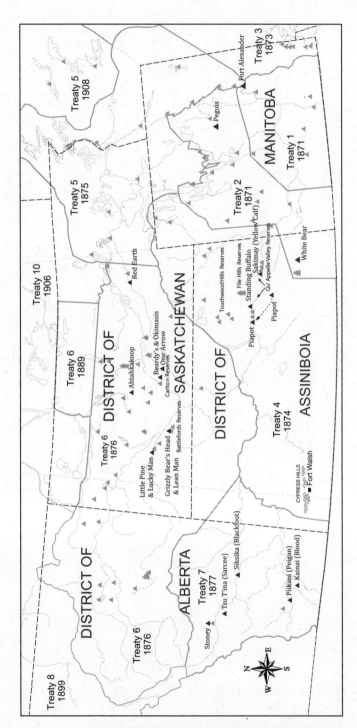

INDIAN RESERVES AND TREATY AREAS TO 1900

NOTES

INTRODUCTION

1   See http://hdrstats.undp.org/indicators/1.html.
2   See http://www.afn.ca/article.asp?id=3809.
3   Dennis Raphael, "Introduction to the Social Determinants of Health," in *Social Determinants of Health: Canadian Perspectives*, edited by Dennis Raphael (Toronto: Scholar's Press, 2004), 6.
4   Maureen Lux, *Medicine that Walks: Disease, Medicine, and Canadian Plains Native People, 1880–1940* (Toronto: University of Toronto Press, 2001), 5–19.
5   Mary-Ellen Kelm, *Colonizing Bodies: Aboriginal Health and Healing in British Columbia* (Vancouver: UBC Press, 1998), xvi–xix.
6   Theodore Binnema, *Common and Contested Ground: A Human and Environmental History of the North American Plains* (Norman: University of Oklahoma Press, 2001), xiii.
7   Immanuel Wallerstein, *The Modern World-System: Capitalist Agriculture and the Origins of European World-Economy in the Sixteenth Century* (New York: Academic Press, 1974).
8   Jason W. Moore, "*The Modern World-System* as Environmental History? Ecology and the Rise of Capitalism," *Theory and Society* 32 (2003): 323.
9   Arthur J. Ray, "At the Cutting Edge: Indians and the Expansion of the Land-Based Fur Trade in Northern North America, 1550–1750," in *The Early-Modern World-System in Geographical Perspective*, edited by Hans-Jurgen Nitz (Stuttgart: Franz Steiner Verlag, 1993), 317–26.
10 Alfred Crosby, *The Columbian Exchange: Biological and Cultural Consequences of 1492* (Westport, CT: Greenwood Publishing Company, 1972), 113, 202.
11 Alfred Crosby, "Virgin Soil Epidemics as a Factor in the Aboriginal Depopulation of America," in *Germs, Seeds, and Animals: Studies in Ecological History* (London: M. E. Sharpe, 1994), 99.
12 Paul Hackett, *"A Very Remarkable Sickness": Epidemics in the Petit Nord, 1670–1846* (Winnipeg: University of Manitoba Press, 2002).
13 Patricia Albers, "Changing Patterns of Ethnicity in the Northwestern Plains, 1780–1870," in *History, Power, and Identity: Ethnogenesis in the Americas, 1492–1992*, edited by Jonathan Hill (Iowa City: University of Iowa Press, 1996), 100.
14 Emmanuel Le Roy Ladurie, "A Concept: The Unification of the Globe by Disease (Fourteenth to Eighteenth Centuries)," *The Mind and Method of the Historian*,(Brighton, UK: Harvester Press, 1981), 28–34.
15 Arthur Ray, "Some Thoughts about the Reasons for Spatial Dynamism in the Early Fur Trade, 1500–1800," in *Three Hundred Prairie Years: Henry Kelsey's "Inland Country of Good Report,"* edited by Henry Epp (Regina: Canadian Plains Research Center, 1993), 113–23.
16 David Mandelbaum, *The Plains Cree: An Ethnographic, Historical, and Comparative Study* (1940; reprint, Regina: Canadian Plains Research Center, 1979).
17 Arthur Ray, *Indians in the Fur Trade: Their Role as Trappers, Hunters, and Middlemen in the Lands Southwest of Hudson Bay, 1660–1870* (Toronto: University of Toronto Press, 1974).
18 Charles Bishop, *The Northern Ojibwa and the Fur Trade: An Historical and Ecological Study* (Toronto: Holt, Rinehart and Winston, 1974).

19   André Gunder Frank, *Capitalism and Underdevelopment in Latin America* (New York: Monthly Review Press, 1967).

20   Paul Thistle, *Indian–European Trade Relations in the Lower Saskatchewan River Region to 1840* (Winnipeg: University of Manitoba Press, 1986).

21   Eleanor M. Blain, "Dependency: Charles Bishop and the Northern Ojibwa," in *Aboriginal Resource Use in Canada: Historical and Legal Aspects,* edited by Kerry Abel and Jean Friesen (Winnipeg: University of Manitoba Press, 1991), 93–106.

22   Laura Peers, *The Ojibwa of Western Canada, 1780–1870* (Winnipeg: University of Manitoba Press, 1994).

23   James G. E. Smith, "The Western Woods Cree: Anthropological Myth and Historical Reality," *American Ethnologist* 14 (1987): 434–48.

24   Dale Russell, *Eighteenth Century Western Cree and Their Neighbours* (Ottawa: Canadian Museum of Civilization, 1991).

25   Michael B. Payne, "Review: Dale R. Russell, *Eighteenth Century Western Cree and Their Neighbours,*" *Manitoba History* 24 (1992): http://www.mhs.mb.ca/docs/mb_history/24/westerncree.shtml; Paul Thistle, "Review: Russell, Dale R., *Eighteenth Century Western Cree and Their Neighbours,*" *Canadian Journal of Native Studies* 11 (1991): 181–83.

26   John Milloy, *The Plains Cree: Trade, Diplomacy, and War, 1790 to 1870* (Winnipeg: University of Manitoba Press, 1988).

27   David Smyth, "Missed Opportunity: John Milloy's *The Plains Cree,*" *Prairie Forum* 17 (1992): 338.

28   Frank Tough, *"As Their Natural Resources Fail": Native Peoples and the Economic History of Northern Manitoba, 1780–1930* (Vancouver: UBC Press, 1996), 300.

29   Robin Brownlie and Mary-Ellen Kelm, "Desperately Seeking Absolution: Native Agency as Colonialist Alibi?," *Canadian Historical Review* 75 (1994): 543–56.

30   Toby Morantz, "The Past and Future of Ethnohistory," *Acta Borealia* 1 (1998): 72.

31   Toby Morantz, *"The White Man's Gonna Getcha": The Colonial Challenge to the Crees in Quebec* (Montreal: McGill-Queen's University Press, 2005).

32   Jeffery Ostler, *The Plains Sioux and U.S. Colonialism from Lewis and Clark to Wounded Knee* (Cambridge, UK: Cambridge University Press, 2004).

33   Arthur Ray, *Indians in the Fur Trade: Their Role as Trappers, Hunters, and Middlemen in the Lands Southwest of Hudson Bay, 1660–1870,* 2nd ed. (Toronto: University of Toronto Press, 1998), xxi.

34   Amartya Sen, *Poverty and Famines: An Essay on Entitlement and Deprivation* (Oxford: Oxford University Press, 1981); see also Amartya Sen, "Food, Economics, and Entitlements," in *The Political Economy of Hunger: Selected Essays,* edited by Jean Dreze, Amartya Sen, and Athar Hussain (Oxford: Oxford University Press, 1998), 50–68.

35   Meredith Thursen, *The Political Ecology of Disease in Tanzania* (New Brunswick, NJ: Rutgers University Press, 1984), xii.

36   Randall Packard, *White Plague—Black Labor: Tuberculosis and the Political Economy of Health and Disease in South Africa* (Berkeley: University of California Press, 1989), 19.

37   Gregory Campbell, "The Changing Dimension of Native American Health: A Critical Understanding of Contemporary Native American Health Issues," in *Native American Resurgence and Renewal: A Reader and Bibliography,* edited by Robert N. Wells (Metuchen, NJ: Scarecrow Press, 1994), 97–104.

38   Gregory Campbell, "Health Patterns and Underdevelopment on the Northern Cheyenne Reservation," in *The Political Economy of North American Indians,* edited by John H. Moore (Norman: University of Oklahoma Press, 1993), 63.

39   James Waldram, Ann Herring, and Kue Young, *Aboriginal Health in Canada,* 2nd ed. (Toronto: University of Toronto Press, 2006), 295.

40. The clause reads, "That in the event hereafter of the Indians comprised within this treaty being overtaken by any pestilence, or by a general famine, the Queen, on being satisfied and certified thereof by Her Indian Agent or Agents, will grant to the Indians assistance of such character and to such extent as Her Chief Superintendent of Indian Affairs shall deem necessary and sufficient to relieve the Indians from the calamity that shall have befallen them." Sourced at: http://www.aadnc-aandc.gc.ca/eng/1100100028710/1100100028783.

CHAPTER 1—INDIGENOUS HEALTH, ENVIRONMENT, AND DISEASE BEFORE EUROPEANS

1   Dobyns, Henry. "Estimating Aboriginal American Population: An Appraisal of Techniques with a New Hemisphere Estimate." *Current Anthropology* 7 (1966): 416.

2   Among the most vociferous critics of Dobyns has been David Henige. See his "On the Current Devaluation of the Notion of Evidence: A Rejoinder to Dobyns," *Ethnohistory* 36 (1989): 304–07, and his *Numbers from Nowhere: The American Indian Contact Population Debate* (Norman: University of Oklahoma Press, 1998).

3   Jane E. Buikstra, ed., *Prehistoric Tuberculosis in the Americas* (Evanston, IL: Northwestern University Archaeological Program, 1981).

4   Kenneth F. Kiple and Stephen V. Beck, "Introduction," in *Biological Consequences of European Expansion, 1450–1800*, edited by Kenneth F. Kiple and Stephen V. Beck, vol. 26 of *Variorum, an Expanding World: The European Impact on World History, 1450–1800* (Ashgate Publishing: Burlington, VT, 1997), xx.

5   John B. Gregg and Larry Zimmerman, "Malnutrition in Fourteenth-Century South Dakota: Osteopathological Manifestations," *North American Archaeologist* (1986): 191–214; Douglas Bamforth, "Climate, Chronology, and the Course of War in the Middle Missouri Region of the North American Plains," in *The Archaeology of Warfare: Prehistories of Raiding and Conquest,* edited by Elizabeth N. Arkush and Mark W. Allen (Gainesville: University of Florida Press, 2006), 90–91.

6   Douglas Bamforth and Curtis Nepstad-Thornberry, "Reconsidering the Occupational History of the Crow Creek Site (39BF 11)," *Plains Anthropologist* 52 (2007): 157.

7   The sudden severe decline in global temperatures is well documented. See Thomas J. Crowley, "Causes of Climate Change over the Past 1000 Years," *Science,* July 14, 2000, 270–77; Brian Fagan, *The Little Ice Age: How Climate Made History, 1300–1500* (New York: Basic Books, 2000), 29–31; Thomas J. Crowley et al., "Volcanism and the Little Ice Age," *Pages News* 16 (2008): 22–23. For its effects in North America, see Reid A. Bryson and Thomas J. Murray, *Climates of Hunger: Mankind and the World's Changing Weather* (Madison: University of Wisconsin Press, 1977), 25–49; James Daschuk, "A Dry Oasis: The Canadian Plains in Late Prehistory," *Prairie Forum* 34 (2009): 1–29.

8   Reid Bryson and Wayne Wendland described the period 900–1200 CE as the "Neo-Atlantic Climatic Episode"; see their "Tentative Climatic Patterns for Some Late Glacial and Post-Glacial Episodes in Central North America," in *Life, Land, and Water: Proceedings of the 1966 Conference on Environmental Studies of the Glacial Lake Agassiz Region,* edited by William J. Mayer-Oakes (Winnipeg: University of Manitoba Press, 1967), 271–98. For a discussion of the period in Europe, see Rudolph Brázdil et al., "Historical Climatology in Europe: The State of the Art," *Climatic Change* 70 (2005): 388–96.

9   Renée Fossett, *In Order to Live Untroubled: Inuit of the Central Arctic, 1550–1940* (Winnipeg: University of Manitoba Press, 2001), 15–19.

10   David Meyer and Scott Hamilton, "Neighbors to the North: Peoples of the Boreal Forest," in *Plains Indians: A.D. 500–1500: The Archaeological Past of Historic Groups,* edited by Karl Schlesier (Norman: University of Oklahoma Press, 1994), 112; Bryson and Wendland, "Tentative Climatic Patterns for Some Late Glacial and Post-Glacial Episodes in Central North America." An important exception to the good conditions of the Neo-Atlantic Climatic Episode was in the American southwest, which experienced severe drought and hardship. Terry L. Jones et al., "Environmental Imperatives Reconsidered: Demographic Crises in Western North America during the Medieval Climatic Anomaly [and Comments and Reply]," *Current Anthropology* 40 (1999): 137–70.

11   James E. Fitting, "Regional Cultural Development, 300 B.C. to A.D. 1000," in *Northeast,* edited by Bruce Trigger, vol. 15 of *Handbook of North American Indians* (Washington, DC: Smithsonian Institution Press, 1978), 44; Guy E. Gibbon, "Cultural Dynamics of the Development of the Oneota Lifeway in Wisconsin," *American Antiquity* 37 (1972): 168.

12   The development of northern flint corn around 800 CE was a major breakthrough in corn production and the spread of the horticulture to new regions. Thomas J. Riley et al., "Cul-

tigens in Prehistoric Eastern North America: Changing Paradigms," *Current Anthropology* 31 (1990): 529.

13   Biloine Whiting Young and Melvin L. Fowler, *Cahokia: The Great American Metropolis* (Urbana: University of Illinois Press, 2000), 316.

14   Thomas E. Emerson, *Cahokia and the Archaeology of Power* (Tuscaloosa: University of Alabama Press, 1997). Some have argued that Cahokia should be seen as the capital of a "state." George R. Milner, "The Late Prehistoric Cahokia Cultural System of the Mississippi River Valley: Foundations, Florescence, and Fragmentation," *Journal of World Prehistory* 4 (1990): 2.

15   James W. Springer and Stanley R. Witkowski, "Siouan Historical Linguistics and Oneota Archaeology," in *Oneota Studies*, edited by Guy Gibbon, Publications in Anthropology 1 (Minneapolis: University of Minnesota Press, 1995), 69–83.

16   Bryan J. Lenius and Dave M. Olinyk, "The Rainy River Composite: Revisions to Late Woodland Taxonomy," in *The Woodland Tradition in the Western Great Lakes: Papers Presented to Elden Johnson*, edited by Guy Gibbon, Publications in Anthropology 4 (Minneapolis: University of Minnesota Press, 1990), 80, Figure 8.3; Meyer and Hamilton, "Neighbors to the North," 112.

17   Lenius and Olinyk, "The Rainy River Composite," 101; Ian Dyck and Richard E. Morlan, "Hunting and Gathering Tradition: Canadian Plains," in *Plains*, edited by Raymond J. DeMallie, vol. 13 of *Handbook of North American Indians* (Washington, DC: Smithsonian Institution Press, 2001), 128–29.

18   R. Peter Winham and Edward J. Lueck, "Cultures of the Middle Missouri," in *Plains Indians, A.D. 500–1500: The Archaeological Past of Historic Groups*, edited by Karl Schlesier (Norman: University of Oklahoma Press, 1994), 159.

19   M. Boyd and C. Surette, "Northernmost Precontact Maize in North America," *American Antiquity* 75 (2010): 130.

20   Dale Walde, "Sedentism and Precontact Tribal Social Organization on the Northern Plains: Colonial Imposition or Indigenous Development?," *World Archaeology* 38 (2006): 298.

21   Ibid., 305.

22   Ibid. 302–03.

23   In archaeology, a phase is "an archaeological unit possessing traits sufficiently characteristic to distinguish it from all other units similarly conceived, whether of the same or other cultures or civilizations, spatially limited to the order of magnitude of a locality or a region and chronologically limited to a relatively brief interval of time." Gordon R. Wiley and Philip Philips, *Method and Theory in American Archaeology* (Chicago: University of Chicago Press, 1963), 23.

24   Dale Walde, "Avonlea and Athapaskan Migrations: A Reconsideration" *Plains Anthropologist* 51 (2006): 193.

25   J. Roderick Vickers, "Cultures of the Northwestern Plains from the Boreal Forest to the Milk River," in *Plains Indians, A.D. 500–1500: The Archaeological Past of Historic Groups*, edited by Karl H. Schlesier (Norman: University of Oklahoma Press, 1994), 28; Trevor Peck and Caroline R. Hudecek-Cuffe, "Archaeology on the Plains: The Last Two Thousand Years," in *Archaeology in Alberta: A View from the New Millennium*, edited by Jack Brink and John F. Dormaar (Medicine Hat: Archaeological Society of Alberta, 2003), 90; Walde, "Sedentism and Precontact Tribal Social Organization on the Northern Plains," 301.

26   Crowley, "Causes of Climate Change over the Past 1000 Years," 271.

27   Ryan C. Bay, Nathan Bramall, and P. Buford Price, "Bipolar Correlation of Volcanism with Millennial Climate Change," *Proceedings of the National Academy of Sciences* 101 (2004): 6341–45; (quotation) Gifford H. Miller et al., "Abrupt Onset of the Little Ice Age Triggered by Volcanism and Sustained by Sea-Ice/Ocean Feedbacks," *Geophysical Research Letters* 39 (2012): LO 2808.

28   Jared Diamond, *Collapse: How Societies Choose to Fail or Succeed* (New York: Penguin, 2005), 267.

29   Dean R. Snow, *The Iroquois* (Oxford: Blackwell, 1994), 31–76.

30   Milner, "The Late Prehistoric Cahokia Cultural System of the Mississippi River Valley," 31–33.

31 Charles R. Cobb and Brian Butler, "The Vacant Quarter Revisited: Late Mississippian Abandonment of the Lower Ohio Valley," *American Antiquity* 67 (2002): 625-41.

32 Lauren W. Ritterbush, "Drawn by the Bison: Late Prehistoric Native Migration into the Central Plains," *Great Plains Quarterly* 22 (2002): 259-70.

33 Beth R. Ritter, "Piecing Together the Ponca Past: Reconstructing Degiha Migrations to the Great Plains," *Great Plains Quarterly* 22 (2002): 271-84.

34 Walde, "Sedentism and Precontact Tribal Social Organization on the Northern Plains," 301; Dale Walde, David Meyer, and Wendy Umfreed, "The Late Period on the Canadian and Adjacent Plains," *Revista de Arqueologica Americana* 9 (1995): 32.

35 Douglas Bamforth, "An Empirical Perspective on the Little Ice Age Climatic Change on the Great Plains," *Plains Anthropologist* 35 (1990): 364.

36 Beverley (Bev) Alistair Nicholson and Scott Hamilton, "Cultural Continuity and Changing Subsistence Strategies during the Late Precontact Period in Southwestern Manitoba," *Canadian Journal of Archaeology* 25 (2001): 69.

37 Catherine Flynn and E. Leigh Syms, "Manitoba's First Farmers," *Manitoba History* 31 (1996): 4-11.

38 Beverley (Bev) Alistair Nicholson et al., "Climatic Challenges and Changes: A Little Ice Age Response to Adversity—the Vickers Focus Forager/Horticulturalists Move On," *Plains Anthropologist* 51 (2006): 325; Keith R. Briffa et al., "Influence of Volcanic Eruptions on Northern Hemisphere Temperature over the Past 600 Years," *Nature* 393 (1998): 453.

39 Nicholson et al., "Climatic Challenges and Changes," 329.

40 Walde, "Sedentism and Precontact Tribal Social Organization on the Northern Plains," 292.

41 Alexander Henry, *Travels and Adventures in Canada and the Indian Territories between the Years 1760 and 1776*, edited by James Bain (Rutland, VT: Charles Tuttle Company, 1969), 295-98.

42 R. Grace Morgan, *An Ecological Analysis of the Northern Plains as Seen through the Garratt Site*, Occasional Papers in Anthropology 7 (Regina: University of Regina, 1979), 111-13, 193.

43 R. Grace Morgan, "Beaver Ecology/Beaver Mythology" (Ph.D. diss., University of Alberta, 1991), 5, 27.

44 James Daschuk, "Who Killed the Prairie Beaver? An Environmental Case for Eighteenth-Century Migration in Western Canada," *Prairie Forum* 37 (2012): 151-72.

45 Richard H. Steckel and Joseph M. Prince, "Tallest in the World: Native Americans of the Great Plains in the Nineteenth Century," paper presented to the International Commission on Historical Demography, Oslo, 1999; Joseph M. Prince and Richard H. Steckel, "Nutritional Success on the Great Plains: Nineteenth-Century Equestrian Nomads," *Journal of Interdisciplinary History* 33 (2003): 353-84.

46 Peter Nabakov, *Indian Running* (Santa Fe: Ancient City Press, 1987), 14-24.

47 Louis Liebenberg, "Persistence Hunting by Modern Hunter-Gatherers," *Current Anthropology* 47 (2006): 1017; Dennis Bramble and Daniel Lieberman, "Endurance Running and the Evolution of *Homo*," *Nature* 432 (2004): 345-52.

48 Ernest G. Walker, "The Woodlawn Site: A Case for Interregional Disease Transmission in the Late Woodland Period," *Canadian Journal of Archaeology* 7 (1983): 49-59.

49 Charlotte A. Roberts and Jane E. Buikstra, *The Bioarchaeology of Tuberculosis: A Global View of a Reemerging Disease* (Gainesville: University of Florida Press, 2003), 191, Figure 4.1.

50 Of the total 255 prehistoric skeletons showing signs of TB from North America, 9 were from the period 1000-1199, 234 were from 1200 to 1399, and only 12 were from 1400 to 1599. Ibid., 194, Figure 4.2.

51 D. A. Ashford et al., "Bovine Tuberculosis: Environmental Public Health Preparedness Considerations for the Future," in *Mycobacterium Bovis Infection in Animals and Humans, Second Edition*, edited by Charles O. Thoen, James H. Steele, and Michael J. Gilsdorf (Ames: Blackwell Publishing, 2006), 305. Other members of the *M. tuberculosis* complex are *M. africanum, M. nicrotti,* and *M. canetti.* On the difficulty of differentiating between

the two main sources of infection, see also Roberts and Buikstra, *The Bioarchaeology of Tuberculosis*, 75, 310.

52 Stacey Tessaro, "Bovine TB and Brucellosis in Animals, Including Man," in *Buffalo*, edited by John Foster, Dick Harrison, and I. S. MacLaren (Edmonton: University of Alberta Press, 1992), 208–09.

53 Matthew Levison, *"Mycobacterium bovis:* An Underappreciated Pathogen," *Current Infectious Disease Reports* 10 (2008): 445; Charlotte Roberts and Keith Manchester, *The Archaeology of Disease, Third Edition* (Ithaca, NY: Cornell University Press, 2005), 187.

54 An important indicator of Pott's disease is a deformity of the spine known colloquially as a "hunchback." Joseph Lichtor and Alexander Lichtor, "Paleopathological Evidence Suggesting Pre-Columbian Tuberculosis of the Spine," *Journal of Bone and Joint Surgery* 39 (1957): 1399; William A. Ritchie, "Paleopathological Evidence Suggesting Pre-Columbian Tuberculosis in New York State," *American Journal of Physical Anthropology* 10 (1952): 305–18.

55 Roberts and Buikstra, *The Bioarchaeology of Tuberculosis*, 189; Roberts and Manchester, *The Archaeology of Disease*, 183.

56 Seymour Hawden, "Tuberculosis in the Buffalo," *Journal of the American Veterinary Medical Association* 100 (1942): 19–22; Roberts and Manchester, *The Archaeology of Disease*, 185.

57 James Daschuk, Paul Hackett, and Scott D. MacNeil, "Treaties and Tuberculosis: First Nations People in Late 19ᵗʰ Century Western Canada, a Political and Economic Transformation," *Canadian Bulletin of the History of Medicine* 23 (2006): 307–30.

CHAPTER 2—THE EARLY FUR TRADE: TERRITORIAL DISLOCATION AND DISEASE

1 Paul Thistle, *Indian–European Trade Relations in the Lower Saskatchewan River Region to 1840*, Manitoba Studies in Native History (Winnipeg: University of Manitoba Press, 1986), 63–64.

2 J. Richtmeier, "Precipitation, Temperature, and Maize Agriculture: Implications for Prehistoric Populations in the Middle Missouri Subarea, 900–1675" (MA thesis, University of Nebraska, 1980), 56.

3 Alfred Crosby, "Virgin Soil Epidemics as a Factor in the Aboriginal Depopulation of America," in *Germs, Seeds, and Animals: Studies in Ecological History* (Armonk, N.J.: M. E. Sharpe, 1993), 97.

4 "Introduction," in *Plains Indians, A.D. 500–1500: The Archaeological Past of Historic Groups*, edited by Karl H. Schlesier (Norman: University of Oklahoma Press, 1994), xxi.

5 David S Jones, "Virgin Soils Revisited," *William and Mary Quarterly* 60 (2003), 742.

6 Conrad Heidenreich, "The Great Lakes Basin, 1600–1653," in *Historical Atlas of Canada, Volume 1: From the Beginning to 1800*, edited by R. Cole Harris (Toronto: University of Toronto Press, 1987), Plate 35.

7 Paul Hackett, *"A Very Remarkable Sickness": Epidemics in the Petit Nord, 1670 to 1846* (Winnipeg: University of Manitoba Press, 2002), 10, 60–61.

8 Heidenreich, "The Great Lakes Basin," Plate 35; Bruce Trigger, *The Children of Aataentsic II: A History of the Huron People to 1660* (Montreal: McGill-Queen's University Press, 1976), 589.

9 Arthur J. Ray, "Some Thoughts about the Reasons for Spatial Dynamism in the Early Fur Trade, 1500–1800," in *Three Hundred Prairie Years: Henry Kelsey's "Inland Country of Good Report*," edited by Henry Epp (Regina: Canadian Plains Research Center, 1993), 118.

10 Hackett, *"A Very Remarkable Sickness*," 69–70.

11 Marcel Trudel, *The Beginnings of New France, 1524–1662* (Toronto: McClelland and Stewart, 1973), 225.

12 Conrad Heidenreich, "Iroquois Disruptions, 1660–1666," in *Historical Atlas of Canada, Volume 1: From the Beginning to 1800*, edited by R. Cole Harris (Toronto: University of Toronto Press, 1987), Plate 37. For the terms of the treaty, see Cornelius Jaenen, ed., *The*

French Regime in the Upper Country of Canada during the Seventeenth Century (Toronto: Champlain Society, 1996), 59–65.

13   Helen Hornbeck Tanner, "The Career of Joseph La France, Coureur de Bois in the Great Lakes," in *The Fur Trade Revisited: Selected Papers of the Sixth North American Fur Trade Conference*, edited by J. S. H. Brown, W. J. Eccles, and Donald P. Feldman (East Lansing: Michigan State University Press, 1994), 182.

14   Hackett, *"A Very Remarkable Sickness,"* 93, traced the source of the epidemic to the arrival of an infected ship in the fall of 1669.

15   Ibid., 48–49, 78–83; E.E. Rich, *A History of the Hudson's Bay Company, 1670–1870*, vol. 1 (London: Hudson's Bay Record Society, 1958), 62.

16   The presence of venereal disease at the bay was noted by Governor John Nixon as early as 1682. Hackett, *"A Very Remarkable Sickness,"* 78.

17   Ray, "Some Thoughts about the Reasons for Spatial Dynamism in the Early Fur Trade," 122.

18   Ibid., 116.

19   Alexander Henry, *Travels and Adventures in Canada and the Indian Territory between the Years 1760 and 1776*, edited by James Bain (Rutland,VT: C. E. Tuttle, 1969), 208–09.

20   Hackett, *"A Very Remarkable Sickness,"* 100.

21   Dale Russell, *Eighteenth-Century Western Cree and Their Neighbours* (Ottawa: Canadian Museum of Civilization, 1991), 127; Arthur Ray and Donald Freeman, *"Give Us Good Measure": An Economic Analysis of Relations between the Indians and the Hudson's Bay Company before 1763* (Toronto: University of Toronto Press, 1978), 45–49.

22   Brian Fagan, *The Little Ice Age: How Climate Made History, 1300–1850* (New York: Basic Books, 2000), 113.

23   Marshall Hurlich, "Historical and Recent Demography of the Algonkians in Northern Ontario," in *Boreal Forest Adaptations: The Northern Algonkians*, edited by Theodore Steegmann (New York: Plenum Press, 1983), 133, 148.

24   Russell, *Eighteenth-Century Western Cree and Their Neighbours*, 127; Ray and Freeman, *"Give Us Good Measure,"* 45–49, 133–36. See also Irma Eckert, "The Early Fur Trade at York and Churchill: Implications for the Native People of the North Central Subarctic," in *Le Castor Fait Tout: Selected Papers of the Fifth North American Fur Trade Conference, 1985*, edited by B. Trigger, T. Morantz, and Louise Dechêne (Montreal: Lake St. Louis Historical Society, 1987), 232.

25   Rupert's Land Research Centre, "An Historical Overview of Aboriginal Lifestyles: The Churchill–Nelson River Drainage Basin," unpublished report, 1992, 91; E. E. Rich, "Trade Habits and Economic Motivation among Indians of North America," in *Sweet Promises: A Reader on Indian-White Relations in Canada*, edited by J. R. Miller (Toronto: University of Toronto Press, 1991), 160–64.

26   Conrad Heidenreich and Françoise Noël, "Trade and Empire, 1697–1739," in *Historical Atlas of Canada, Volume 1: From the Beginning to 1800*, edited by R. Cole Harris (Toronto: University of Toronto Press, 1987), Plate 39.

27   Russell, *Eighteenth-Century Western Cree and Their Neighbours*, 63–78.

28   Ibid., 211. The group might also have succumbed to the disease that was epidemic among the Indians trading at York Factory that summer.

29   Hackett, *"A Very Remarkable Sickness,"* 118; Eckert, "The Early Fur Trade at York and Churchill," 232. Homeguard communities were often adjacent to trading posts and served as provisioners and labourers for Europeans.

30   Eckert, "The Early Fur Trade at York and Churchill," 232.

31   G. Hubert Smith, *The Explorations of the La Vérendryes in the Northern Plains, 1738–43*, edited by W. Raymond Wood (Lincoln: University of Nebraska Press, 1980), 15.

32   Antoine Champagne, *Les La Vérendrye et les postes de l'ouest* (Québec: Les Presses de l'Université Laval, 1968), 123.

33   A. S. Morton, *A History of the Canadian West to 1870–71* (Toronto: University of Toronto Press, 1973), 178.

34   Irene Moore, *Valiant La Vérendrye* (Quebec City: L. A. Proulx, 1927), 154–64.

35   Hackett, *"A Very Remarkable Sickness,"* 137–38.

36 "Smallpox and Climate in the American Southwest," *American Anthropologist*, n.s., 88 (1986): 117.

37 Reuben Gold Thwaites, ed., *The French Regime in Wisconsin Part II—1727–1748*, vol. 18 of *Collections of the Wisconsin State Historical Society* (Madison: Wisconsin Historical Society, 1906), 181–86.

38 Moore, *Valiant La Vérendrye*, 36, 154–77, 251–52.

39 Smith, *The Explorations of the La Vérendryes in the Northern Plains*, 18.

40 Dale Walde, "The Mortlach Phase" (Ph.D. diss., University of Calgary, 1994), 136.

41 Arthur Ray, *Indians in the Fur Trade: Their Role as Trappers, Hunters, and Middlemen in the Lands Southwest of Hudson Bay, 1660–1870* (Toronto: University of Toronto Press, 1974), 39.

42 Russell, *Eighteenth-Century Western Cree and Their Neighbours*, 49–50; Moore, *Valiant La Vérendrye*, 127–28.

43 Russell, *Eighteenth-Century Western Cree and Their Neighbours*, 57.

44 Paul Hackett, "The Monsoni and the Smallpox Epidemic of 1738–39," in *Pushing the Margins: Native and Northern Studies*, edited by Jill Oakes et al. (Winnipeg: Departments of Native Studies and Zoology, University of Manitoba, 2001), 246.

45 Morton, *A History of the Canadian West to 1870–71*, 74; Adolph Greenberg and James Morrison, "Group Identities in the Boreal Forest: The Origin of the Northern Ojibwa," *Ethnohistory* 29 (1982): 77.

46 Hackett, *"A Very Remarkable Sickness,"* 130–34. The estimate is based on a ratio of four people per warrior.

47 Champagne, *Les La Vérendrye et les postes de l'ouest*, 277.

48 Russell, *Eighteenth-Century Western Cree and Their Neighbours*, 56.

49 Greenberg and Morrison, "Group Identities in the Boreal Forest," 97–98n24.

50 Ray and Freeman, *"Give Us Good Measure,"* 42.

51 Charles Bishop, "The Emergence of the Northern Ojibwa: Social and Economic Consequences," *American Ethnologist* 3 (1974): 44.

52 Emöke Szathmary and Franklin Auger, "Biological Distances and Genetic Relationships within Algonkians," in *Boreal Forest Adaptations: The Northern Algonkians*, edited by Theodore Steegmann (New York: Plenum Press, 1983), 311–12.

53 Russell, *Eighteenth-Century Western Cree and Their Neighbours*, 232.

54 Ray, *Indians in the Fur Trade*, 14.

55 Morton, *A History of the Canadian West to 1870–71*, 11.

56 Harold Hickerson, *The Chippewa and Their Neighbours: A Study in Ethnohistory*, Studies in Anthropological Method (Prospect Heights, NJ: Holt, Rinehart and Winston, 1988), 71–72.

57 Hackett, *"A Very Remarkable Sickness,"* 65.

58 Winter counts are pictographic records representing the most important events of each year. The Battiste Good Winter Count presents a yearly record of life among the Dakota from 1700. Garrick Mallery, *Picture-Writing of the American Indians*, vol. 1 (New York: Dover Publications, 1972), 300. For an extended discussion on the value of winter counts for the study of historical disease episodes, see Linea Sundstrom, "Smallpox Used Them Up: References to Epidemic Disease in Northern Great Plains Winter Counts, 1714–1920," *Ethnohistory* 44 (1997): 305–29.

59 J. B. Truteau, "Remarks on the Manners of the Indians Living High Up the Missouri," in *Before Lewis and Clark: Documents Illustrating the History of the Missouri, 1785–1804*, edited by A. P. Nasatir (Lincoln: University of Nebraska Press, 1990), 257–311.

60 Michael K. Trimble, "Chronology of Epidemics among Plains Village Horticulturalists, 1738–1838," *Southwestern Lore* 54 (1988): 26.

61 Tanner, "The Career of Joseph La France," 175.

62 Paul Kelton, "Avoiding the Smallpox Spirits: Colonial Epidemics and Southwestern Indian Survival," *Ethnohistory* 15 (2004): 82–84; William E. Unrau, "The Depopulation of the Dheghia-Siouan Kansa Prior to Removal," *New Mexico Historical Review* 48 (1973): 316.

63 David J. Weber, *The Spanish Frontier in America* (New Haven, CT: Yale University Press, 1992), 192.

64   Ann L. Stodder and Debra L. Martin, "Health and Disease in the Southwest before and after Spanish Contact," in *Disease and Demography in the Americas*, edited by John W. Verano and Douglas H. Uberlaker (Washington, DC: Smithsonian Institution Press, 1992), 67.

65   Frances Lavine and Anna La Bauve, "Examining the Complexity of Historic Population Decline: A Case Study from Pecos Pueblo, New Mexico," *Ethnohistory* 44 (1997): 92.

66   Pekka Hämäläinen, *The Comanche Empire* (New Haven, CT: Yale University Press, 2008).

67   The Ute and Kiowa were also involved in the horse trade along the continental divide. Colin C. Calloway, "Snake Frontiers: The Eastern Shoshones in the Eighteenth Century," *Annals of Wyoming* 63 (1991): 84-86.

68   Clark Wissler, "The Influence of the Horse in the Development of Plains Culture," *American Anthropologist* 16 (1914): 24.

69   Calloway, "Snake Frontiers," 86; Frances Haines, "The Northward Spread of Horses among the Plains Indians," *American Anthropologist*, n.s., 40 (1938): 429-37. The route followed the headwaters of the Colorado, Grand, and Green Rivers to the Snake River in southern Idaho, where horses were traded with the Cayuse, Walla Walla, Yakima, Palouse, Nez Percé, Coeur D'Alêne, Flathead, and others.

70   Theodore Binnema, *Common and Contested Ground: A Human and Environmental History of the North American Plains* (Norman: University of Oklahoma Press, 2001), 91; Calloway, "Snake Frontiers," 86. On the frequency of raids in the 1730s, see Frances L. Swadesh, *Los Primeros Pobladores: Hispanic Americans of the Ute Frontier* (Notre Dame: University of Notre Dame Press, 1974), 128.

71   John Fahey, *The Kalispel Indians* (Norman: University of Oklahoma Press, 1986), 37-39.

72   Bill B. Brunton, "Kootenai," in *Plateau*, edited by Deward E. Walker, vol. 12 of *Handbook of North American Indians* (Washington, DC: Smithsonian Institution Press, 1998), 225. See also Harry Holbert Turney-High, *Ethnography of the Kutenai*, Memoirs of the American Anthropological Association 56 (Menasha, WI: American Anthropological Association, 1941), 11, 18-20.

73   Claude Schaeffer, "Plains Kutenai: An Ethnological Evaluation," *Alberta History* 30 (1982): 5.

74   William E. Farr, "Going to Buffalo: Indian Hunting Migrations across the Rocky Mountains. Part 1, Making Meat and Taking Robes," *Montana: The Magazine of Western History* 53 (2003): 8.

75   Karl H. Schlesier, "Commentary: A History of Ethnic Groups in the Great Plains, A.D. 500-1550," in *Plains Indians, A.D. 500-1500: The Archaeological Past of Historic Groups*, edited by Karl H. Schlesier (Norman: University of Oklahoma Press, 1994), 315; Calloway, "Snake Frontiers," 84. On the drought, see D. W. Stahle et al., "Tree Ring Data Document 16th Century Megadrought over North America," *Eos: Transactions of the American Geophysical Union* 81 (2000): 121-23.

76   J.R. Vickers, "Cultures of the Northwestern Plains from the Boreal Forest Edge to Milk River," in *Plains Indians, A.D. 500-1500: The Archaeological Past of Historic Groups*, edited by Karl H. Schlesier (Norman: University of Oklahoma Press, 1994), 28.

77   Saukamappee's account of his enemy noted that the *mis-stu-tim* ("big dogs") "alarmed us, for we had no idea of horses and could not make out what they were." Thompson, *Travels in Western North America*, 193.

78   Ibid., 199. This passage has been the source of much confusion among contemporary scholars. According to Hopwood, the narrative that included the description of the smallpox outbreak was presented "as nearly as possible as Thompson wrote it, mainly to give the reader a sample of Thompson's unedited prose, but also because there are errors in the transcription of the chapter in the second Champlain Society edition [Glover's]"; ibid., 82. Part of the problem stems from an inept editorial comment by J. B. Tyrrell in 1916. Tyrrell unknowingly merged descriptions of two disease episodes that were actually forty-five years apart. See David Thompson, *David Thompson's Narrative 1784-1812*, edited by Richard Glover (Toronto: Champlain Society, 1962), 252n1. A discussion of the thirty pages of the Thompson narrative missing from the Tyrrell version can be found in Victor C. Hopwood, "New Light on David Thompson," *The Beaver* 288 (1957): 239-45.

79   Russell, *Eighteenth-Century Western Cree and Their Neighbours*, 195.

80   There are no estimates of casualties among the Piikani (Peigan) resulting from the epidemic. Archaeological studies have shown that "the time of the greatest stress upon the Old Woman's [Blackfoot] phase was in the protohistoric period, about A.D. 1700-1750." Vickers, "Cultures of the Northwestern Plains from the Boreal Forest Edge to Milk River," 24.

81   Richard G. Forbis, *Cluny: An Ancient Fortified Village in Alberta*, Occasional Papers in Archaeology 4 (Calgary: University of Calgary Press, 1977), 72-74; Dale Walde, "Mortlach and One Gun: Phase to Phase," in *Archaeology on the Edge: New Perspectives from the Northern Plains*, edited by Brian Kooyman and Jane H. Kelley, Canadian Archaeological Association Occasional Paper 4 (Calgary: University of Calgary Press, 2004), 42-50.

82   James Deetz, *The Dynamics of Stylistic Change in Arikara Ceramics* (Urbana: University of Illinois Press, 1965), 101; Craig Johnson, "The Coalescent Tradition," in *Archaeology on the Great Plains*, edited by W. Raymond Wood (Lawrence: University of Kansas Press, 1998), 327; Walde, "Mortlach and One Gun," 42-50.

83   Forbis, *Cluny*, 6-17.

CHAPTER 3—EARLY COMPETITION AND THE EXTENSION OF TRADE AND DISEASE, 1740-82

1   Elizabeth Fenn, *Pox Americana: The Great Smallpox Epidemic of 1775-82* (New York: Hill and Wang, 2001).

2   Donald J. Lehmer, "Climate and Culture History in the Middle Missouri Valley," in *Pleistocene and Recent Environments of the Central Great Plains*, edited by W. Dort and J.K. Jones (Lawrence: University of Kansas Press, 1970), reprinted in *Selected Writings of Donald J. Lehmer*, Reprints in Anthropology 8 (Lincoln, NB: J and L Reprint Company, 1977), 118.

3   John Milloy, *The Plains Cree: Trade Diplomacy and Warfare, 1790-1870*, Manitoba Studies in Native History (Winnipeg: University of Manitoba Press, 1988), 41; G. Hubert Smith, *The Explorations of the La Vérendryes in the Northern Plains, 1738-43*, edited by W. Raymond Wood (Lincoln: University of Nebraska Press, 1980), 19.

4   D. Rinn, "The Acquisition, Diffusion, and Distribution of the European Horse among Blackfoot Tribes in Western Canada" (MA thesis, University of Manitoba, 1975), 22-24.

5   Dale Miquelon, *New France, 1701-1744: A Supplement to Empire* (Toronto: McClelland and Stewart, 1987), 185.

6   Dale Russell, *Eighteenth-Century Western Cree and Their Neighbours* (Ottawa: Canadian Museum of Civilization, 1991), 61, 91-92.

7   David Meyer and Dale Russell, "'So Fine and Pleasant, beyond Description': The Lands and Lives of the Pegogamaw Crees," *Plains Anthropologist* 49 (2004): 219; David Meyer and Scott Hamilton, "Neighbors to the North: Peoples of the Boreal Forest," in *Plains Indians, A.D. 500-1500: The Archaeological Past of Historic Groups*, edited by Karl H. Schlesier (Norman: University of Oklahoma Press, 1994), 124.

8   Anthony Hendry, "York Factory to the Blackfeet Country: The Journal of Anthony Hendry, 1754-1755," edited by Lawrence J. Burpee, *Proceedings and Transactions of the Royal Society of Canada* Series 1 (1907): 328-30.

9   Smith, *The Explorations of the La Vérendryes in the Northern Plains*, 44, 94. See also Dale Walde, "The Mortlach Phase" (Ph.D. diss., University of Calgary, 1994), 118-19; Dale Walde, David Meyer, and Wendy Umfreed, "The Late Period on the Canadian and Adjacent Plains," *Revista de Archaologia Americana* 9 (1995): 44-45

10   David Smyth, "The Niitsitapi Trade: Euroamericans and the Blackfoot Speaking Peoples to the Mid 1830s" (Ph.D. diss., Carleton University, 2001), 109.

11   Russell, *Eighteenth-Century Western Cree and Their Neighbours*, 197. See also Paul Thistle, *Indian-European Trade Relations in the Lower Saskatchewan River Region to 1840* (Winnipeg: University of Manitoba Press, 1986), 63-64.

12   Alexander Mackenzie, *Voyages from Montreal on the River St. Lawrence through the Continent of North America to the Frozen and Pacific Oceans in the Years 1789 and 1793* (Edmonton: Hurtig Publishers, 1971), 139-40.

13   Hugh Dempsey, "Sarcee," in *Plains*, vol. 13, part 1, of *Handbook of North American Indians*, edited by Raymond J. DeMallie (Washington, DC: Smithsonian Institution Press, 2001), 629.

14   Russell, *Eighteenth-Century Western Cree and Their Neighbours*, 163.

15   Ibid., 114.

16   Samuel Hearne, *A Journey from Prince of Wales Fort in Hudson's Bay to the Northern Ocean* (Edmonton: Hurtig Publishers, 1971).

17   J. C. Yerbury, *The Subarctic Indians and the Fur Trade* (Vancouver: UBC Press, 1986), 48-49, 55. Over 20,000 Made Beaver (the standard of trade) were delivered in the summer of 1772.

18   A. S. Morton, *A History of the Canadian West to 1870-71* (Toronto: University of Toronto Press, 1973), 284-87.

19   Russell, *Eighteenth-Century Western Cree and Their Neighbours*, 105.

20   J. L. Burpee, ed., "An Adventurer from Hudson Bay: The Journal of Matthew Cocking from York Factory to the Blackfoot Country," *Proceedings and Transactions of the Royal Society of Canada*, section 2 (1908): 96-113.

21   Paul Hackett, *"A Very Remarkable Sickness": Epidemics in the Petit Nord, 1670 to 1846* (Winnipeg: University of Manitoba Press, 2002), 83-90.

22   Ibid., 100.

23   Morton, *A History of the Canadian West to 1870-71*, 286.

24   Burpee, ed., "An Adventurer from Hudson Bay," 118, 119.

25   Morton, *A History of the Canadian West to 1870-71*, 286-90; Harry Duckworth, ed., *The English River Book: A Northwest Company Journal and Account Book of 1786* (Montreal: McGill-Queen's University Press, 1990), xiii-xiv.

26   Smyth, "The Niitsitapi Trade," 155.

27   E. E. Rich, ed., "Cumberland House Journal," in *Cumberland House Journals and Inland Journals, 1775-82, First Series* (London: Hudson's Bay Record Society, 1951), 217; Rupert's Land Research Centre, "An Historical Overview of Aboriginal Lifestyles: The Churchill-Nelson River Drainage Basin," unpublished report (Winnipeg: University of Winnipeg, 1992), 99-101.

28   Theodore Binnema, *Common and Contested Ground: A Human and Environmental History of the North American Plains* (Norman: University of Oklahoma Press, 2001), 119; Hudson's Bay Company Archives (hereafter HBCA), Cumberland House Post Journals, B.49/a/1:17b (8 February 1775).

29   Harry Duckworth, ed., *The English River Book: A Northwest Company Account Book of 1786* (Montreal: McGill-Queen's University Press, 1990), xiv; HBCA, Cumberland House Post Journals, B.49/a/1:24 (30 April 1775).

30   HBCA, Cumberland House Post Journals, B.49/a/3 (19 June 1776); Hudson House Post Journals, B.87/a/2:22 (19 December 1779).

31   Duckworth, ed., *The English River Book*, xiv-xv; Russell, *Eighteenth-Century Western Cree and Their Neighbours*, 119.

32   Morton, *A History of the Canadian West to 1870-71*, 315. The location of the Assiniboine was probably along the Carrot River.

33   Alexander Henry, *Travels and Adventures in Canada and the Indian Territories between the Years 1760 and 1776*, edited by James Bain (Rutland, VT: C.E. Tuttle Company, 1969), 317.

34   Arthur Ray, *Indians in the Fur Trade: Their Role as Trappers, Hunters, and Middlemen in the Lands Southwest of Hudson Bay, 1660-1870* (Toronto: University of Toronto Press, 1974), 125-33; Arthur Ray, "The Great Northern Plains: Pantry of the Northwestern Fur Trade, 1774-1885," *Prairie Forum* 9 (1984): 265; George Colpitts, "'Victuals into Their Mouths': Environmental Perspectives on Fur Trade Provisioning Activities at Cumberland House, 1775-1782," *Prairie Forum* 22 (1997): 17.

35   Duckworth, ed., *The English River Book*, xv.

36   HBCA, Cumberland House Post Journals, B.49/a/1:32 (23 June 1775).

37 Hackett, *"A Very Remarkable Sickness,"* 255n1.

38 Heather Rollason Driscoll, "'A Most Important Chain of Connection': Marriage in the Hudson's Bay Company," in *From Rupert's Land to Canada*, edited by Theodore Binnema, Gerhard Enns, and R.C. Macleod (Edmonton: University of Alberta Press, 2001), 91–92.

39 Rich, ed., *Cumberland House Journals and Inland Journals, First Series*, 143–44, 176, 184, 196–97.

40 HBCA, Cumberland House Post Journals, B.49/a/6:41b (17 February 1778).

41 Alexander Mackenzie, *Voyages from Montreal on the River St. Lawrence through the Continent of North America to the Frozen and Pacific Oceans in the Years 1789 and 1793* (Edmonton: Hurtig Publishers, 1971), xii–xiii.

42 HBCA, Cumberland House Post Journals, B.49/a/6:62 (26 May 1778), B.49/a/9:4b (2 July 1779). William Tomison noted that Pond journeyed so far into the interior that "he traded with the northward Indians that Mr. Samuel Hearne was along with Mette na 'pew [Matonabbee?] and his gang."

43 W.A. Sloan, "The Native Response to the Extension of the European Traders into the Athabasca Country and the Mackenzie Basin, 1770–1816," *Canadian Historical Review* 60 (1979): 281.

44 Milloy, *The Plains Cree*, 29.

45 J. G. MacGregor, *Peter Fidler: Canada's Forgotten Surveyor* (Toronto: McClelland and Stewart, 1966), 8.

46 HBCA, Hudson House Post Journals, B.87/a/1:6b (18 December 1778).

47 Morton, *A History of the Canadian West to 1870–71*, 324.

48 MacGregor, *Peter Fidler*, 8; Morton, *A History of the Canadian West to 1870–71*, 331.

49 HBCA, Hudson House Post Journals, B.87/a/1:13b (15 March 1779); Cumberland House Post Journals, B.49/a/7:52b–53 (9 May 1779); Hudson House Post Journals, B.87/a/1:15b (25 April 1779).

50 Smyth, "The Niitsitapi Trade," 158–59; HBCA, Hudson House Post Journals, B.87/a/2:18 (20 November 1779).

51 HBCA, Hudson House Post Journals, B.87/a/2:20 (5 December 1779).

52 HBCA, Hudson House Post Journals, B.87/a/2:21 (10 December 1779), B.87/a/2:30 (12 February 1780), B.87/a/3:6–7b (31 October, 17 and 21 November 1780).

53 HBCA, Hudson House Post Journals, B.87/a/3:6 (31 October 31 1780), B.87/a/3:7–7b (17 and 21 November 1780).

54 HBCA, Hudson House Post Journals, B.87/a/3:6 (31 October 1780), B.87/a/3:7–7b (17 and 21 November 1780). Because the snow was late in coming, the effect of the burning was increased since hunters could not find animal tracks. B.87/a/3:10–13 (17 December 1780, 9 and 17 January 1781). Two weeks later reports came in from the Beaver country "of Indians starving, and have eat up all their Dogs, and cannot come in for want of provisions." B.87/a/26:7b (26 November 1780), B.87/a/3:9b–10 (18 and 22 December 1780), B.87/a/3:13 (18 January 1781), B.87/a/3:13 (22 and 25 January1781), B.87/a/3:14 (7 February 1781), B.87/a/3:15b (4 February 1871), B.87/a/3:16 (27 February 1781), B.87/a/3:16b–17 (2 and 11 March 1781).

55 HBCA, Hudson House Post Journals, B.87/a/3:16b (4 March 1781), B.87/a/3:17 (6 March 1781), B.87/a/3:17b (13 March 1781), B.87/a/3:18 (18 March 1781). No medicine was available for his treatment; the sickness soon spread among the servants; B.87/a/3:18b (24–26 March 1781). Bloody flux is a form of dysentery, a potentially lethal bacterial disease; Hackett, *"A Very Remarkable Sickness,"* 209–10; B.87/a/3:21b (27 April 1781).

56 Adam R. Hodge recently argued that climatic instability undermined the food supply across the northern plains, exaserbating the impact of smallpox in the regions malnourished population. "In Want of Nourishment for to Keep Them Alive": Climate Fluctuations, Bison Scarcity, and the Smallpox Epidemic of 1780-82 on the Northern Great Plains," *Environmental History* 17 (2012): 365-403.

57 HBCA, Hudson House Post Journals, B.87/a/4:5–5b (17 October 1781), B.87/a/4:5b–6 (22 October 1781).

58 John F. Taylor, "Sociocultural Effects of Epidemics on the Northern Plains: 1734–1850," *Western Canadian Journal of Anthropology* 7 (1977): 59; Michael Trimble, "Chronology of Epidemics among Plains Village Horticulturalists: 1738–1838," *Southwestern Lore* 54

(1988): 7; Linea Sundstrom, "Smallpox Used Them Up: References to Epidemic Disease in the Northern Plains Winter Counts, 1714–1920," *Ethnohistory* 44 (1995): 309.

59 In the same month as smallpox was reported on the Saskatchewan River, outbreaks were recorded in California and at Yorktown on the eastern seaboard. Fenn, *Pox Americana: The Great Smallpox Epidemic of 1775-82*, 175.

60 Binnema, *Common and Contested Ground*, 86–106.

61 *David Thompson, Travels in Western North America, 1784–1812*, edited by Victor G. Hopwood (Toronto: Macmillan of Canada, 1971), 191.

62 Colin C. Calloway, "Snake Frontiers: The Eastern Shoshones in the Eighteenth Century," *Annals of Wyoming* 63 (1991): 89–90.

63 Thompson, *David Thompson, Travels in Western North America*, 199.

64 HBCA, Hudson House Post Journals, B.87/a/4:12b–13 (4 December 1781), B.87/a/4:24 (7 March 1782), B.87/a/6:22 (4 January 1783), B.87/a/4:13b (10 December 1781), B.87/a/4:21b (25 February 1782).

65 Russell, *Eighteenth-Century Western Cree and Their Neighbours*, 172.

66 HBCA, Cumberland House Post Journals, B.49/a/11:32 (8 December 1781); Hudson House Post Journals, B.87/a/4:22b (19 February 1782).

67 Thistle, *Indian–European Trade Relations on the Lower Saskatchewan River Region to 1840*, 62–64; David Meyer and Paul Thistle, "Saskatchewan River Rendezvous Centers and Trading Posts: Continuity in a Cree Social Geography," *Ethnohistory* 42 (1995): 421.

68 Thistle, *Indian–European Trade Relations on the Lower Saskatchewan River Region to 1840*, 65, 69.

69 Hackett, *"A Very Remarkable Sickness,"* 93–118. See also Jody Decker, "Tracing Historical Diffusion Patterns: The Case of the 1780–82 Smallpox Epidemic among the Indians of Western Canada," *Native Studies Review* 4 (1988): 1–24; Elliot Coues, ed., *New Light on the Early History of the Greater Northwest: The Manuscript Journals of Alexander Henry and David Thompson, 1799–1814*, vol. 1 (Minneapolis: Ross and Haines, 1965), 46.

70 *Cumberland House Journals and Inland Journals, Second Series*, 298.

71 Hackett, *"A Very Remarkable Sickness,"* 93–118. See also Decker, "Tracing Historical Diffusion Patterns."

72 Laura Peers, *The Ojibwa of Western Canada,1780–1870* (Winnipeg: University of Manitoba Press, 1994), 19n66.

73 Roderick Mackenzie, "Introduction," in Mackenzie, *Voyages from Montreal*, lvii; Victor Lytwyn, "'God Was Angry with Their Country': The Smallpox Epidemic of 1782–83 among the Hudson Bay Lowland Cree," in *Papers of the Thirtieth Algonkian Conference*, edited by David H. Pentland (Winnipeg: University of Manitoba Press, 1999), 157–62.

74 William Walker, Hudson House Journal, 9 April 1782, *Cumberland House Journals and Inland Journals, Second Series*, 285; Russell, *Eighteenth-Century Western Cree and Their Neighbours*, 150–51.

75 MacGregor, *Peter Fidler*, 111–17.

76 G. Nicks, "Native Responses to the Early Fur Trade at Lesser Slave Lake," in *Le Castor Fait Tout: Selected Papers of the Fifth North American Fur Trade Conference*, edited by B. Trigger, Toby Morantz, and Louise Dechêne (Montreal: Lake St. Louis Historical Society, 1987), 285–86; Sloan, "The Native Response to the Extension of the European Traders into the Athabasca and Mackenzie Basin," 288.

77 Russell, *Eighteenth-Century Western Cree and Their Neighbours*, 161, 167.

78 Beryl C. Gillespie, "An Ethnohistory of the Yellowknives: A Northern Athapaskan Tribe," in *Contributions to Anthropology, 1975*, edited by David Brez Carlisle, Mercury Series, Canadian Ethnology Service Paper 31 (Ottawa: National Museum of Man, 1975), 207; Thompson, *David Thompson*, 122; Russell, *Eighteenth-Century Western Cree and Their Neighbours*, 217.

79 Yerbury, *The Subarctic Indians and the Fur Trade*, 147–48. The 90 percent mortality figure is probably an exaggeration; they were able to expand their territory after the epidemic. James G.E. Smith, "Local Band Organization of the Caribou Eater Chipewyan in the Eighteenth and Early Nineteenth Centuries," *Western Canadian Journal of Anthropology* 6 (1976): 77.

80   Sloan, "The Native Response to the Extension of the European Traders into the Athabasca and Mackenzie Basin," 282–83.

81   Gillespie, "An Ethnohistory of the Yellowknives," 208.

82   Mackenzie, *Voyages from Montreal*, liii.

83   HBCA, Cumberland House Post Journals, B.87/a/4:7 (29 October 1781), B.87/a/4:10b (27 November 1781).

84   Cumberland House Journal, 18 December 1781, *Cumberland House Journals and Inland Journals, Second Series*, 226.

85   European immunity was not universal. Canadian Master Bruce and Captain Tuite on the lower Assiniboine died, and a number of traders who were hit by the disease were reported to have starved. Jody Decker, "'We Should Never Be Again the Same People': The Diffusion and Cumulative Impact of Acute Infectious Diseases Affecting the Natives on the Northern Plains of the Western Interior of Canada" (Ph.D. diss., York University, 1989), 60.

86   Ibid., 73.

87   See *Cumberland House Journals and Inland Journals, Second Series*, 16 January 1782 (231); 22 January 1782 (232); 31 January 1782 (234); 5 February 1782 (234–35); 7 February 1782 (235); 14 February 1782 (236); 20 February 1782 (239); 25 February 1782 (240); 11 March 1782 (240); 27 March 1782 (244); Walker to Tomison, May 1782 (254).

88   HBCA, Cumberland House Post Journals, B.49/a/11:36 (25 December 1781), B.87/a/4:25 (18 March 1782), B.87/a/4:27b (16 April 1782).

89   *Cumberland House Journals and Inland Journals, Second Series*, 297.

CHAPTER 4—DESPAIR AND DEATH DURING THE FUR TRADE WARS, 1783-1821

1   Dale Russell, *Eighteenth-Century Western Cree and Their Neighbours* (Ottawa: Canadian Museum of Civilization, 1991), 216. See also Chris Hanks, "The Swampy Cree and the Hudson's Bay Company at Oxford House," *Ethnohistory* 29 (1982): 103–15, 216; Laura Peers, *The Ojibwa of Western Canada, 1780–1870* (Winnipeg: University of Manitoba Press, 1994), 14–21; Jack Frisch, "Some Ethnological and Ethnohistorical Notes of the Iroquois in Alberta," *Man in the Northeast* 7 (1976): 51–64; Gertrude Nicks, "The Iroquois and the Fur Trade in Western Canada," in *Old Trails and New Directions: Papers of the Third North American Fur Trade Conference*, edited by C. M. Judd and A. J. Ray (Toronto: University of Toronto Press, 1980), 85–101.

2   Patricia Albers, "Changing Patterns of Ethnicity in the Northwestern Plains, 1780–1870," in *History, Power, and Identity: Ethnogenesis in the Americas, 1492–1992*, edited by Jonathan Hill (Iowa City: University of Iowa Press, 1996), 100; John Milloy, *The Plains Cree: Trade, Diplomacy, and Warfare, 1790–1870*, Manitoba Studies in Native History (Winnipeg: University of Manitoba Press, 1988); Peers, *The Ojibwa of Western Canada;* Jacqueline Peterson and J. S. H. Brown, eds., *The New Peoples: Being and Becoming Métis in North America*, Manitoba Studies in Native History (Winnipeg: University of Manitoba Press, 1985).

3   A. S Morton, *The Journal of Duncan M'Gillivray of the North West Company at Fort George on the Saskatchewan, 1794–5* (Toronto: Macmillan of Canada, 1927), 166.

4   T. F. Ball, "Historical and Instrumental Evidence of Climate: Western Hudson's Bay, Canada, 1714–1850," in *Climate since A.D. 1500*, edited by Raymond S. Bradley and Philip D. Jones (London: Routledge, 1995), 40–73. For a discussion of the plains drought, 1792–1804, see David Sauchyn and Walter Skinner, "A Proxy Record of Drought Severity for the Southwestern Canadian Plains," *Canadian Water Resources Journal* 26 (2001): 253–72.

5   Elliot Coues, ed., *New Light on the Early History of the Greater Northwest: The Manuscript Journals of Alexander Henry and David Thompson, 1799–1814*, 2 vols. (Minneapolis: Ross and Haines, 1965), 1: 292–93; Alexander Mackenzie, *Voyages from Montreal on the River St. Lawrence through the Continent of North America to the Frozen and Pacific Oceans in the Years 1789 and 1793* (Edmonton: Hurtig Publishers, 1971), xiv; A. S. Morton, *A History of the Canadian West to 1870–71* (Toronto: University of Toronto Press, 1973), 329; John

McDonnell, "The Red River by John McDonnell of the North West Company (about 1797)," in *Les Bourgeois de la Compagnie du Nord-Ouest,* vol. 1, edited by L. R. Masson (New York: Antiquarian Press, 1960), 270–71; Alice M. Johnson, ed., *Saskatchewan Journals and Correspondence: Edmonton House, 1795–1800, Chesterfield House, 1800–1802* (London: Hudson's Bay Record Society, 1967), xviin1.

6 E. E. Rich, *A History of the Hudson's Bay Company, 1670–1870,* 3 vols. (London: Hudson's Bay Record Society, 1959), 2: 83–89.

7 Harry Duckworth, ed., *The English River Book: A Northwest Company Journal and Account Book of 1786* (Montreal: McGill-Queen's University Press, 1990), xvi. See also Morton, *A History of the Canadian West to 1870–71,* 335; J. M. Bumsted, *The Fur Trade Wars: The Founding of Western Canada* (Winnipeg: Great Plains Publications, 1999), 24.

8 Duckworth, ed., *The English River Book,* xxiii; Gerald Friesen, *The Canadian Prairies: A History* (Toronto: University of Toronto Press, 1984), 59.

9 Milloy, *The Plains Cree,* 29.

10 HBCA, Cumberland House Post Journal B.49/a/7:32b (7 January 1779); Theodore Binnema, *Common and Contested Ground: A Human and Environmental History of the North American Plains* (Norman: University of Oklahoma Press, 2001), 109.

11 David G. Mandelbaum, *The Plains Cree: An Ethnographic, Historical, and Comparative Study* (Regina: Canadian Plains Research Center, 1979); Arthur J. Ray, *Indians in the Fur Trade: Their Role as Trappers, Hunters, and Middlemen in the Lands Southwest of Hudson Bay* (Toronto: University of Toronto Press, 1974); Russell, *Eighteenth-Century Western Cree and Their Neighbours.*

12 David Meyer and Dale Russell, "'So Fine and Pleasant, beyond Description': The Lands and Lives of the Pegogamaw Crees," *Plains Anthropologist* 49 (2004): 240–42; Charles Bishop, "Northern Ojibwa Emergence: The Migration," in *Papers of the 33rd Algonquian Conference,* edited by H. C. Wolfart (Winnipeg: University of Manitoba Press, 2002), 14–15.

13 David Meyer and Dale Russell, "The Selkirk Composite of Central Canada: A Reconsideration," *Arctic Anthropology* 24 (1987): 17; Meyer and Russell, "'So Fine and Pleasant, beyond Description,'" 219–35.

14 This northern alliance was in opposition to a southern alliance, led by the Shoshone, who had expanded above the forty-ninth parallel. Milloy, *The Plains Cree,* xv. David Smyth has attacked this view, stating that there was no Blackfoot–Cree alliance in the eighteenth century, though he accepted the notion that they had a common cause in their opposition to the Snakes; see "The Niitsitapi Trade: Euroamericans and the Blackfoot Speaking Peoples to the Mid 1830s" (Ph.D. diss., Carleton University, 2001), 127. Binnema, *Common and Contested Ground,* 15, characterized the relationship between the Cree and Blackfoot through the period as a "coalition," somewhere between the interpretations of Milloy and Smyth.

15 Matthew Cocking, "An Adventurer from Hudson Bay: The Journal of Matthew Cocking from York Factory to the Blackfoot Country," edited by J. L. Burpee, *Proceedings and Transactions of the Royal Society of Canada,* series 3, section 2 (1908): 111.

16 HBCA, Hudson House Post Journal, B.87/a/6:16 (26 October 1782).

17 Binnema, *Common and Contested Ground,* 145.

18 HBCA, B.87/a/5; B.87/a/6:13b–14 (19 October 1782).

19 This was the first documented direct trade with any member of the Niitsitapi alliance, though some trade probably occurred with the French or Canadians at an earlier date. Smyth, "The Niitsitapi Trade," 159.

20 Binnema, *Common and Contested Ground,* 140.

21 Ibid., 108–09, 145.

22 John Nicks, "The Pine Island Posts, 1786–1794: A Study of Competition in the Fur Trade" (MA thesis, University of Alberta, 1975), 152; HBCA, B.121/a/2:35 (1 May 1788). See also Binnema, *Common and Contested Ground,* 149, 153; HBCA, B.205/a/3:10–10b (12 September 1788).

23 Loretta Fowler, *Shared Symbols, Contested Meanings: Gros Ventre Culture and History, 1778–1984* (Ithaca, NY: Cornell University Press, 1987), 42; HBCA, B.205/a/7:21b (14 March 1794); Gary Doige, "Warfare Patterns of the Assiniboine to 1809" (MA thesis, University of Manitoba, 1987), 141.

24   HBCA, B.205/a/8:31 (25 October 1793).

25   HBCA, 205/a/8:32 (8 November 1793).

26   Smyth, "The Niitsitapi Trade," 225.

27   Binnema, *Common and Contested Ground*, 160; University of Toronto, Thomas Fisher Rare Book Room, David Thompson Papers, Thompson Narrative MSS III, reel 1264, 167.

28   Nicks, "The Pine Island Posts," 124ns124-25. The ceremonial role of liquor in the development and maintenance of trade relations is well documented. See Jack O. Waddell, "Malhiot's Journal: An Ethnohistoric Assessment of Chippewa Alcohol Behaviour in the Early Nineteenth Century," *Ethnohistory* 32 (1985): 246-68; Bruce M. White, "A Skilled Game of Exchange: Ojibwa Fur Trade Protocol," *Minnesota History* 50 (1987): 235-36; Morton, *A History of the Canadian West to 1870-71*, 306-07; Marshall G. Hurlich, "Historical and Recent Demography of the Algonkians of Northern Ontario," in *Boreal Forest Adaptations: The Northern Algonkians*, edited by A. T. Steegmann (New York: Plenum Press, 1983), 176-78.

29   Edward Umfreville, *The Present State of Hudson's Bay*, edited by W. S. Wallace (Toronto: Ryerson Press, 1954), 30. Umfreville was a committed opponent of the HBC. See Rich, *The History of the Hudson's Bay Company*, 2: 124, for the company's rebuttal.

30   Nicks, "The Pine Island Posts," 122-23; Rich, *The History of the Hudson's Bay Company*, 2: 227-28.

31   William Tomison to James Swain, 26 April 1796, Johnson, ed., *Saskatchewan Journals and Correspondence*, 57.

32   Harold Hickerson, "The Journal of Charles Jean Baptiste Chaboillez, 1797-1798," *Ethnohistory* 6 (1959): 276-93.

33   Coues, ed., *New Light on the Early History of the Greater Northwest*, 2: 452.

34   *A Narrative of the Captivity and Adventures of John Tanner during Thirty Years Residence among the Indians in the Interior of North America*, edited by Edwin James (Minneapolis: Ross and Haines, 1956), 98.

35   Rich, *The History of the Hudson's Bay Company*, 2: 228-29.

36   Coues, ed., *New Light on the Early History of the Greater Northwest*, 2: 542.

37   Peers, *The Ojibwa of Western Canada*, 17; Hickerson, "Journal of Charles Jean Baptiste Chaboillez," 270.

38   Castoreum is a secretion from glands in the groin of a beaver that, when rubbed on traps, attracts other beavers.

39   Coues, ed., *New Light on the Early History of the Greater Northwest*, 2: 477.

40   Entry of 8 September 1799, Johnson, ed., *Saskatchewan Journals and Correspondence*, 213.

41   Entry of 17 October 1799, ibid., 216; James G. MacGregor, *Peter Fidler: Canada's Forgotten Surveyor, 1769-1822* (Toronto: McClelland and Stewart, 1966), 116, 121-22.

42   Kerry Abel, *Drum Songs: Glimpses of Dene History* (Montreal: McGill-Queen's University Press, 1993), 79-80.

43   Coues, ed., *New Light on the Early History of the Greater Northwest*, 1: 144-45.

44   Morton, *A History of the Canadian West to 1870-71*, 431.

45   Alexander Henry, entry of 1 March 1804, Coues, ed., *New Light on the Early History of the Greater Northwest*, 1: 239.

46   Provincial Archives of Manitoba (hereafter PAM), MG 2 A 1, Selkirk Papers, Coltman to Selkirk, Red River, 17 July 1817, 3814.

47   Rich, *The History of the Hudson's Bay Company, 1670-1870*, 2: 180.

48   Margorie Wilkins Campbell, *The North-West Company* (Toronto: Macmillan, 1955), 108-11.

49   Ray, *Indians in the Fur Trade*, 130.

50   Johnson, ed., *Saskatchewan Journals and Correspondence*, xc; MacGregor, *Peter Fidler*, 238-39.

51   MacGregor, *Peter Fidler*, 156.

52   Gertrude Nicks, "Demographic Anthropology of Native Populations in Western Canada, 1800-1975" (Ph.D. diss., University of Alberta, 1980), 56.

53   Johnson, ed., *Saskatchewan Journals and Correspondence*, xcii. See also Paul Thistle, *Indian-European Trade Relations in the Lower Saskatchewan River Region to 1840*, Manitoba Studies in Native History (Winnipeg: University of Manitoba Press, 1986), 73.

54 John Foster, "Wintering, the Outsider Adult Male, and the Ethnogenesis of the Western Plains Métis," *Prairie Forum* 19 (1994): 7; Johnson, ed., *Saskatchewan Journals and Correspondence*, 311–16; MacGregor, *Peter Fidler*, 140–41; Michael K. Trimble, "Chronology of Epidemics among Plains Village Horticulturalists, 1738–1838," *Southwestern Lore* 54 (1988): 13; Garrick Mallery, *Picture-Writing of the American Indians*, vol. 1 (New York: Dover Publications, 1972), 273, 313. Also see Fowler, *Shared Symbols, Contested Meanings*, 43–46; Decker, "'We Should Never Be Again the Same People,'" 86–89; Frisch, "Some Ethnological and Ethnohistoric Notes on the Iroquois of Alberta," 53.

55 Entry of 13 October 1818, *Sixteen Years in the Indian Country: The Journal of Daniel Williams Harmon, 1800–1816*, edited by W. Kaye Lamb (Toronto: Macmillan, 1957), 193; MacGregor, *Peter Fidler*, 105; Coues, ed., *New Light on the Early History of the Greater Northwest*, 647.

56 Angus Shaw to Joseph Colen, Fort Augustus, 10 May 1797, Johnson, ed., *Saskatchewan Journals and Correspondence*, xxxii–xxxiii.

57 Theodore J. Karamanski, "The Iroquois and the Fur Trade of the Far West," *Beaver* 312 (1982): 7.

58 Entry of 3 May 1797, Johnson, ed., *Saskatchewan Journals and Correspondence*, 92.

59 *A Narrative of the Captivity and Adventures of John Tanner*, 88–89.

60 Robert Brightman, "Conservation and Resource Depletion: The Case of the Boreal Forest Algonkians," in *The Question of the Commons: The Culture and Ecology of Communal Resources*, edited by Bonnie McCay and James Acheson (Tucson: University of Arizona Press, 1987), 133.

61 Ray, *Indians in the Fur Trade*, 119.

62 *A Narrative of the Captivity and Adventures of John Tanner*, 95–98.

63 Calvin Martin, *Keepers of the Game: Indian–Animal Relationships and the Fur Trade* (Berkeley: University of California Press, 1978), 140–41.

64 Ibid., 138–39. *F. tularensis* is transmitted to humans "by the bite of an infected tick or other blood sucking insect; by direct contact with infected animals; by eating inadequately prepared meat or by drinking water that contains the organism." *Taber's Cyclopedic Medical Dictionary*, 16th ed., edited by Clayton L. Thomas (Philadelphia: F. A. Davis, 1989), 1921.

65 Coues, ed., *New Light on the Early History of the Greater Northwest*, 1: 135, 153, 161.

66 Ibid., 203.

67 Paul Hackett, *"A Very Remarkable Sickness": Epidemics in the Petit Nord, 1670 to 1846* (Winnipeg: University of Manitoba Press, 2002), 257.

68 William Tomison, entry of 12 January 1796, Johnson, ed., *Saskatchewan Journals and Correspondence*, 24–25, 128, 161–67.

69 Umfreville, *The Present State of Hudson's Bay*, 19.

70 Simples are concoctions, usually teas or lotions, made from a single medicinal plant; *Voyages from Montreal*, xcv.

71 Coues, ed., *New Light on the Early History of the Greater Northwest*, 2: 516.

72 *Sixteen Years in the Indian Country*, 200.

73 Saskatchewan Archives Board (hereafter SAB), R. G. Ferguson Papers, microfilm 2.391.

74 James Parker, *Emporium of the North: Fort Chipewyan and the Fur Trade to 1835* (Regina: Canadian Plains Research Center, 1987), 47. See also Johnson, ed., *Saskatchewan Journals and Correspondence*, xxvii.

75 Rich, *The History of the Hudson's Bay Company*, 2: 196.

76 Cited in W. A. Sloan, "The Native Response to the Extension of the European Traders into the Athabasca Country and the Mackenzie Basin, 1770–1816," *Canadian Historical Review* 60 (1979): 291.

77 Abel, *Drum Songs*, 78.

78 Sloan, "The Native Response to the Extension of the European Traders," 291.

79 27 March 1807, Masson, ed., *Les Bourgeois de la Compagnie du Nord-Ouest*, 1: 95.

80 James Parker, "Fort Chipewyan and the Early Fur Trade," in *Proceedings of the Fort Chipewyan and Fort Vermilion Bicentennial Conference*, edited by P. McCormack and R. G. Ironside (Edmonton: Boreal Institute for Northern Studies, 1990), 42.

81 NWC fur returns from Athabasca dropped from 648 packs in 1799 to only 182 packs in 1803. Sloan, "The Native Response to the Extension of the European Traders," 293.

82 The second number is a combined total of 16,299 for the NWC and 5,000 for the XY Company. After the merger of the two competitors, the level of alcohol was reduced to an annual average of 9,700 gallons. J. C. Yerbury, *The Subarctic Indians and the Fur Trade, 1680–1860* (Vancouver: UBC Press, 1986), 69; MacGregor, *Peter Fidler*, 148.

83 Letter to Roderick Mackenzie, 27 March 1807, Masson, ed., *Les Bourgeois de la Compagnie du Nord-Ouest*, 1: 95–96.

84 Sloan, "The Native Response to the Extension of the European Traders," 292–93.

85 Yerbury, *The Subarctic Indians and the Fur Trade*, 138.

86 Sloan, "The Native Response to the Extension of the European Traders," 292.

87 Yerbury, *The Subarctic Indians and the Fur Trade*, 71.

88 Sloan, "The Native Response to the Extension of the European Traders," 295.

89 Beryl C. Gillespie, "An Ethnohistory of the Yellowknives: A Northern Athapaskan Tribe," in *Contributions to Anthropology, 1975*, edited by David Brez Carlisle, Mercury Series, Canadian Ethnology Service Paper 31 (Ottawa: National Museum of Man, 1975), 209.

90 Yerbury, *The Subarctic Indians and the Fur Trade*, 73–74.

91 Rich, *The History of the Hudson's Bay Company*, 2: 229.

92 Ibid., 230.

93 Sloan, "The Native Response to the Extension of the European Traders," 295–96; Yerbury, *The Subarctic Indians and the Fur Trade*, 74; MacGregor, *Peter Fidler*, 157; Rich, *The History of the Hudson's Bay Company*, 2: 230; Heather Devine, "Miles Macdonnell and the Decline of the Northwest Company," in *New Faces of the Fur Trade: Selected Papers of the Seventh North American Fur Trade Conference*, edited by J. Fiske, Susan Sleeper-Smith, and William Wicken (East Lansing: Michigan State University Press, 1998), 255.

94 Entry of 10 April 1805, *Sixteen Years in the Indian Country*, 87.

95 MacGregor, *Peter Fidler*, 149, 172.

96 Rich, *The History of the Hudson's Bay Company*, 2: 274; Sloan, "The Native Response to the Extension of the European Traders," 297.

97 Yerbury, *The Subarctic Indians and the Fur Trade*, 107.

98 Letter to Roderick Mackenzie, 27 March 1807, Masson, ed., *Les Bourgeois de la Compagnie du Nord-Ouest*, 1: 86, 92. See also June Helm, "Female Infanticide, European Diseases, and Population Levels among Mackenzie Dene," *American Ethnologist* 7 (1980): 259–85; Shepard Krech III, "The Influence of Disease and the Fur Trade on Arctic Drainage Lowlands Dene, 1800–1850," *Journal of Anthropological Research* 39 (1983): 123–46.

99 Yerbury, *The Subarctic Indians and the Fur Trade*, 102, 150.

100 Shepard Krech III, "The Trade of the Slavey and Dogrib at Fort Simpson in the Early Nineteenth Century," in *The Subarctic Fur Trade: Native Social and Economic Adaptations*, edited by Shepard Krech III (Vancouver: UBC Press, 1984), 107.

101 George Keith to Roderick Mackenzie, 7 January 1807, Masson, ed., *Les Bourgeois de la Compagnie du Nord-Ouest*, 2: 68.

102 George Keith to Roderick Mackenzie, 1 December 1808, ibid., 2: 79.

103 *Sixteen Years in the Indian Country*, 120.

104 Willard Wentzel to Roderick Mackenzie, 30 April 1811, Masson, ed., *Les Bourgeois de la Compagnie du Nord-Ouest*, 1: 106–07.

105 SAB, R. G. Ferguson Papers, microfilm 2.391; Brightman, "Conservation and Resource Depletion," 124–25.

106 George Keith to Roderick Mackenzie, 5 January 1812, Masson, ed., *Les Bourgeois de la Compagnie du Nord-Ouest*, 2: 97.

107 Yerbury, *The Subarctic Indians and the Fur Trade*, 81; George Keith to Roderick Mackenzie, 8 November 1812, Masson, ed., *Les Bourgeois de la Compagnie du Nord-Ouest*, 2: 98; John McDonald of Garth, Autobiographical Notes, ibid., 42.

108 Krech, "The Influence of Disease and the Fur Trade on Arctic Drainage Lowlands Dene," 134; George Keith to Roderick Mackenzie, 15 January 1814, Masson, ed., *Les Bourgeois de la Compagnie du Nord-Ouest*, 2: 125–26.

109 George Keith to Roderick Mackenzie, Mackenzie River Forks, 15 January 1814, Masson, ed., *Les Bourgeois de la Compagnie du Nord-Ouest*, 2: 125–26.

110 Willard Wentzel to Roderick Mackenzie, 28 February 1814, Masson, ed., *Les Bourgeois de la Compagnie du Nord-Ouest*, 1: 109–10. See also Yerbury, *The Subarctic Indians and the Fur Trade*, 81. At Reindeer Lake, rumours circulated that the Chipewyan were plotting to destroy both the Canadian and the HBC posts there. Abel, *Drum Songs*, 81.

111 Theodore J. Karamanski, *Fur Trade and Exploration: Opening the Far Northwest, 1821-1852* (Norman: University of Oklahoma Press 1983), 19.

112 This was the ill-fated "Pemmican Proclamation" issued by Miles Macdonnell of the HBC on 8 January 1814. Bumsted, *Fur Trade Wars*, 93–257; Ann M. Carlos and Elizabeth Hoffman, "The North American Fur Trade: Bargaining to a Joint Profit Maximum under Incomplete Information, 1804-1821," *Journal of Economic History* 46 (1986): 980–81.

113 Edith Burley, *Servants of the Honourable Company: Work, Discipline, and Conflict in the Hudson's Bay Company, 1770-1879* (Don Mills, ON: Oxford University Press, 1997), 225–32.

114 Shirley Ann Smith, "Crossed Swords: Colin Robertson and the Athabasca Campaign," in *Proceedings of the Fort Chipewyan and Fort Vermilion Bicentennial Conference*, edited by Patricia McCormack and R. Geoffrey Ironside (Edmonton: Boreal Institute for Northern Studies, 1990), 69–74; MacGregor, *Peter Fidler*, 173.

115 Rich, *The History of the Hudson's Bay Company*, 2: 316; Carlos and Hoffman, "The North American Fur Trade," 981–82; Ann M. Carlos, "The Birth and Death of Predatory Competition in the North American Fur Trade: 1810-1821," *Explorations in Economic History* 19 (1982): 164n25.

116 Willard Wentzel to George Keith, 28 May 1816, Masson, ed., *Les Bourgeois de la Compagnie du Nord-Ouest*, 1: 117.

117 T. F. Ball, "The Year without a Summer: Its Impact on the Fur Trade and History of Western Canada," in *The Year without a Summer: World Climate in 1816*, edited by C. R. Harington (Ottawa: Canadian Museum of Nature, 1992), 196–202; Roger Stuffling and Ron Fritz, "The Ecology of a Famine: Northwestern Ontario in 1815–17," in *The Year without a Summer: World Climate in 1816*, edited by C. R. Harington (Ottawa: Canadian Museum of Nature, 1992), 203–17.

118 Willard Wentzel to George Keith, 28 May 1816, Masson, ed., *Les Bourgeois de la Compagnie du Nord-Ouest*, 1: 117.

119 Entry of 23 November 1816, *Sixteen Years in the Indian Country*, 65, 189.

120 Peers, *The Ojibwa of Western Canada*, 65, 72.

121 MacGregor, *Peter Fidler*, 208; Krech, "The Influence of Disease and the Fur Trade on Arctic Drainage Lowlands Dene," 133.

122 Milloy, *The Plains Cree*, 62; Jody Decker, "Depopulation of the Northern Plains Natives," *Social Science Medicine* 33 (1991): 386.

123 Krech, "The Influence of Disease and the Fur Trade on Arctic Drainage Lowlands Dene," 133; Yerbury, *The Subarctic Indians and the Fur Trade*, 89; Harmon, entry of 1 September 1817, *Sixteen Years in the Indian Country*, 191.

124 Willard Wentzel to Roderick Mackenzie, 5 April 1819, Masson, ed., *Les Bourgeois de la Compagnie du Nord-Ouest*, 1: 122.

125 Sloan, "The Native Response to the Extension of the European Traders," 299.

126 Hackett, "*A Very Remarkable Sickness*," 274–75.

127 Letter to to Roderick Mackenzie, 23 May 1820, Masson, ed., *Les Bourgeois de la Compagnie du Nord-Ouest*, 1: 130.

128 Milloy, *The Plains Cree*, 87.

129 Ray, *Indians in the Fur Trade*, 108; Hackett, "*A Very Remarkable Sickness*," 275–76.

130 Decker, "Depopulation of the Northern Plains Natives," 385–86; Ray, *Indians in the Fur Trade*, 108.

131 Abel Watetch, *Payepot and His People* (Regina: Saskatchewan History and Folklore Society, 1959), 10–12.

132 Hackett, "*A Very Remarkable Sickness*," 276–85.

133 Ibid., 277, 286–87; Trimble, "Chronology of Epidemics among Plains Village Horticulturalists," 18.

134 Hackett, "*A Very Remarkable Sickness*," 277.

135 Nicks, "Demographic Anthropology of Native Populations in Western Canada," 50.

136 SAB, R. G. Ferguson Papers, microfilm 2.391.
137 HBCA, B.89/a/4:13 (21 November 1819), 16b (25 January 1820).
138 Yerbury, *The Subarctic Indians and the Fur Trade*, 87–89.
139 SAB, R. G. Ferguson Papers, microfilm 2.391.
140 Entry of 13 October 1820, *Journal of Occurrences in the Athabasca Department by George Simpson, 1820 and 1821, and Report*, edited by E. E. Rich (Toronto: Champlain Society, 1938), 81. Rich wrongly attributed the cause of mortality to smallpox.
141 The dispersal of the Chipewyan to avoid contagion might have contributed to the development of the distinct group known after 1821 as the Caribou Eater Chipewyan. James G.E. Smith, "Local Band Organization of the Caribou Eater Chipewyan in the Eighteenth and Early Nineteenth Centuries," *Western Canadian Journal of Anthropology* 6 (1976): 80.
142 Yerbury, *The Subarctic Indians and the Fur Trade*, 150.
143 Letter to Roderick Mackenzie, 23 May 1820, Masson, ed., *Les Bourgeois de la Compagnie du Nord-Ouest*, 1: 127.
144 Carlos, "The Birth and Death of Predatory Competition in the North American Fur Trade," 181.

CHAPTER 5—EXPANSION OF SETTLEMENT AND EROSION OF HEALTH DURING THE HBC MONOPOLY, 1821–69

1 J. C. Yerbury, *The Subarctic Indians and the Fur Trade, 1680–1860* (Vancouver: UBC Press, 1986), 92; James R. Gibson, *Farming the Frontier: The Agricultural Opening of the Oregon Country, 1786–1846* (Seattle: University of Washington Press, 1985), 9–27.
2 Arthur J. Ray, "Some Conservation Schemes of the Hudson's Bay Company, 1821–50: An Examination of the Problems of Resource Management in the Fur Trade," *Journal of Historical Geography* 1 (1975): 53.
3 Edith Burley, *Servants of the Honourable Company: Work, Discipline, and Conflict in the Hudson's Bay Company, 1770–1879* (Don Mills, ON: Oxford University Press, 1997), 6; D. B. Freeman and F. L. Dungey, "A Spatial Duopoly: Competition in Western Canadian Fur Trade, 1770–1835," *Journal of Historical Geography* 7 (1981): 268–70.
4 Carol Judd, "Native Labour and Social Stratification in the Hudson's Bay Northern Department, 1770–1870," *Canadian Review of Sociology and Anthropology* 17 (1980): 307. See also Glen Makahonuk, "Wage Labour in the Economy of the Northwest Fur Economy, 1760–1849," *Saskatchewan History* 41 (1988): 7–8; Ron Bourgeault, "The Indian, the Métis, and the Fur Trade: Class, Sexism, and Racism in the Transition from 'Communism' to Capitalism," *Studies in Political Economy* 12 (1983): 64.
5 *Minutes of Council, Northern Department of Rupert Land, 1821–1831*, edited by R. Harvey Fleming (Toronto: Champlain Society, 1940), 229.
6 Paul Hackett, *"A Very Remarkable Sickness": Epidemics in the Petit Nord, 1670 to 1846* (Winnipeg: University of Manitoba Press, 2002), 156.
7 Renée Fossett, *In Order to Live Untroubled: Inuit of the Central Arctic, 1550–1940*, Manitoba Studies in Native History (Winnipeg: University of Manitoba Press, 2001), 115, 140.
8 R. Grace Morgan, "Beaver Ecology/Beaver Mythology" (Ph.D. diss., University of Alberta, 1991), 156–57.
9 John MacLean, *McDougall of Alberta: A Life of Rev. John McDougall D.D., Pathfinder of Empire and Prophet of the Plains* (Toronto: F.C. Stephenson, 1927), 38; John West, *The Substance of a Journal during a Residence at the Red River Colony, British North America in the Years 1820–1823* (Vancouver: Alcuin Society, 1967), 37; Alfred Crosby, "Virgin Soil Epidemics as a Factor in the Aboriginal Depopulation in America," *William and Mary Quarterly* 33 (1976): 290–91.
10 Paul Hackett, "Averting Disaster: The Hudson's Bay Company and Smallpox in Western Canada during the Eighteenth and Early Nineteenth Centuries," *Bulletin of the History of Medicine* 78 (2004): 594–95.
11 Laura Peers, *The Ojibwa of Western Canada, 1780–1870* (Winnipeg: University of Manitoba Press, 1994), 130.

12 Burley, *Servants of the Honourable Company*, 127.
13 Donna G. Sutherland, *Peguis: A Noble Friend* (St. Andrews, MB: Chief Peguis Heritage Park, 2003), 38.
14 West, *The Substance of a Journal*, 117–19.
15 Laura Peers and Theresa Schenk, eds., *My First Years in the Fur Trade: The Journals of 1802–1804, George Nelson* (Montreal: McGill-Queen's University Press, 2002), 80–81.
16 Caitlin Pepperell et al., "Dispersal of *Mycobacterium tuberculosis* via the Canadian Fur Trade," *Proceedings of the National Academy of Sciences* (2011), 6526-6531.
17 Burley, *Servants of the Honourable Company*, 55–56.
18 A. S. Morton, *A History of the Canadian West to 1870–71* (Toronto: University of Toronto Press, 1973), 640; E. E. Rich, *A History of the Hudson's Bay Company, 1670–1870*, 3 vols. (London: Hudson's Bay Record Society, 1959), 2: 477–78.
19 Peers, *The Ojibwa of Western Canada*, 102; Paul Thistle, *Indian–White Trade Relations in the Lower Saskatchewan River Region to 1840*, (Winnipeg: University of Manitoba Press, 1986), 91–92.
20 Peers, *The Ojibwa of Western Canada*, 101–02.
21 Shepard Krech III, "The Influence of Disease and the Fur Trade on Arctic Drainage Lowlands Dene, 1800–1850," *Journal of Anthropological Research* 39 (1983): 132–33; Gertrude Nicks, "Demographic Anthropology of Native Populations in Western Canada, 1800–1975" (Ph.D. diss., University of Alberta, 1980), 51.
22 Rich, *A History of the Hudson's Bay Company*, 2: 471–72.
23 Arthur J. Ray, "Periodic Shortages, Native Welfare, and the Hudson's Bay Company, 1670–1930," in *The Subarctic Fur Trade: Native Social and Economic Adaptations*, edited by Shepard Krech III (Vancouver: UBC Press, 1984), 6.
24 Nicks, "Demographic Anthropology of Native Populations in Western Canada," 31.
25 Robin Ridington, "Changes of Mind: Dunne-za Resistance to Empire," *B.C. Studies* 43 (1979): 68; Nicks, "Demographic Anthropology of Native Populations in Western Canada," 51.
26 Peers, *The Ojibwa of Western Canada*, 103.
27 Ray, "Some Conservation Schemes of the Hudson's Bay Company," 55–57.
28 Barry Cooper, *Alexander Kennedy Isbister: A Respectable Critic of the Honourable Company* (Ottawa: Carleton University Press, 1988), 72; Glyndwr Williams, "Introduction," in *Peter Skene Ogden's Snake Country Journals 1827–28 and 1828–29* (London: Hudson's Bay Record Society, 1971), xiv.
29 Knut Fladmark, "Early Fur-Trade Forts of the Peace River Area of British Columbia," *B.C. Studies* 65 (1985): 51–52; David V. Burley, J. Scott Hamilton, and Knut Fladmark, *Prophecy of the Swan: The Upper Peace River Fur Trade of 1794–1823* (Vancouver: UBC Press, 1996), 126, 129; Shepard Krech III, "The Banditte of St. John's," *The Beaver* 313 (1982): 36–41; Shepard Krech III, "The Beaver Indians and the Hostilities at Fort St. John's," *Arctic Anthropology* 20 (1983): 35–45.
30 Ray, "Some Conservation Schemes of the Hudson's Bay Company," 54–55.
31 Milloy, *The Plains Cree: Trade, Diplomacy, and Warfare, 1790–1870*, 65; Hugh Dempsey, *Big Bear: The End of Freedom* (Vancouver: Douglas and McIntyre, 1984), 12–15; Susan Sharrock, "Crees, Cree–Assiniboines, and Assiniboines: Interethnic Social Organization on the far Northern Plains," *Ethnohistory* 21 (1974): 111–15.
32 Jody Decker, "Depopulation of the Northern Plains Natives," *Social Science Medicine* 33 (1991): 388–90.
33 Laura Peers, "Changing Resource-Use Patterns of Saulteaux Trading at Fort Pelly, 1821–1870," in *Aboriginal Resource Use in Canada: Historical and Legal Aspects*, edited by Kerry Abel and Jean Friesen (Winnipeg: University of Manitoba Press, 1991), 105–18.
34 E. S. Rogers, "Cultural Adaptations: The Northern Ojibwa of the Boreal Forest 1670–1980," in *Boreal Forest Adaptations: The Northern Algonkians*, edited by A.T. Steegmann (New York: Plenum Press, 1983), 108.
35 Marshall Hurlich, "Historical and Recent Demography of the Algonkians of Northern Ontario," in *Boreal Forest Adaptations: The Northern Algonkians*, edited by A.T. Steegmann (New York: Plenum Press, 1983), 170.

36   Ray, "Periodic Shortages, Native Welfare, and the Hudson's Bay Company," 10.

37   Judd, "Native Labour and Social Stratification in the Hudson's Bay Company's Northern Department," 307.

38   Morton, *A History of the Canadian West to 1870–71*, 698; Robert Brightman, "Conservation and Resource Depletion: The Case of the Boreal Forest Algonkians," in *The Question of the Commons: The Culture and Ecology of Communal Resources*, edited by Bonnie McCay and James Acheson (Tucson: University of Arizona Press, 1987), 137.

39   Brightman, "Conservation and Resource Depletion," 135.

40   Katherine L. Reedy-Maschner and Herbert D. G. Maschner, "Marauding Middlemen: Western Expansion and Violent Conflict in the Subarctic," *Ethnohistory* 46 (1999): 712.

41   Shepard Krech III, *The Ecological Indian: Myth and History* (New York: W.W. Norton and Company, 1999), 194; Thistle, *Indian–European Trade Relations in the Lower Saskatchewan River Region to 1840*, 88.

42   Martha McCarthy, *To Evangelize the Nations: Roman Catholic Missions in Manitoba, 1818–1870* (Winnipeg: Manitoba Culture, Heritage and Recreation, Historic Resources, 1990), 51.

43   Burley, *Servants of the Honourable Company*, 102, 107–08.

44   Aborigines' Protection Society, *Canada West and the Hudson's Bay Company: A Political and Humane Question of Vital Importance to the Honour of Great Britain, to the Prosperity of Canada, and to the Existence of the Native Tribes; Being an Address to the Right Honourable Henry Labouchere, Her Majesty's Principal Secretary of State for the Colonies* (London: William Tweedie, 1856), 3.

45   McCarthy, *To Evangelize the Nations*,16. See also David McCrady, "Living with Strangers: The Nineteenth-Century Sioux and the Canadian–American Borderlands" (Ph.D. diss., University of Manitoba, 1998), 20–27; Milloy, *The Plains Cree*, 111; Ron Rivard and Catherine Littlejohn, *The History of the Métis of Willow Bunch* (Saskatoon: Apex Graphics, 2003), 58–68.

46   Milloy, *The Plains Cree*, 99; Ray, "Periodic Shortages, Native Welfare, and the Hudson's Bay Company," 5.

47   Frank G. Roe, *The North American Buffalo: A Critical Study of the Species in Its Wild State* (Toronto: University of Toronto Press, 1970), 396.

48   Jeffrey Ostler, *The Plains Sioux and U.S. Colonialism from Lewis and Clark to Wounded Knee* (Cambridge, UK: Cambridge University Press, 2004), 57–58.

49   John Foster, "Wintering, the Outsider Adult Male, and the Ethnogenesis of the Western Plains Métis," *Prairie Forum* 19 (1994): 1–15.

50   J.G. MacGregor, *John Rowand: Czar of the Prairies* (Saskatoon: Western Producer Prairie Books, 1978), 88–89.

51   Milloy, *The Plains Cree*, 105.

52   Hackett, *"A Very Remarkable Sickness,"* 172. See also Arthur J. Ray, "Diffusion of Diseases in the Western Interior of Canada, 1830–1850," *Geographical Review* 66 (1976): 139–57.

53   Hackett, *"A Very Remarkable Sickness,"* 161.

54   Samuel G. Morton, *Illustrations of Pulmonary Consumption: Its Anatomical Characters, Causes, Symptoms, and Treatment* (Philadelphia: E.C. Biddle, 1837), 312–13.

55   Hackett, *"A Very Remarkable Sickness,"* 162–63.

56   Milloy, *The Plains Cree*, 65.

57   Fossett, *In Order to Live Untroubled*, 140.

58   Michael K. Trimble, "Chronology of Epidemics among Plains Village Horticulturalists, 1738–1838," *Southwestern Lore* 54 (1988): 23.

59   Morton, *Illustrations of Pulmonary Consumption*, 312–13. The account hinted at the emergence of the disease in the British territory to the north.

60   Michael K. Trimble, "The 1832 Inoculation Program on the Missouri River," in *Disease and Demography in the Americas*, edited by John W. Verano and Douglas Uberlaker (Washington, DC: Smithsonian Institution Press, 1992), 260–63.

61   Ostler, *The Plains Sioux and U.S. Colonialism from Lewis and Clark to Wounded Knee*, 31.

62   Trimble, "The 1832 Inoculation Program on the Missouri River," 257. The epidemic of 1837 is probably the best-documented disease episode on the plains in the nineteenth century.

In the American context, see Milo M. Quaife, ed., "The Smallpox Epidemic on the Upper Missouri," *Mississippi Valley Historical Review* 17 (1930–31): 278–99; Clyde D. Dollar, "The High Plains Smallpox Epidemic of 1837–38," *Western Historical Quarterly* 8 (1977): 15–38; Michael K. Trimble, "The 1837–1838 Smallpox Epidemic on the Upper Missouri," in *Skeletal Biology in the Great Plains: Migration, Warfare, Health, and Subsistence*, edited by Douglas Owsley and Richard Jantz (Washington, DC: Smithsonian Institution Press, 1994): 81–89; K. C. Tessendorf, "Red Death on the Missouri," *American West* 14 (1977): 48–53; R. G. Robertson, *Rotting Face: Smallpox and the American Indian* (Caldwell, ID: Claxton Press, 2001).

63 Ostler, *The Plains Sioux and U.S. Colonialism from Lewis and Clark to Wounded Knee*, 31.

64 Ray, "Diffusion of Diseases in the Western Interior of Canada," 155–56.

65 Arthur J. Ray, *Indians in the Fur Trade: Their Role as Trappers, Hunters, and Middlemen in the Lands Southwest of Hudson Bay* (Toronto: University of Toronto Press, 1974), 193n11.

66 Paul Kane, *Wanderings of an Artist among the Indians of North America, from Canada to Vancouver's Island and Oregon through the Hudson's Bay Territory and Back Again* (Edmonton: Hurtig, 1968), 90.

67 Hackett, *"A Very Remarkable Sickness,"* 447–48; Ray, "Periodic Shortages, Native Welfare, and the Hudson's Bay Company," 1–20.

68 Library and Archives Canada (hereafter LAC), MG 29 B 15, Robert Bell Papers, vol. 61, f. 34, Anonymous, "Reminiscences of One of the Last Descendants of a Bourgeois of the Northwest Company," n.d., 29; Arthur J. Ray, "Smallpox: The Epidemic of 1837," *The Beaver* 306 (1975): 9–11.

69 Peers, *The Ojibwa of Western Canada*, 142.

70 Patricia Albers, "Changing Patterns of Ethnicity in the Northeastern Plains, 1780–1870," in *History, Power, and Identity: Ethnogenesis in the Americas, 1492–1992*, edited by Jonathan Hill (Iowa City: University of Iowa Press, 1996), 104.

71 HBCA, B.159/a/17, Dr. Todd's Journal, 22–23 October 1837, 5; 15 November 1837, 8; 8 December 1837, 9b.

72 Decker, "Depopulation of the Northern Plains Natives," 388.

73 Dan Kennedy, *The Recollections of an Assiniboine Chief/Dan Kennedy (Ochankugahe)*, edited by James Stevens (Toronto: McClelland and Stewart, 1972), 72–73; Ray, *Indians in the Fur Trade*, 187–88.

74 Hugh A. Dempsey, "Smallpox: Scourge of the Plains," in *In Harm's Way: Disasters in Western Canada*, edited by Anthony Rasporich and Max Foran (Calgary: University of Calgary Press, 2004), 26; William Barr, "Lieutenant Aemilius Simpson's Survey: York Factory to Fort Vancouver, 1826," in *Selected Papers of Rupert's Land Colloquium 2000*, compiled by David G. Malaher (Winnipeg: Centre for Rupert's Land Studies, University of Winnipeg, 2000), 7.

75 Hugh A. Dempsey, ed., "Simpson's Essay on the Blackfoot," *Alberta History* 38 (1990): 3.

76 Kennedy stated that the Assiniboine population in 1947 was a mere 3,000, a tenth of what had been estimated at the beginning of the nineteenth century. SAB, Mary Weekes Papers, R-100, vol. 3, f. 40, Dan Kennedy to Mary Weekes, 9 December 1947.

77 James Hector and W. S. W. Vaux, "Notice of the Indians Seen by the Exploring Expedition under the Command of Captain Palliser," *Transactions of the Ethnological Society of London* 1 (1860): 251.

78 Kennedy, *The Recollections of an Assiniboine Chief*, 72–73.

79 Douglas R. Parks and Raymond J. DeMallie, "Sioux, Assiniboine, and Stoney Dialects: A Classification," *Anthropological Linguistics* 34 (1992): 248.

80 Ian A.L. Getty and Erik Gooding, "Stoney," in *The Plains*, edited by Raymond J. DeMallie, vol. 13, part 1, of *Handbook of North American Indians* (Washington, DC: Smithsonian Institution Press, 2001), 596.

81 Gary Doige, "Warfare Patterns of the Assiniboine to 1809" (MA thesis, University of Manitoba, 1987), 172.

82 HBCA, B.159/a/17:9b (8 December 1837), 16b (5 March 1838).

83 HBCA, B.159.a/17:3 (25 September 1837), 3b (5 October 1837).

84 E. Wagner Stearn and Allen E. Stearn, *The Effect of Smallpox on the Destiny of the Amerindian* (Boston: Bruce Humphries Publishers, 1945), 56–57; Hackett, "Averting Disaster," 591.

85 Hackett, "Averting Disaster," 593–606.

86 Arthur J. Ray, "William Todd: Doctor and Trader of the Hudson's Bay Company, 1816–51," *Prairie Forum* 9 (1984): 23.

87 Hackett, "Averting Disaster," 602–06.

88 Michael Payne, *The Most Respectable Place in the Territory: Everyday Life in the Hudson's Bay Service, 1788 to 1870* (Ottawa: Environment Canada, Parks Canada Service, National Historic Parks and Sites, 1989), 93–105.

89 Ibid., 104.

90 Hackett, *"A Very Remarkable Sickness,"* 189.

91 Ray, *Indians in the Fur Trade,* 189.

92 Fritz Pannekoek, "The Reverend James Evans and the Social Antagonisms of Fur Trade Society, 1840–1846," in *Religion and Society and the Prairie West,* edited by Richard Allen (Regina: Canadian Plains Research Center, 1974), 2–3.

93 McCarthy, *To Evangelize the Nations,* 133–40.

94 Ibid., 113.

95 SAB, R-E2033, Edward Ahenakew Papers, "Stanley Mission," 2.

96 Robert Jarvenpa, "The Hudson's Bay Company, the Roman Catholic Church, and the Chipewyan in the Late Fur Trade Period," in *Le Castor Fait Tout: Selected Papers of the Fifth North American Fur Trade Conference, 1985,* edited by B. Trigger, T. Morantz, and L. Dechene (Montreal: Lake St. Louis Historical Society, 1987), 491–92; Ray, "Periodic Shortages, Native Welfare, and the Hudson's Bay Company," 10.

97 J. M. Bumsted, *Trials and Tribulations: The Red River Settlement and the Emergence of Manitoba, 1811–1870* (Winnipeg: Great Plains Publications, 2003), 97–99.

98 John S. Galbraith, "The Hudson's Bay Company under Fire, 1847–62," *Canadian Historical Review* 30 (1949): 322–35, and especially Cooper, *Alexander Kennedy Isbister.* See also A.A. den Otter, "The 1857 Parliamentary Inquiry, the Hudson's Bay Company, and Rupert's Land's Aboriginal People," *Prairie Forum* 24 (1999): 143–70.

99 Cooper, *Alexander Kennedy Isbister,* 107.

100 Ibid., 36, 108–10.

101 For a full discussion of the difficult climatic period in the Arctic, see Fossett, *In Order to Live Untroubled,* 149.

102 J. H. Lefroy to Anna (Lefroy), Fort Simpson, 29 March 1844, in *John Henry Lefroy, in Search of the Magnetic North: A Soldier–Surveyor's Letters from the North-West 1843–1844,* edited by G. F. G. Stanley (Toronto: Macmillan, 1955), 110–11; Morton, *A History of the Canadian West to 1870–71,* 821.

103 Bumsted, *Trials and Tribulations,* 103.

104 John S. Galbraith, *The Hudson's Bay Company as an Imperial Factor, 1821–1869* (Toronto: University of Toronto Press, 1957), 313–16, and especially Frederick Merk, *The Oregon Question: Essays in Anglo-American Diplomacy and Politics* (Cambridge, MA: Harvard University Press, 1967).

105 Hackett, *"A Very Remarkable Sickness,"* 154, 199–236.

106 Paul Hackett, "Historical Mourning Practices Observed among the Cree and Ojibwa Indians of the Central Subarctic," *Ethnohistory* 52 (2005): 522.

107 Hackett, *"A Very Remarkable Sickness,"* 193.

108 Shepard Krech III, "The Early Fur Trade in the Northwestern Subarctic: The Kutchin and the Trade in Beads," in *Le Castor Fait Tout: Selected Papers of the Fifth North American Fur Trade Conference, 1985,* edited by B. Trigger, T. Morantz, and L. Dechêne (Montreal: Lake St. Louis Historical Society, 1987), 264–65.

109 Hackett, *"A Very Remarkable Sickness,"* 199–211.

110 Ibid., 199.

111 Alexander Ross, *The Red River Settlement: Its Rise, Progress, and Present State. With Some Account of the Native Races and Its General History, to the Present Day* (Edmonton: Hurtig, 1972), 362–63.

112 John F. Taylor, "Sociocultural Effects of Epidemics on the Northern Plains: 1734–1850," *Western Canadian Journal of Anthropology* 7 (1977): 56.

113 Ostler, *The Plains Sioux and U.S. Colonialism from Lewis and Clark to Wounded Knee*, 32–33. Among the Brulé Lakota, 500 of a pre-epidemic population of 3,500 died in 1849.

114 Burley, *Servants of the Honourable Company*, 155.

115 Judd, "Native Labour and Social Stratification in the Hudson's Bay Company's Northern Department," 311.

116 Galbraith, *The Hudson's Bay Company as an Imperial Factor*, 61–62; William S. Gladstone, *The Gladstone Diary: Travels in the Early West*, edited by Bruce Haig (Lethbridge: Historic Trails Society of Alberta, 1985), 43; Peers, *The Ojibwa of Western Canada*, 176–79.

117 John Milloy, "Our Country: The Significance of the Buffalo Resource for a Plains Cree Sense of Territory," in *Aboriginal Resource Use in Canada: Historical and Legal Aspects*, edited by Kerry Abel and Jean Friesen (Winnipeg: University of Manitoba Press, 1991), 64; Roe, *The North American Buffalo*, 410.

118 See Henry Youle Hind, *Narrative of the Canadian Red River Exploring Expedition of 1857 and of the Assiniboine and Saskatchewan Expedition of 1858*, 2 vols. (Edmonton: Hurtig, 1971), 1: 99–100.

119 Rupert's Land Research Centre, *An Historical Overview of Aboriginal Lifestyles: The Churchill-Nelson River Drainage Basin* (Winnipeg: Rupert's Land Research Centre, 1992), 133; Peers, *The Ojibwa of Western Canada*, 198; Sutherland, *Peguis*, 139–43.

120 Hind, *Narrative of the Canadian Red River Exploring Expedition of 1857*, 1: 361.

121 Irene Spry, "The Great Transformation: The Disappearance of the Commons in Western Canada," in *Man and Nature on the Prairies*, edited by Richard Allen, Canadian Plains Studies 6 (Regina: Canadian Plains Research Center, 1976), 27; Milloy, *The Plains Cree*, 107.

122 Hector and Vaux, "Notice of the Indians Seen by the Exploring Expedition under the Command of Captain Palliser," 251.

123 Ray, "Diffusion of Diseases in the Western Interior of Canada," 150.

124 Hurlich, "Historical and Recent Demography of the Algonkians of Northern Ontario," 161.

125 John MacLean, *McDougall of Alberta: A Life of Rev. John McDougall D.D., Pathfinder of Empire and Prophet of the Plains* (Toronto: F. C. Stephenson, 1927), 38.

126 Winona Stevenson, "The Journals and Voices of a Church of England Native Catechist: Askenootow (Charles Pratt), 1851–1884," in *Reading beyond Words: Contexts for Native History*, edited by Jennifer S.H. Brown and Elizabeth Vibert (Peterborough: Broadview Press, 1996), 309.

127 A vaccination campaign was undertaken by Dr. William Cowan in 1852. LAC, MG 29 E 8, Robert Bell Papers, Diary of William Cowan, Surgeon to Enrolled Army Pensioners at Fort Garry, 22.

128 Katherine Hughes, *Father Lacombe: The Blackrobe Voyageur* (New York: Moffat, Yard and Company, 1911), 71–72.

129 Hector and Vaux, "Notice of the Indians Seen by the Exploring Expedition under the Command of Captain Palliser," 258–59.

130 David Sauchyn and Walter Skinner, "A Proxy Record of Drought Severity for the Southwestern Canadian Plains," *Canadian Water Resources Journal* 26 (2001): 266.

131 David Smyth, "The Niitsitapi Trade: Euroamericans and the Blackfoot Speaking Peoples to the Mid 1830s" (Ph.D. diss., Carleton University, 2001), 529.

132 Richard T. Wright, *Overlanders: The Epic Cross-Canada Treks for Gold* (Williams Lake, BC: Winter Quarters Press, 2000).

133 Galbraith, "The Hudson's Bay Company under Fire," 333–35.

134 Margaret A. Ormsby, *British Columbia: A History* (Vancouver: Macmillan of Canada, 1958), 134–63; Robin Fisher, *Contact and Conflict: Indian-European Relations in British Columbia, 1774–1890* (Vancouver: UBC Press, 1977), 95–118.

135 Robert T. Boyd, "Demographic History, 1774–1874," in *Northwest Coast*, edited by Wayne Suttles, vol. 7 of *Handbook of North American Indians* (Washington, DC: Smithsonian Institution Press, 1990), 142; Edward Sleigh Hewlett, "The Chilcotin Uprising of 1864," *B.C. Studies* 19 (1973): 63.

136 W. A. Cheadle, *Cheadle's Journal of a Trip across Canada, 1862–63* (Edmonton: Hurtig, 1971), 222.

137 Galbraith, "The Hudson's Bay Company under Fire," 335; Doug Owram, *The Promise of Eden: The Canadian Expansionist Movement and the Idea of the West, 1856–1900* (Toronto: University of Toronto Press, 1980), 38–58.

138 Peers, *The Ojibwa of Western Canada*, 199. See also Cheadle, *Cheadle's Journal of a Trip across Canada*, 121.

139 See, for example, "The Liquor Nuisance," *The Nor' Wester*, 14 August 1860; LAC, MG 19 A 48, Fort Garry Correspondence, Letter to Lawrence Clarke, 9 November 1867, Letter 4, 2.

140 Milloy, *The Plains Cree*, 105.

141 James M. MacGregor, *Senator Hardisty's Prairies, 1849–1889* (Saskatoon: Western Producer Prairie Books, 1978), 68–69. In 1857, the HBC established the first "provisioning" farm at Red River. Carolyn Podruchny, "Farming the Frontier: Agriculture in the Fur Trade, a Case Study of the Provisional Farm at Lower Fort Garry, 1857–1870" (MA thesis, McGill University, 1990).

142 Wayne Moodie and Barry Kaye, "The Northern Limit of Indian Agriculture in North America," *Geographical Review* 59 (1969): 521; Sarah Carter, *Lost Harvests: Prairie Indian Reserve Farmers and Government Policy* (Montreal: McGill-Queen's University Press, 1990), 42–43; Hector and Vaux, "Notice of the Indians Seen by the Exploring Expedition under the Command of Captain Palliser," 248.

143 McCarthy, *To Evangelize the Nations*, 222; T. R. Allsopp, *Agricultural Weather in the Red River Basin of Southern Manitoba over the period 1800 to 1975*, Atmospheric Environment Report CLI-3-77 (Downsview, ON: Fisheries and Environment Canada, 1977), 11–12; Sauchyn and Skinner, "A Proxy Record of Drought Severity for the Southwestern Canadian Plains," 266.

144 Galbraith, *The Hudson's Bay Company as an Imperial Factor*, 387–90.

145 Owram, *Promise of Eden*, 69–80.

146 Gladstone, *The Gladstone Diary*, 68–72.

147 Ibid., 75–81; John S. Collins, *Across the Plains in '64: Incidents of Early Days West of the Missouri River—Two Thousand Miles in an Open Boat from Fort Benton to Omaha—Reminiscences of the Pioneer Period of Galena, General Grant's Old Home* (Omaha: National Printing Company, 1904), 21–23; James Fisk, "Expedition from Fort Abercrombie to Fort Benton," US House of Representatives, 37th Congress, 1863, 22, 29.

148 Milloy, *The Plains Cree*, 114; Abel Watetch, "History of Piapot Reserve," SAB, microfilm 2.75, *School Histories of 35 Indian Reserves*, 1955; Paul M. Raczka, *Winter Count: A History of the Blackfoot People* (Brocket, AB: Oldman River Cultural Centre, 1979), 57.

149 Raczka, *Winter Count*, 55, 60.

150 Hugh A. Dempsey, *A Blackfoot Winter Count*, Occasional Paper 1 (Calgary: Glenbow Museum, 1965), 14; Raczka, *Winter Count*, 56.

151 Martha McCarthy, *From the Great River to the Ends of the Earth: Oblate Missions to the Dene* (Edmonton: University of Alberta Press, 1995), 197.

152 Milloy, *The Plains Cree*, 114.

153 G. Herman Sprenger, "The Métis Nation: Buffalo Hunting vs. Agriculture in the Red River Settlement (circa 1810–1870)," *Western Canadian Journal of Anthropology* 3 (1972): 167; Allsopp, *Agricultural Weather in the Red River Basin of Southern Manitoba over the Period 1800 to 1975*, 12–13.

154 Allsopp, *Agricultural Weather in the Red River Basin of Southern Manitoba over the Period 1800 to 1975*, 12; Bumsted, *Trials and Tribulations*, 178.

155 McCarthy, *To Evangelize the Nations*, 204.

156 Funds were raised in Minnesota, England, and by subscription in Canada. Bumsted, *Trials and Tribulations*, 180–83.

CHAPTER 6—CANADA, THE NORTHWEST, AND THE TREATY PERIOD, 1869–76

1 "Report of the Board of Health, 27 Apr. 1871," in *Mission among the Buffalo: The Labours of the Reverend George M. and John C. McDougall in the Canadian Northwest, 1860–1876*, by James Ernest Nix (Toronto: Ryerson Press, 1960), 67.

2 Paul Sharp, *Whoop-Up Country: The Canadian-American West, 1865–1885* (Norman: University of Oklahoma Press, 1973), 39, 104, 145.

3 John C. Ewers, *The Blackfeet: Raiders on the Northwestern Plains* (Norman: University of Oklahoma Press, 1958), 246–53.

4 Robert M. Utley, *Bluecoats and Redskins: The United States Army and the Indian, 1866–1891* (London: Cassell, 1973), 191.

5 Ewers, *The Blackfeet*, 246–53. See also Utley, *Bluecoats and Redskins*, 188–218; J.P. Dunn, *Massacres of the Mountains: A History of the Indian Wars of the Far West, 1815–1875* (London: Eyer and Spottiswoode, 1963), 448–55.

6 John MacLean, *McDougall of Alberta: A Life of Rev. John McDougall D.D., Pathfinder of Empire and Prophet of the Plains* (Toronto: F. C. Stephenson, 1927), 37.

7 Sharp, *Whoop-Up Country*, 27.

8 William Butler, *The Great Lone Land: A Narrative of Travel and Adventure in the Northwest of America* (Edmonton: Hurtig, 1968), 360.

9 Margaret A. Kennedy, *The Whiskey Trade of the Northwestern Plains: A Multidisciplinary Study* (New York: Lang, 1997), 32.

10 Hugh Dempsey, "Smallpox: Scourge of the Plains" in *Harm's Way: Disasters in Western Canada*, edited by Anthony Rasporich and Max Foran (Calgary: University of Calgary Press, 2004), 37. Although belief in the infested blanket story is widespread, there is only a single documented case of the deliberate infection of aboriginal people by Europeans in North America, by British troops under the command of General Amherst during the Pontiac uprising of 1763. For a discussion of that incident and persistent belief in the use of smallpox as a weapon of war during revolutionary times, see Elizabeth Fenn, "Biological Warfare in Eighteenth-Century North America: Beyond Jeffrey Amherst," *Journal of American History* 86 (2000): 1552–80. For an analysis of the legend of the infested blanket, see Adrienne Mayor, "The Nessus Shirt in the New World: Smallpox Blankets in History and Legend," *Journal of American Folklore* 108 (1995): 54–77.

11 E. Wagner Stearn and Allen E. Stearn, *The Effect of Smallpox on the Destiny of the Amerindian* (Boston: Bruce Humphries Publishers, 1945), 101–03, attributed the source of the epidemic to construction of the Pacific Railroad.

12 Kennedy, *The Whiskey Trade of the Northwestern Plains*, 32.

13 Hugh Dempsey, *Red Crow: Warrior Chief* (Saskatoon: Western Producer Prairie Books, 1980), 69.

14 Dempsey, "Smallpox," 29; Treaty 7 Elders and Tribal Council with Walter Hildebrandt, Sarah Carter, and Dorothy First Rider, *The True Spirit and Original Intent of Treaty 7* (Montreal: McGill-Queen's University Press, 1996), 30.

15 Frank G. Roe, *The North American Buffalo: A Critical Study of the Species in Its Wild State*, 2nd ed. (Toronto: University of Toronto Press, 1970), 757n159.

16 George McDougall, 1 April 1871, in *George Millward McDougall: The Pioneer, Patriot, and Missionary*, by John McDougall (Toronto: William Briggs, 1888), 175.

17 LAC, MG 29 E 39, Robertson-Ross Papers, f. 1, "Field Notebook," 14 September 1872, 28–29. Alcohol-related deaths varied within the nations that made up the alliance. Among the Piikani, thirty-four died of disease and twenty-seven from liquor; among the Omak-sikimi-tapix, the Northern Piikani, twelve died of disease and thirteen from alcohol; among the Tsuu T'ina, whom he called the "Plains Beaver Indians," seven deaths were caused by disease, but none was attributed to alcohol.

18 Patrick Robertson-Ross, *Report of Colonel Robertson-Ross, Adjutant-General of the Militia on the Territories of the Dominion* (Ottawa: Queen's Printer, 1872), 28–29.

19 Robertson-Ross, "Field Notebook," 15 September 1872, 35.

20   John McDougall, *On Western Trails in the Early Seventies* (Toronto: William Briggs, 1911), 129; Hugh Dempsey, *Firewater: The Impact of the Whiskey Trade on the Blackfoot Nation* (Calgary: Fifth House Publishers, 2002), 66.

21   Hugh Dempsey, *The Amazing Death of Calf Shirt and Other Blackfoot Stories: Three Hundred Years of Blackfoot History* (Saskatoon: Fifth House Publishers, 1994), 47–59; Ewers, *The Blackfeet*, 259–60.

22   Carlton R. Stewart, ed., *The Last Great (Inter-Tribal) Indian Battle* (Lethbridge: Lethbridge Historical Society, 1997).

23   Unknown to the Cree-led alliance, the Blackfoot camp had been augmented by survivors of the American Army attack on the Marias River and by some northern Blackfoot when the attack occurred on 25 October. Alex Johnston, "The Last Great Indian Battle," in ibid., 8. The victory of the Blackfoot at Belly River was also partially the result of superior weaponry acquired from the Montana trade. Their repeating rifles far outpowered the flintlocks and bows and arrows of the HBC-supplied northern alliance. Adolf Hungry Wolf, *The Blood People: A Division of the Blackfoot Confederacy* (New York: Harper and Row, 1977), 255. See also Ewers, *The Blackfeet*, 260–61.

24   Treaty 7 Elders et al., *The True Spirit and Original Intent of Treaty 7*, 9.

25   Butler, *The Great Lone Land*, 368.

26   Hugh Dempsey, ed., "Smallpox Epidemic of 1869–70," *Alberta History* 11 (1963): 17.

27   For a discussion of the relief effort, dispatched after spring breakup, see E.R. Young, *By Canoe and Dog Train: Among the Cree and Salteaux Indians* (Toronto: William Briggs, 1890), 197–205.

28   John McDougall, *In the Days of the Red River Rebellion*, edited by Susan Jaeckel (Edmonton: University of Alberta Press, 1983), 117; Peter Erasmus, *Buffalo Days and Nights* (Calgary: Fifth House Publishers, 1999), 200.

29   Isaac Cowie, *The Company of Adventurers: A Narrative of Seven Years in the Service of the Hudson's Bay Company during 1867–1874* (Lincoln: University of Nebraska Press, 1993), 382.

30   Ibid. The epidemic appears to have struck along the upper Assiniboine River even though Chief Factor Campbell claimed that he and his wife vaccinated more than 100 people there. Clifford Wilson, *Campbell of the Yukon* (Toronto: Macmillan of Canada, 1970), 169–70. Butler, *The Great Lone Land*, 227–28, reported that half of the people attached to Fort Pelly died during the outbreak.

31   W. D. Smiley, "'The Most Good to the Indians': The Reverend James Nisbet and the Prince Albert Mission," *Saskatchewan History* 46 (1994): 42.

32   Ibid.; Katherine Pettipas, "Introduction," in *The Diary of the Reverend Henry Budd, 1870–1875*, edited by Katherine Pettipas (Winnipeg: Hignell Printing, 1974), xxxviii.

33   SAB, Campbell Innes Papers, A-113, John McKay Papers, f. 1, Diary 1870–84, entry of 8 February 1871; HBCA, Search File: "Smallpox Epidemic, 1870," Extract 25, D.A. Smith to W. Armit, Fort Garry, 5 March 1871.

34   See W. J. Christie, "Smallpox Report," *The Manitoban*, 16 September 1871, in Dempsey, ed., "Smallpox Epidemic of 1869–70," 17.

35   Smiley, "'The Most Good to the Indians,'" 40–41; *The Manitoban*, 21 January 1871, in Dempsey, ed., "Smallpox Epidemic of 1869–70," 14.

36   Butler, *The Great Lone Land*, 368–69.

37   James G. MacGregor, *Senator Hardisty's Prairies, 1849–1889* (Saskatoon: Western Producer Prairie Books, 1978), 75–76; Young, *By Canoe and Dog Train*, 198.

38   McDougall, *In the Days of the Red River Rebellion*, 127; MacGregor, *Senator Hardisty's Prairies*, 76.

39   HBCA, Search File: "Smallpox Epidemic, 1869–1870," Extract 6, W. J. Christie to D. A. Smith, Carlton House, 6 September 1870.

40   Several Europeans were infected, but only four succumbed to the disease during the outbreak. See MacGregor, *Senator Hardisty's Prairies*, 78–79. Although most of the aboriginal population was susceptible to the infection, those who had been infected in earlier outbreaks were immune. The Métis catechist Peter Erasmus was assisted during the epidemic by a

Stoney elder, Pan-eza Sa-win, who "was not afraid of the sickness as he had got over it several years earlier." Erasmus, *Buffalo Days and Nights*, 211–12.

41 Young, *By Canoe and Dog Train*, 202–05.

42 MacGregor, *Senator Hardisty's Prairies*, 74. Sinclair apparently attempted to make his own serum for use at Fort Pitt with lymph taken from a Saulteaux who had been vaccinated at the Prince Albert mission. Unfortunately for the surrounding Cree, the procedure was unsuccessful. SAB, W. Traill Papers, A-104, 4.

43 Butler, *The Great Lone Land*, 250–51, 369. The inhabitants of the fort were immunized by Sinclair from scabs from the Saulteaux vaccinated by Nisbet at Prince Albert. Christie, "Smallpox Report," in Dempsey, ed., "Smallpox Epidemic of 1869–70," 16–17; HBCA, Search File: "Smallpox Epidemic, 1869–1870," Extract 6, W. J. Christie to D. A. Smith, Carlton House, 6 September 1870.

44 HBCA, Search File: "Smallpox Epidemic, 1869–1870," Extract 6, W. J. Christie to D. A. Smith, Carlton House, 6 September 1870.

45 Butler, *The Great Lone Land*, 250. A similar account is provided by MacLean, *McDougall of Alberta*, 44.

46 HBCA, Search File: "Smallpox Epidemic, 1869–1870," Extract 6, W. J. Christie to D. A. Smith, Carlton House, 6 September 1870. Three women and a "good many children" perished at Carlton House.

47 SAB, W. Traill Papers, A-104, 5.

48 Butler, *The Great Lone Land*, 369.

49 Christie, "Smallpox Report," in Dempsey, ed., "Smallpox Epidemic of 1869–70," 16.

50 Frank J. Dolphin, *Indian Bishop of the West: Vital Justin Grandin, 1829–1902* (Ottawa: Novalis, 1986), 121–24. The journal of the St. Paul mission in Alberta recorded 2,000 baptisms on the plains that terrible summer. Katherine Hughes, *Father Lacombe: The Blackrobe Voyageur* (New York: Moffat, Yard and Company, 1911), 187.

51 Dolphin, *Indian Bishop of the West*, 121.

52 Smiley, "'The Most Good to the Indians,'" 42; Erasmus, *Buffalo Days and Nights*, 210–11.

53 Nix, *Mission among the Buffalo*, 64; Young, *By Canoe and Dog Train*, 198; MacLean, *McDougall of Alberta*, 44; Erasmus, *Buffalo Days and Nights*, 209; Henry Budd, "Entry of 6 Sep. 1870," in *The Diary of Henry Budd, 1870–1875*, edited by Katherine Pettipas (Winnipeg: Hignell Printing, 1974), 39.

54 MacLean, *McDougall of Alberta*, 44.

55 Edward McCourt, *Remember Butler: The Story of William Butler* (Toronto: McClelland and Stewart, 1967), 60–64; David Meyer and Robert Hutton, "Pasquatinow and the Red Earth Crees," *Prairie Forum* 23 (1998): 103.

56 SAB, microfilm 2.75, "Nut Lake Indians, 1905–1955," *School Histories of 35 Indian Reserves*, 1955; Butler, *The Great Lone Land*, 227–28. Unfortunately, no records of Fort Pelly for 1870 exist in the HBCA collection.

57 St. Albert Historical Society, *The Black Robe's Vision: A History of the St. Albert District* (St. Albert, AB: St. Albert Historical Society, 1985), 58.

58 HBCA, Search File: "Smallpox Epidemic, 1869–1870," Extract 4, Edmonton House Journal.

59 James G. MacGregor, *Edmonton: A History* (Edmonton: Hurtig, 1975), 79.

60 George McDougall, 21 October 1871, in John McDougall, *George Millward McDougall*, 159.

61 Nix, *Mission among the Buffalo*, 65; MacLean, *McDougall of Alberta*, 40–41.

62 McDougall, *George Millward McDougall*, 155.

63 Butler, *The Great Lone Land*, 369–70.

64 A.G. Morice, *History of the Catholic Church in Western Canada from Lake Superior to the Pacific (1659–1895)* (Toronto: Musson Book Company, 1910), 86.

65 MacLean, *McDougall of Alberta*, 41; McDougall, *George Millward McDougall*, 176.

66 MacLean, *McDougall of Alberta*, 41. The child, Antoine Gibeault, was nine years old at the time. J. E. Dion, "A Short History of Moose Lake in 1907," in *Echoes of the Past: History of Bonnyville and District*, edited by Real Girard (Bonnyville, AB: Bonnyville Historical Society, 1984), 13–14.

67 SAB, R. A. Mayson Papers 4, A-M455, Dr. Andrew Everett Porter, 2.

68   Alexander Morris stated that the prompt action of the company during the epidemic "saved the Indians from entire destruction." Stephen Sliwa, "Standing the Test of Time: A History of the Beardy's/Okemasis Reserve, 1876–1951" (MA thesis, Trent University, 1993), 52.

69   The board was made up of the following: W. J. Christie, the chairman; Richard Hardisty and John Bunn of the HBC; Protestant clerics George McDougall, his son John, Peter Campbell, and Henry Steinhauer; and Catholic priests Leduc, Lacombe, André, and Furmond. Dempsey, ed., "Smallpox Epidemic of 1869–70," 18.

70   James Mochoruk, "The Political Economy of Northern Development: Governments and Capital along Manitoba's Resource Frontier, 1870–1930" (Ph.D. diss., University of Manitoba, 1992), 19–20.

71   SAB, John A. Macdonald Papers, A-70, Adams Archibald to John A. Macdonald, 6 December 1870.

72   For a full description of Butler's orders, see *The Great Lone Land*, 353–55, and Canada, *Sessional Papers 1871*, No. 20, George Hill to William Butler, Fort Garry, 10 October 1870, 62–63.

73   HBCA, Search File: "Smallpox Epidemic, 1870," Extract 12, D. A. Smith to G. G. Smith, Fort Garry, 19 October 1870; R. M. Gorsline, "The Medical Services of the Red River Expeditions, 1870–71," *Medical Services Journal, Canada* 23 (1967): 169; Canada, *Sessional Papers 1871*, No. 20, Adams Archibald, Fort Garry, 13 October 1870, 58–59, and Adams Archibald to Joseph Howe, Fort Garry, 24 October 1870, 66–67.

74   Butler, *The Great Lone Land*, 239.

75   Young, *By Canoe and Dog Train*, 200.

76   HBCA, Search File: "Smallpox Epidemic, 1869–1870," Extract 10, W. J. Christie to W. G. Smith, Edmonton House, 11 October 1870.

77   Christie, "Smallpox Report," in Dempsey, ed., "Smallpox Epidemic of 1869–70," 15; HBCA, Search File: "Smallpox Epidemic, 1869–1870," Extract 20, W. J. Christie to the Chief Factors and Chief Traders, Northern Department, Edmonton House, 5 January 1871.

78   George McDougall, 21 October 1870, in John McDougall, *George Millward McDougall*, 165.

79   HBCA, Search File: "Smallpox Epidemic, 1869–1870," Extract 19, Horace Boulanger, Clerk in Charge of Cumberland House, to the Governor, Chief Factors, and Chief Traders, Cumberland House, 5 January 1870; Cowie, *The Company of Adventurers*, 425.

80   HBCA, Search File: "Smallpox Epidemic, 1869–1870," Extract 20, W. J. Christie to the Chief Factors and Chief Traders, Northern Department, Edmonton House, 5 January 1871. McDonald was expected to have arrived at Edmonton between 1 and 10 December. D. A. Smith to W. G. Smith, Fort Garry, 28 December 1870.

81   HBCA, Search File: "Smallpox Epidemic, 1869–1870," Extract 21, D. A. Smith to W. G. Smith, Fort Garry, 22 January 1871.

82   SAB, Campbell Innes Papers, A-113, vol. 5, Archdeacon MacKay Papers, Diary 1870–84, 8 February 1871.

83   Martha McCarthy, *From the Great River to the Ends of the Earth: Oblate Missions to the Dene, 1847–1921* (Edmonton: University of Alberta Press, 1995), 126n39; LAC, Church Missionary Society (hereafter CMS), microfilm A-80, Reverend Day to the Secretaries, Fort Simpson, November 1870; William Hardisty to William McMurray, Fort Chipewyan, 12 January 1870, in "Private Letters from the Fur Trade," by Clifford Wilson, in *Papers Read before the Historical and Scientific Society of Manitoba*, Series 3, edited by W. L. Morton and J. A. Jackson (Winnipeg: Historical and Scientific Society of Manitoba, 1950), 45.

84   HBCA, Search File: "Smallpox Epidemic, 1869–1870," Extract 9, D. A. Smith to W. G. Smith, Fort Garry, 10 October 1870.

85   HBCA, Search File: "Smallpox Epidemic, 1869–1870," Extract 19, Horace Belanger to the Governor, Chief Factors, and Chief Traders, Northern Department, Cumberland House, 5 January 1871.

86   HBCA, Search File: "Smallpox Epidemic, 1869–1870," Extract 20, W. J. Christie to the Chief Factors and Chief Traders, Northern Department, Edmonton, 5 January 1871.

87 George McDougall to Dr. Wood, Victoria Mission, 1 March 1871, in John McDougall, *George Millward McDougall*, 168.

88 *The Manitoban*, 16 September 1871, in Dempsey, ed., "Smallpox Epidemic of 1869–70," 18–19.

89 Christie, "Smallpox Report," in ibid., 17.

90 Cowie, *The Company of Adventurers*, 428–30.

91 Butler, *The Great Lone Land*, 205.

92 HBCA, Search File: "Smallpox Epidemic, 1869–1870," Extract 26, J.H. McTavish to W. Armit, Fort Garry, 14 June 1871; Extract 27, J. H. McTavish to W. Armit, Fort Garry, 29 July 1871; Extract 28, J. H. McTavish to W. Armit, Fort Garry, 7 August 1871.

93 McDougall, *George Millward McDougall*, 172.

94 HBCA, Search File: "Smallpox Epidemic, 1869–1870," Extract 20, W. J. Christie to the Chief Factors and Chief Traders, Northern Department, Edmonton, 5 January 1871.

95 McDougall, *George Millward McDougall*, 150–52.

96 David McCrady, "Beyond Boundaries: Aboriginal Peoples and the Prairie West, 1850–1885" (MA thesis, University of Victoria, 1992), 70–77. Of the forty-three chiefs who signed Treaty 7, seven had been signatories to the US Blackfoot Treaty in 1855.

97 Butler, *The Great Lone Land*, 380–86.

98 James G. MacGregor, *Father Lacombe* (Edmonton: Hurtig, 1975), 210. The request by Sweet Grass for a treaty was dated 13 April 1871. Christie forwarded it to Archibald. Alexander Morris, *The Treaties of Canada with the Indians of Manitoba and the North-West Territories* (Saskatoon: Fifth House Publishers, 1991), 169–71.

99 Morris, *The Treaties of Canada*, 170.

100 Ibid.

101 Jean Friesen, "Magnificent Gifts: The Treaties of Canada with the Indians of the Northwest 1869–76," *Transactions of the Royal Society of Canada*, Series 5 (1986): 43, 46. See also Frank Tough, *"As Their Natural Resources Fail": Native Peoples and the Economic History of Northern Manitoba, 1870–1930* (Vancouver: UBC Press, 1996), 79–81; Frank Tough, "Aboriginal Rights versus the Deed of Surrender: The Legal Rights of Native Peoples and Canada's Acquisition of the Hudson's Bay Company Territory," *Prairie Forum* 17 (1992) : 230.

102 Wemyss Simpson to the Secretary of State for the Provinces, 3 November 1871, in Morris, *The Treaties of Canada*, 168.

103 Allen Ronaghan, "Charles Mair and the North-West Emigration Aid Society," *Manitoba History* 14 (1987): 14.

104 Frank Tough, "Economic Aspects of Aboriginal Title in Northern Manitoba: Treaty 5 Adhesions and Métis Scrip," *Manitoba History* 15 (1988): 7.

105 Peter Naylor, "Index to Aboriginal Issues Found in the Records of the North-West Mounted Police RG 18, National Archives of Canada" (typescript) (Saskatoon: Office of the Treaty Commissioner, 1994), Extract 590, Adams Archibald to Joseph Howe, Fort Garry, 6 March 1872, 215.

106 LAC, John A. Macdonald Papers, microfilm C-1670, 110702, Gilbert McMicken to John A. Macdonald, Winnipeg, 22 June 1872.

107 Cowie, *The Company of Adventurers*, 441, 445; Frank Tough, "Indian Economic Behaviour, Exchange, and Profits in Northern Manitoba during the Decline of Monopoly, 1870–1930," *Journal of Historical Geography* 16 (1990): 390.

108 Arthur J. Ray, J. R. Miller, and Frank Tough, *Bounty and Benevolence: A History of Saskatchewan Treaties* (Montreal: McGill-Queen's University Press, 2000), 139, 146.

109 LAC, MG 29 A 6, Robert Bell Papers, Hudson's Bay Company, Northern Department, "Journal of a Voyage from Fort Garry to Fort Simpson, Mackenzie River, by Land and Water, and of Its Return by Dog Train to Carlton Performed on a Tour of Inspection of Posts from 22nd August, 1872, to 28th January, 1873 by Hon. William Joseph Christie, Inspecting Chief Factor of the Hudson's Bay Company," 26 January 1873.

110 Ray, Miller, and Tough, *Bounty and Benevolence*, 130.

111 George M. Grant, *Ocean to Ocean: Sandford Fleming's Expedition through Canada in 1872* (Toronto: Coles Publishing Company, 1970), 96.

112 Ibid., 190.
113 Ibid., 97–99, 133; John Webster Grant, *Moon of Wintertime: Missionaries and the Indians of Canada in Encounter since 1534* (Toronto: University of Toronto Press, 1984), 155.
114 LAC, John A. Macdonald Papers, microfilm C-1670, 110809, Gilbert McMicken to John A. Macdonald, Fort Garry, 18 April 1873.
115 Sharp, *Whoop-Up Country*, 79.
116 LAC, MG 29 B 15, Robert Bell Papers, vol. 27, f. 103, "Confidential Report to Alexander Morris from Robert Bell, Fort Garry," 14 October 1873.
117 Ibid.
118 Ibid., Enclosure No. 2.
119 Ibid., Alexander Morris to Minister of the Interior, Fort Garry, 23 October 1873.
120 Margaret Complin, "Calling Valley of the Crees and the Buffalo," *The Beaver* 265 (1935): 23; Sarah Carter, *Lost Harvests: Prairie Indian Reserve Farmers and Government Policy* (Montreal: McGill-Queen's University Press, 1990), 56; Ray, Miller, and Tough, *Bounty and Benevolence*, 107–11.
121 Ray, Miller, and Tough, *Bounty and Benevolence*, 156.
122 Morris, *The Treaties of Canada*, 106.
123 Abel Watetch, *Payepot and His People* (Regina: Saskatchewan History and Folklore Society, 1959), 16.
124 Ibid., 48; CMS, microfilm A-81, 275, J.A. Mackay to Secretaries, 20 August 1873.
125 D. Aidan McQuillan, "Creation of Indian Reserves on the Canadian Prairies, 1870–1885," *Geographical Review* 70 (1980): 389n29.
126 SAB, R. G. Ferguson Papers, microfilm R-2.391, 39.
127 Ibid., 36, Extract of Acting Indian Superintendent Provencher's Annual Report, Department of Indian Affairs, 1877.
128 Ibid., 38, Extract of J. A. N. Provencher, Report of the Manitoba Indian Commissioner's Office, Winnipeg, 30 October 1875. On the link between the severity of measles and malnutrition, see David C. Morley, "Nutrition and Infectious Disease," in *Disease and Urbanization: Symposia for the Study of Human Biology*, vol. 20, edited by E. J. Clegg and J. P. Garlick (London: Taylor and Francis, 1980), 37.
129 SAB, R. G. Ferguson Papers, microfilm R-2.391, 37, Extract of J. A. N. Provencher, Report of the Manitoba Indian Commissioner's Office, Winnipeg, 30 October 1875.
130 HBCA, Search File: "Battleford," Lawrence Clarke to James Graham, Carlton House, 24 June 1874; Arlean MacPherson, *The Battlefords: A History* (Saskatoon: Modern Press, 1967), 66.
131 LAC, MG 27 ID 10, David Laird Papers, Indian Affairs, NWT, David Laird Letterbook, 1874–75, 18, copy of letter from C. N. Bell, Winnipeg, 23 March 1874.
132 LAC, John A. Macdonald Papers, microfilm C-1523, 41,896, David Laird to Minister of the Interior, Fort Garry, 9 June 1874.
133 Jim Wallace, *A Double Duty: The Decisive First Decade of the North-West Mounted Police* (Winnipeg: Bunker to Bunker Books, 1997), 123–24.
134 John McDougall to A. Morris, 23 October 1875, in Morris, *The Treaties of Canada*, 174.
135 Erasmus, *Buffalo Days and Nights*, 228.
136 Noel E. Dyck, "The Administration of Federal Indian Aid in the Northwest Territories, 1879–1885" (MA thesis, University of Saskatchewan, 1970), 85n33.
137 Ray, Miller, and Tough, *Bounty and Benevolence*, 130.
138 Butler, *The Great Lone Land*, 242.
139 Ray, Miller, and Tough, *Bounty and Benevolence*, 146.
140 Erasmus, *Buffalo Days and Nights*, 248–49.
141 Ibid., 249.
142 An alternative view is that those leaders who favoured treaty "betrayed" those who opposed it, such as Big Bear. Neil McLeod, "Exploring Cree Narrative Memory" (Ph.D. diss., University of Regina, 2005), 98–101.
143 Ray, Miller, and Tough, *Bounty and Benevolence*, 136, 146.
144 Chief John Snow, *These Mountains Are Our Sacred Places: The Story of the Stoney Indians* (Toronto: Samuel Stevens, 1977), 30.

145 Morris, *The Treaties of Canada*, 241.
146 A. G. Jackes, Narrative of Proceedings, 27 August 1876, in ibid., 228.
147 Erasmus, *Buffalo Days and Nights*, 215, 251.
148 Walter Hildebrandt, *Views from Fort Battleford: Constructed Visions of an Anglo-Canadian West* (Regina: Canadian Plains Research Center, 1994), 16–17.
149 Ray, Miller, and Tough, *Bounty and Benevolence*, 143.

CHAPTER 7—TREATIES, FAMINE, AND EPIDEMIC TRANSITION ON THE PLAINS, 1877–82

1 Jill St. Germain, *Indian Treaty Making in the United States and Canada, 1867–1877* (Toronto: University of Toronto Press, 2001), 124.
2 Peter Erasmus, *Buffalo Days and Nights* (Calgary: Fifth House Publishers, 1999), 249.
3 Alexander Morris, *The Treaties of Canada with the Indians of Manitoba and the North-West Territories* (Saskatoon: Fifth House Publishers, 1991), 178, 185, 212, 215, 216, 218, 228.
4 Laurie Meijer Drees, "Reserve Hospitals in Southern Alberta, 1890 to 1930," *Native Studies Review* 9 (1993–94): 93.
5 Jane Buikstra, ed., *Prehistoric Tuberculosis in the Americas* (Evanston, IL: Northwestern University Archaeological Program, 1981); Peter H. Bryce, "The History of the American Indians in Relation to Health," *Ontario Historical Society Papers and Records* 12 (1914): 137–39.
6 George A. Clark, Marc Kelley, John M. Grange, and M. Cassandra Hill, "The Evolution of Mycobacterial Disease in Human Populations," *Current Anthropology* 28 (1987): 45, 46, 48, 51.
7 William D. Johnston, "Tuberculosis," in *The Cambridge World History of Human Disease*, edited by Kenneth F. Kiple (Cambridge, UK: Cambridge University Press, 1993), 1059; Nevin Scrimshaw, Carl Taylor, and John Gordon, *Interactions of Nutrition and Infection* (Geneva: World Health Organization, 1968), 16.
8 Charlotte A. Roberts and Jane E. Buikstra, *The Bioarchaeology of Tuberculosis: A Global View on a Reemerging Disease*, 20. Servants of the HBC were often returned home to convalesce when they showed signs of the disease, as did William Tomison, who took sick leave during the winter of 1788–89 to prevent his sickness from leading to a "consummated state." John Nicks, "The Pine Island Posts, 1786–1794: A Study of Competition in the Fur Trade" (MA thesis, University of Alberta, 1975), 78. A recent study has shown the connection between French Canadian voyageurs and strains of TB that persist to the present in isolated indigenous populations in the west. Caitlin Pepperell et al., "Dispersal of *Mycobacterium tuberculosis* via the Canadian Fur Trade," *Proceedings of the National Academy of Sciences* (2011), www.pnas.org/cgi/doi/10.1073/pnas.1016708108, 1.
9 Joseph M. Prince and Richard H. Steckel, "Nutritional Success on the Great Plains: Nineteenth-Century Equestrian Nomads," *Journal of Interdisciplinary History* 33 (2003): 367–75. See also Joseph M. Prince, "Intersection of Economics, History, and Human Biology: Secular Trends in Stature in Nineteenth-Century Sioux Indians," *Human Biology* 67 (1995): 387–406; Richard H. Steckel and Joseph M. Prince, "Tallest in the World: Native Americans of the Great Plains in the Nineteenth Century," paper presented to the International Commission on Historical Demography, Oslo, Norway, 1999.
10 Johnston, "Tuberculosis," 1061; R. G. Ferguson, *Studies in Tuberculosis* (Toronto: University of Toronto Press, 1955), 6.
11 SAB, R. G. Ferguson Papers, microfilm R-2.391, vi–vii.
12 J. W. Daschuk, Paul Hackett, and Scott McNeil, "Treaties and Tuberculosis: First Nations People in Late 19th Century Western Canada, a Political and Economic Transformation," *Bulletin of the History of Medicine* 23, 2 (2006): 307–30.
13 Noel E. Dyck, "The Administration of Federal Indian Aid in the Northwest Territories, 1879–1885" (MA thesis, University of Saskatchewan, 1970), 27.
14 In the early 1870s, developments in tanning technology allowed bison hides to be used in the manufacture of industrial belts for the burgeoning economy of the American east.

This "spasm of industrial expansion was the primary cause of the bison's near extinction." Andrew C. Isenberg, *The Destruction of the Bison: An Environmental History, 1750–1920* (Cambridge, UK: Cambridge University Press, 2000), 130–31; Arthur J. Ray, "The Northern Great Plains: Pantry of the Northwestern Fur Trade, 1774–1885," *Prairie Forum* 9 (1984): 277–78; Frank G. Roe, *The North American Buffalo: A Critical Study of the Species in Its Wild State*, 2nd ed. (Toronto: University of Toronto Press, 1970), 473.

15　D. Aidan McQuillan, "Creation of Indian Reserves on the Canadian Prairies, 1870–1885," *Geographical Review* 70 (1980): 383n11.

16　CMS, microfilm A-80, Joseph Reader to Reverend Fenn, 29 July 1874, 221. See also Nan Shipley, "Printing Press at Oonikup," *The Beaver* 290 (1960): 48–49.

17　Report of Surgeon John Kittson, Swan River, 19 December 1875, in *A Chronicle of the West: North-West Mounted Police Reports for 1875*, edited by S. W. Horral (Calgary: Historical Society of Alberta, 1975), 23; Hugh Dempsey, ed., *R. B. Nevitt: A Winter at Fort Macleod* (Calgary: McClelland and Stewart West, 1974), 47–48; Jody Decker, "Country Distempers: Deciphering Disease and Illness in Rupert's Land before 1870," in *Reading beyond Words: Contexts for Native History*, edited by J. S. H. Brown and Elizabeth Vibert (Peterborough: Broadview Press, 1996), 158.

18　George M.Grant, *Ocean to Ocean: Sandford Fleming's Expedition through Canada in 1872* (Toronto: Coles Publishing Company, 1970), 96.

19　R. V. Pierce, *The People's Common Sense Medical Adviser*, 61st ed. (Buffalo: World's Dispensary Medical Association, 1895), 447.

20　Dyck, "The Administration of Federal Indian Aid in the Northwest.Territories," 21.

21　Canada, *Sessional Papers* [hereafter CSP], 1876, No. 9, Indian Commissioner's Office, Winnipeg, 30 October 1875, 33.

22　CSP, 1877, No. 11, David Mills, Report of the Department of the Interior for the Year Ended 30 June 1876, xii.

23　McQuillan, "Creation of Indian Reserves on the Canadian Prairies," 383.

24　William T. Hornaday, *The Extermination of the American Bison with a Sketch of Its Discovery and Life History* (Washington, DC: Government Printing Bureau, 1889), 505–06.

25　Dyck, "The Administration of Federal Indian Aid in the Northwest Territories," 22; A.J. Looy, "Saskatchewan's First Indian Agent: M.G. Dickieson," *Saskatchewan History* 32 (1979): 111.

26　Isenberg, *The Destruction of the Bison*, 140–43.

27　B. Byron Price, "Introduction," in *The Trail Drivers of Texas*, edited by J. Marvin Hunter (Austin: University of Texas Press, 1985), v; Terry Jordan, *North-American Cattle Ranching Frontier: Origins, Diffusions, and Differentiation.* (Albuquerque: University of New Mexico Press, 1993), 222.

28　Both cattle and bison are "primary hosts" of bovine tuberculosis. They are susceptible to the disease and propagate it under natural circumstances. Tessaro, "Bovine Tuberculosis and Brucellosis in Animals, Including Man," 209.

29　Ibid., 210.

30　Thomas E. Mails, *The Mystic Warriors of the Plains* (New York: Mallard Press, 1991), 536.

31　As is the case in humans, sickness with bovine tuberculosis is separate from simple infection with *M. bovis*. The persistence of latent TB "is a major reason why tuberculosis is so tenacious in populations of primary hosts." Tessaro, "Bovine Tuberculosis and Brucellosis in Animals, Including Man," 212. On the failure of Texas longhorns and the Texas system of ranching on the northern plains, see Terry Jordan, *North American Cattle-Ranching Frontiers* (Albuquerque: University of New Mexico Press, 1993), 236–40.

32　Although overshadowed by *M. tuberculosis*, *M. bovis* remains a significant source of morbidity and mortality in the developing world, especially among those infected with HIV. W.Y. Ayele et al., "Bovine Tuberculosis: An Old Disease but a New Threat to Africa," *International Journal of Tuberculosis and Lung Disease* 8 (2004): 927.

33　Cattle infected with actinomycosis, a fungal disease known colloquially as "big jaw," were often provided to "placate" Indians during cattle drives since they had no commercial value. A.B. Holder, "Papers on Diseases among Indians," *Medical Record: A Weekly Journal of Medicine and Surgery*, 13 August 1892, 181–82.

34 The bacterium that causes tuberculosis was not identified until 1882. The danger posed by bovine tuberculosis to human populations was not universally accepted until 1895. Keir Waddington, "Unfit for Human Consumption: Tuberculosis and the Problem of Infected Meat in Late Victorian Britain," *Bulletin of the History of Medicine* 73 (2003): 650.

35 William H. Quinn, Victor Neal, and Santiago E Anutez De Mayolo, "El Niño Occurrences over the Past Four and a Half Centuries," *Journal of Geophysical Research* 92 (1987): 14,451; Cesar N. Caviedes, *El Niño in History: Storming through the Ages* (Gainesville: University Press of Florida, 2001), Table 1.1, 10.

36 SAB, Campbell Innes Papers, A-113, vol. 3, Canadian Northwest Historical Society Papers, Subject File 12, Ruth Matheson notes, n.d.

37 Tessaro, "Bovine Tuberculosis and Brucellosis in Animals, Including Man," 209.

38 John Hines, *The Red Indians of the Plains: Thirty Years Missionary Experience in the Saskatchewan* (London: Society for Promoting Christian Knowledge, 1915), 146.

39 Dyck, "The Administration of Federal Indian Aid in the Northwest Territories," 26.

40 Roe, *The North American Buffalo*, 477–79; David D. Smits, "The Frontier Army and the Destruction of the Buffalo: 1865–1883," *Western Historical Quarterly* 25 (1994): 334–38; William A. Dobak, "The Army and the Buffalo: A Demur," *Western Historical Quarterly* 26 (1995): 202. Prime ministerial correspondence indicates that the American Army contributed to the demise of herds. LAC, John A. Macdonald Papers, microfilm C-1673, p. 114,313, Morris to Macdonald, Toronto, 6 July 1879; microfilm C-1590, p. 81,299, Campbell to Macdonald, Ottawa, 10 August 1879.

41 Gudjon Arngrimsson, *Nyja Island: Saga of the Journey to New Iceland* (Winnipeg: Turnstone Press, 1997), 152–53.

42 Morris, *The Treaties of Canada*, 144, 148, 153; Winona Stevenson, "Icelanders and Indians in the Interlake: John Ramsay and the White Mud River," typescript (Winnipeg: University of Winnipeg, 1986); LAC, RG 10, vol. 3646, file 8064, Report of Dr. Lynch on Indians of Lake Winnipeg, 12 April 1877.

43 Nelson Gerrard, *The Icelandic River Saga* (Arborg, MB: Saga Publications, 1985), 37.

44 One source estimated that 200 Indians died at the community of Sandy River alone. E.L.M. Thorpe, *Culture, Evolution, and Disease*, Anthropology Paper 30 (Winnipeg: University of Manitoba, 1989), 49. By the end of January 1877, the aboriginal death toll on the west side of Lake Winnipeg was estimated to be at least 300. Jim Mochoruk, *Formidable Heritage: Manitoba's North and the Cost of Development, 1870 to 1930* (Winnipeg: University of Manitoba Press, 2004), 40.

45 Provincial Archives of Manitoba (hereafter PAM), Alexander Morris Papers, Ketcheson Collection, MG 12,Telegram Book 3, No. 23, R. W. Scott to Alexander Morris, 29 November 1876.

46 PAM, Alexander Morris Papers, Ketcheson Collection, MG 12, Telegram Book 3, No. 10, attachment of a message from Morris to Mackenzie, 24 November 1876.

47 Mochoruk, *Formidable Heritage*, 40.

48 James Mochoruk, "The Political Economy of Northern Development: Governments and Capital along Manitoba's Resource Frontier, 1870–1930" (Ph.D. diss., University of Manitoba, 1992), 55.

49 LAC, RG 10, microfilm C-10113, vol. 3648, file 8138, David Mills, Department of the Interior Memorandum, 14 May 1877; S.D. Cote to J.A. Macdonald, 14 June 1880; LAC, RG 10, vol. 3643, file 7708, Extract from Report of Surgeon B. Nevitt, Fort Macleod, 2 January 1877.

50 LAC, RG 10, microfilm C-10113, vol. 3648, file 8138, S.D. Cote to J.A. Macdonald, 14 June 1880.

51 John L. Tobias, "Canada's Subjugation of the Plains Cree, 1879–1885," in *Sweet Promises: A Reader on Indian-White Relations in Canada*, edited by J. R. Miller (Toronto: University of Toronto Press, 1991), 215.

52 SAB, R-E1883, Frederick Tarr and Larry Peterson, "The Coming of the Queen," in "Little Pine/Lucky Man Band #116" (typescript, n.d.).

53 Grant MacEwan, *Sitting Bull: The Years in Canada* (Edmonton: Hurtig, 1973), 90–91.

54 Treaty 7 Elders and Tribal Council with Walter Hildebrandt, Sarah Carter, and Dorothy First Rider, *The True Spirit and Original Intent of Treaty 7* (Montreal: McGill-Queen's University Press, 1996), viii.

55 David Chalmers, *Laird of the West* (Calgary: Detselig Enterprises, 1981), 99.

56 Hugh Dempsey, *Crowfoot: Chief of the Blackfeet* (Norman: University of Oklahoma Press, 1972), 110.

57 John Snow, *These Mountains Are Our Sacred Places: The Story of the Stoney Indians* (Toronto: Samuel Stevens, 1977), 31.

58 A. J. Looy, "The Indian Agent and His Role in the Administration of the Northwest Superintendency, 1876–1893" (Ph.D. diss., Queen's University, 1977), 61.

59 LAC, RG 10, vol. 3643, file 7708, Report of Surgeon B. Nevitt of the North-West Mounted Police, Fort Macleod, 2 January 1877.

60 Father Scollen to the Lieutenant Governor, Fort Pitt, 8 September 1876, in Morris, *The Treaties of Canada*, 248–49.

61 Dempsey, *Crowfoot*, 96; Morris, *The Treaties of Canada*, 256; L.V. Kelly, *The Range Men: The Story of the Ranchers and Indians of Alberta* (Toronto: Coles, 1980), 119.

62 Looy, "Saskatchewan's First Indian Agent," 112–13.

63 Maureen Lux, *Medicine that Walks: Disease, Medicine, and Canadian Plains Native People, 1880–1940* (Toronto: University of Toronto Press, 2001), 33. The notion that it was "cheaper to feed [Indians] than to fight them" was echoed by Dr. Duncan McEachran, a prominent early rancher and chief veterinary inspector in the early 1880s. David Breen, *The Canadian Prairie West and the Ranching Frontier, 1874–1924* (Toronto: University of Toronto Press, 1983), 15.

64 SAB, microfilm 2.563, Alphonse Little Poplar, "Miscellaneous Documents Relating to the Sweet Grass Reserve" (typescript, 1974).

65 Looy, "Saskatchewan's First Indian Agent," 111.

66 Mary Weekes, *The Last Buffalo Hunter* (Toronto: Macmillan of Canada, 1945), 173–87.

67 Dempsey, *Crowfoot*, 108–09.

68 LAC, RG 10, microfilm C-10119, vol. 3678, file 11683, Report of Dr. Hagarty, Battleford, 20 February 1879.

69 HBCA, Search File: "Prince Albert," Lawrence Clarke to Commissioner James Graham, Carlton House, 26 November 1878, 32.

70 Looy, "Saskatchewan's First Indian Agent," 113.

71 Walter Hildebrandt, *Views from Fort Battleford: Constructed Visions of an Anglo-Canadian West* (Regina: Canadian Plains Research Center, 1994), 42.

72 James Walker, "Incidents of Indian Events," in *The Sands of Time*, edited by Ross Innes (North Battleford: Turner-Warwick Publications, 1986), 124.

73 *Saskatchewan Herald*, 16 December 1878, 3.

74 Ibid., 21 October 1878, 10 February 1879, 24 February 1879; SAB, R.A. Mayson Papers, A.M-455, 4, 3.

75 Looy, "Saskatchewan's First Indian Agent," 110; Tobias, "Canada's Subjugation of the Plains Cree," 212–39.

76 D. N. Sprague noted the connection between completion of the CPR, the centrepiece of the National Policy, and subjugation of the Métis; see *Canada and the Métis, 1869–1885* (Waterloo: Wilfrid Laurier University Press, 1988), 157–77. Joyce Green stated that the subjugation of First Nations was the fourth, though unstated, plank of the National Policy, along with the building of the CPR, the protective tariff, and the agricultural settlement of the west; see "Towards a Detente with History: Confronting Canada's Colonial Legacy," *International Journal of Canadian Studies* 12 (1995): 91–92.

77 Canada, Privy Council Office, *Guide to Canadian Ministries since Confederation, July 1, 1867–February 1, 1982* (Ottawa: Government of Canada, Privy Council Office, Public Archives of Canada, 1982), 13.

78 Sarah Carter, *Lost Harvests: Prairie Indian Reserve Farmers and Government Policy* (Montreal: McGill-Queen's University Press, 1990), 78, 80.

79 *Saskatchewan Herald*, 24 March 1879, 2.

80 McQuillan, "Creation of Indian Reserves on the Canadian Prairies," 384.

81 Looy, "The Indian Agent and His Role in the Administration of the Northwest Superintendency," 51.

82 *Saskatchewan Herald*, 7 May 1879, 2.

83 Dyck, "The Administration of Federal Indian Aid in the Northwest Territories," 45.

84 From 1882 on, food made up 50 percent or more of the total spending on Indian affairs in the northwest. Carl Beal, "Money, Markets, and Economic Development in Saskatchewan Indian Reserve Communities, 1870–1930s" (Ph.D. diss., University of Manitoba, 1994), 139–40.

85 Hugh Shewell, *"Enough to Keep Them Alive": Indian Welfare in Canada* (Toronto: University of Toronto Press, 2004), 73–75.

86 SAB, A. E. Forget Papers, R-39, vol. 6, file 7, Henriette A. Forget, "Reminiscences of Fort Battleford," 2; *Saskatchewan Herald*, 2 June 1879, 2; Arlean McPherson, *The Battlefords: A History* (Saskatoon: Modern Press, 1967), 67.

87 *Saskatchewan Herald*, 30 June 1879, 1.

88 McPherson, *The Battlefords*, 60.

89 Lux, *Medicine that Walks*, 34.

90 SAB, R-E1883, Laird to Macdonald, 30 June 1879, in Tarr and Peterson, "Little Pine/Lucky Man Band #116."

91 SAB, Campbell Innes Papers, A-113, vol. 5, McKay Papers, f. 1, Diary 1870–84.

92 Looy, "Saskatchewan's First Indian Agent," 109.

93 *Saskatchewan Herald*, 30 June 1879, 2.

94 Ibid.; Looy, "Saskatchewan's First Indian Agent," 108–09.

95 *Saskatchewan Herald*, 25 August 1879, 2.

96 Ibid., 14 July 1879, 2.

97 CSP, 1881, Report to the Superintendent of Indian Affairs, Edmonton, 21 August 1880, 102; Jean Larmour, "Edgar Dewdney, Commissioner of Indian Affairs and Lieutenant Governor of the Northwest Territories, 1879–1888" (MA thesis, University of Saskatchewan, Regina Campus, 1969), 43; Looy, "The Indian Agent and His Role in the Administration of the Northwest Superintendency," 63.

98 CSP, 1880, Report of the Indian Commissioner, Ottawa, 2 January 1880, 78.

99 Hugh Dempsey, ed., "The Starvation Year: Edgar Dewdney's Diary for 1879, Part 1," *Alberta History* 31 (1983): 9 (entries for 17 and 19 July 1879).

100 Jim Wallace, *A Double Duty: The Decisive First Decade of the North-West Mounted Police* (Winnipeg: Bunker to Bunker Books, 1997), 210.

101 John Macoun, *Autobiography of John Macoun, M.A.: Canadian Explorer and Naturalist, 1831–1920* (Ottawa: Ottawa Field-Naturalists Club, 1922), 149–50.

102 Dempsey, ed., "The Starvation Year, Part 1," 11 (entry of 24 July 1879).

103 *Saskatchewan Herald*, 1 December 1879, 1.

104 CSP, 1879, Part 3, North-West Mounted Police Force, Commissioner's Report, 1879, Report of Surgeon Kennedy, Fort Macleod, 30 November 1879, 34. Mortality is generally higher among females than males in populations "where tuberculosis epidemics are just beginning." Johnston, "Tuberculosis," 1060.

105 Adolph Hungry Wolf, The Blackfoot Papers-Volume 4 Pikunni Biographies (Skookumchuk, B.C.: The Good Medicine Cultural Foundation), 1260-1261.

106 Mountain fever is spread from contact with ticks infected with the mite *Rickittsia*. A recent discussion reported that between 20 and 25 percent of untreated victims die, though mortality from an outbreak was reported to be as high as 75 percent. Victoria A. Harden, "Rocky Mountain Spotted Fever and the Spotted Fever Group Diseases," in *Cambridge World History of Human Disease*, edited by Kenneth Kiple (Cambridge, UK: Cambridge University Press, 1993), 982, 984.

107 Ibid., 982; Kelly, *The Range Men*, 125; CSP, 1880, North-West Mounted Police Force, Commissioner's Report, 1879, Report of Surgeon Kittson, Fort Macleod, 30 January 1880, 29.

108 LAC, MG 29 B 15, Robert Bell Papers, vol. 24, f. 88, McDonald to Bell, 16 April 1879.

109 CSP, 1880, Report of Lawrence Vankoughnet, Deputy Superintendent General of Indian Affairs, Ottawa, 31 December 1879, 12.

110 CSP, 1880, Report of the Acting Superintendent, Battleford, 21 July 1879, 105.

111 LAC, RG 10, vol. 3678, file 11683, Report on the Indians of White Bear's Band, 5–6 August 1879.

112 LAC, RG 10, vol. 3678, file 11683, Report on the Indians of Day Star's Band and Yellow Quill's Band, 15 August 1879.

113 Lux, *Medicine that Walks,* 34.

114 LAC, RG 10, vol. 3678, file 11683, Report on the Indians of Loud Voice's Band, 29 August 1879; Report on the Indians of Chicock's Band, 30 August 1879.

115 Thomas Malthus, *An Essay on the Principle of Population, Volume 1,* edited by Patricia James (Cambridge, UK: Cambridge University Press, 1989), 11.

116 Amartya Sen, *Poverty and Famines: An Essay on Entitlement and Deprivation* (Oxford: Clarendon Press, 1981), 1. The notion of entitlement relations in the context of food is developed further in Sen's essay "Food, Economics, and Entitlements," in *The Political Economy of Hunger: Selected Essays,* edited by Jean Dreze, Amartya Sen, and Athar Hussain (Oxford: Clarendon Press, 1995), 50–68. See also Louise A. Titley, "Food Entitlement, Famine, and Conflict," *Journal of Interdisciplinary History* 14 (1983): 333–49.

117 See Breen, *The Canadian Prairie West and the Ranching Frontier,* 10–15; Paul Sharp, *Whoop-Up Country: The Canadian–American West, 1865–1885* (Norman: University of Oklahoma Press, 1973), 96–97.

118 *Saskatchewan Herald,* 1 December 1879, 1.

119 Commissioners of the Royal North-West Mounted Police, *Opening Up the West: Being the Official Reports of the Royal North-West Mounted Police Force from 1874 to 1881* (Toronto: Coles, 1973), 3.

120 Hildebrandt, *Views from Fort Battleford,* 98.

121 Stephen Sliwa, "Standing the Test of Time: A History of the Beardy's/Okemasis Reserve, 1876–1951" (MA thesis, Trent University, 1993), 54–57.

122 SAB, RCE-1120, Indians of North America, Clippings File, Yesteryears, No. 22, "Disquieting News from Duck Lake," 2 May 1938 (reprint of *Saskatchewan Herald,* 14 January 1879).

123 Sliwa, "Standing the Test of Time," 58–59; James Walker, Report, Battleford, 19 December 1879, in Commissioners of the Royal North-West Mounted Police, *Opening the West,* 21; *Saskatchewan Herald,* 27 January 1879, 1.

124 Gary Abrams, *Prince Albert: The First Century, 1866–1966* (Saskatoon: Modern Press, 1966), 26–27.

125 *Saskatchewan Herald,* 16 August 1880, 1. Beardy and his co-accused were later acquitted of the charges.

126 Sliwa, "Standing the Test of Time," 61–62.

127 HBCA, Search File: "Prince Albert," Lawrence Clarke to James Graham, 3 March 1880.

128 *Saskatchewan Herald,* 19 July 1880. Bands that expressed disaffection with the dominion included those of Poundmaker, Strike Him on the Back, Samson, Ermine Skin, and Bob Tail; ibid., 5 July 1880, 2–3.

129 Ibid., 16 August 1880, 2.

130 Dyck, "The Administration of Federal Indian Aid in the Northwest Territories"; Tobias, "Canada's Subjugation of the Plains Cree."

131 Looy, "The Indian Agent and His Role in the Administration of the Northwest Superintendency," 112.

132 Tobias, "Canada's Subjugation of the Plains Cree," 235n30.

133 Dempsey, ed., "The Starvation Year, Part 2," 8. Less than two years later the dominion's own surveyor refused to delineate the reserve set aside for Strike Him on the Back because of the poor quality of the land. *Saskatchewan Herald,* 5 June 1881, 1.

134 Kelly, *The Range Men,* 128.

135 Sharp, *Whoop-Up Country,* 221.

136 LAC, John A. Macdonald Papers, microfilm C-1590, 81299, Campbell to Macdonald, Ottawa, 10 August 1879.

137 Ibid.

138 Ibid., 81309–10, Campbell to Macdonald, Ottawa, 12 August 1879.

139 Ibid., 81312; George Duck, "Letters from the West," *The Beaver* 282 (1951): 24; SAB, Campbell Innes Papers, A-113, vol. 2, f. 3, "Lives of the Early Pioneers," 15 April 1920, 31.

140 McQuillan, "Creation of Indian Reserves on the Canadian Prairies," 385.
141 Dempsey, *Crowfoot*, 112–14.
142 Tobias, "Canada's Subjugation of the Plains Cree," 216–21.
143 Carter, *Lost Harvests*, 79.
144 Hildebrandt, *Views from Fort Battleford*, 40.
145 SAB, Tarr and Peterson, "Little Pine/Lucky Man Band #116"; Looy, "Saskatchewan's First Indian Agent," 112.
146 Carter, *Lost Harvests*, 81–82.
147 Ibid., 85–86; Looy, "The Indian Agent and His Role in the Administration of the Northwest Superintendency," 87–132; Brian Titley, *The Frontier World of Edgar Dewdney* (Vancouver: UBC Press, 1999), 45.
148 Dyck, "The Administration of Federal Indian Aid in the Northwest Territories," 34–37.
149 *CSP*, 1880, Report of the Deputy Superintendent General of Indian Affairs, Ottawa, 31 December 1879, 12.
150 Dyck, "The Administration of Federal Indian Aid in the Northwest Territories," 34, 41; Hugh Dempsey, "The Fearsome Fire Wagons," in *The CPR West: The Iron Road and the Making of a Nation*, edited by Hugh Dempsey (Vancouver: Douglas and McIntyre, 1984), 55–70; Carter, *Lost Harvests*, 99–102.
151 *CSP*, 1881, Report to the Superintendent General of Indian Affairs, Ottawa, 31 December 1880, 93.
152 Lux, *Medicine that Walks*, 36.
153 SAB, R. G. Ferguson Papers, microfilm R-2.391, Appendix: "Housing," 1.
154 *CSP*, 1881, James Smart, Report to the Superintendent of Indian Affairs, Edmonton, 21 August 1880, 102; Brian Titley, "The Fate of the Sharphead Stonies," *Alberta History* 39 (1991): 2; H.B. MacDonald, "The Killing of the Buffalo," *The Beaver* 266 (1935): 22.
155 *CSP*, 1880, Report of the Deputy Superintendent General of Indian Affairs, Ottawa, 31 December 1879, 13.
156 Carter, *Lost Harvests*, 89.
157 HBCA, Search File: "Prince Albert," Clarke to Graham, 3 March 1880, 3.
158 *CSP*, 1881, Report to the Superintendent General of Indian Affairs, Fort Walsh, 30 September 1880, 106.
159 *CSP*, 1881, Report of the Superintendent General of Indian Affairs, Extract of Fort Ellice Report, 25 January 1881, xxxi.
160 *CSP*, 1883, Report of C. E. Denny, Indian Agent, Fort Macleod, 10 November 1882, 176.
161 Hugh Dempsey, "The Bull Elk Affair," *Alberta History* 40 (1992): 2–9.
162 *CSP*, 1880, Lawrence Vankoughnet, Report of the Deputy Superintendent General of Indian Affairs, Ottawa, 31 December 1879, 13.
163 Lux, *Medicine that Walks*, 36. Heavy blizzards in the nearby eastern parklands were reported to have caused the final extermination of a remnant bison herd in the Kamsack area of eastern Saskatchewan. MacDonald, "The Killing of the Buffalo," 22.
164 Report of Major Walsh, Brockville, 31 December 1880, in Commissioners of the Royal North-West Mounted Police, *Opening the West*, 26.
165 Report of Superintendent L. N. F. Crozier, Wood Mountain, December 1880, in ibid., 30–31.
166 Report of Surgeon George A. Kennedy, Fort Walsh, 23 December 1880, in ibid., 47. Kennedy reported a scarlet fever epidemic in October.
167 LAC, RG 10, reel C-10126, vol. 3726, file 24811, "Report from Dr. Kittson of the North-West Mounted Police Stationed at Fort Macleod, Concerning the Insufficiency of Rations Issued to the Indians of the Northwest Territories, 1880–1915," Kittson to Macleod, 1 July 1880, 2.
168 *CSP*, 1881, Report to the Superintendent General of Indian Affairs, Ottawa, 31 December 1880, 91–93.
169 Carter, *Lost Harvests*, 89, 99.
170 *Saskatchewan Herald*, 12 January 1880, 1; *CSP*, 1882, W. Anderson, Edmonton, 13 December 1881, 84.
171 *Saskatchewan Herald*, 5 July 1880, 1; *CSP*, 1880, Report of Battleford Agency, 21 July 1879, 104.
172 Tobias, "Canada's Subjugation of the Plains Cree," 528.

173 Brian Hubner, "Horse Stealing and the Borderline: The NWMP and the Control of Indian Movement," *Prairie Forum* 20 (1995): 296.

174 *CSP*, 1881, Report to the Superintendent General of Indian Affairs, Ottawa, 31 December 1880, 92.

175 Bruce Peel, "The Last Battle," *The Beaver* 297 (1966): 12; Robert Stewart, *Sam Steele: Lion of the Frontier* (Regina: Centax Books, 1999), 92–93; Carter, *Lost Harvests*, 76–77.

176 Peel, "The Last Battle," 12–14.

177 *CSP*, 1881, Edgar Dewdney, Report of the Indian Commissioner, 31 December 1880, 92.

178 Nettie McLennan, "Starting Out with the Indians," in *Early History of Saskatchewan Churches*, edited by Meredith B. Banting (Regina: Banting Publishers, 1975), 176.

179 HBCA, Search File: "Prince Albert," Clarke to James Graham, Fort Carlton, 3 March 1880, 3.

180 Hagarty was officially dismissed on 14 June 1880. LAC, RG 10, vol. 3648, file 8138, J. Cote, Report of a Committee of the Privy Council, 14 June 1880.

181 MacPherson, *The Battlefords*, 60; LAC, RG 10, vol. 3678, file 11683, Robert Sinclair (Accountant) to Lawrence Vankoughnet, 7 August 1879.

182 *CSP*, 1881, Report of Edwin Allen, Indian Agent, Fort Walsh, 30 September 1880, 106. Lux, *Medicine that Walks,* 37, noted that overcrowding, an inadequate diet, and the constant movement in search of food "produced an out-of-control synergism between infection and hunger."

183 *CSP*, 1881, Edgar Dewdney, Report of the Indian Commissioner, Ottawa, 31 December 1880, 92. For a discussion of the Montana outbreak, and a subsequent epidemic of mumps, see Lux, *Medicine that Walks,* 37. Mortality of the combined outbreak was greatest among children. *CSP*, 1882, John A. Macdonald, Superintendent of Indian Affairs, Fort Macleod, 30 May 1881, xxiv.

184 Dempsey, *Crowfoot,* 131–38; Dyck, "The Administration of Federal Aid in the Northwest Territories," 45.

185 *CSP*, 1882, Report of the Department of Indian Affairs, Fort Carlton, 23 March 1881, x.

186 Lux, *Medicine that Walks,* 59.

187 Dempsey, "The Bull Elk Affair," 4–5, 8. Some meagre improvements were made to the ration system, including the distribution of cattle heads and offal gratis to the Indian population and the maintenance of an adequate supply of beef and flour to allay fears of imposed starvation.

188 Stewart, *Sam Steele,* 96; Lux, *Medicine that Walks,* 40.

189 *Saskatchewan Herald,* 11 April 1881, 1.

190 Tessaro, "Bovine Tuberculosis and Brucellosis in Animals, Including Humans," 213.

191 Lux, *Medicine that Walks,* 36.

192 *Saskatchewan Herald,* 25 April 1881, 1.

193 *CSP*, 1882, Report of the Department of Indian Affairs, Extract of Report, Humboldt, 18 November 1881, xiii.

194 *Saskatchewan Herald,* 4 July 1881, 1.

195 Ibid., 31 December 1881, 1. The human variant of mange, a mite-borne disease, is scabies. Clayton L. Thomas, ed., *Taber's Cyclopedic Medical Dictionary,* 16th ed. (Philadelphia: F.A. Davis Company, 1989), 1079. The mange epidemic among the remaining Indian horses continued until at least the summer of 1882, when Cree leader Mistawassis implored the governor general for help because their horses had been traded for food or died of disease. MacPherson, *The Battlefords,* 68.

196 Larmour, "Edgar Dewdney," 35–37.

197 Dyck, "The Administration of Federal Indian Aid in the Northwest Territories," 42.

198 Titley, *The Frontier World of Edgar Dewdney,* 47–49; Larmour, "Edgar Dewdney," 31–32.

199 Robert Nestor, "Hayter Reed, Severality, and the Subdivision of Indian Reserves on the Canadian Prairies" (MA thesis, University of Regina, 1997), 33.

200 *CSP*, 1882, Hayter Reed, Report of the Superintendent General of Indian Affairs, Battleford, 9 July 1881, xviii.

201 Looy, "The Indian Agent and His Role in the Administration of the Northwest Superintendency," 94.

202 MacPherson, *The Battlefords*, 71.
203 Tobias, "Canada's Subjugation of the Plains Cree," 528–29.
204 Beal, "Money, Markets, and Economic Development in Saskatchewan Indian Reserve Communities," 145.
205 MacPherson, *The Battlefords*, 69.
206 McQuillan, "Creation of Indian Reserves on the Canadian Prairies," 385.
207 With the exception of the Wood Mountain Dakota, whose reserve was established near the international boundary, the only reserve in southwestern Saskatchewan is Nekaneet, near Maple Creek. The small Cree community was granted reserve status in 1913. David Lee, "Foremost Man and His Band," *Saskatchewan History* 36 (1983): 100.
208 *Saskatchewan Herald*, 27 May 1882, 2; 24 June 1882, 1.
209 Lux, *Medicine that Walks*, 69–70.
210 Hugh Dempsey, *Big Bear: The End of Freedom* (Vancouver: Douglas and McIntyre, 1984), 109–11.
211 The localized nature of tuberculosis infection was highlighted by the observation that, in the 1920s, the treaty Indian population of the Qu'Appelle Valley had a TB mortality rate twenty times higher than the Euro-Canadian population of the area. R.G. Ferguson, *Tuberculosis among the Indians of the Great Plains: Preliminary Report of an Investigation Being Carried Out by the National Research Council of Canada* (London: Adlard and Son, 1929), 45.
212 David McCrady, "Living with Strangers: The Nineteenth-Century Sioux and the Canadian–American Borderlands" (Ph.D. diss., University of Manitoba, 1998), 1.
213 Peter D. Elias, *The Dakota of the Canadian Northwest: Lessons for Survival* (Winnipeg: University of Manitoba Press, 1988), 57.
214 Mark Deidrich, *The Odyssey of Chief Standing Buffalo and the Northern Sisseton Sioux* (Minneapolis: Coyote Books, 1988), 37. In his study of TB among treaty inhabitants of the Qu'Appelle Valley, R.G. Ferguson postulated that the band might have introduced the disease to the region. See "A Study of the Epidemiology in a Primitive People," *Edinburgh Medical Journal* 36 (1929): 204–05. Ferguson based his studies on population data gathered from annuity payment records of the Department of Indian Affairs. Because the Dakota were not treaty Indians, they did not receive annuity payments and were not included in the studies.
215 Elias, *The Dakota of the Canadian Northwest*, 57.
216 LAC, RG 10, reel C-10119, vol. 3678, file 11683. The physician reported on 7 January 1879 that the men were employed cutting wood while the women "were doing a great deal of work around the settlers' houses."
217 Ibid., 8 September 1879.
218 Elias, *The Dakota of the Canadian Northwest*, 56–57.
219 Ibid., 155.
220 "Positive deviance" was a concept developed in the field of nutrition to account for successful behaviours of healthy individuals within otherwise impoverished populations. Daschuk, Hackett, and MacNeil, "Treaties and Tuberculosis," 307–30.

CHAPTER 8—DOMINION ADMINISTRATION OF RELIEF, 1883–85

1 By 1883, 91 percent of the Treaty 4 population had settled on reserves. The members of a single band led by Foremost Man made up three-quarters of those absent in the statistics for Treaty 4. In the Battleford and Carlton districts, over 98 percent of the treaty population were on their appointed reserves. Although listed among the settled, Big Bear's band stayed on the move until 1885. Carl Beal, "Money, Markets, and Economic Development in Saskatchewan Indian Reserve Communities, 1870–1930s" (Ph.D. diss., University of Manitoba, 1994), 126–27.
2 LAC, MG 26, John A. Macdonald Papers, Vankoughnet to Macdonald, 2 November 1882.
3 Glenbow Archives, M 320, Dewdney Papers, Series 10, Fred White to Edgar Dewdney, 29 August 1882, 737–41.

4   John P. Turner, *The North-West Mounted Police*, vol. 2 (Ottawa: King's Printer, 1950), 31; Jim Wallace, *A Double Duty: The Decisive First Decade of the North-West Mounted Police* (Winnipeg: Bunker to Bunker Books, 1997), 244.

5   Paul Sharp, "Merchant Princes of the Plains," *Montana: Magazine of History* 5 (1955): 6.

6   Beal, "Money, Markets, and Economic Development in Saskatchewan Indian Reserve Communities," 130–40.

7   Sharp, "Merchant Princes of the Plains," 5–7. The head office was moved to St. Louis in 1874.

8   Paul Sharp, *Whoop-Up Country: The Canadian–American West, 1865–1885* (Norman: University of Oklahoma Press, 1973), 222.

9   Alan Wilson, "Introduction," in *The Letters of Charles John Brydges, 1879–1882, Hudson's Bay Company Land Commissioner*, edited by Hartwell Bowsfield (Winnipeg: Hudson's Bay Record Society, 1977), xxxiv.

10   Cecil Denny, *The Law Marches West* (Toronto: J. M. Dent and Sons, 1972), 190–91. On completion of the railway, Indian agents were supplied with boxes of uncut one-dollar bills to prepare as cash for treaty payments.

11   Sharp, "Merchant Princes of the Plains," 8.

12   C. J. Brydges to William Armit, 28 September 1882, in Bowsfield, ed., *The Letters of Charles John Brydges*, 202. On one occasion, Brydges himself had to purchase food for his own use from a Baker store at Fort Ellice "because we had none." C.J. Brydges to Eden Colville, 29 August 1881, in ibid., 264.

13   Brydges to Armit, 28 September 1882, in ibid., 267. Much of Baker's success can be attributed to its ability to maintain a low cost for freight. Goods delivered to Calgary from Montreal cost five and a half cents a pound, whereas the HBC paid three cents a pound for freight between Edmonton and Calgary, a distance of only 200 miles.

14   Sharp, "Merchant Princes of the Plains," 12.

15   L. V. Kelly, *The Range Men: The Story of the Ranchers and Indians of Alberta* (Toronto: Coles, 1980), 142.

16   Brydges to Colville, 6 May 1881, in Bowsfield, ed., *The Letters of Charles John Brydges*, 157.

17   Brydges to Armit, 8 January 1880, in ibid., 46n3. See also Brydges to Armit, 12 May 1881, in ibid., 162.

18   Brydges to Armit, 28 September 1882, in ibid., 265.

19   Improvements in navigation were the responsibility of the dominion Department of Public Works. Bruce Peel, *Steamboats on the Saskatchewan* (Saskatoon: Western Producer Prairie Books, 1972), 111–23.

20   Ibid., 124–34. In 1883, the *Northcote* ran aground several times and was forced to leave seventy-seven tons of cargo destined for Edmonton at Pitt.

21   Theodore Barris, *Fire Canoe: Prairie Steamboat Days Revisited* (Toronto: McClelland and Stewart, 1977), 70–71. The steamer loaded its cargo at Medicine Hat, where the railway crossed the South Saskatchewan River.

22   Peel, *Steamboats on the Saskatchewan*, 140.

23   *Saskatchewan Herald*, 13 October 1883, 1.

24   Peel, *Steamboats on the Saskatchewan*, 105–09.

25   Peel, *Steamboats on the Saskatchewan*, 105–09.

26   Hugh Dempsey, *Crowfoot: Chief of the Blackfeet* (Norman: University of Oklahoma Press, 1972), 140. During the standoff between the police and the Blackfoot, oats and flour in the ration house were piled against the walls of the detachment as fortification. Hugh Dempsey, "The Bull Elk Affair," *Alberta History* 40 (1992): 7–8.

27   The inability of the HBC to fill orders beyond those provided for in the yearly tendering process was a serious deficiency in its quest for dominion contracts. Because Baker could meet the pressing need for food in cases of starvation, the dominion turned to the American company. Wilson, "Introduction," lxvi.

28   Noel E. Dyck, "The Administration of Federal Indian Aid in the North-West Territories, 1879–1885" (MA thesis, University of Saskatchewan, 1970), 39–43.

29   In the Treaty 4 area, reserve land under cultivation increased fivefold, grain production increased eightfold, and root crops tripled between 1880 and 1884. In that time, the reserve

population more than tripled. In the Treaty 6 area, the Battleford reserves increased their grain production by more than 600 percent and doubled their production of root crops during the four-year period. Although the reserve population increased, it was not as great as that in the Treaty 4 region. Beal, "Money, Markets, and Economic Development in Saskatchewan Indian Reserve Communities," 154–55.

30 Both home farms and European-manned supply farms were cancelled, though farm instructors remained on reserves. Brian Titley, *The Frontier World of Edgar Dewdney* (Vancouver: UBC Press, 1999), 53; Beal, "Money, Markets, and Economic Development in Saskatchewan Indian Reserve Communities," 151.

31 Beal, "Money, Markets, and Economic Development in Saskatchewan Indian Reserve Communities," 158.

32 *Saskatchewan Herald,* 10 November 1883, 2. On the Poundmaker Reserve in 1882, people were reported to be starving beside ample supplies of grain because there was no mill to turn the wheat into food. Sarah Carter, *Lost Harvests: Prairie Indian Reserve Farmers and Government Policy* (Montreal: McGill-Queen's University Press, 1990), 99.

33 SAB, John A. Macdonald Papers, reel C 1524, Dewdney to Macdonald, 4 February 1885, 193–94.

34 Dyck, "The Administration of Federal Indian Aid in the Northwest Territories," 32.

35 In the fall of 1882, rations were withheld from Poundmaker's band for over forty days. Canada, House of Commons, *Debates,* 15 April 1886, 723. DIA employees were a "major source of intelligence about the Cree and their plans." John L. Tobias, "Canada's Subjugation of the Plains Cree, 1879–1885," *Canadian Historical Review* 64 (1983): 533.

36 Jean Larmour, "Edgar Dewdney, Commissioner of Indian Affairs and Lieutenant Governor of the North-West Territories, 1879–1888" (MA thesis, University of Saskatchewan, Regina Campus, 1969), 35.

37 George F. G. Stanley, *The Birth of Western Canada: A History of the Riel Rebellions* (Toronto: University of Toronto Press, 1960), 269–70; Dyck, "The Administration of Federal Indian Aid in the Northwest Territories," 57, 69, 81; Maureen Lux, *Medicine that Walks: Disease, Medicine, and Canadian Plains Native People, 1880–1940* (Toronto: University of Toronto Press, 2001), 42; Beal, "Money, Markets, and Economic Development in Saskatchewan Indian Reserve Communities," 140.

38 Douglas Leighton, "A Victorian Civil Servant at Work: Lawrence Vankoughnet and the Canadian Indian Department, 1873–1893," in *As Long as the Sun Shines and Water Flows: A Reader in Canadian Native Studies,* edited by Ian A. L. Getty and Antoine Lussier (Vancouver: UBC Press, 1983), 104–19.

39 Sandra Gwyn, *"A Private Capital": Love and Ambition in the Age of Macdonald and Laurier* (Toronto: McClelland and Stewart, 1984), 128.

40 Denny, *The Law Marches West,* 204; *Saskatchewan Herald,* 29 September 1883, 2.

41 Leighton, "A Victorian Civil Servant at Work," 106–07.

42 In 1883, Reed was appointed to the second highest office of the DIA bureaucracy in the northwest after only two years of experience in the department. Robert Nestor, "Hayter Reed, Severality, and the Subdivision of Indian Reserves on the Canadian Prairies" (MA thesis, Saskatchewan Indian Federated College, University of Regina, 1998), 33–34.

43 Robert Jefferson, *Fifty Years on the Saskatchewan* (Battleford: Canadian North-West Historical Society, 1929), 126.

44 Leighton, "A Victorian Civil Servant at Work," 107; Stanley, *The Birth of Western Canada,* 270–71.

45 Simon Winchester, *Krakatoa: The Day the Earth Exploded: Aug. 27, 1883* (New York: HarperCollins, 2003), 291.

46 The eruption of Krakatoa measured 6 on the Volcanic Explosivity Index. K. R. Briffa et al., "Influence of Volcanic Eruptions on Northern Hemisphere Summer Temperature over the Past 600 Years," *Nature* 393 (1998): 451, 453.

47 Gerald Friesen, "Imports and Exports in the Manitoba Economy 1870–1890," *Manitoba History* 16 (1988): 39; Donald Creighton, *John A. Macdonald: The Old Chieftain* (Toronto: Macmillan of Canada, 1955), 370.

48 Qu'Appelle Valley Farming Company, "Annual Meeting of the Qu'Appelle Valley Farming Company, Limited" (president's report), Winnipeg, 9 January 1884, 2.

49 B.E. Anderson, "Relief Problem Existed Here in 1883 When William Hunter Drove to Duck Lake for Flour Supply," *Saskatoon Daily Star* (press clipping, 1932?), SAB, Campbell Innes Papers, A-113, vol. 2, f. 18.

50 At Lake Athabasca, the hunger was so extreme that there were reports of cannibalism. In 1884, famine was also reported at Rupert's House. SAB, R. G. Ferguson Papers, reel R.2.391, Appendix "Scarcity of Food of Northern Indians," 4. At Moose Factory, cold, wet summers in 1883 and 1884 meant that "all garden operations are next to a failure." Shipping in Hudson Bay was also delayed by severe ice conditions. A. J. W. Catchpole and Irene Hanuta, "Severe Summer Ice in Hudson Strait and Hudson Bay Following Major Volcanic Eruptions, 1751 to 1889 A.D.," *Climatic Change* 14 (1989): 72.

51 David Meyer, *The Red Earth Crees, 1860–1960*, Mercury Series, Canadian Ethnology Service Paper No. 100 (Ottawa: National Museum of Man, 1985), 169.

52 LAC, MG 17, Records of the Church Missionary Society, microfilm A-112, James Settee, The Pas (Devon) Journal, 20 February 1884.

53 Glenbow Archives, M 320, Dewdney Papers, Series 8, Macdonald to Dewdney, 17 September 1883, 443–44.

54 Lux, *Medicine that Walks*, 40.

55 CSP, John A. Macdonald, Annual Report of the Department of Indian Affairs, 1 January 1884, x–xi.

56 Stanley, *The Birth of Western Canada*, 272.

57 Glenbow Archives, M 320, Dewdney Papers, Series 8, Macdonald to Dewdney, 17 November 1883, 471–72.

58 Isabel Andrews, "The Crooked Lakes Reserves: A Study in Indian Policy in Practice from the Qu'Appelle Treaty to 1900" (MA thesis, University of Regina, 1972), 63.

59 Glenbow Archives, M 320, Dewdney Papers, Series 8, Macdonald to Dewdney, 8 December 1883, 475–76.

60 Andrews, "The Crooked Lakes Reserves," 64.

61 Hugh Dempsey, *Big Bear: The End of Freedom* (Vancouver: Douglas and McIntyre, 1984), 121.

62 Titley, *The Frontier World of Edgar Dewdney*, 53–54.

63 Dempsey, *Big Bear*, 121.

64 SAB, John A. Macdonald Papers, R-70, Macdonald to Dewdney, 28 November 1883, 51.

65 Titley, *The Frontier World of Edgar Dewdney*, 54.

66 Larmour, "Edgar Dewdney, Commissioner of Indian Affairs and Lieutenant Governor of the Northwest Territories," 60–61.

67 Anthony J. Looy, "The Indian Agent and His Role in the Administration of the Northwest Superintendency, 1876–1893" (Ph.D. diss., Queen's University, 1977), 104.

68 The total expenditure for relief of all the destitute Indians of Manitoba and the Northwest Territories was approximately $500,000. Canada, *Public Accounts of Canada, Fiscal Year Ended 30th June 1883* (Ottawa: Queen's Printer), iii, 62.

69 In 1881, a "Mr. Smith" offered to withdraw his tender in exchange for $5,000 from the HBC; Baker acquired his withdrawal for a mere $1,000. The HBC estimated that bribes paid by Baker to Smith and another firm under "Kavanaugh" led to significant profits. Brydges to Colville, 6 May 1881, in Bowsfield, ed., *The Letters of Charles John Brydges*, 155–57.

70 C. J. Brydges to Eden Colville, 2 May 1881, in ibid., 153.

71 Sharp, "Merchant Princes of the Plains," 15.

72 Sharp, *Whoop-Up Country*, 221.

73 Titley, *The Frontier World of Edgar Dewdney*, 143.

74 LAC, MG 26, John A. Macdonald Papers, microfilm C-1596, Dewdney to Macdonald, 9 August 1882, 89718–19. Dewdney was reportedly given $10,000 in stocks of the Bell Farming Company. Canada, House of Commons, *Debates*, M. C. Cameron, 15 April 1886, 719.

75 Jean Larmour, "Edgar Dewdney, Indian Commissioner in the Transition Period of Indian Settlement, 1897–1885," *Saskatchewan History* 33 (1980): 14.

76   A liberal newspaper, the *Stratford Beacon,* noted that "Mr. Dewdney went out west as poor as a church mouse ... and now he is reputed to be worth half a million. He is certainly a very wealthy man. He did not save this out of his salary. How did he get it?" Cited in Dempsey, *Big Bear,* 117.

77   Canada, House of Commons, *Debates,* Mr. Patterson, 16 April 1886, 734.

78   Lux, *Medicine that Walks,* 59–60.

79   Canada, House of Commons, *Debates,* 15 April 1886, 734.

80   Ibid., A.W. Ogilvy and Company to I.G. Baker and Company, 17 May 1884, 736.

81   Lux, *Medicine that Walks,* 143–44.

82   Larmour, "Edgar Dewdney, Commissioner of Indian Affairs and Lieutenant Governor of the North-West Territories," 52–53.

83   Dempsey, *The Amazing Death of Calf Shirt and other Blackfoot Stories,* 162.

84   In one case, over 43,000 pounds of beef were bought from Baker in a single day for the approximately 2,100 inhabitants of the reserve. Canada, House of Commons, *Debates,* 11 July 1885, 3220, 3319.

85   Canada, House of Commons, *Debates,* M.C. Cameron, 13 July 1885, 3319; LAC, MG 26, John A. Macdonald Papers, microfilm C-1523, 42237.

86   An outbreak of typhoid fever killed a large number of Niitsitapi in the fall of 1883. CSP, John A. Macdonald, Report of the Department of Indian Affairs, 1 January 1884, liii.

87   Canada, House of Commons, *Debates,* C. F. Ferguson, 15 April 1886, 739–40.

88   The contract for supplies with Baker amounted to almost half of the total expenses for Farm 17. The HBC supplied no food to Farm 17 during the period identified in the Wadsworth report. Canada, *Public Accounts of Canada, Fiscal Year Ended 30th June 1883* (Ottawa: Queen's Printer), 84–85.

89   LAC, MG 26, John A. Macdonald Papers, microfilm C-1523, 42228.

90   In 1883, fresh beef sold for eight cents a pound in the northwest, while bacon cost three times as much. In the Treaty 4 area, the dominion spent $15,290.92 on salted pork but only $1,288.45 on fresh beef, prompting Indian Agent Herchmer to report that "A great deal of sickness has visited them lately caused by the want of fresh meat ... although it is known that beef is life to the Indian, while salt pork is disease and death to him." Canada, House of Commons, *Debates,* 15 April 1886, 722–23.

91   Lux, *Medicine that Walks,* 38.

92   LAC, RG 10, vol. 3744, file 29507-2, Report of A. MacDonald, Qu'Appelle, 20 June 1882.

93   Lux, *Medicine that Walks,* 39; David Lee, "Piapot: Man and Myth," *Prairie Forum* 17 (1992): 257. For a regional perspective on the returns to Cypress, see Tobias, "Canada's Subjugation of the Plains Cree," 219–20.

94   CSP, 1884, DIA Annual Report for 1883, Report of T. P. Wadsworth, Inspector of Indian Agencies, Edmonton, 9 October 1883, 117.

95   Lux, *Medicine that Walks,* 40. Agent MacDonald continued to withhold rations to control his charges and on one occasion wrote that "a little starvation will do them good." Canada, House of Commons, *Debates,* M.C. Cameron, 15 April 1886, 729.

96   Piapot's acceptance of a reserve adjacent to the Assiniboine Reserve created a concentration of more than 2,000 Indians, and the chief intended the mass of people to serve as a power base from which to negotiate revisions to Treaty 4. Tobias, "Canada's Subjugation of the Plains Cree," 220.

97   Lee, "Piapot," 256.

98   *Regina Leader,* 16 August 1883, 2.

99   Ibid., 23 August 1883, 2.

100   Ibid., 22 November 1883, 4.

101   Statement regarding the food riot at the Sakimay Reserve, ibid., 28 February 1884, 4.

102   SAB, microfilm 2.75, *School Histories of Thirty-Five Indian Reserves,* Abel Watetch, "History of Piapot Reserve," 5; Abel Watetch, *Payepot and His People* (Regina: Saskatchewan History and Folklore Society, 1959), 17.

103   W. W. Gibson, *Silver Cloud: Condensed from "The Last Buffalo"* (n.p.: self-published, 1940?), 2–3. Official reports of the mortality were lower but still horrendous. Dr. O.C. Edwards reported that the death toll was forty-two Crees and thirty-three Assiniboines; LAC, RG

10, vol. 3745, file 29506-4, Part 1, O.C. Edwards to A. MacDonald, 13 May 1884. M. C. Cameron asserted that 10 percent of the Indians at the Indian Head reserves died in the span of six months during the winter of 1883–84; Canada, House of Commons, *Debates*, M.C. Cameron, 15 April 1886, 724. Katherine Pettipas, *Severing the Ties that Band: Government Repression of Indigenous Religious Ceremonies on the Prairies*, Manitoba Studies in Native History (Winnipeg: University of Manitoba Press, 1994), 13, estimated the death toll to be 30 percent.

104 Canada, House of Commons, *Debates*, 15 April 1886, 719.

105 Ibid., 745. Detailed accounts of the Indian department are not available for 1883–84.

106 Canada, House of Commons, *Debates*, 11 July 1885, 3320.

107 Glenbow Archives, M 320, Dewdney Papers, Series 8, CPR Telegraph, 8 February 1884, 485.

108 LAC, MG 26, John A. Macdonald Papers, microfilm C-1523, file 11175, 42224, handwritten note, 19 March 1884, "Action Taken by Department on Matters Complained Of." In Parliament, it was charged that Edwards' report was suppressed by Dewdney for almost two years because it was "so scandalous and outrageous." Canada, House of Commons, *Debates*, 15 April 1886, 725.

109 LAC, RG 10, vol. 3745, file 29506-4, Part 1, Commissioner A.G. Irvine to Fred White, Regina, 27 May 1884.

110 LAC, MG 26, John A. Macdonald Papers, microfilm C-1523, 42224, Re: Sickness of Piapot Reserve.

111 LAC, RG 10, vol. 3745, file 29506-4, Part 1, Commissioner A. G. Irvine to Fred White, Regina, 18 May 1884. The corpses had been lashed to trees in accordance with traditional practices, but Irvine reported that a fire had caused the "bodies to drop on the ground where they remained."

112 LAC, RG 10, vol. 3745, file 29506-4, Part 1, Edwards to MacDonald, Indian Head, 13 May 1884. Lux, *Medicine that Walks*, 44, noted that Edwards' designation of the ailment as "land scurvy" was probably a misdiagnosis of scrofula (cervical lymphadenitis).

113 LAC, RG 10, vol. 3745, file 29506-4, Part 1, Edwards to MacDonald, Indian Head, 13 may 1884. See also, Lux, *Medicine that Walks*, 4.

114 LAC, RG 10, vol. 3745, file 29506-4, Part 1, Irvine to White, 18 May 1884; W. A. Waiser, *La Police a Cheval du Nord-Ouest, de 1874 a 1889: Étude statistique*, Bulletin de recherche 117 (Ottawa: Parcs Canada, 1979), 13.

115 LAC, RG 10, vol. 3745, file 29506-4, Part 1, Irvine to White, 18 May 1884.

116 Lux, *Medicine that Walks*, 51.

117 Canada, House of Commons, *Debates*, M. C. Cameron, 15 April 1886, 724–25.

118 LAC, MG 26, John A. Macdonald Papers, microfilm C-1690, 132745, Vankoughnet to Macdonald, 10 December 1883.

119 Andrews, "The Crooked Lakes Reserves," 58–59.

120 Before being fired, Setter fed 567 inhabitants of the reserve primarily under the leadership of Chief Sakimay. Another band that shared the reserve, under the leadership of She Sheep, comprised of 355 people, was self-supporting through hunting and fishing in the parklands and required no food assistance. Ibid., 48–76.

121 Isabel Andrews, "Indian Protest against Starvation: The Yellow Calf Incident of 1884," *Saskatchewan History* 28 (1975): 41–51.

122 Ibid., 46–47.

123 Lux, *Medicine that Walks*, 43; *Saskatchewan Herald*, 28 June 1884, 2.

124 Peter Naylor, "Index to Aboriginal Issues Found in the Records of the North West Mounted Police RG 18, National Archives of Canada" (typescript) (Saskatoon: Office of the Treaty Commissioner, 1994), 189, document 497, Lawrence Vankoughnet to Fred White, 2 May 1884.

125 Andrews, "The Crooked Lakes Reserves," 92.

126 Glenbow Archives, M 320, Dewdney Papers, Series 8, Macdonald to Dewdney, 11 August 1884, 509–10.

127 LAC, MG 26, John A. Macdonald Papers, microfilm C-1523, file 4624, 4225. Crowfoot also complained of inadequate flour rations; see file 15040, 41873, 14 August 1884. The total

estimated death toll among the Blackfoot between 1883 and 1886 was 600; Tom McHugh, *The Time of the Buffalo* (New York: Knopf, 1972), 286.

128 LAC, RG 10, vol. 3745, file 29506-4, Part 1, Reed to Macdonald, 20 May 1884.

129 Lux, *Medicine that Walks*, 65; Dyck, "The Administration of Federal Indian Aid in the Northwest Territories," 74.

130 *Saskatchewan Herald*, 28 June 1884, 1.

131 Ibid., 19 April 1884, 1. Judge C. B. Rouleau admonished Dewdney to provide the Indians with food and clothing for the good of "the Government and the Country." Blair Stonechild and Bill Waiser, *Loyal till Death: Indians and the North-West Rebellion* (Calgary: Fifth House, 1997), 61.

132 *Saskatchewan Herald*, 3 May 1884, 1.

133 Ross Innes, *The Sands of Time* (Battleford: Turner-Warwick Publications, 1986), 31–43.

134 In 1884, the dominion began providing children in the mission schools with "a biscuit each for their dinner." CMS, microfilm A-112, John Hines Journal, 9 June 1884.

135 Louis Cochin, *Reminiscences: A Veteran Missionary of Cree Indians and a Prisoner in Poundmaker's Camp* (Battleford: Battleford Historical Society, 1927), 26.

136 Jefferson, *Fifty Years on the Saskatchewan*, 125.

137 D. Aidan McQuillan, "Creation of Indian Reserves on the Canadian Prairies, 1870–1885," *Geographical Review* 70 (1980): 392. The successful reserves might well have been in the parklands, where a mixed economy was still feasible. Yellow Quill's band, on the northern margins of Treaty 4, were able to purchase blankets, clothing, and flour with their ample harvest of furs. CSP, 1884, A. MacDonald, Report of Qu'Appelle Agency, Treaty 4, 6 July 1883, 73.

138 McQuillan, "Creation of Indian Reserves on the Canadian Prairies," 392.

139 *Saskatchewan Herald*, 31 May 1884, 3.

140 Kelly, *The Range Men*, 175–76.

141 CMS, microfilm A-112, John Hines, Assissippi Journal, 9 March 1884.

142 Ibid.

143 CSP, 1885, J. A. Macrae, Report of Carlton Agency, 11 August 1884, 79–80. At Prince Albert, the scarcity of processing equipment was compounded by the destruction of two mills from fires in 1884. *Saskatchewan Herald*, 6 April 1884, 1; 14 June 1884, 3.

144 CMS, microfilm A-112, James Settee to Reverend Fenn, 22 November 1884.

145 CMS, microfilm A-112, James Settee to Reverend Fenn, 8 December 1884.

146 Frank Tough, "The Establishment of a Commercial Fishing Industry and the Demise of Native Fisheries in Northern Manitoba," *Canadian Journal of Native Studies* 4 (1984): 303–19.

147 CSP, 1885, J. A. Macrae, Report of Carlton Agency, 11 August 1884, 83.

148 CSP, 1885, Thomas Quinn, Acting Indian Sub-Agent, Report for Fort Pitt, 21 July 1884, 86.

149 Anderson reported that the Ste. Anne fishery had declined from as much as 40,000 or 50,000 pounds per winter during the HBC period to less than 8,000 pounds; CSP, 1885, W. Anderson, Indian Agent, Report for Edmonton, 26 August 1884, 137. By 1887, exports of fish to the United States from the northwest amounted to 1.5 million pounds; SAB, R. G. Ferguson Papers, microfilm R.391, Appendix 3: "Food," 53. A year later the estimated catch on Lake Winnipeg was 2 million pounds, described as a "wholesale slaughter of fish"; James Mochoruk, "The Political Economy of Northern Development: Governments and Capital along Manitoba's Resource Frontier, 1870–1930" (Ph.D. diss., University of Manitoba, 1992), 135–36.

150 CSP, 1885, T. P. Wadsworth, Battleford, 25 October 1884, 150. By the turn of the century, Jackfish Lake was so depleted that people abandoned it, going to Meadow Lake and Big River in search of fish. Meota History Book Committee, *Footsteps in Time* (Meota, SK: Meota History Book Committee, 1980), 95.

151 *Saskatchewan Herald*, 4 June 1887, 2.

152 Tobias, "Canada's Subjugation of the Plains Cree," 222.

153 SAB, John A. Macdonald Papers, R-70, Dewdney to Macdonald, 5 September 1884.

154 In 1883, expenditures for provisions in the northwest amounted to $530,982; the following year the total rose to $547,595. Beal, "Money, Markets, and Economic Development in Saskatchewan Indian Reserve Communities," 140.

155 Glenbow Archives, M 320, Dewdney Papers, Series 10, Fred White to Edgar Dewdney, 22 November 1884, 799–802.

156 *Saskatchewan Herald,* 20 March 1885, 2.

157 Canada, House of Commons, *Debates,* M. C. Cameron, 15 April 1886, 720.

158 Stonechild and Waiser, *Loyal till Death,* 4.

159 Although most accounts list nine deaths, Allen Ronaghan has argued that a tenth murder has gone unrecognized. See his "Who Was the 'Fine Young Man'? The Frog Lake 'Massacre' Revisited," *Saskatchewan History* 43 (1995): 18.

160 Stonechild and Waiser, *Loyal till Death,* 117.

161 Ibid., 108. Quinn, a trainee of Reed, was described as "the most stubborn and obnoxious of the Indian Department's employees." Bob Beal and Rod Macleod, *Prairie Fire: The 1885 North-West Rebellion* (Edmonton: Hurtig Publishers, 1984), 79.

162 William B. Cameron, *The War Trail of Big Bear* (London: Duckworth, 1927), 19.

163 Jean Goodwill and Norma Sluman, *John Tootoosis* (Winnipeg: Pemmican Publications, 1984), 54–55. See also Joseph Dion, *My Tribe, the Crees* (Calgary: Glenbow Museum, 1979), 92.

164 For another discussion of "big lie day," see Dempsey, *Big Bear,* 152–53.

165 Stonechild and Waiser, *Loyal till Death,* 117.

166 Agnes C. Laut, "Reverend 'Jack' Matheson: The Sky Pilot of the Crees," *Toronto Saturday Night,* Christmas 1911, 29.

167 Ibid. Four years earlier Delaney was involved in a similar situation on the Makaoo Reserve. Stonechild and Waiser, *Loyal till Death,* 108.

168 Lux, *Medicine that Walks,* 54.

169 Goodwill and Sluman, *John Tootoosis,* 54.

170 Verne Dusenbury, *The Montana Cree: A Study in Religious Persistence* (Norman: University of Oklahoma Press, 1999), 39.

171 Canada, House of Commons, *Debates,* M. C. Cameron, 15 April 1886, 729.

172 Ibid., 721.

173 Ibid.

174 CSP, 1883, W. Pocklington, Blackfoot Crossing, 20 July 1883, 86; ibid., Appendix, 193–94, extract of the *Macleod Gazette,* 16 March 1886.

175 Ibid., Appendix, 193–94, extract of the *Macleod Gazette,* 16 March 1886.

176 S. W. Horrall, "The (Royal) North-West Mounted Police and Prostitution on the Canadian Prairies," in *The Mounted Police and Prairie Society, 1873–1919,* edited by William M. Baker (Regina: Canadian Plains Research Center, 1998), 173.

177 CSP, 1883, Report of the North-West Mounted Police, Appendix A, Report of Surgeon Jukes, Fort Walsh, 29 November 1882, 25–26.

178 Waiser, "La police à cheval du Nord-Ouest," 11, 20–21.

179 LAC, MG 29 E 48, Diary of Inspector Deane, 1883, n. pag.

180 Pamela M. White, "Restructuring the Domestic Sphere—Prairie Indian Women on Reserves: Image, Ideology, and State Policy, 1880–1930" (Ph.D. diss., McGill University, 1987), 119.

181 John Gray, *Red Lights on the Prairies* (Toronto: Macmillan of Canada, 1971), 12.

182 Titley, *The Frontier World of Edgar Dewdney,* 50; Sarah Carter, "First Nations Women of Prairie Canada in the Early Reserve Years, the 1870s to the 1920s: A Preliminary Inquiry," in *Women of the First Nations: Power, Wisdom, and Strength,* edited by Christine Miller et al., Manitoba Studies in Native History (Winnipeg: University of Manitoba Press, 1996), 70.

183 J. W. Molson was the instructor at Morley at the time; CSP, 1883, 200.

184 LAC, RG 10, microfilm C-10136, vol. 3772, file 34938, William Donovan to Lawrence Vankoughnet, 30 October 1886.

185 The woman was reported to be the sister of Henry Pratt, Reed's servant and interpreter. Pratt stated that the charges against his master were "pure fabrications." LAC, RG 10, microfilm C-10136, vol. 3772, file 34938, Statement of Henry Pratt, Regina, 28 December 1886.

186 LAC, RG 10, microfilm C-10136, vol. 3772, file 34938, Donovan to Vankoughnet, 30 October 1886.

187 On 14 April, prior to the taking of Fort Pitt, Big Bear dictated a message to Sergeant Martin: "[S]ince I met you long ago we have always been good friends ... so please try to get off from Pitt as soon as you can. And tell your Captain that I remember him well, for since the Canadian Government had left me to starve in this country he sometimes gave me food, and I don't forget the blankets he gave me, and that is the reason I want you all to get off without bloodshed." Cited in W. L. Clink, *Battleford Beleaguered: The Story of the Riel Uprising from the* Saskatchewan Herald (Willowdale, ON: privately printed, 1984), 29. Jefferson, *Fifty Years on the Saskatchewan*, 155, noted that at Frog Lake "[t]he employees of the Hudson's Bay Company were the only men they spared, a fact which speaks volumes."

188 Walter Hildebrandt, *Views from Fort Battleford: Constructed Visions of an Anglo-Canadian West* (Regina: Canadian Plains Research Center, 1994), 85.

189 *Saskatchewan Herald*, 23 April 1885, 1.

190 Beal and Macleod, *Prairie Fire*, 183.

191 Hildebrandt, *Views from Fort Battleford*, 85.

192 Stonechild and Waiser, *Loyal till Death*, 98. See also Kenneth J. Tyler, "Interim Report: The History of the Mosquito, Grizzly Bear's Head, and Lean Man Bands, 1878–1920" (typescript) (Regina: Indian Studies Resource Centre, Saskatchewan Indian Federated College, University of Regina, 1974), 4. In her discussion of the Battleford trials, Sandra Bingaman reported that Itka had gotten into a serious confrontation with Payne "over an extra bag of flour." See her "The North-West Rebellion Trials, 1885" (MA thesis, University of Regina, 1971), 123.

193 *Saskatchewan Herald*, 5 October 1885, 2.

194 Hildebrandt, *Views from Fort Battleford*, 84.

195 *Saskatchewan Herald*, 23 April 1885, 2.

196 Ibid., 4 May 1885, 2.

197 Recent examples include Sarah Carter, "Introduction," in *Two Months in the Camp of Big Bear: The Life and Adventures of Theresa Gowanlock and Theresa Delaney* (Regina: Canadian Plains Research Center, 1999); Allen Ronaghan, "Father Fafard and the Fort Pitt Mission," *Alberta History* 46 (1998): 13–18; and Ronaghan, "Who Was the 'Fine Young Man'?" Hildebrandt, *Views from Fort Battleford*, 79, notes about rebellion historiography that "[t]he episodic portrayal of these events has always focussed on battles and killings, not on the long term factors of starvation and the sense of frustration felt by the Cree."

198 *Saskatchewan Herald*, 15 June 1885, 2.

199 The band never returned to their reserve; Tyler, "Interim Report," 5–6.

200 Lewis Redman Ord, "Reminiscences of a Bungle by One of the Bunglers," in *Reminiscences of a Bungle by One of the Bunglers and Two Other Stories of the Rebellion*, edited by R.C. Macleod (Edmonton: University of Alberta Press, 1983), 76. Ord was a member of Sam Steele's scouts. The woman who took her own life rather than risk capture was Sits-by-the-Door; Wayne F. Brown, *Steele's Scouts: Samuel Benfield Steele and the North-West Rebellion* (Surrey, BC: Heritage House, 2001), 145.

201 Ord, "Reminiscences of a Bungle by One of the Bunglers," 65.

202 Harold Panryn Rusden, "Suppression of the Northwest Insurrection," in Macleod, ed., *Reminiscences of a Bungle by One of the Bunglers*, 308.

203 On the criticism of Rouleau's actions during the rebellion, see Bingaman, "The North-West Rebellion Trials," 113–14. Stonechild and Waiser, *Loyal till Death*, 90, described the judge's flight as "running for his life."

204 Stonechild and Waiser, *Loyal till Death*, 221.

205 E. Brian Titley, "Hayter Reed and Indian Administration in the West," in *Swords and Ploughshares: War and Agriculture in Western Canada*, edited by R. C. Macleod (Edmonton: University of Alberta Press, 1993), 117.

206 Stonechild and Waiser, *Loyal till Death*, 221.

207 *Saskatchewan Herald*, 30 November 1885, 2.

208 Jefferson, *Fifty Years on the Saskatchewan*, 153.

209 Tobias, "Canada's Subjugation of the Plains Cree," 232.

210 Canada, House of Commons, *Debates*, M.C. Cameron, 15 April 1886, 745.

CHAPTER 9—THE NADIR OF INDIGENOUS HEALTH, 1886–91

1 Carl Beal, "Money, Markets, and Economic Development in Saskatchewan Indian Reserve Communities, 1870–1930s" (Ph.D. diss., University of Manitoba, 1994), 179.

2 CSP, 1886, Edgar Dewdney, Report of the Indian Commissioner, 17 November 1886, 106. The statement was a "tacit admission" that the source of "the temptation to commit outrages" was the government's "starvation policy side by side with storehouses of food and clothing." Beal, "Money, Markets, and Economic Development in Saskatchewan Indian Reserve Communities," 179.

3 Brian Titley, "Hayter Reed and Indian Administration in the West," in *Swords and Ploughshares: War and Agriculture in Western Canada*, edited by R.C. Macleod (Edmonton: University of Alberta Press, 1993), 117–18.

4 Robert Nestor, "Hayter Reed, Severality, and the Subdivision of Indian Reserves on the Canadian Prairies" (MA thesis, Saskatchewan Indian Federated College, University of Regina, 1998), 34–40.

5 For a discussion of the policy see, Sarah Carter, "Two Acres and a Cow: 'Peasant' Farming for the Indians of the Northwest, 1889–1897," in *Sweet Promises: A Reader in Indian-White Relations in Canada*, edited by J. R. Miller (Toronto: University of Toronto Press, 1991), 353–77.

6 Ibid., 83–97.

7 Peter Douglas Elias, *The Dakota of the Canadian Northwest: Lessons for Survival*, Manitoba Studies in Native History (Winnipeg: University of Manitoba Press, 1988), 83.

8 Zachary M. Hamilton and Marie Albina Hamilton, *These Are the Prairies* (Regina: School Aids and Textbook Publishers,1955), 3.

9 Blair Stonechild and Bill Waiser, *Loyal till Death: Indians and the North-West Rebellion* (Calgary: Fifth House, 1997), 132.

10 CSP, 1886, William Pocklington, Annual Report, Blood Agency, 1 July 1886, 136.

11 *Saskatchewan Herald*, 17 May 1886, 1–3. In August 2007, his remains were returned to the reserve that bears his name.

12 Ibid., 12 July 1886, 2.

13 Ibid. As Poundmaker visited his adopted father, Crowfoot, he choked, "blood gushed from his mouth[,] and in a few moments he was dead." Hugh Dempsey, *Crowfoot: Chief of the Blackfeet* (Norman: University of Oklahoma Press, 1972), 200.

14 Joyce Sowby, "Macdonald the Administrator: Department of the Interior and Indian Affairs, 1878–1887" (MA thesis, Queen's University, 1984), 185.

15 William Beahen and Stan Horral, *Red Coats on the Prairies: The Northwest Mounted Police, 1886–1900* (Regina: Centax Books, 1999), 57.

16 The effects of the pass system are well documented. See Laurie Barron, "The Indian Pass System in the Canadian West, 1882–1935," *Prairie Forum* 13 (1988): 25–42; and Sarah Carter, "Controlling Indian Movement: The Pass System," *NeWest Review* 10 (1985): 8–9. The non-treaty Dakota maintained their position in the cash economy of the plains. During the late 1880s, as reserve populations were inhibited in terms of movement and employment, the Standing Buffalo Dakota assisted in construction of the Qu'Appelle–Long Lake Railway, the first major branch line of the CPR in Saskatchewan. Elias, *The Dakota of the Canadian Northwest*, 153.

17 SAB, John A. Macdonald Papers, R-70, Dewdney to Macdonald, 9 September 1885, 376. Brian Hubner suggested that all levels of Canadian authority knew that the pass law had no legal foundation and violated the spirit of Treaty 7. See his "Horse Stealing and the Borderline: The NWMP and the Control of Indian Movement," *Prairie Forum* 20 (1995): 295.

18 Police opposition to enforcement of the act was such that by 1892 Commissioner Herchmer of the NWMP sought legal advice on the issue and circulated an order to his staff not to prosecute Indians without legal justification. Barron, "The Indian Pass System in the Canadian West," 36.

19 John Peter Turner, *The North-West Mounted Police* (Ottawa: King's Printer, 1950), 2: 284.

20 Father André to Colonel Herchmer, Assistant Commissioner, 5 November 1888, in Peter Naylor, "Index to Aboriginal Issues Found in the Records of the North West Mounted Police RG 18, National Archives of Canada" (typescript) (Saskatoon: Office of the Treaty Commissioner, 1994), entry no. 000.

21 Maureen Lux, *Medicine that Walks: Disease, Medicine, and Canadian Plains Native People, 1880–1940* (Toronto: University of Toronto Press, 2001), 45–56.

22 Grizzly Bear's Head left Canada with over 100 followers. Kenneth J. Tyler, "Interim Report: The History of the Mosquito, Grizzly Bear's Head, and Lean Man Bands, 1878–1920" (typescript) (Regina: Indian Studies Resource Centre, Saskatchewan Indian Federated College, University of Regina, 1974), 5.

23 On 30 December 1885, the *Benton River Press* reported that 137 Crees under Little Bear (Imases) had been apprehended and taken to Fort Assiniboine. James Dempsey, "Little Bear's Band: Canadian or American Indians?," *Alberta History* 41 (1993): 3; Verne Dusenbury, *The Montana Cree: A Study in Religious Persistence* (Norman: University of Oklahoma Press, 1999), 32, 37.

24 *Saskatchewan Herald*, 5 February 1887, 1. Later in the year, the newspaper reported that fugitive Canadian Indians were taking refuge in the mountains rather than obey an American military directive ordering them back to Canada. Ibid., 12 November 1887, 3.

25 Little Poplar was killed in Montana in 1886. Ibid., 16 August 1886, 1.

26 The 500 does not include the band under Grizzly Bear's Head, who "apparently never returned to his reserve." Tyler, "Interim Report," 5. According to Titley, "Hayter Reed and Indian Administration in the West," 120, between 10 and 15 percent of the rebels "were restored to department favour" in 1888. Many of the returnees to Alberta took up residence on the reserve set aside for Chief Bobtail and were known as the Montana Band. David Lupul, "The Bobtail Land Surrender," *Alberta History* 26 (1978): 29.

27 Charlie White Weasel, *Pembina and Turtle Mountain Ojibway (Chippewa) History from the Personal Collection and Writings of Charlie White Weasel* (Belcourt, ND: self-published, 1994), 150.

28 *Saskatchewan Herald*, 26 July 1886, 2. In August, the newspaper reported that so many were being placed on the half-breed list that "the Indian population on the Saskatchewan will present a very small appearance on paper." Ibid., 16 August 1886, 1.

29 Ken Hatt, "The North-West Rebellion Scrip Commissions, 1885–1889," in *1885 and After: Native Society in Transition*, edited by F. L. Barron and James Waldram (Regina: Canadian Plains Research Center, 1985), 197; CSP, 1887, John A. Macdonald, Report of the Superintendent General of Indian Affairs, 1 January 1887, lii.

30 The population of the Pecaysees band fell from 992 to 521. CSP, 1887, John A. Macdonald, Report of the Superintendent General of Indian Affairs, 1 January 1887, li. So many took scrip among Passpassche's band that the remainder were merged with Enoch's band in 1887. CSP, 1888, Edgar Dewdney, Report of the Indian Commissioner, 23 December 1887, 192.

31 *Saskatchewan Herald*, 5 March 1888, 4.

32 Five hundred people withdrew from treaty. CSP, 1887, John A. Macdonald, Report of the Superintendent General of Indian Affairs, 1 January 1887, xlvi.

33 The agency population fell from 814 to 386. Ibid., xlix–l.

34 CSP, 1888, John A. Macdonald, Report of the Superintendent General, 3 January 1888, lii.

35 Beal, "Money, Markets, and Economic Development in Saskatchewan Indian Reserve Communities," 197.

36 Similar destitution was reported along Carrot River, the forks of the Saskatchewan, Fort à la Corne, and Birch Hills. LAC, RG 18, vol. 32, f. 262, Relief of Destitute Halfbreeds at Prince Albert, John Cotton, Memorandum to the Commissioner, 10 February 1890, 238.

37 In 1884, $547,595 was spent on food; the following year the total dropped to $504,255. Beal, "Money, Markets, and Economic Development in Saskatchewan Indian Reserve Communities," 140.

38 SAB, John A. Macdonald Papers, R-70, Macdonald to Dewdney, 5 July 1885, n. pag.

39 Lux, *Medicine that Walks*, 58. To illustrate the magnitude of mortality in the area, the author provided the rate of 31.6 deaths per 1,000 for Montreal and 20.0 deaths per 1,000 for Paris and London.

40 Surviving members of the band were integrated with Ironhead's band in 1895. Brian Titley, "The Fate of the Sharphead Stonies," *Alberta History* 39 (1991): 8.

41 Dempsey, *Crowfoot*, 181.

42 Turner, *The North-West Mounted Police*, 2: 483.

43 LAC, CMS, microfilm A-113, Assissippi Journal, 3 August and 23 August 1885, 2–3.

44 SAB, John A. Macdonald Papers, R-70, Macdonald to Dewdney, telegram, 24 August 1884, 363; Dewdney to Macdonald, deciphered telegram, 25 August 1885, 365.

45 *Saskatchewan Herald*, 20 September 1886, 1.

46 CSP, 1887, W. Anderson, Report of the Edmonton Agency, n.d., 104.

47 Hartwell Bowsfield, ed., *The Letters of Charles John Brydges, 1883–1889, Hudson's Bay Company Land Commissioner* (Winnipeg: Hudson's Bay Record Society, 1981), C. J. Brydges to William Armit, 19 September 1887, 293.

48 Lux, *Medicine that Walks*, 65.

49 David C. Morley, "Nutrition and Infectious Disease," in *Disease and Urbanization: Symposia for the Study of Human Biology*, vol. 20, edited by E. J. Clegg and J. P. Garlick (London: Taylor and Francis, 1980), 37. See also David C. Morley, "Severe Measles," in *Changing Disease Patterns and Human Behaviour*, edited by N. F. Stanley and R. A. Joske (London: Academic Press, 1980), 124–25. The measles epidemic persisted until 1889 and reportedly took a large toll in both Canada and the United States. See E. Wagner Stearn and Allen E. Stearn, *The Effect of Smallpox on the Destiny of the Amerindian* (Boston: Bruce Humphries Publishers, 1945), 107.

50 William Hornaday, *The Extermination of the American Bison* (Washington, DC: Smithsonian Institution, 1889), 526–27.

51 *Saskatchewan Herald*, 25 September 1889, 4.

52 Ibid., 1 November 1886, 4; 6 August 1887, 3; 20 March 1889, 2.

53 Ibid., 5 March 1888, 4.

54 John Hines, *The Red Indians of the Plains: Thirty Years Missionary Experience in the Saskatchewan* (London: Society for Promoting Christian Knowledge, 1915), 216–17. See also *Saskatchewan Herald*, 12 February 1887, 1.

55 SAB, Anglican Diocese of Saskatchewan, Parish Register of Burials, Assissippi Mission. In 1887 alone, thirteen funerals were recorded.

56 SAB, Anglican Diocese of Saskatchewan, Parish Register of Burials, Stanley Mission. In 1887, twenty-five burials were reported.

57 Helen Buckley, *From Wooden Ploughs to Welfare: Why Indian Policy Failed in the Prairie Provinces* (Montreal: McGill-Queen's University Press, 1992), 37.

58 Lux, *Medicine that Walks*, 147–48.

59 Ibid., 64.

60 CSP, 1887, T. P. Wadsworth, Inspector of Indian Agencies, Battleford, 20 October 1887, 144.

61 Titley, "The Fate of the Sharphead Stonies," 6–7, reported that forty-seven of the dead were boys and girls under the age of fifteen.

62 Laurel Schenstead-Smith, "Disease Patterns and Factors Relating to the Transmission of Disease among the Residents of the Onion Lake Agency," *Na Pao: A Saskatchewan Anthropological Journal* 12 (1982): 3–4.

63 Richard Gallagher, *Diseases that Plague Modern Man: A History of Ten Communicable Diseases* (New York: Oceana Publications, 1969), 46. The disease might have originated in China, prompting some to call the epidemic the Chinese Distemper.

64 See http://www.globalsecurity.org/security/ops/hsc-scen-3_pandemic-influenza.htm.

65 CSP, 1890, Edgar Dewdney, Report of the Superintendent General, 13 January 1890, xi. Catarrhal infections refer to infections of the mucous membranes accompanied by discharges

from the mouth or throat. Lesley Brown, ed., *The New Shorter Oxford English Dictionary on Historical Principles* (Oxford: Clarendon Press, 1993), 351.

66 CSP, 1891, Report of the Indian Commissioner, Regina, October 1890, 136.

67 CSP, 1891, 30 August 1890, 38; 1 September 1890, 41; 18 August 1890, 42; A. M. Muckle, Clandeboyne, MB, 30 August 1890, 32. According to Lux, *Medicine that Walks*, 87, the most common cause of death associated with the epidemic was bacterial pneumonia.

68 *Saskatchewan Herald*, 23 January 1889, 1.

69 "The Indian Epidemic," ibid., 6 February 1889, 2.

70 Lux, *Medicine that Walks*, 87.

71 CSP, 1890, Edgar Dewdney, Report of the Superintendent General, 13 January 1890, xxviii.

72 Sarah Carter, *Lost Harvests: Prairie Indian Reserve Farmers and Government Policy* (Montreal: McGill-Queen's University Press, 1990), 193–236; Sarah Carter, "Two Acres and a Cow: 'Peasant' Farming for the Indians of the Northwest, 1889–1897," in *Sweet Promises: A Reader in Indian-White Relations in Canada*, edited by J. R. Miller (Toronto: University of Toronto Press, 1991), 353–77. Robert Nestor argued that fiscal imperatives were the key motivation for the scheme; "Hayter Reed, Severality, and the Subdivision of Indian Reserves on the Canadian Prairies," 121.

73 Buckley, *From Wooden Ploughs to Welfare*, 52–53.

74 David Sauchyn and Walter Skinner, "A Proxy Record of Drought Severity for the Southwestern Canadian Plains," *Canadian Water Resources Journal* 26 (2001): 266.

75 Carter, *Lost Harvests*, 181–90.

76 *Saskatchewan Herald*, 13 November 1889, 1. In the new year, the number of destitute farmers in northern Dakota was estimated at 4,000. Ibid., 5 February 1890, 3.

77 Ibid., 18 August 1888, 3–4; 8 September 1888, 2. The subsistence economy of northern Alberta was seriously undermined by extermination of the remaining northern bison herd. Ibid., 20 March 1889, 4.

78 Stephen Sliwa, "Standing the Test of Time: A History of the Beardy's/Okemasis Reserve, 1876–1951" (MA thesis, Trent University, 1993), 93. The band had no chief until 1936, over forty years later. SAB, reel 2.75, *School Histories of 35 Indian Reserves*, "Beardy's Reserve," 20.

79 *Saskatchewan Herald*, 12 February 1890, 1.

80 Dempsey, *Crowfoot*, 208–16.

81 Lux, *Medicine that Walks*, 83–84.

82 CSP, 1889, Report of the Manitoba Superintendency, E. McColl, Winnipeg, 14 November 1888, 160. The *midewiwin* ceremony had probably been ongoing in the northern parklands of Saskatchewan. In 1884, John Hines reported that "the heathen Indians are congregating around Pelican Lake for their annual 'Metahawin,' it is at this festival that they practice all their superstitious ceremonies." LAC, CMS, microfilm A-112, Assissippi Journal, 6 June 1884, n. pag.

83 Pahkahkos was also known as Bony Spectre, believed to have "sacrificed itself so that others may live" and associated with starvation. Katherine Pettipas, *Severing the Ties that Bind: Government Repression of Indigenous Religious Ceremonies on the Prairies*, Manitoba Studies in Native History (Winnipeg: University of Manitoba Press, 1994), 55.

84 Hubner, "Horse Stealing and the Borderline," 285; Pettipas, *Severing the Ties that Bind*, 99.

85 For a discussion of the curative aspect of the ceremony, and of its suppression by Canadian authorities, see Pettipas, *Severing the Ties that Bind*, 183–85.

86 Alice B. Kehoe, *The Ghost Dance: Ethnohistory and Revitalization* (Fort Worth: Holt, Rinehart and Winston, 1989), 4–5. See also Ronald Niezen, *Spirit Wars: Native North American Religion in the Age of Nation Building* (Berkeley: University of California Press, 2000), 130–36.

87 Kehoe, *The Ghost Dance*, 5. There was a total eclipse of the sun on 1 January 1889.

88 Henry Dobyns and Robert Euler, *The Ghost Dance of 1889 among the Pai Indians of Northwestern Arizona* (Prescott, AZ: Prescott College Press, 1967), 1–2.

89 James Mooney, *The Ghost Dance Religion and the Sioux Outbreak of 1890* (Lincoln: University of Nebraska Press, 1991), 786.

90 Ibid., 826–27.

91 Ibid., 845–46.

92 Ibid., 857. A different account of Sitting Bull's death appears in Dee Brown, *Bury My Heart at Wounded Knee: An Indian History of the American West* (New York: Bantam Books, 1970), 441.

93 Mooney, *The Ghost Dance Religion and the Sioux Outbreak of 1890*, 869. See also Brown, *Bury My Heart at Wounded Knee*, 417–18. The mobilization of between 6,000 and 7,000 troops was the largest operation conducted by the US Army since the end of the Civil War. For a discussion of the reasons for the American government's show of force, see Jeffrey Ostler, *The Plains Sioux and U.S. Colonialism from Lewis and Clark to Wounded Knee* (Cambridge, UK: Cambridge University Press, 2004), 288.

94 Mooney, *The Ghost Dance Religion and the Sioux Outbreak of 1890*, 869–70.

95 Russell Thornton, *We Shall Live Again: The 1870 and 1890 Ghost Dance Movements as Demographic Revitalization* (Cambridge, UK: Cambridge University Press, 1986), 45–46.

96 Beahen and Horral, *Red Coats on the Prairies*, 60.

97 L. W. Herchmer to Superintendent Steele, telegram, 7 December 1890, in Naylor, "Index to Aboriginal Issues Found in the Records of the North West Mounted Police," entry no. 152.

98 SAB, reel R-2.563, Alphonse Little Poplar, *Miscellaneous Indian Policy Documents Relating to the Sweet Grass Reserve*, 4. For further discussion on confinement to mitigate the spread of the Ghost Dance and other outside religious movements, see Barron, "The Indian Pass System in the Canadian West," 31.

99 LAC, RG 18, vol. 46, file 15, Report of G. E. Sander, Inspector, to E. W. Jarvis, Superintendent, 19 December 1890, in Naylor, "Index to Aboriginal Issues Found in the Records of the North West Mounted Police," entry no. 151.

100 Letter from L. W. Herchmer, Commissioner, to unknown, 22 December 1890, in ibid., entry no. 155.

101 Beahen and Horral, *Red Coats on the Prairies*, 60.

102 Barron, "The Indian Pass System in the Canadian West," 33–34.

103 CSP, 1892, Edgar Dewdney, Report of the Superintendent General, January 1892, x.

104 Members of Sitting Bull's band living at Wood Mountain were reported to be practising the dance in 1895. During the late 1890s, the Saskatchewan Dakota gave up the actual dance but incorporated the belief system into existing religious practices in a movement that became known as New Tidings. It persisted on the Wahpeton Reserve near Prince Albert until the 1960s. Kehoe, *The Ghost Dance*, 44–46, 129–34.

105 Pettipas, *Severing the Ties that Bind*, 101–02; Ronald Niezen, *Spirit Wars*, 136–40.

106 Pettipas, *Severing the Ties that Bind*, 102.

107 Deanna Christensen, *Ahtahkakoop: The Epic Account of a Plains Cree Head Chief, His People, and Their Struggle for Survival, 1816–1896* (Shell Lake, SK: Ahtahkakoop Publishing, 2000), 650.

108 F. Laurie Barron, "The Indian Pass System in the Canadian West," 33.

109 Nestor, "Hayter Reed, Severality, and the Subdivision of Indian Reserves on the Canadian Prairies," 102.

110 SAB, reel R-2.563, Alphonse Little Poplar, *Miscellaneous Indian Policy Documents Relating to the Sweet Grass Reserve*, 4–5. See also Barron, "The Indian Pass System in the Canadian West," 36.

111 Thornton, *We Shall Live Again*, 46; R. G. Ferguson, *Tuberculosis among the Indians of the Great Canadian Plains* (London: Adlard and Son, 1929), 10.

112 Beal, "Money, Markets, and Economic Development in Saskatchewan Indian Reserve Communities," 200.

113 CSP, 1895, Hayter Reed, Report of the Deputy Superintendent General, 2 December 1895, xx–xxi.

114 LAC, RG 10, reel 10,166, vol. 3949, file 126,345, Hayter Reed to A. E. Forget, 14 February 1895.

115 Ibid., Dr. John Hutchinson to Hayter Reed, 28 May 1895.

116 CSP, 1886, Edgar Dewdney, Report of the Indian Commissioner, 17 November 1886, 108.

117 Nestor, "Hayter Reed, Severality, and the Subdivision of Indian Reserves on the Canadian Prairies," 100–02.

118 LAC, RG 10 reel 10,166,vol. 3949, f. 126,345, Dr. F. X. Girard to Indian Commissioner, 1 April 1895.

119 Ferguson, *Tuberculosis among the Indians of the Great Canadian Plains*, 12.

120 *CSP*, 1903, Blackfoot Agency, Gleichen, AB, 7 August 1902, 124.

121 *CSP*, 1893, E. McColl, Inspector, Manitoba Superintendency, 18 October 1893, 46.

122 LAC, RG 10, reel 10,151, vol. 3855, file 79,963, "Manitoba—Dr. G. Orton's Report on the Deleterious Effects of Civilization and Subsequent Effort to Ventilate Schools as a Protection against Tuberculosis, 1891-1897."

123 *CSP*, 1895, J. J. Campbell, Moose Mountain Agency, 30 June 1895, 53.

124 Laurie Meijer Drees, "Reserve Hospitals in Southern Alberta, 1890 to 1930," *Native Studies Review* 9 (1993-94): 93-112; Laurie Meijer Drees, "Reserve Hospitals and Medical Officers: Health Care and Indian Peoples in Southern Alberta, 1890s-1930," *Prairie Forum* 21 (1996): 149-76.

125 *CSP*, 1895, Dr. George Orton, Medical Superintendent, Manitoba Superintendency, 28 August 1895, 139.

126 LAC, RG 10, reel 10,151, vol. 3855, file 79,963, Hayter Reed to A. E. Forget, 10 April 1895.

127 LAC, RG 10, reel 10,166, vol. 3949, file 126,345, Dr. T. A. Patrick to Assistant Commissioner, 10 June 1985, 2.

128 For a detailed discussion of health conditions at the schools, see John Milloy, "*A National Crime*": *The Canadian Government and the Residential School System, 1879 to 1986* (Winnipeg: University of Manitoba Press, 1999), 77-108.

129 The younger the individual, the more likely that primary infection will become active disease and result in death. William D. Johnston, "Tuberculosis," in *The Cambridge World History of Human Diseases*, edited by Kenneth Kiple (Cambridge, UK: Cambridge University Press, 1993), 1060.

130 LAC, RG 10, reel 10,166, vol. 3949, file 126,345, M. M. Seymour to Indian Commissioner, Fort Qu'Appelle, 28 May 1895, 3.

131 Four were from consumption, and one resulted from pleurisy. *CSP*, 1892, J. Hugonnard, Principal, Qu'Appelle Industrial School, 1 October 1890, 202.

132 Of a total enrolment of 795 pupils, 153 perished. Milloy, "*A National Crime*," 92.

133 *CSP*, 1894, J. Hugonnard, Qu'Appelle Industrial School, 22 August 1893, 88. The following year he reported consumption as the cause of most of the deaths at the institution, "though in nearly every case it has clearly been hereditary," and "Pure blooded children appear to be more affected by it than those with white blood, and they rally much better after any sickness." *CSP*, 1894, J. Hugonnard, Qu'Appelle Industrial School, 4 August 1894, 344.

134 *CSP*, 1887, Edgar Dewdney, Report of the Indian Commissioner, 17 November 1886, 110.

135 See, for example, *CSP*, 1898, Thomas Carruthers, Touchwood Hills, 20 July 1897, 176.

136 Milloy, "*A National Crime*," 86.

137 David Meyer, *The Red Earth Crees, 1860-1960*, Mercury Series, Canadian Ethnology Service Paper No. 100 (Ottawa: National Museum of Man, 1985), 89.

138 P. H. Bryce, "The History of the American Indians in Relation to Health," *Ontario Historical Society Papers and Records* 12 (1914): 141.

139 A. B. Cook, R. G. Ferguson, and J. F. Cairns, *Report to the Government of Saskatchewan by the Anti-Tuberculosis Commission* (Regina: Saskatchewan Anti-Tuberculosis Commission, 1922), 15. For further discussion on the belief in the racial susceptibility of First Nations people to tuberculosis, see Maureen Lux, "Perfect Subjects: Race, Tuberculosis, and the Qu'Appelle BCG Trial," *Canadian Bulletin of Medical History* 15 (1998): 277-95; and Lux, *Medicine that Walks*, 5-9.

140 Ferguson, *Tuberculosis among the Indians of the Great Canadian Plains*; Robert G. Ferguson, *Studies in Tuberculosis* (Toronto: University of Toronto Press, 1955). For accounts of his work, see Lux, "Perfect Subjects," 277-95; and C. Stuart Houston, *R. G. Ferguson: Crusader against Tuberculosis* (Toronto: Hannah Institute and Dundurn Press, 1991), 91-100.

141 Annuity payment lists would not account for those who opted out of treaty and took scrip. Beal showed that 15 percent of the File Hills population did so in 1886; "Money, Markets, and Economic Development in Saskatchewan Indian Reserve Communities," 197. If Ferguson

was guilty of this oversight, then his mortality figures would be too high for some years, but the general trend in mortality remains legitimate.

142 Ferguson, *Studies in Tuberculosis*, 4–8.

143 Between 1893 and 1904, the maximum death rate from tuberculosis in European prisons was 1,910 per 100,000; in 1887, the maximum rate for asylums was 2,300 per 100,000. Ferguson added that "Even the tuberculosis death rate of 1,400 per 100,000 during the First World War ... did not approximate that of the Indian tuberculosis epidemic"; ibid., 7–8.

144 Ibid., 6–9. Ferguson accepted the notion of racial susceptibility. For further discussion, see Lux, "Perfect Subjects"; and Michael Worboys, "Tuberculosis and Race in Britain and Its Empire, 1900–50," in *Race, Science, and Medicine, 1700–1960*, edited by Waltraus Ernst and Bernard Harris (London: Routledge, 1999), 144–67. There were dissenting opinions, however, even in the 1920s; see Committee of the National Tuberculosis Association, *Tuberculosis among the North American Indians: Report of a Committee of the National Tuberculosis Association Appointed on Oct. 28, 1921* (Washington, DC: Government Printing Bureau, 1923), 16.

145 The estimated mortality in the Warsaw ghetto in April 1942 of 11.0 per 1,000, if extended to a year, provides a rate of 143.2 per 1,000. Charles Roland, "Mortality among Warsaw Jewry: Selected Months," in *Courage under Siege: Starvation, Disease, and Death in the Warsaw Ghetto* (New York: Oxford University Press, 1992), 225.

146 Ferguson, *Tuberculosis among Indians of the Great Canadian Plains*, 45.

147 James B. Waldram, D. Ann Herring and T. Kue Young, *Aboriginal Health in Canada: Historical, Cultural and Epidemiological Perspectives* Second Edition (Toronto: University of Toronto Press, 2006), 190.

148 T. K. Young, *The Health of Native Americans: Toward a Biocultural Epidemiology* (New York: Oxford University Press, 1994), 59.

149 George A. Clark et al., "The Evolution of Mycobacterial Disease in Human Populations: A Reevaluation," *Current Anthropology* 28 (1987): 51. The study was based in part on Ferguson's research on the reserve population of the Qu'Appelle Valley.

150 Charcoal was convicted of Sergeant Wilde's death but not on the initial charge since there was not enough evidence to prove his guilt. Adolph Hungry Wolf, *The Blood People: A Division of the Blackfoot Confederacy* (New York: Harper and Row, 1977), 281.

151 Hugh Dempsey, *Charcoal's World* (Saskatoon: Western Producer Prairie Books, 1978), 155.

CONCLUSION

1 Alexander Morris, 26 August 1876, in *The Treaties of Canada with the Indians of Manitoba and the North-West Territories* (Saskatoon: Fifth House Publishers, 1991), 228.

2 Gregory Campbell, "The Changing Dimension of Native American Health: A Critical Understanding of Contemporary Native American Health Issues," in *Native American Resurgence and Renewal: A Reader and Bibliography*, edited by Robert N. Wells (Metuchen, NJ: Scarecrow Press, 1994), 94–118.

3 D. Ann Herring, James B. Waldram, and T. Kue Young, *Aboriginal Health in Canada: Historical, Cultural, and Epidemiological Perspectives*, 2nd ed. (Toronto: University of Toronto Press, 2006), 297.

BIBLIOGRAPHY

ARCHIVAL SOURCES

Glenbow Archives
M320, Edgar Dewdney Papers

Hudson's Bay Company Archives (HBCA)
Biography Files
    Search File: Battleford
    Search File: Prince Albert
    Search File: Smallpox Epidemic, 1870
Brandon House Post Journals
    B.22/a/1, 1793–94
Chesterfield House Post Journals
    B.34/a/2, 1800–01
    B.34/a/3, 1801–02
Cumberland House Post Journals
    B.49/a/1, 1774–75
    B.49/a/3, 1775–76
    B.49/a/4, 1776–77
    B.49/a/6, 1777–78
    B.49/a/7, 1778–79
    B.49/a/9, 1779–80
    B.49/a/11, 1781–82
    B.49/a/31, 1801–02
Hudson House Post Journals
    B.87/a/1, 1778–79
    B.87/a/2, 1779–80
    B.87/a/3, 1780–81
    B.87/a/4, 1781–82

B.87/a/5, 1782
B.87/a/6, 1782–83
Fort Pelly Post Journals
B.159/a/17, 1837–38
Ile-à-la-Crosse Post Journals
B.89/a.4, 1819–20
Manchester House Post Journal
B.121/a/1, 1786–87
B.121/a/2, 1787–88
B.121/a/3, 1788–89
B.121/a/4, 1789–90
South Branch House
B.205/a/3, 1788–89
B.205/a/7, 1792–93
B.205/a/8, 1793–94

Library and Archives Canada (LAC)
MG 17, Records of the Church Missionary Society
MG 19 A 48, Fort Garry Correspondence
MG 26, John A. Macdonald Papers
MG 27, David Laird Papers
MG 29, Robert Bell Papers
RG 10, Records of the Department of Indian Affairs
RG 18, Records of the North West Mounted Police

Provincial Archives of Manitoba (PAM)
MG 2 A 1, Selkirk Papers
MG 12, Alexander Morris Papers

University of Toronto, Thomas Fisher Rare Book Room
MS 21, David Thompson Papers
MS 26, J. B. Tyrrell Papers
Reel 1264, David Thompson Narrative

Saskatchewan Archives Board (SAB)
A-104, W. Traill Papers
A-113, Campbell Innes Papers
R.2.75, *School Histories of Thirty-Five Indian Reserves*
R.2.391, R. G. Ferguson Papers
R.2.563, Sweet Grass Reserve Papers
R-39, A. E. Forget Papers

R-70, John A. Macdonald Papers
R-100, Mary Weekes Papers
RE-1120, Indians of North America
RE-2033, Edward Ahenakew Papers
RE-1888, Little Pine/Lucky Man Band
R-1.124, Anglican Diocese of Saskatchewan—Parish Records of the Church Missionary Society

Western University (WU)
D. B. Weldon Regional Library Regional Collection, David Mills Letterbooks, 1876–78

BOOKS AND ARTICLES

Abel, Annie H., ed. *Chardon's Journal at Fort Clark, 1834–1839.* Freeport, NY: Books for Libraries Press, 1970.

Abel, Kerry. *Drum Songs: Glimpses of Dene History.* Montreal: McGill-Queen's University Press, 1993.

Aborigines' Protection Society. *Canada West and the Hudson's Bay Company: A Political and Humane Question of Vital Importance to the Honour of Great Britain, to the Prosperity of Canada, and to the Existence of the Native Tribes; Being an Address to the Right Honorable Henry Labouchere, Her Majesty's Principal Secretary of State for the Colonies.* London: William Tweedie, 1856.

Abrams, Gary. *Prince Albert: The First Century, 1866–1966.* Saskatoon: Modern Press, 1966.

Ahenakew, Edward. "An Opinion of the Frog Lake Massacre." *Alberta Historical Review* 8 (1960): 9–15.

——. *Voices of the Plains Cree.* Edited by Ruth M. Buck. Toronto: McClelland and Stewart, 1973.

Akrigg, G. P. V., and Helen B. Akrigg. *British Columbia Chronicle, 1778–1846: Adventures by Land and Sea.* Vancouver: Discovery Press, 1975.

Albers, Patricia. "Changing Patterns of Ethnicity in the Northeastern Plains, 1780–1870." In *History, Power, and Identity: Ethnogenesis in the Americas, 1492–1992,* edited by Jonathan Hill, 90–118. Iowa City: University of Iowa Press, 1996.

——. "Plains Ojibwa." In *Plains,* edited by Raymond J. DeMallie, 652–60. Vol. 13, Part 1, of *Handbook of North American Indians.* Washington, DC: Smithsonian Institution Press, 2001.

Allsopp, T. R. *Agricultural Weather in the Red River Basin of Southern Manitoba over the Period 1800 to 1975*. Atmospheric Environment Report CLI-3-77. Downsview, ON: Fisheries and Environment Canada, 1977.

Anderson, Ian. *Sitting Bull's Boss: Above the Medicine Line with James Morrow Walsh*. Surrey, BC: Heritage House, 2000.

Andrews, Isabel. "The Crooked Lakes Reserves: A Study in Indian Policy in Practice from the Qu'Appelle Treaty to 1900." MA thesis, University of Regina, 1972.

——. "Indian Protest against Starvation: The Yellow Calf Incident of 1884." *Saskatchewan History* 28 (1975): 41–51.

Angel, Barbara. "Fur Trade Relations with Native People at Fort Vermilion, 1821–1846." In *Proceedings of the Fort Chipewyan and Fort Vermilion Bicentennial Conference*, edited by Patricia A. McCormack and R. Geoffrey Ironside, 86–93. Edmonton: Boreal Institute for Northern Studies, University of Alberta, 1990.

Arndt, Katherine L. "Dynamics of the Fur Trade on the Middle Yukon River, 1839 to 1868." Ph.D. diss., University of Alaska, 1996.

Arngrimsson, Gudjon. *Nyja Island: Saga of the Journey to New Iceland*. Winnipeg: Turnstone Press, 1997.

Asch, Michael. "Some Effects of the Late Nineteenth Century Modernization of the Fur Trade on the Economy of the Slavey Indians." *Western Canadian Journal of Anthropology* 6 (1976): 7–15.

Ashford, D. A., et al. "Bovine Tuberculosis: Environmental Public Health Preparedness Considerations for the Future." In *Mycobacterium Bovis Infection in Animals and Humans*, 2nd ed., edited by Charles O. Thoen, James H. Steele, and Michael J. Gilsdorf, 305–15. Ames: Blackwell Publishing, 2006.

Askenazy, Hans. *Cannibalism: From Sacrifice to Survival*. Amherst: Prometheus Books, 1994.

Atton, F. Melvyn. "Fish Resources and the Fisheries Industry of the Canadian Plains." *Prairie Forum* 9 (1984): 315–25.

——. "The Life: Fish and Water." In *Three Hundred Prairie Years: Henry Kelsey's "Inland Country of Good Report,"* edited by Henry Epp, 17–26. Regina: Canadian Plains Research Center, 1993.

Ayele, W. Y., S. D. Neill, J. Zinsstag, M. G. Weiss, and I. Pavlik. "Bovine Tuberculosis: An Old Disease but a New Threat to Africa." *International Journal of Tuberculosis and Lung Disease* 8 (2004): 924–37.

Ball, T. F. "Historical and Instrumental Evidence of Climate: Western Hudson's Bay, Canada, 1714–1850." In *Climate since A.D. 1500*, edited by Raymond S. Bradley and Philip D. Jones, 40–73. London: Routledge, 1995.

———. "The Year without a Summer: Its Impact on the Fur Trade and History of Western Canada." In *The Year without a Summer: World Climate in 1816*, edited by C. R. Harington, 196–202. Ottawa: Canadian Museum of Nature, 1992.

Ballantyne, Philip, et al. "Aski-Puko-the Land Alone: A Report on the Expected Effects of the Proposed Hydro-Electric Installation at Wintego Rapids upon the Cree of the Peter Ballantyne and Lac la Ronge Bands." Regina: Saskatchewan Indian Federated College Library, 1976.

Bamforth, Douglas B. "Climate, Chronology, and the Course of War in the Middle Missouri Region of the North American Plains." In *The Archaeology of Warfare: Prehistories of Raiding and Conquest,* edited by Elizabeth N. Arkush and Mark W. Allen, 66–100. Gainesville: University of Florida Press, 2006.

———. "An Empirical Perspective on Little Ice Age Climatic Change on the Great Plains." *Plains Anthropologist* 35 (1990): 359–66.

———. "Indigenous People, Indigenous Violence: Precontact Warfare on the North American Great Plains." *Man,* n.s., 29 (1994): 95–115.

Bamforth, Douglas, and Curtis Nepstad-Thornberry. "Reconsidering the Occupational History of the Crow Creek Site (39BF 11)." *Plains Anthropologist* 52 (2007): 153–73.

Banting, Meredith B., ed. *Early History of Saskatchewan Churches.* Regina: Banting Publishers, 1975.

Barkun, Michael. *Disaster and the Millennium.* New Haven, CT: Yale University Press, 1974.

Barkwell, Peter A. "The Medicine Chest Clause in Treaty No. 6." *Canadian Native Law Review* 4 (1981): 1–21.

Barr, William. "Lieutenant Aemilius Simpson's Survey: York Factory to Fort Vancouver, 1826." In *Selected Papers of Rupert's Land Colloquium 2000,* compiled by David G. Malaher, 1–8. Winnipeg: Centre for Rupert's Land Studies, University of Winnipeg, 2000.

Barris, Theodore. *Fire Canoe: Prairie Steamboat Days Revisited.* Toronto: McClelland and Stewart, 1977.

Barron, F. Laurie. "Indian Agents and the North-West Rebellion." In *1885 and After: Native Society in Transition,* edited by F. Laurie Barron and James Waldram, 139–54. Regina: Canadian Plains Research Center, 1985.

———. "The Indian Pass System in the Canadian West, 1882–1935." *Prairie Forum* 13 (1988): 25–42.

Barsh, Russel L. "The Substitution of Cattle for Bison on the Great Plains." In *The Struggle for the Land: Indigenous Insight and Industrial Empire in the Semiarid World*, edited by Paul A. Olson, 103–26. Lincoln: University of Nebraska Press, 1990.

Baumgartner, Frederic J. *Longing for the End: A History of Millennialism in Western Civilization*. New York: St. Martin's Press, 1999.

Bay, Ryan C., Nathan Bramall, and P. Buford Price. "Bipolar Correlation of Volcanism with Millennial Climate Change." *Proceedings of the National Academy of Sciences* 101 (2004): 6341–45.

Beahen, William, and Stan Horral. *Red Coats on the Prairies: The Northwest Mounted Police, 1886–1900*. Regina: Centax Books, 1999.

Beal, Bob, and Rod Macleod. *Prairie Fire: The 1885 North-West Rebellion*. Edmonton: Hurtig Publishers, 1984.

Beal, Carl. "Money, Markets, and Economic Development in Saskatchewan Indian Reserve Communities, 1870–1930s." Ph.D. diss., University of Manitoba, 1994.

Beaudoin, Alwynne. "What They Saw: The Climatic and Environmental Context for Euro-Canadian Settlement in Alberta." *Prairie Forum* 24 (1999): 1–40.

Belyea, Barbara, ed. *David Thompson: Columbia Journals*. Montreal: McGill-Queen's University Press, 1994.

——, ed. *A Year Inland: The Journal of a Hudson's Bay Company Winterer*. Waterloo: Wilfrid Laurier University Press, 2000.

Benenson, Abram S. "Smallpox." In *Viral Infections of Humans: Epidemiology and Control*, 2nd ed., edited by Alfred S. Evans, 541–68. New York: Plenum Medical Book Company, 1982.

Bilson, Geoffrey. *A Darkened House: Cholera in Nineteenth Century Canada*. Toronto: University of Toronto Press, 1980.

Bingaman, Sandra. "The North-West Rebellion Trials, 1885." MA thesis, University of Regina, 1971.

Binnema, Theodore. *Common and Contested Ground: A Human and Environmental History of the Northwestern Plains*. Norman: University of Oklahoma Press, 2001.

Bishop, Charles. "The Emergence of the Northern Ojibwa: Social and Economic Consequences." *American Ethnologist* 3 (1976): 39–54.

——. "Northern Ojibwa Emergence: The Migration." In *Papers of the Thirty-Third Algonquian Conference*, edited by H. C. Wolfart, 13–109. Winnipeg: University of Manitoba Press, 2002.

——. *The Northern Ojibwa and the Fur Trade: An Historical and Ecological Study*. Culture and Communities: A Series of Monographs. Toronto: Holt, Rinehart and Winston, 1974.

Bishop, Charles, and Estelle Smith. "Early Historic Populations in Northwestern Ontario: Archaeological and Ethnohistorical Interpretations." *American Antiquity* 40 (1975): 54–63.

Black Rogers, Mary. "Varieties of 'Starving': Semantics and Survival in the Subarctic Fur Trade, 1750–1850." *Ethnohistory* 33 (1986): 353–83.

Blain, Eleanor. "Dependency: Charles Bishop and the Northern Ojibwa." In *Aboriginal Resource Use in Canada: Historical and Legal Aspects*, edited by K. Abel and J. Friesen, 93–106. Winnipeg: University of Manitoba Press, 1991.

Bliss, Michael. *Plague: A Story of Smallpox in Montreal.* Toronto: HarperCollins Publishers, 1991.

Boulton, Charles A. *I Fought Riel: A Military Memoir.* Edited by Heather Robertson. Toronto: Lorimer, 1985.

Bourgeault, Ron. "The Indian, the Métis, and the Fur Trade: Class, Sexism, and Racism in the Transition from 'Communism' to Capitalism." *Studies in Political Economy* 12 (1983): 45–80.

Bowsfield, Hartwell, ed. *The Letters of Charles John Brydges, 1879–1882, Hudson's Bay Company Land Commissioner.* Hudson's Bay Record Society, vol. 31. Winnipeg: Hudson's Bay Record Society, 1977.

——, ed. *The Letters of Charles John Brydges, 1883–1889, Hudson's Bay Company Land Commissioner.* Hudson's Bay Record Society, vol. 33. Winnipeg: Hudson's Bay Record Society, 1981.

Boyd, Robert T. "Demographic History, 1774–1874." In *Northwest Coast*, edited by Wayne Suttles, 135–48. Vol. 7 of *Handbook of North American Indians*. Washington, DC: Smithsonian Institution Press, 1990.

Boyd, M., and C. Surette. "Northernmost Precontact Maize in North America." *American Antiquity* 75 (2010): 117–33.

Brázdil, Rudolph, Christian Pfister, Heinz Wanner, Hans Von Storch, and Jürg Luterbacher. "Historical Climatology in Europe: The State of the Art." *Climatic Change* 70 (2005): 363–430.

Breen, David. *The Canadian Prairie West and the Ranching Frontier, 1874–1924.* Toronto: University of Toronto Press, 1983.

Brewer, Anthony. *Marxist Theories of Imperialism: A Critical Survey.* London: Routledge, 1980.

Briffa, K. R., P. D. Jones, F. H. Shwingruber, and T. J. Osborn. "Influence of Volcanic Eruptions on Northern Hemisphere Summer Temperature over the Past 600 Years." *Nature* 393 (1998): 450–55.

Brightman, Robert. "Conservation and Resource Depletion: The Case of the Boreal Forest Algonkians." In *The Question of the Commons: The Culture and Ecology of Communal Resources*, edited by

Bonnie McCay and James Acheson, 121–42. Tucson: University of Arizona Press, 1987.

Brinker, J. A. H. "A Historical, Epidemiological, and Aetiological Study of Measles (Morbilli; Rubeola)." *Proceedings of the Royal Society of Medicine* 31 (1938): 807–28.

Brown, Dee. *Bury My Heart at Wounded Knee: An Indian History of the American West*. New York: Bantam Books, 1970.

Brown, Wayne F. *Steele's Scouts: Samuel Benfield Steele and the North-West Rebellion*. Surrey, BC: Heritage House, 2001.

Brunton, Bill B. "Kootenai." In *Plateau*, edited by Deward E. Walker, 223–37. Vol. 12 of *Handbook of North American Indians*. Washington, DC: Smithsonian Institution Press, 1998.

Bryce, P. H. "The History of the American Indians in Relation to Health." *Ontario Historical Society Papers and Records* 12 (1914): 128–41.

Bryson, Reid, and Thomas Murray. *Climates of Hunger: Mankind and the World's Changing Weather*. Madison: University of Wisconsin Press, 1977.

Bryson, Reid, and Wayne Wendland. "Tentative Climatic Patterns for Some Glacial and Post-Glacial Episodes in Central North America." In *Life, Land, and Water: Proceedings of the 1966 Conference on Environmental Studies of the Glacial Lake Agassiz Region*, edited by William J. Mayer-Oakes, 271–98. Winnipeg: University of Manitoba Press, 1967.

Buck, Ruth Matheson. *The Doctor Rode Side-Saddle*. Toronto: McClelland and Stewart, 1974.

Buckley, Helen. *From Wooden Ploughs to Welfare: Why Indian Policy Failed in the Prairie Provinces*. Montreal: McGill-Queen's University Press, 1992.

Buikstra, Jane E., ed. *Prehistoric Tuberculosis in the Americas*. Evanston, IL: Northwestern University Archaeological Program, 1981.

Bumsted, J. M. *Floods of the Centuries: A History of Flood Disasters in the Red River Valley, 1776–1997*. Winnipeg: Great Plains Publications, 1997.

——. *Fur Trade Wars: The Founding of Western Canada*. Winnipeg: Great Plains Publications, 1999.

——. *Trials and Tribulations: The Red River Settlement and the Emergence of Manitoba, 1811–1870*. Winnipeg: Great Plains Publications, 2003.

Burley, Edith. *Servants of the Honourable Company: Work, Discipline, and Conflict in the Hudson's Bay Company, 1770–1879*. Don Mills, ON: Oxford University Press, 1997.

Burley, David V., J. Scott Hamilton, and Knut Fladmark. *Prophecy of the Swan: The Upper Peace River Fur Trade of 1794–1823.* Vancouver: UBC Press, 1996.

Bushnell, G. E. *Epidemiology of Tuberculosis.* Baltimore: William Hood and Company, 1930.

Butler, William Francis. *The Great Lone Land: A Narrative of Travel and Adventure in the Northwest of America.* Edmonton: Hurtig Publishers, 1968.

Calloway, Colin C. "The Inter-Tribal Balance of Power on the Great Plains, 1760–1850." *American Studies* 16 (1982): 25–47.

——. "Snake Frontiers: The Eastern Shoshones in the Eighteenth Century." *Annals of Wyoming* 63 (1991): 82–92.

Cameron, William B. *The War Trail of Big Bear.* London: Duckworth, 1927.

Camp, Gregory S. "The Chippewa Fur Trade in the Red River Valley of the North, 1790–1830." In *The Fur Trade in North Dakota,* edited by Virginia L. Heidenreich, 33–46. Bismark: State Historical Society of North Dakota, 1990.

Campbell, Gregory. "The Changing Dimension of Native American Health: A Critical Understanding of Contemporary Native American Health Issues." In *Native American Resurgence and Renewal: A Reader and Bibliography,* edited by Robert N. Wells, 94–118. Metuchen, NJ: Scarecrow Press, 1994.

——. "Health Patterns and Economic Underdevelopment on the Cheyenne Reservation." In *The Political Economy of North American Indians,* edited by John H. Moore, 60–86. Norman: University of Oklahoma Press, 1993.

——. "The Political Economy of Ill-Health: Changing Northern Cheyenne Health Patterns and Economic Underdevelopment." Ph.D. diss., University of Oklahoma, 1987.

——, ed. *Plains Indian Historical Demography and Health: Perspectives, Interpretations, and Critiques.* Special issue of *Plains Anthropologist* 34 (1989).

Campbell, Marjorie Wilkins. *The North West Company.* Toronto: Macmillan, 1955.

Campbell, Sarah K. *Post-Columbian Culture History in the Northern Columbia Plateau A.D. 1500–1900.* New York: Garland Publishing, 1990.

Canada. House of Commons. *Debates.*

——. ——. *Sessional Papers.*

——. Privy Council Office. *Guide to Canadian Ministries since Confederation, July 1, 1867 to February 1, 1982.* Ottawa: Canadian Government Publishing Centre, 1982.

Cardinal, Harold, and Walter Hildebrandt. *Treaty Elders of Saskatchewan: Our Dream Is that Our Peoples Will One Day Be Clearly Recognized as Nations.* Calgary: University of Calgary Press, 2000.

Carley, Caroline D. "Historical and Archaeological Evidence of 19th Century Fever Epidemics and Medicine at Hudson's Bay Company's Fort Vancouver." *Historical Archaeology* 15 (1981): 19–35.

Carlos, Ann. "The Birth and Death of Predatory Competition in the North American Fur Trade: 1810–1821." *Explorations in Economic History* 19 (1982): 156–83.

Carlos, Ann M., and Elizabeth Hoffman. "The North American Fur Trade: Bargaining to a Joint Profit Maximum under Incomplete Information, 1804–1821." *Journal of Economic History* 46 (1986): 967–86.

Carter, Sarah. "Controlling Indian Movement: The Pass System." *NeWest Review* 10 (1985): 8–9.

——. "First Nations Women of Prairie Canada in the Early Reserve Years, the 1870s to the 1920s: A Preliminary Inquiry." In *Women of the First Nations: Power, Wisdom, and Strength,* edited by Christine Miller and Patricia Chuchryk, with Marie Smallface Marule, Brenda Manyfingers, and Cheryl Deering, 51–76. Manitoba Studies in Native History. Winnipeg: University of Manitoba Press, 1996.

——. "Introduction." In *Two Months in the Camp of Big Bear: The Life and Adventures of Theresa Gowanlock and Theresa Delaney,* by Theresa Gowanlock and Theresa Delaney, vii–xxii. Regina: Canadian Plains Research Center, 1999.

——. *Lost Harvests: Prairie Indian Reserve Farmers and Government Policy.* Montreal: McGill-Queen's University Press, 1990.

——. "Two Acres and a Cow: 'Peasant' Farming for the Indians of the Northwest, 1889–1897." *Canadian Historical Review* 70 (1989): 27–52. Reprinted in *Sweet Promises: A Reader in Indian–White Relations in Canada,* edited by J.R. Miller, 353–77. Toronto: University of Toronto Press, 1991.

Case, R. A., and G. M. MacDonald. "Tree Ring Reconstructions of Streamflow for Three Canadian Prairie Rivers." *Journal of the American Water Resources Association* 39 (2003): 707–16.

Catchpole, A. J. W., and Irene Hanuta. "Severe Summer Ice in Hudson Strait and Hudson Bay Following Major Volcanic Eruptions, 1751 to 1889 A.D." *Climatic Change* 14 (1989): 61–79.

Caviedes, Cesar N. *El Niño in History: Storming through the Ages.* Gainesville: University of Florida Press, 2001.

Chalmers, David. *Laird of the West.* Calgary: Detselig Enterprises, 1981.

Champ, Joan. "'Difficult to Make Hay': Early Attempts at Agriculture on the Montreal Lake Reserve." *Saskatchewan History* 47 (1995): 27–35.

Champagne, Antoine. *Les La Vérendrye et le poste de l'ouest.* Québec: Les Presses de l'Université Laval, 1968.

———. *Nouvelles études sur les La Vérendrye et le poste de l'ouest.* Québec: Les Presses de l'Université Laval, 1971.

Cheadle, W. A. *Cheadle's Journal of a Trip across Canada, 1862–63.* Edmonton: Hurtig Publishers, 1971.

Christensen, Deanna. *Ahtahkakoop: The Epic Account of a Plains Cree Head Chief, His People, and Their Struggle for Survival, 1816–1896.* Shell Lake, SK: Ahtahkakoop Publishing, 2000.

———. "Selected Aspects of Fort Pitt's History." Regina: Saskatchewan Parks and Renewable Resources, Historic Parks, Parks Visitor Services, 1984.

Clark, George A., Marc Kelley, J. M. Grange, and Cassandra Hill. "The Evolution of Mycobacterial Disease in Human Populations: A Reevaluation." *Current Anthropology* 28 (1987): 45–62.

Clink, W.L., ed. *Battleford Beleaguered: 1885, the Story of the Riel Uprising from the Columns of the* Saskatchewan Herald. Willowdale, ON: privately printed, 1984.

Coates, Kenneth. "Furs along the Yukon: Hudson's Bay Company–Native Trade in the Yukon River Basin, 1830–1893." *B.C. Studies* 55 (1982): 50–78.

Cobb, Charles R., and Brian Butler. "The Vacant Quarter Revisited: Late Mississippian Abandonment of the Lower Ohio Valley." *American Antiquity* 67 (2002): 625–41.

Cochin, Louis. *Reminiscences: A Veteran Missionary of Cree Indians and a Prisoner in Poundmaker's Camp.* Battleford: North-West Historical Society, 1927.

Cocking, Matthew. "An Adventurer from Hudson Bay: The Journal of Matthew Cocking from York Factory to the Blackfoot Country." Edited by J. L. Burpee. *Proceedings and Transactions of the Royal Society of Canada,* Series 3, Section 2 (1908): 91–121.

Cohn, Norman. *The Pursuit of the Millennium: Revolutionary Millenarians and Mystical Anarchists of the Middle Ages.* New York: Oxford University Press, 1970.

Collins, John S. *Across the Plains in '64: Incidents of Early Days West of the Missouri River—Two Thousand Miles in an Open Boat from Fort Benton to Omaha—Reminiscences of the Pioneer Period of Galena, General Grant's Old Home.* Omaha: National Printing Company, 1904.

Colpitts, George. "'Victuals into Their Mouths': Environmental Perspectives on Fur Trade Provisioning Activities at Cumberland House, 1775–1782." *Prairie Forum* 22 (1997): 1–22.

Commissioners of the Royal North-West Mounted Police. *Opening the West: Official Reports of the Royal North-West Mounted Police.* Toronto: Coles, 1973.

Complin, Margaret. "Calling Valley of the Crees and the Buffalo." *The Beaver* 265 (1935): 20–23, 58.

Comstock, George W. "Frost Revisited: The Modern Epidemiology of Tuberculosis." *American Journal of Epidemiology* 101 (1975): 363–82.

Comstock, George W., and Richard J. O'Brien. "Tuberculosis." In *Bacterial Infections of Humans: Epidemiology and Control,* 3rd ed., edited by Alfred S. Evans and Philip S. Brachman, 777–804. New York: Plenum Medical Book Company, 1998.

Cook, A. B., R. G. Ferguson, and J. F. Cairns. *Report to the Government of Saskatchewan by the Anti-Tuberculosis Commission.* Regina: Saskatchewan Anti-Tuberculosis Commission, 1922.

Cook, Ramsay, ed. *The Voyages of Jacques Cartier.* Toronto: University of Toronto Press, 1993.

Cooper, Barry. *Alexander Kennedy Isbister: A Respectable Critic of the Honourable Company.* Ottawa: Carleton University Press, 1988.

Cornish, F. C. "The Blackfeet and the Rebellion." *Alberta Historical Review* 6 (1958): 20–25.

Coues, Elliot, ed. *Forty Years a Fur Trader on the Upper Missouri: The Personal Narrative of Charles Larpenteur, 1833–1872.* 2 vols. Minneapolis: Ross and Haines, 1962.

——, ed. *New Light on the Early History of the Greater Northwest: The Manuscript Journals of Alexander Henry and David Thompson, 1799–1814.* 2 vols. Minneapolis: Ross and Haines, 1965.

Cowie, Isaac. *The Company of Adventurers: A Narrative of Seven Years in the Service of the Hudson's Bay Company during 1867–1874.* Introduction by David R. Miller. Lincoln: University of Nebraska Press, 1993.

Creighton, Donald. *John A. Macdonald: The Old Chieftain.* Toronto: Macmillan Company of Canada, 1955.

Crosby, Alfred W. *Biological Imperialism: The Biological Expansion of Europe, 900–1900.* Cambridge, UK: Cambridge University Press, 1986.

——. *The Columbian Exchange: Biological and Cultural Consequences of 1492.* Westport, CT: Greenwood Publishing Company, 1972.

——. *Germs, Seeds, and Animals: Studies in Ecological History.* London: M.E. Sharpe, 1994.

——. "Influenza." In *Cambridge World History of Human Diseases,* edited by Kenneth Kiple, 807–11. Cambridge, UK: Cambridge University Press, 1993.

——. "Virgin Soil Epidemics as a Factor in the Aboriginal Depopulation in America." *William and Mary Quarterly* 33 (1976): 289–99.

Crouse, Nellis M. *La Vérendrye: Fur Trader and Explorer.* Toronto: Ryerson Press, 1956.

Crowley, Thomas J. "Causes of Climate Change over the past 1000 Years." *Science,* 14 July 2000, 270–78.

Crowley, Thomas J., G. Zielinski, B. Vinther, R. Udisti, K. Kreutz, J. Cole-Dai, and E. Castellano. "Volcanism and the Little Ice Age." *Pages News* 16 (2008): 22–23.

Cummings, S. Lyle. *Primitive Tuberculosis.* London: John Bale Medical Publications, 1939.

Daniels, Roy. *Alexander Mackenzie and the North West.* Toronto: Mc-Clelland and Stewart, 1971.

Daschuk, James. "A Dry Oasis: The Canadian Plains in Late Prehistory." *Prairie Forum* 34 (2009): 1–29.

——. "Who Killed the Prairie Beaver? An Environmental Case for Eighteenth Century Migration in Western Canada." *Prairie Forum* 37 (2012): 151–72.

Daschuk, J. W., Paul Hackett, and Scott McNeil. "Treaties and Tuberculosis: First Nations People in the Late Nineteenth Century, a Political and Economic Transformation." *Bulletin of the History of Medicine* 23 (2006): 307–30.

Dawson, R. MacGregor. "The Gerrymander of 1882." *Canadian Journal of Economics and Political Science* 1 (1935): 197–221.

Decker, Jody. "Country Distempers: Deciphering Disease and Illness in Rupert's Land before 1870." In *Reading beyond Words: Contexts for Native History,* edited by J.S.H. Brown and Elizabeth Vibert, 156–81. Peterborough: Broadview Press, 1996.

——. "Depopulation of the Northern Plains Natives." *Social Science Medicine* 33 (1991): 381–93.

——. "Scurvy at York." *The Beaver* 69 (1989): 42–48.

——. "Tracing Historical Diffusion Patterns: The Case of the 1780–82 Smallpox Epidemic among the Indians of Western Canada." *Native Studies Review* 4 (1988): 1–24.

——. "'We Should Never Be Again the Same People': The Diffusion and Cumulative Impact of Acute Infectious Diseases Affecting the Natives on the Northern Plains of the Western Interior of Canada." Ph.D. diss., York University, 1989.

Deetz, James. *The Dynamics of Stylistic Change in Arikara Ceramics.* Urbana: University of Illinois Press, 1965.

Dempsey, Hugh. *The Amazing Death of Calf Shirt and Other Blackfoot Stories: Three Hundred Years of Blackfoot History.* Saskatoon: Fifth House, 1994.

——. *Big Bear: The End of Freedom.* Vancouver: Douglas and McIntyre, 1984.

——. *A Blackfoot Winter Count.* Glenbow Foundation Paper 1. Calgary: Glenbow Foundation, 1965.

——. "The Bull Elk Affair." *Alberta History* 40 (1992): 2–9.

——. *Charcoal's World.* Saskatoon: Western Producer Prairie Books, 1987.

——. *Crowfoot: Chief of the Blackfeet.* Norman: University of Oklahoma Press, 1972.

——. *Firewater: The Impact of the Whiskey Trade on the Blackfoot Nation.* Calgary: Fifth House, 2002.

——. *Red Crow: Warrior Chief.* Saskatoon: Western Producer Prairie Books, 1980.

——. "Sarcee." In *Plains,* edited by Raymond J. DeMallie, 629–37. Vol. 13, Part 1, of *Handbook of North American Indians.* Washington, DC: Smithsonian Institution Press, 2001.

——. "Smallpox: Scourge of the Plains." In *In Harm's Way: Disasters in Western Canada,* edited by Anthony Rasporich and Max Foran, 15–40. Calgary: University of Calgary Press, 2004.

——. "The Sweet Grass Hills Massacre." *Montana: The Magazine of Western History* 7 (1957): 12–18.

——. "An Unwilling Diary." *Alberta Historical Review* 7 (1955): 7–10.

——, ed. *The CPR West: The Iron Road and the Making of a Nation.* Vancouver: Douglas and McIntyre, 1984.

——, ed. *R. B. Nevitt, a Winter at Fort Macleod.* Calgary: Alberta–Glenbow Institute, McClelland and Stewart West, 1974.

——, ed. "Simpson's Essay on the Blackfoot." *Alberta History* 38 (1990): 1–14.

——, ed. "Smallpox Epidemic of 1869–70." *Alberta History* 11 (1963): 13–19.

——, ed. "The Starvation Year: Edgar Dewdney's Diary for 1879." Part 1. *Alberta History* 31 (1983): 1–15.

——, ed. "The Starvation Year: Edgar Dewdney's Diary for 1879." Part 2. *Alberta History* 31 (1983): 1–12.

Dempsey, James. "Little Bear's Band: Canadian or American Indians?" *Alberta History* 41 (1993): 2–10.

den Otter, A. A. "The 1857 Parliamentary Inquiry, the Hudson's Bay Company, and Rupert's Land Aboriginal People." *Prairie Forum* 24 (1999): 143–69.

Denny, Cecil. *The Law Marches West*. Toronto: J.M. Dent and Sons, 1972.

Devine, Heather. "Ambition versus Loyalty: Miles Macdonnell and the Decline of the Northwest Company." In *New Faces of the Fur Trade: Selected Papers of the Seventh North American Fur Trade Conference, Halifax, Nova Scotia 1995*, edited by J. Fiske, Susan Sleeper-Smith, and William Wicken, 247–82. East Lansing: Michigan State University Press, 1998.

Diamond, Jared. *Collapse: How Societies Choose to Fail or Succeed*. New York: Penguin, 2005.

——. *Guns, Germs, and Steel: The Fates of Human Societies*. New York: W.W. Norton and Company, 1997.

Dickason, Olive. *Canada's First Nations: A History of Founding Peoples from the Earliest Times*. Toronto: McClelland and Stewart, 1992.

Diedrich, Mark. *The Odyssey of Chief Standing Buffalo and the Northern Sisseton Sioux*. Minneapolis: Coyote Books, 1988.

Dion, Joseph. *My Tribe, the Crees*. Calgary: Glenbow Museum, 1979.

——. "A Short History of Moose Lake in 1907." In *Echoes of the Past: History of Bonnyville and District*, edited by Real Girard, 13–14. Bonnyville, AB: Bonnyville and District Historical Society, 1984.

Dixon, C. W. *Smallpox*. London: J. and A. Churchill, 1962.

Dobak, William A. "The Army and the Buffalo: A Demur." *Western Historical Quarterly* 26 (1995): 197–202.

Dobyns, Henry. "Estimating Aboriginal American Population: An Appraisal of Techniques with a New Hemisphere Estimate." *Current Anthropology* 7 (1966): 395–416.

——. "Native American Trade Centers as Contagious Disease Foci." In *Disease and Demography in the Americas*, edited by John W. Verano and Douglas H. Uberlaker, 215–22. Washington, DC: Smithsonian Institution Press, 1992.

——. *Their Number Become Thinned: Native American Population Dynamics in Eastern North America.* Knoxville: University of Tennessee Press, 1983.

Dobyns, Henry, and Robert Euler. *The Ghost Dance of 1889 among the Pai Indians of Northwestern Arizona.* Prescott, AZ: Prescott College Press, 1967.

Doige, Gary. "Warfare Patterns of the Assiniboine to 1809." MA thesis, University of Manitoba, 1987.

Dollar, Clyde D. "The High Plains Smallpox Epidemic of 1837–38." *Western Historical Quarterly* 8 (1977): 15–38.

Dolphin, Frank J. *Indian Bishop of the West: Vital Justin Grandin, 1829–1902.* Ottawa: Novalis, 1986.

Driscoll, Heather Rollason. "A Most Important Chain of Connection: Marriage in the Hudson's Bay Company." In *From Rupert's Land to Canada,* edited by Theodore Binnema, Gerhard Enns, and R. C. Macleod, 81–107. Edmonton: University of Alberta Press, 2001.

Duck, George. "Letters from the West." *The Beaver* 282 (1951): 20–24.

Duckworth, Harry, ed. *The English River Book: A Northwest Company Account Book of 1786.* Montreal: McGill-Queen's University Press, 1990.

Dunn, J. P. *Massacres of the Mountains: A History of the Indian Wars of the Far West, 1815–1875.* London: Eyer and Spottiswoode, 1963.

Dusenbury, Verne. *The Montana Cree: A Study in Religious Persistence.* Norman: University of Oklahoma Press, 1999.

Dyck, Noel E. "The Administration of Federal Indian Aid in the Northwest Territories, 1879–1885." MA thesis, University of Saskatchewan, 1970.

Dyck, Ian, and Richard E. Morlan. "Hunting and Gathering Tradition: Canadian Plains." In *Plains,* edited by Raymond J. DeMallie, 115–30. Vol. 13, Part 1, of *Handbook of North American Indians.* Washington, DC: Smithsonian Institution Press, 2001.

Eckert, Irma. "The Early Fur Trade at York and Churchill: Implications for the Native People of the North Central Subarctic." In *Le Castor Fait Tout: Selected Papers of the Fifth North American Fur Trade Conference, 1985,* edited by B. Trigger, T. Morantz, and L. Dechene, 223–35. Montreal: Lake St. Louis Historical Society, 1987.

Elias, Peter Douglas. *The Dakota of the Canadian Northwest: Lessons for Survival.* Manitoba Studies in Native History. Winnipeg: University of Manitoba Press, 1988.

Emerson, Thomas E. *Cahokia and the Archaeology of Power.* Tuscaloosa: University of Alabama Press, 1997.

Erasmus, Peter. *Buffalo Days and Nights*. Calgary: Fifth House, 1999.

Evans, R. G. *Outlaws and Lawmen of Western Canada*. Surrey, BC: Frontier Books, 1983.

Evans, Simon M. *The Bar U and Canadian Ranching History*. Calgary: University of Calgary Press, 2004.

Ewers, John C. *The Blackfeet: Raiders on the Northwestern Plains*. Norman: University of Oklahoma Press, 1958.

———. "The Influence of Epidemics on the Indian Populations and Cultures of Texas." *Plains Anthropologist* 18 (1973): 104–15.

Ewart, William B. "Causes of Mortality in a Subarctic Settlement (York Factory, Man.), 1714–1946." *Canadian Medical Association Journal* 129 (1983): 571–74.

Fagan, David. *The Little Ice Age: How Climate Shaped History, 1300–1500*. New York: Basic Books, 2000.

Fahey, John. *The Kalispel Indians*. Norman: University of Oklahoma Press, 1986.

Farmer, Paul. *Infections and Inequalities: The Modern Plagues*. Berkeley: University of California Press, 1999.

Farr, William E. "Going to Buffalo: Indian Hunting Migrations across the Rocky Mountains. Part 1, Making Meat and Taking Robes." *Montana: The Magazine of Western History* 53 (2003): 2–21.

Fenn, Elizabeth. "Biological Warfare in Eighteenth-Century North America: Beyond Jeffrey Amherst." *Journal of American History* 86 (2000):1552–80.

———. *Pox Americana: The Great Smallpox Epidemic of 1775–82*. New York: Hill and Wang, 2001.

Ferguson, R. G. *Studies in Tuberculosis*. Toronto: University of Toronto Press, 1955.

———. "A Study of the Epidemiology in a Primitive People." *Edinburgh Medical Journal* 36 (1929): 199–206.

———. *Tuberculosis among Indians of the Great Canadian Plains: Preliminary Report of an Investigation Being Carried Out by the National Research Council of Canada*. London: Adlard and Son, 1929.

Finlay, John, and D. N. Sprague. *The Structure of Canadian History*. 2nd ed. Scarborough: Prentice-Hall Canada, 1984.

Fisher, Robin. *Contact and Conflict: Indian–European Relations in British Columbia, 1774–1890*. Vancouver: UBC Press, 1977.

Fitting, James E. "Regional Cultural Development, 300 B.C. to A.D. 1000." In *Northeast*, edited by Bruce Trigger, 44–57. Vol. 15 of *Handbook of North American Indians*. Washington, DC: Smithsonian Institution Press, 1978.

Fladmark, Knut. "Early Fur-Trade Forts of the Peace River Area of British Columbia." *B.C. Studies* 65 (1985): 48–65.

Fleming, R. Harvey, ed. *Minutes of Council, Northern Department of Rupert's Land, 1821–1831*. Toronto: Champlain Society, 1940.

Flores, Dan. "Bison Ecology and Bison Diplomacy: The Southern Plains from 1800 to 1850." *Journal of American History* 78 (1991): 465–85.

Flynn, Catherine, and E. Leigh Syms. "Manitoba's First Farmers." *Manitoba History* 31 (1996): 4–11.

Forbis, Richard G. *Cluny: An Ancient Fortified Village in Alberta*. Occasional Papers 4. Calgary: Department of Archaeology, University of Calgary, 1977.

Fossett, Renée. *In Order to Live Untroubled: Inuit of the Central Arctic, 1550–1940*. Manitoba Studies in Native History. Winnipeg: University of Manitoba Press, 2001.

Foster, John. "Missionaries, Mixed-Bloods, and the Fur Trade: Four Letters of the Rev. William Cockran, Red River Settlement, 1830–1831." *Western Canadian Journal of Anthropology* 3 (1972): 104–25.

——. "The Origins of the Mixed Bloods in the Canadian West." In *Essays in Western History*, edited by L. G. Thomas, 71–82. Edmonton: University of Alberta Press, 1976.

——. "Wintering, the Outsider Adult Male, and the Ethnogenesis of the Western Plains Métis." *Prairie Forum* 19 (1994): 1–15.

---, ed. "Rupert's Land and the Red River Settlement, 1820–70." In *The Prairie West to 1905: A Canadian Sourcebook*, edited by Lewis G. Thomas, 19–69. Toronto: Oxford University Press, 1975.

Fowler, Loretta. *Shared Symbols, Contested Meanings: Gros Ventre Culture and History, 1778–1984*. Ithaca, NY: Cornell University Press, 1987.

Francis, Daniel. *Battle for the West: Fur Traders and the Birth of Canada*. Edmonton: Hurtig Publishers, 1982.

Frank, André Gunder. *Capitalism and Underdevelopment in Latin America: Historical Studies of Chile and Brazil*. New York: Monthly Review Press, 1967.

Frauenthal, James C. *Smallpox: When Should Routine Vaccination Be Discontinued?* Boston: Birkhauser, 1981.

Freeman, D. B., and F. L. Dungey. "A Spatial Duopoly: Competition in the Western Canadian Fur Trade, 1770–1835." *Journal of Historical Geography* 7 (1981): 252–70.

Friesen, Gerald. *The Canadian Prairies: A History*. Toronto: University of Toronto Press, 1984.

——. "Imports and Exports in the Manitoba Economy 1870–1890." *Manitoba History* 16 (1988): 31–41.

Friesen, Jean. "Magnificent Gifts: The Treaties of Canada with the Indians of the Northwest, 1869–76." *Transactions of the Royal Society of Canada*, Series 5 (1986): 41–51.

Frisch, Jack. "Some Ethnological and Ethnohistorical Notes of the Iroquois in Alberta." *Man in the Northeast* 7 (1976): 51–64.

Galbraith, John S. *The Hudson's Bay Company as an Imperial Factor, 1821–1869.* Toronto: University of Toronto Press, 1957.

——. "The Hudson's Bay Company under Fire, 1847–62." *Canadian Historical Review* 30 (1949): 322–35.

Gallagher, Richard. *Diseases that Plague Modern Man: A History of Ten Communicable Diseases.* New York: Oceana Publications, 1969.

Gentilcore, R. L., ed. *The Land Transformed, 1800–1891.* Vol. 2 of *Historical Atlas of Canada.* Toronto: University of Toronto Press, 1993.

Gerrard, Nelson. *The Icelandic River Saga.* Arborg, MB: Saga Publications, 1985.

Getty, Ian A. L., and Erik Gooding. "Stoney." In *Plains,* edited by Raymond J. DeMallie, 596–603. Vol. 13, Part 1, of *Handbook of North American Indians.* Washington, DC: Smithsonian Institution Press, 2001.

Gibbon, Guy E. "Cultural Dynamics of the Development of the Oneota Lifeway in Wisconsin." *American Antiquity* 37 (1972): 166–85.

Gibson, James R. *Farming the Frontier: The Agricultural Opening of the Oregon Country, 1786–1846.* Seattle: University of Washington Press, 1985.

——. *The Lifeline of the Oregon Country: The Fraser–Columbia Brigade System, 1811–47.* Vancouver: UBC Press, 1997.

——. "Smallpox on the Northwest Coast, 1835–1838." *B.C. Studies* 56 (1982–83): 61–81.

Gibson, W.W. *Silver Cloud: Condensed from "The Last Buffalo."* N.p.: privately printed, n.d. [circa 1940].

Gillespie, Beryl. "An Ethnohistory of the Yellowknives: A Northern Athapaskan Tribe." In *Contributions to Canadian Ethnology, 1975,* edited by David B. Carlisle, 191–245. Mercury Series, Canadian Ethnology Service Paper 31. Ottawa: National Museum of Man, 1975.

——. "Territorial Groups before 1821: Athapaskans of the Shield and the Mackenzie Drainage." In *Subarctic,* edited by June Helm, 161–68. Vol. 6 of *Handbook of North American Indians.* Washington, DC: Smithsonian Institution Press, 1981.

——. "Yellowknife." In *Subarctic,* edited by June Helm, 285–90. Vol. 6 of *Handbook of North American Indians.* Washington, DC: Smithsonian Institution Press, 1981.

Gillese, John Patrick. "The Bears that Killed the Buffalo." *The Beaver* 293 (1962): 43–49.

Gilman, Rhoda, Carolyn Gilman, and Deborah Stultz. *The Red River Trails: Oxcart Routes between St. Paul and the Selkirk Settlement, 1820–1870.* St. Paul: Minnesota Historical Society, 1979.

Gladstone, William S. *The Gladstone Diary: Travels in the Early West.* Edited by Bruce Haig. Lethbridge: Historic Trails Society of Alberta, 1985.

Glazebrook, G. P. de T., ed. *The Hargrave Correspondence, 1821–1843.* Toronto: Champlain Society, 1938.

Gluek, Alvin. *Minnesota and the Manifest Destiny of the Canadian Northwest: A Study in Canadian–American Relations.* Toronto: University of Toronto Press, 1965.

Goldring, Phillip. "The Cypress Hills Massacre: A Century's Retrospect." *Saskatchewan History* 26 (1973): 81–102.

——. "Labour Records of the Hudson's Bay Company, 1821–1870." *Archivaria* 11 (1980): 53–86.

——. *Whiskey, Horses, and Death: The Cypress Hills Massacre and Its Sequel.* Occasional Papers in Archaeology and History, Canadian Historic Sites 21. Ottawa: Parks Canada, 1973.

Goodwill, Jean, and Norma Sluman. *John Tootoosis.* Winnipeg: Pemmican Publications, 1984.

Gorsline, R. M. "The Medical Services of the Red River Expeditions, 1870–71." *Medical Services Journal Canada* 3 (1967): 167–74.

Grabowski, Jan, and Nicole St. Onge. "Montreal Iroquois *Engagés* in the Western Fur Trade, 1800–1821." In *From Rupert's Land to Canada,* edited by Theodore Binnema, Gerhard J. Ens, and R.C. Macleod, 23–58. Edmonton: University of Alberta Press, 2001.

Graham-Cumming, G., and C. R. Maundrell. "Health of the Original Canadians, 1867–1967." *Medical Services Journal Canada* 3 (1967): 115–66.

Grange, J. M., M. Gandy, P. Farmer, and A. Zumia. "Historical Declines in Tuberculosis: Nature, Nurture, and the Biosocial Model." *International Journal of Tuberculosis and Lung Disease* 5 (2001): 208–12.

Grant, George M. *Ocean to Ocean: Sandford Fleming's Expedition through Canada in 1872.* Toronto: Coles Publishing Company, 1970.

Grant, John Webster. *Moon of Wintertime: Missionaries and the Indians of Canada in Encounter since 1534.* Toronto: University of Toronto Press, 1984.

Gray, John. *Red Lights on the Prairies.* Toronto: Macmillan of Canada, 1971.

Green, Joyce. "Towards a Detente with History: Confronting Canada's Colonial Legacy." *International Journal of Canadian Studies* 12 (1995): 85–105.

Greenberg, Adolph, and James Morrison. "Group Identities in the Boreal Forest: The Origin of the Northern Ojibwa." *Ethnohistory* 29 (1982): 75–102.

Gregg, John B., and Larry Zimmerman. "Malnutrition in Fourteenth-Century South Dakota: Osteopathological Manifestations." *North American Archaeologist* 7 (1986): 191–214.

Greibach, W. A. "The Narrative of James Gibson." Part 2. *Alberta History* 6 (1958): 10–16.

Grinnell, George Bird. *Blackfoot Lodge Tales: The Story of a Prairie People.* Lincoln: University of Nebraska Press, 1962.

Grove, Jean M. *The Little Ice Age.* London: Methuen, 1988.

Gulig, Anthony. "In Whose Interest? Government–Indian Relations in Northern Saskatchewan and Wisconsin, 1900–1940." Ph.D. diss., University of Saskatchewan, 1997.

———. "Sizing Up the Catch: Native–Newcomer Resource Competition and the Early Years of Saskatchewan's Northern Commercial Fishery." *Saskatchewan History* 47 (1995): 3–11.

Gullason, Lynda. "'No Less than 7 Different Nations': Ethnicity and Culture Contact at Fort George–Buckingham House." In *The Fur Trade Revisited: Papers of the Sixth North American Fur Trade Conference, Mackinac Island, Michigan, 1991,* edited by J.S.H. Brown, W. Eccles, and D.P. Feldman, 117–43. East Lansing: Michigan State University Press, 1994.

Gwyn, Sandra. *"A Private Capital": Love and Ambition in the Age of Macdonald and Laurier.* Toronto: McClelland and Stewart, 1984.

Hackett, Paul. "Averting Disaster: The Hudson's Bay Company and Smallpox in Western Canada during the Late Eighteenth and Early Nineteenth Centuries." *Bulletin of the History of Medicine* 78 (2004): 575–609.

———. "Historical Mourning Practices Observed among the Cree and Ojibway Indians of the Central Subarctic." *Ethnohistory* 52 (2005): 503–32.

——. "The Monsoni and the Smallpox of 1737–39." In *Pushing the Margins: Native and Northern Studies,* edited by Jill Oakes, Rick Riewe, Marilyn Bennet, and Brenda Chisholm, 244–57. Winnipeg: Departments of Native Studies and Zoology, University of Manitoba, 2001.

——. "'A Very Remarkable Sickness': The Diffusion of Directly Transmitted, Acute Infectious Diseases in the Petit Nord, 1670–1846." Ph.D. diss., University of Manitoba, 1999.

——. *"A Very Remarkable Sickness": Epidemics in the Petit Nord, 1670 to 1846.* Winnipeg: University of Manitoba Press, 2002.

Haines, Francis. "The Northward Spread of Horses among the Plains Indians." *American Anthropologist,* n.s., 40 (1938): 429–37.

Hall, D. J. "'A Serene Atmosphere?' Treaty 1 Revisited." *Canadian Journal of Native Studies* 4 (1987): 321–58.

Hämäläinen, Pekka. *The Comanche Empire.* New Haven, CT: Yale University Press, 2008.

Hamilton, Zachary M., and Marie Albina Hamilton. *These Are the Prairies.* Regina: School Aids and Textbook Publishers, 1955.

Hanks, Chris. "The Swampy Cree and the Hudson's Bay Company at Oxford House." *Ethnohistory* 29 (1982): 103–15.

Hara, Hiroko Sue. *The Hare Indians and Their World.* Mercury Series, Canadian Ethnology Service Paper 63. Ottawa: National Museum of Man, 1980.

Harden, Victoria A. "Rocky Mountain Spotted Fever and the Spotted Fever Group of Diseases." In *Cambridge World History of Human Disease,* edited by Kenneth Kiple, 982–84. Cambridge, UK: Cambridge University Press, 1993.

Harington, C. R., ed. *The Year without a Summer? World Climate in 1816.* Ottawa: Canadian Museum of Nature, 1992.

Harper, Frank B. *Fort Union and Its Neighbors on the Upper Missouri: A Chronological Record of Events.* St. Paul: Great Northern Railway, 1925.

Harris, R. C., ed. *From the Beginning to 1800.* Vol. 1 of *Historical Atlas of Canada.* Toronto: University of Toronto Press, 1987.

Hatt, Ken. "The North-West Rebellion Scrip Commissions, 1885–1889." In *1885 and After: Native Society in Transition,* edited by F.L. Barron and James Waldram, 189–204. Regina: Canadian Plains Research Center, 1985.

Hawden, Seymour. "Tuberculosis in the Buffalo." *Journal of the American Veterinary Medical Association* 100 (1942): 19–22.

Hays, Robert G. *A Race at Bay:* New York Times *Editorials on "the Indian Problem," 1860–1900.* Carbondale: Southern Illinois University Press, 1997.

Hearne, Samuel. *A Journey from Prince of Wales Fort in Hudson's Bay to the Northern Ocean in the Years 1769, 1770, 1771, 1772.* Edmonton: Hurtig Publishers, 1971.

Hector, James, and W. S. W. Vaux. "Notice of the Indians Seen by the Exploring Expedition under the Command of Captain Palliser." *Transactions of the Ethnological Society of London* 1 (1860): 245–61.

Helm, June. "Female Infanticide, European Diseases, and Population Levels among Mackenzie Dene." *American Ethnologist* 7 (1980): 259–85.

Helm, June, and Beryl Gillespie. "Dogrib Oral Tradition as History: War and Peace in the 1820s." *Journal of Anthropological Research* 37 (1981): 8–27.

Hendry [Henday], Anthony. "York Factory to the Blackfeet Country: The Journal of Anthony Hendry, 1754–1755." Edited by J.L. Burpee. *Proceedings and Transactions of the Royal Society of Canada,* 3rd Series, 1 (1907): 307–64.

Henige, David. *Numbers from Nowhere: The American Indian Contact Population Debate.* Norman: University of Oklahoma Press, 1998.

——. "On the Current Devaluation of the Notion of Evidence: A Rejoinder to Dobyns." *Ethnohistory* 36 (1989): 304–07.

Henry, Alexander [the Elder]. *Travels and Adventures in Canada and the Indian Territory between the Years 1760 and 1776.* Edited by James Bain. Rutland, VT: C. E. Tuttle Company, 1969.

Henry, Alexander [the Younger]. *The Journal of Alexander Henry the Younger, 1799–1814.* Vol. 1. Edited by Barry Gough. Toronto: Champlain Society, 1988.

Hewlett, Edward S. "The Chilcotin Uprising of 1864." *B.C. Studies* 19 (1973): 50–72.

Hickerson, Harold. *The Chippewa and Their Neighbours: A Study in Ethnohistory.* Rev. and expanded ed. Studies in Anthropological Method. Prospect Heights, IL: Waveland Press, 1988.

——. "Journal of Charles Jean Baptiste Chaboillez, 1797–1798." *Ethnohistory* 6 (1959): 265–316, 363–427.

Hildebrandt, Walter. *Views from Fort Battleford: Constructed Visions of an Anglo-Canadian West.* Regina: Canadian Plains Research Center, 1994.

Hind, Henry Youle. *Narrative of the Canadian Red River Exploring Expedition of 1857 and of the Assiniboine and Saskatchewan Expedition of 1858.* 2 vols. Edmonton: Hurtig Publishers, 1971.

——. "Of Some of the Superstitions and Customs Common among the Indians in the Valley of the Assiniboines and the Saskatchewan." *Canadian Journal,* n.s., 22 (1859): 253–62.

Hines, John. *The Red Indians of the Plains: Thirty Years Missionary Experience in the Saskatchewan.* London: Society for Promoting Christian Knowledge, 1915.

Hodge, Adam R. "In Want of Nourishment for to Keep Them Alive":Climate Fluctuations, Bison Scarcity, and the Smallpox Epidemic of 1780-82 on the Northern Great Plains," *Environmental History* 17 (2012): 365-403.

Hodgetts, J. E., William McCloskey, Reginald Whitaker, and V. Seymour Wilson. *The Biography of an Institution: The Civil Service Commission of Canada, 1908–1967.* Montreal: McGill-Queen's University Press, 1972.

Holder, A. B. "Papers on Diseases among Indians." *Medical Record: A Weekly Journal of Medicine and Surgery,* 13 August 1892, 177–82.

Honigmann, John. *Ethnography and Acculturation of the Fort Nelson Slave.* Yale University Publications in Anthropology 33. New Haven, CT: Yale University Press, 1946.

Hopwood, Victor C. "New Light on David Thompson." *The Beaver* 288 (1957): 239–45.

Hornaday, William T. *The Extermination of the American Bison with a Sketch of Its Discovery and Life History.* Washington, DC: Smithsonian Institution, Government Printing Bureau, 1889.

Hornbeck Tanner, Helen. "The Career of Joseph La France, Coureur de Bois in the Great Lakes." In *The Fur Trade Revisited: Selected Papers of the Sixth North American Fur Trade Conference, Mackinac Island, Michigan, 1991,* edited by J.S.H. Brown, W.J. Eccles, and D.P. Feldman, 171–88. East Lansing: Michigan State University Press, 1994.

Horral, S. W. *A Chronicle of the West: Northwest Mounted Police Report for 1875.* Calgary: Historical Society of Alberta, 1975.

——. "The (Royal) Northwest Mounted Police and Prostitution on the Canadian Prairies." *Prairie Forum* 10 (1985): 105–28.

——. "The (Royal) Northwest Mounted Police and Prostitution on the Canadian Prairies." In *The Mounted Police and Prairie Society, 1873–1919,* edited by William M. Baker, 173–92. Regina: Canadian Plains Research Center, 1998.

Hubner, Brian. "Horse Stealing and the Borderline: The NWMP and the Control of Indian Movement." *Prairie Forum* 20 (1995): 281–300.

Hughes, Katherine. *Father Lacombe: The Blackrobe Voyageur.* New York: Moffat, Yard and Company, 1911.

——. *Father Lacombe: The Blackrobe Voyageur.* Toronto: McClelland and Stewart, 1920.

Hungry Wolf, Adolf. *The Blood People: A Division of the Blackfoot Confederacy.* New York: Harper and Row, 1977.

Hungry Wolf, Adolph The Blackfoot Papers: Four Volumes. Skookumchuk, B.C.: The Good Medicine Cultural Foundation, 2006.

Hurlich, Marshall. "Historical and Recent Demography of the Algonkians of Northern Ontario." In *Boreal Forest Adaptations: The Northern Algonkians,* edited by A.T. Steegmann, 143–200. New York: Plenum Press, 1983.

Innes, Ross. *The Sands of Time.* North Battleford: Turner-Warwick Publications, 1986. [Originally published as Campbell Innes, *The Cree Rebellion of 1884* (Battleford: Canadian North-West Historical Society, 1927).]

Innis, H. A. *The Fur Trade in Canada: An Introduction to Canadian Economic History.* 1930; reprint, Toronto: University of Toronto Press, 1999.

Isenberg, Andrew C. *The Destruction of the Bison: An Environmental History, 1750–1920.* Cambridge, UK: Cambridge University Press, 2000.

Ives, John W. *A Theory of Athapaskan Prehistory.* Calgary: University of Calgary Press, 1990.

Jaenen, Cornelius, ed. *The French Regime in the Upper Country during the Seventeenth Century.* Toronto: Champlain Society, 1996.

Janes, Robert R. "Observations on Crisis Cult Activities in the Mackenzie Basin." In *Problems in the Prehistory of the North American Subarctic: The Athapaskan Question,* edited by J.W. Helmer, S. Van Dyke, and F.J. Kense, 153–64. Calgary: University of Calgary Press, 1977.

Jarvenpa, Robert. "The Hudson's Bay Company, the Roman Catholic Church, and the Chipewyan in the Late Fur Trade Period." In *Le Castor Fait Tout: Selected Papers of the Fifth North American Fur Trade Conference, 1985,* edited by B. Trigger, T. Morantz, and L. Dechene, 485–517. Montreal: Lake St. Louis Historical Society, 1987.

Jefferson, Robert. *Fifty Years on the Saskatchewan.* Battleford: Canadian North-West Historical Society, 1929.

Jennings, John. "The North West Mounted Police and Indian Policy after the Rebellion." In *1885 and After: Native Society in Transition,* edited by F.L. Barron and James Waldram, 225–40. Regina: Canadian Plains Research Center, 1985.

Johnson, Alice M., ed. *Saskatchewan Journals and Correspondence: Edmonton House 1795–1800, Chesterfield House, 1800–1802.* Hudson's Bay Record Society 26. London: Hudson's Bay Record Society, 1967.

Johnson, Craig M. "The Coalescent Tradition." In *Archaeology on the Great Plains,* edited by W. Raymond Wood, 308–44. Lawrence: University of Kansas Press, 1998.

Johnston, Susan. "Epidemics, the Forgotten Factor in Seventeenth Century Native Warfare in the St. Lawrence Region." In *Native People, Native Lands: Canadian Indians, Inuit, and Métis,* edited by Bruce Cox, 14–31. Ottawa: Carleton University Press, 1987.

Johnston, William D. "Tuberculosis." In *The Cambridge World History of Human Disease,* edited by Kenneth F. Kiple, 1059–68. Cambridge, UK: Cambridge University Press, 1993.

Jones, Terry L., G. M. Brown, L. M. Raab, J. L. McVickar, W. G. Spaulding, D. J. Kennett, A. York, and P. L. Walker. "Environmental Imperatives Reconsidered: Demographic Crises in Western North America during the Medieval Climatic Anomaly [and Comments and Reply]." *Current Anthropology* 40 (1999): 137–70.

Jones, David S. "Virgin Soils Revisited," *William and Mary Quarterly* 60 (2003): 703-742.

Jordan, Terry. *North American Cattle-Ranching Frontiers.* Albuquerque: University of New Mexico Press, 1993.

Judd, Carol. "Native Labour and Social Stratification of the Hudson's Bay Company's Northern Department, 1770–1870." *Canadian Review of Sociology and Anthropology* 17 (1980): 305–14.

——. "Sakie, Esquawenoe, and the Foundation of the Dual-Native Tradition at Moose Factory." In *The Subarctic Fur Trade: Native Social and Economic Adaptations,* edited by Shepard Krech III, 81–98. Vancouver: UBC Press, 1984.

Kane, Paul. *Wanderings of an Artist among the Indians of North America, from Canada to Vancouver's Island and Oregon through the Hudson's Bay Territory and Back Again.* Edmonton: Hurtig Publishers, 1968.

Karamanski, Theodore J. *Fur Trade and Exploration: Opening the Far Northwest, 1821–1852.* Norman: University of Oklahoma Press, 1983.

——. "The Iroquois and the Fur Trade of the Far West." *The Beaver* 312 (1982): 4–13.

Karlen, Arlo. *Man and Microbes: Disease and Plagues in History and Modern Times*. New York: Putnam, 1995.

Kehoe, Alice B. *The Ghost Dance: Ethnohistory and Revitalization*. Case Studies in Cultural Anthropology. Fort Worth: Holt, Rinehart and Winston, 1989.

Keith, Lloyd B. *Wildlife's Ten Year Cycle*. Madison: University of Wisconsin Press, 1963.

——, ed. *North of Athabasca: Slave Lake and Mackenzie River Documents of the North West Company, 1800–1821*. Montreal: McGill-Queen's University Press, 2001.

Kelly, L. V. *The Range Men: The Story of the Ranchers and Indians of Alberta*. Toronto: Coles, 1980.

Kelm, Mary-Ellen. *Colonizing Bodies: Aboriginal Health and Healing in British Columbia, 1900–50*. Vancouver: UBC Press, 1998.

Kelton, Paul. "Avoiding the Smallpox Spirits: Colonial Epidemics and Southwestern Indian Survival." *Ethnohistory* 15 (2004): 45–71.

Kemp, D. D. "The Drought of 1804–1805 in Central North America." *Weather* 37 (1982): 34–41.

Kennedy, Dan. *Recollections of an Assiniboine Chief/Dan Kennedy (Ochankugahe)*. Edited by James Stevens. Toronto: McClelland and Stewart, 1972.

Kennedy, Margaret A. *The Whiskey Trade of the Northwestern Plains: A Multidisciplinary Study*. New York: P. Lang, 1997.

Keys, Ancel, Josef Brozek, Austin Henschel, Olaf Mickelsen, and Henry L. Taylor. *The Biology of Human Starvation*. 2 vols. Minneapolis: University of Minnesota Press, 1950.

King, Richard. *Narrative of a Journey to the Shores of the Arctic Ocean in 1833, 1834, and 1835*. 2 vols. London: Richard Bentley, 1836.

Kiple, Kenneth F., and Stephen V. Beck. "Introduction." In *Biological Consequences of European Expansion, 1450–1800*, edited by Kenneth F. Kiple and Stephen V. Beck, xv–xxix. Vol. 26 of *An Expanding World: The European Impact on World History, 1450–1800*. Burlington, VT: Ashgate, 1997.

Klein, Alan M. "Political Economy of the Buffalo Hide Trade: Race and Class on the Plains." In *The Political Economy of North American Indians*, edited by John H. Moore, 137–60. Norman: University of Oklahoma Press, 1993.

Koucky, Rudolph W. "The Buffalo Disaster of 1882." *North Dakota History* 50 (1983): 23–30.

Krech, Shepard III. "The Banditte of St. John's." *The Beaver* 313 (1982): 36–41.

——. "The Beaver Indians and the Hostilities at Fort St. John's." *Arctic Anthropology* 20 (1983): 35–45.

——. "Disease, Starvation, and Northern Athapaskan Social Organization." *American Ethnologist* 5 (1978): 710–32.

——. "The Early Fur Trade in the Northwestern Subarctic: The Kutchin and the Trade in Beads." In *Le Castor Fait Tout: Selected Papers of the Fifth North American Fur Trade Conference, 1985,* edited by B. Trigger, T. Morantz, and L. Dechene, 236–77. Montreal: Lake St. Louis Historical Society, 1987.

——. *The Ecological Indian: Myth and History.* New York: W.W. Norton and Company, 1999.

——. "The Influence of Disease and the Fur Trade on Arctic Drainage Lowlands Dene, 1800–1850." *Journal of Anthropological Research* 39 (1983): 123–46.

——. "On the Aboriginal Population of the Kutchin." *Arctic Anthropology* 15 (1978): 89–104.

——. "Throwing Bad Medicine: Sorcery, Disease, and the Fur Trade among the Kutchin and other Northern Athapaskans." In *Indians, Animals, and the Fur Trade: A Critique of* Keepers of the Game, edited by Shepard Krech III, 73–108. Athens: University of Georgia Press, 1981.

——. "The Trade of the Slavey and Dogrib at Ft. Simpson in the Early 19th Century." In *The Subarctic Fur Trade: Native Social and Economic Adaptations,* edited by Shepard Krech III, 99–146. Vancouver: UBC Press, 1984.

Lamb, W. Kaye, ed. *Sixteen Years in Indian Country: The Journal of Daniel Harmon, 1800–1816.* Toronto: Macmillan, 1957.

Lamb, H.H. *Climate, History, and the Modern World.* London: Methuen, 1982.

Larmour, Jean. "Edgar Dewdney, Commissioner of Indian Affairs and Lieutenant Governor of the Northwest Territories, 1879–1888." MA thesis, University of Saskatchewan, Regina Campus, 1969.

Laut, Agnes C. "Reverend 'Jack' Matheson: The Sky Pilot of the Crees." *Toronto Saturday Night* (Christmas 1911): 26–30.

Lavine, Frances, and Anna La Bauve. "Examining the Complexity of Historic Population Decline: A Case Study from Pecos Pueblo, New Mexico." *Ethnohistory* 44 (1997): 75–113.

LeBaron, Charles W., and David W. Taylor. "Typhoid Fever." In *The Cambridge World History of Human Disease*, edited by Kenneth F. Kiple, 1071–76. Cambridge, UK: Cambridge University Press, 1993.

Lee, David. "Foremost Man and His Band." *Saskatchewan History* 36 (1983): 94–101.

———. "Piapot: Man and Myth." *Prairie Forum* 17 (1992): 251–62.

Lehmer, Donald J. "Climate and Culture History in the Middle Missouri Valley." In *Pleistocene and Recent Environments of the Central Great Plains*, edited by W. Dort and J.K. Jones, 117–29. Lawrence: University of Kansas Press, 1970. Reprinted in *Selected Writings of Donald J. Lehmer*, Reprints in Anthropology 8, 59–72. Lincoln: J and L Reprint Company, 1977.

Leighton, Douglas. "A Victorian Civil Servant at Work: Lawrence Vankoughnet and the Canadian Indian Department, 1873–1893." In *As Long as the Sun Shines and Water Flows: A Reader in Canadian Native Studies*, edited by Ian A.L. Getty and Antoine Lussier, 104–19. Vancouver: UBC Press, 1983.

Lenius, Bryan J., and Dave M. Olinyk. "The Rainy River Composite: Revisions to Late Woodland Taxonomy." In *The Woodland Tradition in the Western Great Lakes: Papers Presented to Elden Johnson*, edited by Guy Gibbon, 77–112. Publications in Anthropology 4. Minneapolis: University of Minnesota Press, 1990.

Le Roy Ladurie, Emmanuel. *The Mind and Method of the Historian*. Brighton, UK: Harvester Press, 1981.

———. *The Territory of the Historian*. Chicago: University of Chicago Press, 1979.

Levison, Matthew. "*Mycobacterium bovis:* An Underappreciated Pathogen." *Current Infectious Disease Reports* 10 (2008): 444–46.

Lichtor, Joseph, and Alexander Lichtor. "Paleopathological Evidence Suggesting Pre-Columbian Tuberculosis of the Spine." *Journal of Bone and Joint Surgery* 39 (1957): 1398–99.

Liebenberg, Louis. "Persistence Hunting by Modern Hunter-Gatherers." *Current Anthropology* 47 (2006): 1017–26.

Looy, Anthony J. "The Indian Agent and His Role in the Administration of the Northwest Superintendency, 1876–1893." Ph.D. diss., Queen's University, 1977.

———. "Saskatchewan's First Indian Agent: M.G. Dickieson." *Saskatchewan History* 32 (1979): 104–15.

Lott, Dale F. *American Bison: A Natural History*. Berkeley: University of California Press, 2003.

Lupul, David. "The Bobtail Land Surrender." *Alberta History* 26 (1978): 29–39.

Lux, Maureen. "Beyond Biology: Disease and Its Impact on the Canadian Plains Native People 1880–1930." Ph.D. diss., Simon Fraser University, 1996.

———. *Medicine that Walks: Disease, Medicine, and Canadian Plains Native People, 1880–1940.* Toronto: University of Toronto Press, 2001.

———. "Perfect Subjects: Race, Tuberculosis, and the Qu'Appelle BCG Vaccine Trial." *Canadian Bulletin of Medical History* 15 (1998): 277–95.

———. "Prairie Indians and the 1918 Influenza Epidemic." *Native Studies Review* 8 (1992): 23–34.

Lytwyn, Victor P. "'God Was Angry with Their Country': The Smallpox Epidemic of 1782–83 among the Hudson Bay Lowland Cree." In *Papers of the Thirtieth Algonkian Conference*, edited by David H. Pentland, 142–65. Winnipeg: University of Manitoba Press, 1999.

———. *Muskekowuck Athinuwick: Original People of the Great Swampy Land.* Manitoba Studies in Native History. Winnipeg: University of Manitoba Press, 2002.

MacDonald, H. B. "The Killing of the Buffalo." *The Beaver* 266 (1935): 20–24.

MacEwan, Grant. *Cornerstone Colony: Selkirk's Contributions to the Canadian West.* Saskatoon: Western Producer Prairie Books, 1977.

———. *Sitting Bull: The Years in Canada.* Edmonton: Hurtig Publishers, 1973.

MacGregor, James G. *Edmonton: A History.* Edmonton: Hurtig Publishers, 1975.

———. *Father Lacombe.* Edmonton: Hurtig Publishers, 1975.

———. *A History of Alberta.* Edmonton: Hurtig Publishers, 1972.

———. *John Rowand: Czar of the Prairies.* Saskatoon: Western Producer Prairie Books, 1978.

———. *Peter Fidler: Canada's Forgotten Surveyor, 1769–1822.* Toronto: McClelland and Stewart, 1966.

———. *Senator Hardisty's Prairies, 1849–1889.* Saskatoon: Western Producer Prairie Books, 1978.

Mackenzie, Alexander. *Voyages from Montreal on the River St. Lawrence through the Continent of North America to the Frozen and Pacific Oceans in the Years 1789 and 1793.* Edmonton: Hurtig Publishers, 1971.

MacLean, John. *McDougall of Alberta: A Life of Rev. John McDougall D.D., Pathfinder of Empire and Prophet of the Plains.* Toronto: F.C. Stephenson, 1927.

Macleod, R. D. "The North West Mounted Police, 1873–1905: Law Enforcement and the Social Order in the Canadian Northwest." Ph.D. diss., Duke University, 1972.

Macoun, John. *Autobiography of John Macoun, M.A.: Canadian Explorer and Naturalist 1831–1920.* Ottawa: Ottawa Field-Naturalists Club, 1922.

Mails, Thomas E. *The Mystic Warriors of the Plains.* New York: Mallard Press, 1991.

Makahonuk, Glen. "Wage Labour in the Northwest Fur Trade Economy, 1760–1849." *Saskatchewan History* 41 (1988): 1–18.

Malainey, Mary E. "The Gros Ventre/Fall Indians in Historical and Archaeological Interpretation." *Canadian Journal of Native Studies* 25 (2005): 155–83.

Mallery, Garrick. *Picture-Writing of the American Indians.* 2 vols. New York: Dover Publications, 1972.

Malthus, Thomas R. *T.R. Malthus, an Essay on the Principle of Population, or, a View of Its Past and Present Effect on Human Happiness: With an Inquiry into Our Prospects Respecting the Future Removal or Mitigation of the Evils which It Occasions.* Edited by Patricia James. Cambridge, UK: Cambridge University Press, 1989.

Mandelbaum, David. *The Plains Cree: An Ethnographic, Historical, and Comparative Study.* Regina: Canadian Plains Research Center, 1979.

Marsh, James. "Grand Portage." In *The 1997 Canadian Encyclopaedia Plus.* Toronto: McClelland and Stewart, 1996. CD-rom.

Martin, Calvin. *Keepers of the Game: Indian–Animal Relationships and the Fur Trade.* Berkeley: University of California Press, 1978.

Masson, L.R., ed. *Les Bourgeois de la Compagnie du Nord-Ouest: Recit de voyages, lettres, et rapports inedits relatif au nord-ouest canadien.* 2 vols. New York: Antiquarian Press, 1960.

Matthews, Washington. "Consumption among the Indians." *Transactions of the American Climatological Association* 3 (1886): 234–41.

Mayor, Adrienne. "The Nessus Shirt in the New World: Smallpox Blankets in History and Legend." *Journal of American Folklore* 108 (1995): 54–77.

McCarthy, Martha. *From the Great River to the Ends of the Earth: Oblate Missions to the Dene, 1847–1921.* Edmonton: University of Alberta Press, 1995.

——. *To Evangelize the Nations: Roman Catholic Missions in Manitoba, 1818–1870.* Winnipeg: Manitoba Culture, Heritage and Recreation, Historic Resources, 1990.

McColl, Frances. *Ebenezer McColl: "Friend to the Indians." Superinten-dent of Indian Affairs for Manitoba and Northwest Territories, a Biography 1835–1902.* Winnipeg: self-published, 1989.

McCormack, Patricia. "The Athabasca Influenza Epidemic of 1835." In *Issues in the North,* edited by Jill Oakes and Rick Riewe, 33–42. Edmonton: Canadian Circumpolar Institute, 1996.

McCourt, Edward. *Remember Butler: The Story of William Butler.* Toronto: McClelland and Stewart, 1967.

McCrady, David. "Beyond Boundaries: Aboriginal Peoples and the Prairie West, 1850–1885." MA thesis, University of Victoria, 1992.

——. "Living with Strangers: The Nineteenth-Century Sioux and the Canadian–American Borderlands." Ph.D. diss., University of Manitoba, 1998.

McDougall, John. *George Millward McDougall: The Pioneer, Patriot, and Missionary.* Toronto: William Briggs, 1888.

——. *In the Days of the Red River Rebellion.* Edited by Susan Jaeckel. Edmonton: University of Alberta Press, 1983.

——. *On Western Trails in the Early Seventies: Frontier Life in the Cana-dian North-West.* Toronto: William Briggs, 1911.

McHugh, Tom. *The Time of the Buffalo.* New York: Knopf, 1972.

McLeod, Malcolm, ed. *Archibald McDonald, Peace River: A Canoe Voy-age from Hudson's Bay to Pacific by Sir George Simpson, Journal of the Late Chief Factor, Archibald McDonald ... Who Accompanied Him.* Edmonton: Hurtig Publishers, 1971.

McLeod, Neil. "Exploring Cree Narrative Memory." Ph.D. diss., Uni-versity of Regina, 2005.

McNeill, William. "Historical Patterns of Migration." *Current Anthro-pology* 20 (1979): 95–98.

——. *Plagues and Peoples.* Garden City, NY: Anchor Press, 1976.

McPherson, Arlean. *The Battlefords: A History.* Saskatoon: Modern Press, 1967.

McQuillan, D. Aidan. "Creation of Indian Reserves on the Canadian Prairies, 1870–1885." *Geographical Review* 70 (1980): 379–96.

Meijer Drees, Laurie. "Reserve Hospitals and Medical Officers: Health Care and Indian Peoples in Southern Alberta, 1890s–1930." *Prairie Forum* 21 (1996): 149–76.

——. "Reserve Hospitals in Southern Alberta, 1890 to 1930." *Native Studies Review* 9 (1993–94): 93–112.

Meota History Book Committee. *Footsteps in Time.* Meota, SK: Meota History Book Committee, 1980.

Merk, Frederick. *The Oregon Question: Essays in Anglo-American Diplomacy and Politics.* Cambridge, MA: Harvard University Press, 1967.

——, ed. *Fur Trade and Empire: George Simpson's Journal Entitled Remarks Connected with the Fur Trade in the Course of a Voyage from York Factory to Fort George and Back to York Factory, 1824–25.* Cambridge, MA: Harvard University Press, Belknap Press, 1968.

Meyer, David. *The Red Earth Crees, 1860–1960.* Mercury Series, Canadian Ethnology Service Paper 100. Ottawa: National Museum of Man, 1985.

Meyer, David, and Scott Hamilton. "Neighbors to the North: Peoples of the Boreal Forest." In *Plains Indians, A.D. 500–1500: The Archaeological Past of Historic Groups,* edited by Karl H. Schlesier, 96–127. Norman: University of Oklahoma Press, 1994.

Meyer, David, and Robert Hutton. "Pasquatinow and the Red Earth Crees." *Prairie Forum* 23 (1998): 93–112.

Meyer, David, and Dale Russell. "The Selkirk Composite of Central Canada: A Reconsideration." *Arctic Anthropology* 24 (1987): 1–31.

——. "'So Fine and Pleasant, beyond Description': The Lands and Lives of the Pegogamaw Crees." *Plains Anthropologist* 49 (2004): 217–52.

Meyer, David, and Paul Thistle. "Saskatchewan River Rendezvous Centres and Trading Posts: Continuity in a Cree Social Geography." *Ethnohistory* 42 (1995): 403–44.

Mikulencak, Angelina. "Mandan–Hidatsa and Sioux Cultural Dynamics: The Competitive Exclusion Principle on the Northern Plains." MA thesis, University of Arlington, 1995.

Miller, David Reed. "Fused Identities and Ethnogenesis, Cooperation versus Autonomy: Susan Sharrock's Ideas Revisited." Paper presented at the Rupert's Land Colloquium, Kenora, ON, 2004.

Miller, Gifford H., et al. "Abrupt Onset of the Little Ice Age Triggered by Volcanism and Sustained by Sea-Ice/Ocean Feedbacks." *Geophysical Research Letters* 39 (2012).

Miller, Harry B. *These Too Were Pioneers: The Story of the Key Indian Reserve No. 64 and the Centennial of the Church.* Melville, SK: Senior's Consultant Service, 1984.

Miller, James R. *Shingwauk's Vision: A History of Native Residential Schools.* Toronto: University of Toronto Press, 1996.

Milloy, John. *"A National Crime": The Canadian Government and the Residential School System, 1879 to 1896.* Manitoba Studies in Native History. Winnipeg: University of Manitoba Press, 1999.

——. "Our Country: The Significance of the Buffalo Resource for a Plains Cree Sense of Territory." In *Aboriginal Resource Use in Canada: Historical and Legal Aspects,* edited by Kerry Abel and Jean Friesen, 51–70. Manitoba Studies in Native History. Winnipeg: University of Manitoba Press, 1991.

——. *The Plains Cree: Trade, Diplomacy, and Warfare, 1790–1870.* Manitoba Studies in Native History. Winnipeg: University of Manitoba Press, 1988.

Milner, George R. "Late Prehistoric Cahokia Cultural System of the Mississippi River Valley: Foundations, Florescence, and Fragmentation." *Journal of World Archaeology* 4 (1990): 1–43.

Miquelon, Dale. *New France 1701–1744: A Supplement to Empire.* Toronto: McClelland and Stewart, 1987.

Mitchell, Ross. "Early Doctors of Red River and Manitoba." In *Papers Read before the Historical and Scientific Society of Manitoba,* Series 3, edited by W.L. Morton and J.A. Jackson, 37–47. Winnipeg: Historical and Scientific Society of Manitoba, 1948.

Mochoruk, James. *Formidable Heritage: Manitoba's North and the Cost of Development, 1870 to 1930.* Winnipeg: University of Manitoba Press, 2004.

——. "The Political Economy of Northern Development: Governments and Capital along Manitoba's Resource Frontier, 1870–1930." Ph.D. diss., University of Manitoba, 1992.

Moodie, D. W., and Barry Kaye. "The Northern Limit of Indian Agriculture in North America." *Geographical Review* 59 (1969): 513–29.

Mooney, James. *The Ghost Dance Religion and the Sioux Outbreak of 1890.* Introduction by Raymond J. DeMallie. Lincoln: University of Nebraska Press, 1991.

Moore, Irene. *Valiant La Vérendrye.* Quebec: L.A. Proulx, 1927.

Moore, Jason W. "The Modern World-System as Environmental History? Ecology and the Rise of Capitalism." *Theory and Society* 32 (2003): 307–77.

Morantz, Toby. *The White Man's Gonna Getcha: The Colonial Challenge to the Crees in Quebec.* Montreal: McGill-Queen's University Press, 2002.

Morgan, E. C. "The North-West Mounted Police, 1873–1883." MA thesis, University of Regina, 1970.

Morgan, R. Grace. "Beaver Ecology/Beaver Mythology." Ph.D. diss., University of Alberta, 1991.

——. *An Ecological Analysis of the Northern Plains as Seen through the Garratt Site*. Occasional Papers in Anthropology 7. Regina: University of Regina, 1979.

Morice, A.G. *History of the Catholic Church in Western Canada from Lake Superior to the Pacific (1659–1895)*. Toronto: Musson Book Company, 1910.

Morley, David C. "Nutrition and Infectious Disease." In *Disease and Urbanization: Symposia for the Study of Human Biology*, vol. 20, edited by E.J. Clegg and J.P. Garlick, 37–45. London: Taylor and Francis, 1980.

——. "Severe Measles." In *Changing Disease Patterns and Human Behaviour*, edited by N.F. Stanley and R.A. Joske, 115–28. London: Academic Press, 1980.

Morris, Alexander. *The Treaties of Canada with the Indians of Manitoba and the North-West Territories*. Saskatoon: Fifth House, 1991.

Morse, Eric W. *Fur Trade Canoe Routes of Canada: Then and Now*. Ottawa: Queen's Printer, 1971.

Morton, A. S. *A History of the Canadian West to 1870–71*. Toronto: University of Toronto Press, 1973.

Morton, Samuel George. *Illustrations of Pulmonary Consumption: Its Anatomical Characters, Causes, Symptoms, and Treatment*. Philadelphia: E.C. Biddle, 1837.

Nabakov, Peter. *Indian Running*. Santa Fe: Ancient City Press, 1987.

Nasatir, A.P., ed. *Before Lewis and Clark: Documents Illustrating the History of the Missouri, 1785–1804*. 2 vols. Lincoln: University of Nebraska Press, 1990.

Naylor, Peter. "Index to Aboriginal Issues Found in the Records of the North West Mounted Police RG 18, National Archives of Canada." Saskatoon: Office of the Treaty Commissioner, 1994. Typescript.

Nestor, Robert. "Hayter Reed, Severality, and the Subdivision of Indian Reserves on the Canadian Prairies." MA thesis, Saskatchewan Indian Federated College, University of Regina, 1998.

Newman, Peter C. *A Company of Adventurers*. Markham, ON: Penguin Books Canada, 1986.

Nicholson, Beverley (Bev) Alistair, and Scott Hamilton. "Cultural Continuity and Changing Subsistence Strategies during the Late Precontact Period in Southwestern Manitoba." *Canadian Journal of Archaeology* 25 (2001): 53–73.

Nicholson, Beverley (Bev) Alistair, Scott Hamilton, Garry Running, and Sylvia Nicholson. "Climatic Challenges and Changes: A Little

Ice Age Response to Adversity—the Vickers Focus Forager/Horticulturalists Move On." *Plains Anthropologist* 51 (2006): 325–34.

Nicks, Gertrude. "Demographic Anthropology of Native Populations in Western Canada, 1800–1975." Ph.D. diss., University of Alberta, 1980.

———. "The Iroquois and the Fur Trade in Western Canada." In *Old Trails and New Directions: Papers of the Third North American Fur Trade Conference,* edited by C.M. Judd and A.J. Ray, 85–101. Toronto: University of Toronto Press, 1980.

———. "Native Responses to the Early Fur Trade at Lesser Slave Lake." In *Le Castor Fait Tout: Selected Papers of the Fifth North American Fur Trade Conference, 1985,* edited by B. Trigger, T. Morantz, and L. Dechene, 278–310. Montreal: Lake St. Louis Historical Society, 1987.

Nicks, John. "The Diary of a Young Fur Trader: The 1789–90 Journal of Thomas Staynor." In *Essays in Western Canadian History,* edited by L.H. Thomas, 17–33. Edmonton: University of Alberta Press, 1976.

———. "The Pine Island Posts, 1786–1794: A Study of Competition in the Fur Trade." MA thesis, University of Alberta, 1975.

Niezen, Ronald. *Spirit Wars: Native North American Religion in the Age of Nation Building.* Berkeley: University of California Press, 2000.

Nix, James Ernest. *Mission among the Buffalo: The Labours of the Reverend George M. and John C. McDougall in the Canadian Northwest, 1860–1876.* Toronto: Ryerson Press, 1960.

Oliver, E. H., ed. *The Canadian Northwest: Its Early Development and Legislative Records.* 2 vols. Ottawa: Government Printing Bureau, 1914.

Ord, Lewis Redman. "Reminiscences of a Bungle by One of the Bunglers." In *Reminiscences of a Bungle by One of the Bunglers and Two Other Stories of the Rebellion,* edited by R.C. Macleod, 1–102. Edmonton: University of Alberta Press, 1983.

Ormsby, Margaret A. *British Columbia: A History.* Vancouver: Macmillan of Canada, 1958.

Osgood, Cornelius. *Contributions to the Ethnography of the Kutchin.* Yale University Publications in Anthropology 14. New Haven, CT: Yale University Press, 1936.

Osler, William. *The Principles and Practice of Medicine.* New York: D. Appleton and Company, 1892.

Ostler, Jeffrey. *The Plains Sioux and U.S. Colonialism from Lewis and Clark to Wounded Knee*. Cambridge, UK: Cambridge University Press, 2004.

Owram, Doug. *The Promise of Eden: The Canadian Expansionist Movement and the Idea of the West, 1856–1900*. Toronto: University of Toronto Press, 1980.

Palombard, Joseph. *Bureaucracy and Political Development*. Princeton, NJ: Princeton University Press, 1963.

Pannekoek, Fritz. "The Reverend James Evans and the Social Antagonisms of the Fur Trade Society, 1840–1846." In *Religion and Society and the Prairie West*, edited by Richard Allen, 1–16. Canadian Plains Studies. Regina: Canadian Plains Research Center, 1974.

Parkard, Randall. *White Plague, Black Labor: Tuberculosis and the Political Economy of Health and Disease in South Africa*. Berkeley: University of California Press, 1989.

Parker, James. *Emporium of the North: Fort Chipewyan and the Fur Trade to 1835*. Regina: Canadian Plains Research Center, 1987.

——. "Fort Chipewyan and the Early Fur Trade." In *Proceedings of the Fort Chipewyan and Fort Vermilion Bicentennial Conference*, edited by Patricia A. McCormack and R. Geoffrey Ironside, 41–44. Edmonton: Boreal Institute for Northern Studies, 1990.

Parks, Douglas R., and Raymond J. DeMallie. "Sioux, Assiniboine, and Stoney Dialects: A Classification." *Anthropological Linguistics* 34 (1992): 233–56.

Payne, Michael. *The Most Respectable Place in the Territory: Every Day Life in the Hudson's Bay Company Service York Factory, 1788 to 1870*. Ottawa: Environment Canada, Parks Canada Service, National Historic Parks and Sites, 1989.

——. "Review: Dale R. Russell, *Eighteenth-Century Western Cree and Their Neighbours*," *Manitoba History* 24 (1992): n. pag. www.mhs.mb.ca/docs/mb_history/24/westerncree.shtml.

Peck, Trevor, and Caroline R. Hudecek-Cuffe. "Archaeology on the Plains: The Last Two Thousand Years." In *Archaeology in Alberta: A View from the New Millennium*, edited by Jack Brink and John F. Dormaar, 72–103. Medicine Hat: Archaeological Society of Alberta, 2003.

Peel, Bruce. "The Last Battle." *The Beaver* 297 (1966): 12–14.

——. *Steamboats on the Saskatchewan*. Saskatoon: Western Producer Prairie Books, 1972.

Peers, Laura. "Changing Resource-Use Patterns of Saulteaux Trading at Fort Pelly, 1821–1870." In *Aboriginal Resource Use in Canada:*

Historical and Legal Aspects, edited by Kerry Abel and Jean Friesen, 107–18. Manitoba Studies in Native History. Winnipeg: University of Manitoba Press, 1991.

——. *The Ojibwa of Western Canada, 1780–1870.* Manitoba Studies in Native History. Winnipeg: University of Manitoba Press, 1994.

Peers, Laura, and Theresa Schenck, eds. *George Nelson, My First Years in the Fur Trade: The Journals of 1802–1804.* Montreal: McGill-Queen's University Press, 2002.

Pepperell, Caitlin S., et al. "Dispersal of *Mycobacterium tuberculosis* via the Canadian Fur Trade." *Proceedings of the National Academy of Sciences* 108 (2011): 6526-6531. www.pnas.org/cgi/doi/10.1073/pnas.1016708108.

Peterson, Hans. "Imases and His Band: Canadian Refugees after the North West Rebellion." *Western Canadian Journal of Anthropology* 7 (1978): 21–37.

Peterson, Jacqueline. "Gathering at the River: The Métis Peopling of the Northern Plains." In *The Fur Trade in North Dakota,* edited by Virginia L. Heidenreich, 47–65. Bismark: State Historical Society of North Dakota, 1990.

——. "Many Roads to Red River: Métis Genesis in the Great Lakes Region, 1680–1815." In *The New Peoples: Being and Becoming Métis in North America,* edited by J.S.H. Brown and J. Peterson, 37–73. Manitoba Studies in Native History. Winnipeg: University of Manitoba Press, 1985.

Pettipas, Katherine. *The Diary of the Reverend Henry Budd, 1870–1875.* Winnipeg: Hignell Printing, 1974.

——. *Severing the Ties that Bind: Government Repression of Indigenous Religious Ceremonies on the Prairies.* Manitoba Studies in Native History. Winnipeg: University of Manitoba Press, 1994.

Pickering, Kathleen. "Articulation of the Lakota Mode of Production and the Euro-American Fur Trade." In *The Fur Trade Revisited: Selected Papers of the Sixth North American Fur Trade Conference, Mackinac Island, Michigan, 1991,* edited by J.S.H. Brown, W.J. Eccles, and D.P. Feldman, 57–70. East Lansing: Michigan State University Press, 1994.

Pierce, R. V. *The People's Common Sense Medical Adviser.* 61st ed. Buffalo: n.p., 1895.

Post, John D. "Famine, Mortality, and Epidemic Disease in the Process of Modernization." *Economic History Review,* Second Series, 29 (1976): 14–37.

Price, B. Byron. "Introduction." In *The Trail Drivers of Texas,* edited by J. Marvin Hunter. Austin: University of Texas Press, 1985. http://www.utexas.edu/utpress/excerpts/exhuntra.html#ex1.

Prince, Joseph M. "Intersection of Economics, History, and Human Biology: Secular Trends in Stature in Nineteenth-Century Sioux Indians." *Human Biology* 67 (1995): 387–406.

Prince, Joseph M., and Richard H. Steckel. "Nutritional Success on the Great Plains: Nineteenth-Century Equestrian Nomads." *Journal of Interdisciplinary History* 33 (2003): 353–84.

Produchny, Caroline. "Farming the Frontier: Agriculture in the Fur Trade, a Case Study of the Provisional Farm at Lower Fort Garry, 1857–1870." MA thesis, McGill University, 1990.

Provo, Daniel J. *Fort Esperance in 1793–1795: A North West Company Provisioning Post.* Lincoln: J and L Reprints in Anthropology, vol. 28, 1984.

Quaife, Milo M., ed. "The Smallpox Epidemic on the Upper Missouri." *Mississippi Valley Historical Review* 17 (1930–31): 278–99.

Qu'Appelle Valley Farming Company. "Annual Meeting of the Qu'Appelle Valley Farming Company, Limited" (president's report), Winnipeg, 9 January 1884.

Quinn, William H., Victor Neal, and Santiago E. Anutez De Mayolo. "El Niño Occurrences over the Past Four and a Half Centuries." *Journal of Geophysical Research* 92 (1987): 14449–61.

Rackza, Paul M. *Winter Count: A History of the Blackfoot People.* Brocket, AB: Oldman River Cultural Centre, 1979.

Rae, John. "A Visit to the Red River and the Saskatchewan, 1861." Edited by Irene Spry. *Geographical Journal* 140 (1974): 1–17.

Ramenovsky, Ann F. *Vectors of Death: The Archaeology of European Contact.* Albuquerque: University of New Mexico Press, 1987.

Rannie, W. F. "'Awful Splendour': Historical Accounts of Prairie Fire in Southern Manitoba Prior to 1870." *Prairie Forum* 26 (2001): 17–46.

——. "The Role of Frost as a Limiting Factor to Wheat Production in the Red River Settlement." *Prairie Forum* 17 (1992): 1–12.

Ray, Arthur J. *The Canadian Fur Trade in the Industrial Age.* Toronto: University of Toronto Press, 1990.

——. "Diffusion of Diseases in the Western Interior of Canada, 1830–1850." *Geographical Review* 66 (1976): 139–57.

——. *Indians in the Fur Trade: Their Role as Trappers, Hunters, and Middlemen in the Lands Southwest of Hudson's Bay, 1660–1870.* Toronto: University of Toronto Press, 1974.

——. *Indians in the Fur Trade: Their Role as Trappers, Hunters, and Middlemen in the Lands Southwest of Hudson's Bay, 1660–1870.* 2nd ed. Toronto: University of Toronto Press, 1998.

——. "The Northern Great Plains: Pantry of the Northwestern Fur Trade, 1774–1885." *Prairie Forum* 9 (1984): 263–80.

——. "Periodic Shortages, Native Welfare, and the Hudson's Bay Company, 1670–1930." In *The Subarctic Fur Trade: Native Social and Economic Adaptations,* edited by Shepard Krech III, 1–20. Vancouver: UBC Press, 1984.

——. "Smallpox: The Epidemic of 1837–38." *The Beaver* 306 (1975): 8–13.

——. "Some Conservation Schemes of the Hudson's Bay Company, 1821–50: An Examination of the Problems of Resource Management in the Fur Trade." *Journal of Historical Geography* 1 (1975): 49–68.

——. "Some Thoughts about the Reasons for Spatial Dynamism in the Early Fur Trade, 1500–1800." In *Three Hundred Prairie Years: Henry Kelsey's "Inland Country of Good Report,"* edited by Henry Epp, 113–23. Regina: Canadian Plains Research Center, 1993.

——. "William Todd: Doctor and Trader, for the Hudson's Bay Company, 1816–51." *Prairie Forum* 9 (1984): 13–26.

Ray, Arthur J., and Donald Freeman. *"Give Us Good Measure": An Economic Analysis of Relations between the Indians and the Hudson's Bay Company before 1763.* Toronto: University of Toronto Press, 1978.

Ray, Arthur J., J. R. Miller, and Frank Tough. *Bounty and Benevolence: A History of Saskatchewan Treaties.* Montreal: McGill-Queen's University Press, 2000.

Reedy-Maschner, Katherine L., and Herbert D.G. Maschner. "Marauding Middlemen: Western Expansion and Violent Conflict in the Subarctic." *Ethnohistory* 46 (1999): 703–43.

Reff, Daniel T. *Disease, Depopulation, and Culture Change in Northwestern New Spain, 1518–1764.* Salt Lake City: University of Utah Press, 1991.

Reid, John Phillip. *Contested Empire: Peter Skene Ogden and the Snake River Expeditions.* Norman: University of Oklahoma Press, 2002.

Rich, E. E. *A History of the Hudson's Bay Company, 1670–1870, Volume 2, 1673–1870.* Hudson's Bay Record Society Publications 22. London: Hudson's Bay Record Society, 1959.

——. *Hudson's Bay Company, 1670–1870, Volume 3: 1821–1870.* Toronto: McClelland and Stewart, 1960.

——. "Trade Habits and Economic Motivation among Indians of North America." *Canadian Journal of Economics and Political Science*

26 (1960): 35–53. Reprinted in *Sweet Promises: A Reader on Indian-White Relations in Canada*, edited by J.R. Miller, 157–79. Toronto: University of Toronto Press, 1991.

——, ed. *Cumberland House Journals and Inland Journals, 1775–82*. First Series, 1775–79. Hudson's Bay Record Society Publications 15. London: Hudson's Bay Record Society, 1951.

——, ed. *Cumberland House Journals and Inland Journals 1775–82*. Second Series, 1779–82. Hudson's Bay Record Society Publications 15. London: Hudson's Bay Record Society, 1952.

——, ed. *John Rae's Arctic Correspondence with the Hudson's Bay Company on Arctic Exploration, 1844–1855*. Hudson's Bay Record Society Publications 16. London: Hudson's Bay Record Society, 1953.

——, ed. *Journal of Occurrences in the Athabasca Department by George Simpson, 1820 and 1821, and Report*. Toronto: Champlain Society, 1938.

Richardson, John. "Dr. Richardson's Residence at Cumberland House: His Account of the Cree Indians." In *Narrative of a Journey to the Shores of the Polar Sea in the Years 1819-20-21-22*, 2nd ed., by John Franklin, 2 vols, 1: 91–145. London: John Murray, 1824.

Richtmeier, J. "Precipitation, Temperature, and Maize Agriculture: Implications for Prehistoric Populations in the Middle Missouri Subarea, 900–1675." MA thesis, University of Nebraska, 1980.

Ridington, Robin. "Changes of Mind: Dunne-za Resistance to Empire." *B.C. Studies* 43 (1979): 65–80.

Riley, Thomas J., Richard Edging, and Jack Rosen. "Cultigens in Prehistoric Eastern North America: Changing Paradigms." *Current Anthropology* 31 (1990): 525–41.

Rinn, Dennis. "The Acquisition, Diffusion, and Distribution of the European Horse among the Blackfoot Tribes in Western Canada." MA thesis, University of Manitoba, 1975.

Ritchie, William A. "Paleopathological Evidence Suggesting Pre-Columbian Tuberculosis in New York State." *American Journal of Physical Anthropology* 10 (1952): 305–18.

Ritter, Beth R. "Piecing Together the Ponca Past: Reconstructing Degiha Migrations to the Great Plains." *Great Plains Quarterly* 22 (2002): 271–84.

Ritterbush, Lauren W. "Drawn by the Bison: Late Prehistoric Native Migration into the Central Plains." *Great Plains Quarterly* 22 (2002): 259–70.

Rivard, Ron, and Catherine Littlejohn. *The History of the Métis of Willow Bunch*. Saskatoon: Apex Graphics, 2003.

Roberts, Charlotte A., and Jane E. Buikstra. *The Bioarchaeology of Tuberculosis: A Global View of a Reemerging Disease.* Gainesville: University of Florida Press, 2003.

Roberts, Charlotte, and Keith Manchester. *The Archaeology of Disease.* 3rd ed. Ithaca, NY: Cornell University Press, 2005.

Robertson, R. G. *Rotting Face: Smallpox and the American Indian.* Caldwell, ID: Claxton Press, 2001.

Robertson-Ross, Patrick. *Report of Colonel Robertson-Ross, Adjutant-General of the Militia on the Territories of the Dominion.* Ottawa: Queen's Printer, 1872.

Roe, Frank G. *The Indian and the Horse.* Norman: University of Oklahoma Press, 1962.

———. *The North American Buffalo: A Critical Study of the Species in Its Wild State.* Toronto: University of Toronto Press, 1970.

Rogers, E. S. "Cultural Adaptations: The Northern Ojibwa of the Boreal Forest 1670–1980." In *Boreal Forest Adaptations: The Northern Algonkians,* edited by A.T. Steegmann, 85–142. New York: Plenum Press, 1983.

Rogers, E. S., and Mary B. Black. "Subsistence Strategy in the Fish and Hare Period, Northern Ontario: The Weagamow Ojibwa, 1880–1920." *Journal of Anthropological Research* 32 (1976): 1–43.

Rogers, E. S., and James G. E. Smith. "Environment and Culture in the Shield and Mackenzie Borderlands." In *Subarctic,* edited by June Helm, 130–45. Vol. 6 of *Handbook of North American Indians.* Washington, DC: Smithsonian Institution Press, 1981.

Roland, Charles. *Courage under Siege: Starvation, Disease, and Death in the Warsaw Ghetto.* New York: Oxford University Press, 1992.

Ronaghan, Allen. "Charles Mair and the North-West Emigration Aid Society." *Manitoba History* 14 (1987): 10–14.

———. "Father Fafard and the Fort Pitt Mission." *Alberta History* 46 (1998): 13–18.

———. "Who Was the 'Fine Young Man'? The Frog Lake 'Massacre' Reconsidered." *Saskatchewan History* 47 (1995): 12–19.

Ross, Alexander. *The Red River Settlement: Its Rise, Progress, and Present State. With Some Account of the Native Races and Its General History, to the Present Day.* Edmonton: Hurtig Publishers, 1972.

Rupert's Land Research Centre. *An Historical Overview of Aboriginal Lifestyles: The Churchill–Nelson River Drainage Basin.* Winnipeg: Rupert's Land Research Centre, 1992.

Rusden, Harold Panryn. "Suppression of the Northwest Insurrection." In *Reminiscences of a Bungle by One of the Bunglers and Two*

Other Stories of the Rebellion, edited by R.C. Macleod, 241–312. Edmonton: University of Alberta Press, 1983.

Russell, Dale. *Eighteenth-Century Western Cree and Their Neighbours.* Mercury Series, Archaeological Survey of Canada Paper 143. Ottawa: Canadian Museum of Civilization, 1991.

——. "The Puzzle of Henry Kelsey and His Journey." In *Three Hundred Prairie Years: Henry Kelsey's "Inland Country of Good Report,"* edited by Henry Epp, 74–88. Regina: Canadian Plains Research Center, 1993.

Sahlins, Marshall. "Notes on the Original Affluent Society." In *Man the Hunter,* edited by Richard B. Lee and Irven DeVore, 85–89. Chicago: Aldine Publishing Company, 1968.

——. *Stone Age Economics.* Chicago: Aldine-Atherton, 1972.

Satzewich, Vic, and Terry Wotherspoon. *First Nations: Race, Class, and Gender Relations.* Scarborough, ON: Nelson Canada, 1993.

Sauchyn, David, and Walter Skinner. "A Proxy Record of Drought Severity for the Southwestern Canadian Plains." *Canadian Water Resources Journal* 26 (2001): 253–72.

Sauchyn, David, Jennifer Stroich, and Antoine Beriault. "A Paleoclimatic Context for the Drought of 1999–2001 in the Northern Great Plains of North America." *Geographical Journal* 169 (2003): 158–67.

Savishinsky, Joel S., and Hiroko Sue Hara. "Hare." In *Subarctic,* edited by June Helm, 314–25. Vol. 6 of *Handbook of North American Indians.* Washington, DC: Smithsonian Institution Press, 1981.

Schaeffer, Claude E. "Plains Kutenai: An Ethnological Evaluation." *Alberta History* 30 (1982): 1–9.

Schenstead-Smith, Laurel. "Disease Pattern and Factors Relating to the Transmission of Disease among the Residents of the Onion Lake Agency." *Na Pao: A Saskatchewan Anthropological Journal* 12 (1982): 1–10.

Schiltz, Thomas F. "Brandy and Beaver Pelts: Assiniboine–European Trading Patterns, 1695–1805." *Saskatchewan History* 37 (1984): 95–102.

——. "The Gros Ventres and the Canadian Fur Trade." *American Indian Quarterly* 12 (1988): 41–56.

Schlesier, Karl H. "Commentary: A History of Ethnic Groups in the Great Plains, A.D. 500–1550." In *Plains Indians, A.D. 500–1500: The Archaeological Past of Historic Groups,* edited by Karl H. Schlesier, 308–446. Norman: University of Oklahoma Press, 1994.

Scott, Leslie M. "Indian Diseases as Aids to Pacific Northwest Settlement." *Oregon Historical Society Quarterly* 29 (1928): 144–61.

Scrimshaw, Nevin, Carl Taylor, and John Gordon. *Interactions of Nutrition and Infection*. Geneva: World Health Organization, 1968.

Sen, Amartya. "Food, Economics, and Entitlements." In *The Political Economy of Hunger: Selected Essays*, edited by Jean Dreze, Amartya Sen, and Athar Hussain, 50–68. Oxford: Clarendon Press, 1995.

——. *Poverty and Famines: An Essay on Entitlement and Deprivation*. Oxford: Clarendon Press, 1981.

Sharp, Paul. "Merchant Prince of the Plains." *Montana: The Magazine of Western History* 5 (1955): 2–20.

——. *Whoop-Up Country: The Canadian–American West, 1865–1885*. Norman: University of Oklahoma Press, 1973.

Sharrock, Susan. "Crees, Cree–Assiniboines, and Assiniboines: Interethnic Social Organization on the Far Northern Plains." *Ethnohistory* 21 (1974): 95–122.

Shewell, Hugh. *"Enough to Keep Them Alive": Indian Welfare in Canada, 1873–1965*. Toronto: University of Toronto Press, 2004.

Shipley, Nan. "Printing Press at Oonikup." *The Beaver* 290 (1960): 48–53.

Shkilnyk, Anastasia M. *A Poison Stronger than Love: The Destruction of an Ojibwa Community*. New Haven, CT: Yale University Press, 1985.

Silversides, Brock. *The Face Pullers: Photographing Native Canadians 1871–1939*. Saskatoon: Fifth House, 1994.

Simpson, Thomas. *Narrative of the Discoveries on the North Coast of America, Affected by the Officers of the Hudson's Bay Company during the Years 1836–39*. 2 vols. 1843; reprint, Toronto: Canadiana House, 1970.

Sliwa, Stephen. "Standing the Test of Time: A History of the Beardy's/Okemasis Reserve, 1876–1951." MA thesis, Trent University, 1993.

Sloan, W. A. "The Native Response to the Extension of the European Traders into the Athabasca Country and the Mackenzie Basin, 1770–1816." *Canadian Historical Review* 60 (1979): 281–99.

Smiley, W. D. "'The Most Good to the Indians': The Reverend James Nisbett and the Prince Albert Mission." *Saskatchewan History* 46 (1994): 34–51.

Smith, G. Hubert. *The Explorations of the La Vérendryes in the Northern Plains, 1738–43*. Edited by W. Raymond Wood. Lincoln: University of Nebraska Press, 1980.

Smith, James G. E. "Chipewyan and Fur Traders' Views of Rupert's Land." In *Rupert's Land: A Cultural Tapestry*, edited by R. Davies, 131–46. Waterloo: Wilfrid Laurier University Press, 1988.

——. "Economic Uncertainty in an 'Original Affluent Society': Caribou and Caribou Eater Chipewyan Adaptive Strategies." *Arctic Anthropology* 15 (1978): 68–88.

——. "Local Band Organization of the Caribou Eater Chipewyan in the Eighteenth and Early Nineteenth Centuries." *Western Canadian Journal of Anthropology* 6 (1976): 72–90.

——. "The Western Woods Cree: Anthropological Myth and Historical Reality." *American Ethnologist* 14 (1987): 434–48.

Smith, Shirley Ann. "Crossed Swords: Colin Robertson and the Athabasca Campaign." In *Proceedings of the Fort Chipewyan and Fort Vermilion Bicentennial Conference*, edited by Patricia McCormack and R. Geoffrey Ironsides, 69–74. Edmonton: Boreal Institute for Northern Studies, 1990.

Smits, David D. "The Frontier Army and the Destruction of the Buffalo: 1865–1883." *Western Historical Quarterly* 25 (1994): 313–38.

Smyth, David. "Missed Opportunity: John Milloy's *The Plains Cree*." *Prairie Forum* 17 (1992): 337–54.

——. "The Niitsitapi Trade: Euroamericans and the Blackfoot Speaking Peoples to the Mid 1830s." Ph.D. diss., Carleton University, 2001.

Snow, Dean R. *The Iroquois*. Oxford: Blackwell, 1994.

Snow, John. *These Mountains Are Our Sacred Places: The Story of the Stoney Indians*. Toronto: Samuel Stevens, 1977.

Sowby, Joyce. "Macdonald the Administrator: Department of the Interior and Indian Affairs, 1882–1887." MA thesis, Queen's University, 1984.

Sprague, D. N. *Canada and the Métis, 1869–1885*. Waterloo: Wilfred Laurier University Press, 1988.

Sprenger, G. Herman. "The Métis Nation: Buffalo Hunting vs. Agriculture in the Red River Settlement. Circa 1810–1870." *Western Canadian Journal of Anthropology* 3 (1972): 158–78.

Springer, James W., and Stanley R. Witkowski. "Siouan Historical Linguistics and Oneota Archaeology." In *Oneota Studies*, edited by Guy Gibbon, 69–83. Publications in Anthropology 1. Minneapolis: University of Minnesota Press, 1995.

Spry, Irene. "The Great Transformation: The Disappearance of the Commons in Western Canada." In *Man and Nature on the Prairies*, edited by Richard Allen, 21–45. Canadian Plains Studies 6. Regina: Canadian Plains Research Center, 1976.

——. "Matthew Cocking." *Dictionary of Canadian Biography*. www.biographi.ca/EN/ShowBIOPrintable.asp?BioID=35934.

——. "The 'Private Adventurers' of Rupert's Land." In *The Developing West,* edited by John Foster, 49–70. Edmonton: University of Alberta Press, 1983.

——, ed. *The Papers of the Palliser Expedition, 1857–1860.* Toronto: Champlain Society, 1968.

St. Albert Historical Society. *The Black Robe's Vision: A History of the St. Albert District.* St. Albert, AB: St. Albert Historical Society, 1985.

St. Germain, Jill. *Indian Treaty Making in the United States and Canada, 1867–1877.* Toronto: University of Toronto Press, 2001.

Stahle, D. W., et al. "Tree Ring Data Document 16th Century Megadrought over North America." *Eos: Transactions of the American Geophysical Union* 81 (2000): 121–23.

Stanley, George F. G. *The Birth of Western Canada: A History of the Riel Rebellions.* Toronto: University of Toronto Press, 1960.

——. "The Fur Trade Party: Part 1 Storm Warnings." *The Beaver* 284 (1953): 35–39.

——, ed. *John Henry Lefroy, in Search of the Magnetic North: A Soldier-Surveyor's Letters from the North-West 1843–1844.* Toronto: Macmillan, 1955.

Stearn, E. Wagner, and Allen E. Stearn. *The Effect of Smallpox on the Destiny of the Amerindian.* Boston: Bruce Humphries Publishers, 1945.

Steckel, Richard H., and Joseph M. Prince. "Tallest in the World: Native Americans of the Great Plains in the Nineteenth Century." Paper presented at the International Commission on Historical Demography, Oslo, 1999. www.scribd.com/.

Steegmann, Theodore. "Hazards and Adaptations: The Past." In *Boreal Forest Adaptations: The Northern Algonkians,* edited by Theodore Steegmann, 243–68. New York: Plenum Press, 1983.

Stevenson, Winona. "Icelanders and Indians in the Interlake: John Ramsay and the White Mud River." Winnipeg: University of Winnipeg, 1986.

——. "The Journals and Voices of a Church of England Native Catechist: Askenootow (Charles Pratt), 1851–1884." In *Reading beyond Words: Contexts for Native History,* edited by Jennifer S.H. Brown and Elizabeth Vibert, 304–29. Peterborough: Broadview Press, 1996.

Stewart, Carlton R., ed. *The Last Great (Inter-Tribal) Indian Battle.* Lethbridge: Lethbridge Historical Society, 1997.

Stewart, Robert. *Sam Steele: Lion of the Frontier.* Regina: Centax Books, 1999.

Stodder, Ann L.W., and Debra L. Martin. "Health and Disease in the Southwest before and after Spanish Contact." In *Disease and Demography in the Americas,* edited by John W. Verano and Douglas H. Uberlaker, 55–73. Washington, DC: Smithsonian Institution Press, 1992.

Stonechild, Blair, and Bill Waiser. *Loyal till Death: Indians and the North-West Rebellion.* Calgary: Fifth House, 1997.

Sutherland, Donna G. *Peguis: A Noble Friend.* St. Andrews, MB: Chief Peguis Heritage Park, 2003.

Swadesh, Frances Leon. *Los Primeros Pobladores: Hispanic Americans of the Ute Frontier.* Notre Dame: University of Notre Dame Press, 1974.

Szathmary, Emöke, and Franklin Auger. "Biological Distances and Genetic Relationships within Algonkians." In *Boreal Forest Adaptations: The Northern Algonkians,* edited by Theodore Steegmann, 289–316. New York: Plenum Press, 1983.

Tanner, John. *A Narrative of the Captivity and Adventures of John Tanner during Thirty Years Residence among the Indians in the Interior of North America.* Edited by Edwin James. Minneapolis: Ross and Haines, 1956.

Taylor, Carl E. "Synergy among Mass Infections, Famines, and Poverty. *Journal of Interdisciplinary History* 14 (1983): 483–501.

Taylor, J. L. "Two Views on the Meaning of Treaties Six and Seven." In *The Spirit of the Alberta Indian Treaties,* edited by Richard Price, 9–46. Montreal: Institute for Research on Public Policy; Edmonton: Indian Association of Alberta, 1980. Also published by University of Alberta Press, 1999.

Taylor, John F. "Sociocultural Effects of Epidemics on the Northern Plains: 1734–1850." *Western Canadian Journal of Anthropology* 7 (1977): 55–81.

Tessaro, Stacey V. "Bovine Tuberculosis and Brucellosis in Animals: Including Man." In *Buffalo,* edited by John Foster, Dick Harrison, and I.S. MacLaren, 207–24. Edmonton: University of Alberta Press, 1992.

Tessendorf, K. C. "Red Death on the Missouri." *American West* 14 (1977): 48–53.

Thistle, Paul. *Indian–White Trade Relations in the Lower Saskatchewan River Region to 1840.* Manitoba Studies in Native History. Winnipeg: University of Manitoba Press, 1986.

——. "Review: Russell, Dale R., *Eighteenth-Century Western Cree and Their Neighbours*," *Canadian Journal of Native Studies* 11 (1991): 181–83.

Thomas, Clayton L., ed. *Taber's Cyclopedic Medical Dictionary*. 16th ed. Philadelphia: F.A. Davis Company, 1989.

Thompson, Albert Edward. *Chief Peguis and His Descendants*. Winnipeg: Peguis Publishers, 1973.

Thompson, David. *David Thompson's Narrative of His Exploration of Western America, 1784–1812*. Edited by Joseph Burr Tyrrell. Toronto: Champlain Society, 1916.

——. *David Thompson's Narrative 1784–1812*. 2nd ed. Edited by Richard Glover. Toronto: Champlain Society, 1962.

——. *David Thompson: Travels in North America, 1784–1812*. Edited by Victor G. Hopwood. Toronto: Macmillan of Canada, 1971.

Thornton, Russell. *We Shall Live Again: The 1870 and 1890 Ghost Dance Movements as Demographic Revitalization*. Cambridge, UK: Cambridge University Press, 1986.

Thorpe, E. L. M. "Culture, Evolution, and Disease." Anthropology Department Paper 30. Winnipeg: University of Manitoba, 1989.

Thursen, Meredith. *The Political Ecology of Disease in Tanzania*. New Brunswick, NJ: Rutgers University Press, 1984.

Titley, Brian. "The Fate of the Sharphead Stonies." *Alberta History* 39 (1991): 1–8.

——. *The Frontier World of Edgar Dewdney*. Vancouver: UBC Press, 1999.

——. "Hayter Reed and Indian Administration in the West." In *Swords and Ploughshares: War and Agriculture in Western Canada*, edited by R.C. Macleod, 109–48. Edmonton: University of Alberta Press, 1993.

——. "Unsteady Debut: J. A. N. Provencher and the Beginnings of Indian Administration in Manitoba." *Prairie Forum* 22 (1997): 21–46.

Titley, Louise A. "Food Entitlement, Famine, and Conflict." *Journal of Interdisciplinary History* 14 (1983): 333–49.

Tobias, John L. "Canada's Subjugation of the Plains Cree, 1879–1885." *Canadian Historical Review* 64 (1983): 519–48.

——. "Canada's Subjugation of the Plains Cree, 1879–1885." In *Sweet Promises: A Reader on Indian-White Relations in Canada*, edited by J. R. Miller, 212–40. Toronto: University of Toronto Press, 1991.

Tough, Frank. "Aboriginal Rights versus the Deed of Surrender: The Legal Rights of the Native Peoples and Canada's Acquisition of the Hudson's Bay Company Territory." *Prairie Forum* 17 (1992): 225–50.

——. "As Their Natural Resources Fail": Native Peoples and the Economic History of Northern Manitoba, 1870–1930. Vancouver: UBC Press, 1996.

——. "Economic Aspects of Aboriginal Title in Northern Manitoba: Treaty 5 Adhesions and Métis Scrip." Manitoba History 15 (1988): 3–16.

——. "The Establishment of a Commercial Fishing Industry and the Demise of Native Fisheries in Northern Manitoba." Canadian Journal of Native Studies 4 (1984): 303–19.

——. "Indian Economic Behaviour, Exchange, and Profits in Northern Manitoba during the Decline of Monopoly, 1870–1930." Journal of Historical Geography 16 (1990): 385–401.

——. "The Northern Fur Trade: A Review of Conceptual and Methodological Problems." Musk Ox 36 (1988): 66–79.

Treaty 7 Elders and Tribal Council, with Walter Hildebrandt, Sarah Carter, and Dorothy First Rider. The True Spirit and Original Intent of Treaty 7. Montreal: McGill-Queen's University Press, 1996.

Trimble, Michael K. "Chronology of Epidemics among Plains Village Horticulturalists 1738–1838." Southwestern Lore 54 (1988): 4–31.

——. "The 1832 Inoculation Program on the Missouri River." In Disease and Demography in the Americas, edited by John W. Verano and Douglas Uberlaker, 257–64. Washington, DC: Smithsonian Institution Press, 1992.

——. "The 1837–1838 Smallpox Epidemic on the Upper Missouri." In Skeletal Biology in the Great Plains: Migration, Warfare, Health, and Subsistence, edited by Douglas Owsley and Richard Jantz, 81–89. Washington, DC: Smithsonian Institution Press, 1994.

Trudel, Marcel. The Beginnings of New France, 1524–1662. Canadian Centenary Series 2. Toronto: McClelland and Stewart, 1973.

Truteau, J. B. "Remarks on the Manners of the Indians Living High Up the Missouri." In Before Lewis and Clark: Documents Illustrating the History of the Missouri, 1785–1804, edited by A.P. Nasatir, 257–311. Lincoln: University of Nebraska Press, 1990.

Tsey, Komla, and Stephanie Short. "From Headloading to the Iron Horse: The Unequal Health Consequences of Railway Expansion in the Gold Coast, 1898–1929." Social Science Medicine 40 (1995): 613–21.

Tucker, Sarah. The Rainbow in the North: A Short Account of the First Establishment of Christianity in Rupert's Land by the Church Missionary Society. London: J. Nisbet and Company, 1851.

Turner, John Peter. The North-West Mounted Police. 2 vols. Ottawa: King's Printer, 1950.

Turney-High, Harry Holbert. *Ethnography of the Kutenai.* Memoirs of the American Anthropological Association 56. Menasha, WI: American Anthropological Association, 1941.

Turpel-Lafond, M. E. *Maskéko–Sákahinanihk: 100 Years for a Saskatchewan First Nation.* Saskatoon: Houghton Boston, 2004.

Tyler, Kenneth J. "Interim Report: The History of the Mosquito, Grizzly Bear's Head, and Lean Man Bands, 1878–1920." Regina: Indian Studies Resource Centre, Saskatchewan Indian Federated College, 1974.

Ulijaszek, S. J. "Nutritional Status and Susceptibility to Infectious Disease." In *Diet and Disease in Traditional and Developing Societies,* edited by G. A. Harrison and J.C. Waterlow, 137–54. Cambridge, UK: Cambridge University Press, 1990.

Umfreville, Edward. *The Present State of Hudson's Bay.* Edited by W. S. Wallace. Toronto: Ryerson Press, 1954.

United States. Senate Committee on Indian Affairs. *Tuberculosis among the North American Indians: Report of a Committee of the National Tuberculosis Association Appointed on October 28, 1921.* Washington, DC: Government Printing Office, 1923.

Unrau, William E. "The Depopulation of the Dheghia–Siouan Kansa Prior to Removal." *New Mexico Historical Review* 48 (1973): 313–28.

Utley, Robert M. *Frontier Regulars: The United States Army and the Indian, 1866–1891.* New York: Macmillan, 1973.

Van Kirk, Sylvia. *"Many Tender Ties": Women in Fur-Trade Society in Western Canada, 1670–1870.* Winnipeg: University of Manitoba Press, 1980.

Verano, John W., and Douglas H. Uberlaker, eds. *Disease and Demography in the Americas.* Washington, DC: Smithsonian Institution Press, 1992.

Vickers, J. Roderick. "Cultures of the Northwestern Plains from the Boreal Forest to the Milk River." In *Plains Indians, A.D. 500–1500: The Archaeological Past of Historic Groups,* edited by Karl H. Schlesier, 3–33. Norman: University of Oklahoma Press, 1994.

Waddell, Jack O. "Malhiot's Journal: An Ethnohistoric Assessment of Chippewa Alcohol Behaviour in the Early Nineteenth Century." *Ethnohistory* 32 (1985): 246–68.

Waddington, Keir. "'Unfit for Human Consumption': Tuberculosis and the Problem of Infected Meat in Late Victorian Britain." *Bulletin of the History of Medicine* 77 (2003): 636–61.

Waiser, W. A. *La Police à Cheval du Nord-Ouest, de 1874 à 1889: Étude statistique.* Bulletin de recherches 117. Ottawa: Parcs Canada, 1979.

——. "A Willing Scapegoat: John Macoun and the Route of the CPR." *Prairie Forum* 10 (1985): 65–82.

Walde, Dale. "Avonlea and Athapaskan Migrations: A Reconsideration." *Plains Anthropologist* 51 (2006): 185–97.

——. "Mortlach and One Gun: Phase to Phase." In *Archaeology on the Edge: New Perspectives from the Northern Plains,* edited by Brian Kooyman and Jane H. Kelley, 39–51. Canadian Archaeological Association Occasional Paper 4. Calgary: University of Calgary Press, 2004.

——. "The Mortlach Phase." Ph.D. diss., University of Calgary, 1994.

——. "Sedentism and Precontact Tribal Social Organization on the Northern Plains: Colonial Imposition or Indigenous Development?" *World Archaeology* 38 (2006): 291–310.

Walde, Dale, David Meyer, and Wendy Umfreed. "The Late Period on the Canadian and Adjacent Plains." *Revista de Arquaologia Americana* 9 (1995): 7–66.

Walker, E. G. "The Woodlawn Site: A Case for Interregional Disease Transmission in the Late Pre-Historic Period." *Canadian Journal of Archaeology* 7 (1983): 49–59.

Wallace, Jim. *A Double Duty: The Decisive First Decade of the North-West Mounted Police.* Winnipeg: Bunker to Bunker Books, 1997.

Wallerstein, Immanuel. *The Modern World System III: The Second Era of Great Expansion of the Capitalist World Economy, 1730–1840s.* San Diego: Academic Press, 1989.

Wasylow, Walter J. "History of Battleford Industrial School for Indians." MA thesis, University of Saskatchewan, 1972.

Watetch, Abel. *Payepot and His People.* Regina: Saskatchewan History and Folklore Society, 1959.

Watson, Bruce M. "The Effects of the 1847–48 Measles Epidemic on the Servants of the Hudson's Bay Company Working on the Pacific Slopes." In *Selected Papers of the Rupert's Land Colloquium 2000,* compiled by David G. Malaher, 203–13. Winnipeg: Centre for Rupert's Land Studies, University of Winnipeg, 2000.

Watt, Sheldon J. *Epidemics and History: Disease, Power, and Imperialism.* New Haven, CT: Yale University Press, 1997.

Weber, David J. *The Spanish Frontier in America.* New Haven, CT: Yale University Press, 1992.

Weekes, Mary. *The Last Buffalo Hunter.* Toronto: Macmillan of Canada, 1945.

Weekes, Mary, and William Cornwallis King. *Trader King: The Thrilling Story of Forty Years in the North-West Territories, Related by One of the Last of the Old Time Wintering Partners of the Hudson's Bay Company.* Regina: School Aids and Textbook Publishing Company, 1949.

West, John. *The Substance of a Journal during a Residence at the Red River Colony, British North America, in the Years 1820–1823.* Vancouver: Alcuin Society, 1967.

White, Bruce M. "A Skilled Game of Exchange: Ojibwa Fur Trade Protocol." *Minnesota History* 50 (1987): 229–40.

White, Pamela M. "Restructuring the Domestic Sphere—Prairie Indian Women on Reserves: Image, Ideology, and State Policy, 1880–1930." Ph.D. diss., McGill University, 1987.

White Weasel, Charlie. *Pembina and Turtle Mountain Ojibway (Chippewa) History from the Personal Collection and Writings of Charlie White Weasel.* Belcourt, ND: self-published, 1994.

Whiting Young, Biloine, and Melvin L. Fowler. *Cahokia: The Great American Metropolis.* Urbana: University of Illinois Press, 2000.

Wien, Tom. "Coureur de Bois." In *The 1997 Canadian Encyclopaedia Plus.* Toronto: McClelland and Stewart, 1996. CD-rom.

Wiley, Gordon R., and Philip Philips. *Method and Theory in American Archaeology.* Chicago: University of Chicago Press, 1963.

Williams, Glyndwr, ed. *Peter Skene Ogden's Snake Country Journals 1827–28 and 1828–29.* Hudson's Bay Record Society Publication 28. London: Hudson's Bay Record Society, 1971.

Williamson, Norman James. "Abishabis the Cree." *Studies in Religion* 9 (1980): 217–45.

Wilson, Clifford. *Campbell of the Yukon.* Toronto: Macmillan of Canada, 1970.

——. "Private Letters from the Fur Trade." In *Papers Read before the Historical and Scientific Society of Manitoba,* Series 3, edited by W.L. Morton and J.A. Jackson, 39–45. Winnipeg: Historical and Scientific Society of Manitoba, 1950.

Winchester, Simon. *Krakatoa, the Day the Earth Exploded: August 27, 1883.* New York: HarperCollins, 2003.

Winham, R. Peter, and Edward J. Lueck. "Cultures of the Middle Missouri." In *Plains Indians, A.D. 500–1500: The Archaeological Past of Historic Groups,* edited by Karl Schlesier, 149–75. Norman: University of Oklahoma Press, 1994.

Wissler, Clark. "The Influence of the Horse in the Development of Plains Culture." *American Anthropologist* 16 (1914): 1–25.

Wood, Charles A. "Climatic Effects of the 1783 Laki Eruption." In *The Year without a Summer? World Climate in 1816*, edited by C.R. Harington, 58–77. Ottawa: Canadian Museum of Nature, 1992.

Wood, W. Raymond. *Biesterfeldt: A Post-Contact Coalescent Site on the Northeastern Plains*. Smithsonian Contributions to Anthropology 15. Washington, DC: Smithsonian Institution Press, 1971.

Worboys, Michael. "Tuberculosis and Race in Britain and Its Empire, 1900–50." In *Race, Science, and Medicine, 1700–1960*, edited by Waltraus Ernst and Bernard Harris, 144–67. London: Routledge, 1999.

Wright, Richard Thomas. *Overlanders*. Williams Lake, BC: Winter Quarters Press, 2000.

Yerbury, J. C. "The Post-Contact Chipewyan: Trade Rivalries and Changing Territorial Boundaries." *Ethnohistory* 23 (1976): 237–64.

——. *The Subarctic Indians and the Fur Trade, 1680–1860*. Vancouver: UBC Press, 1986.

Young, E. R. *By Canoe and Dog Train: Among the Cree and Salteaux Indians*. Toronto: William Briggs, 1890.

Young, T. K. *The Health of Native Americans: Toward a Biocultural Epidemiology*. New York: Oxford University Press, 1994.

INDEX

Page numbers in italics refer to photographs. Page numbers with a **t** refer to tables and with an **m** refer to maps.

INDEX

Fidler, Peter, 38, 47, 49, 56
File Hills, 146–47, 162, 163, 193m, 249n141
Finlay's Fort, 30–31
fires
    for control of food supply,
        7, 35, 36, 206n54
    drought and, 103–4, 107
Fish Eaters, 82
fishing
    commercial harvesting, 150, 241n149
    media coverage, 150
    subsistence harvesting, 53, 56, 64,
        89, 95, 110, 150–51, 241n149
Flathead, 24, 60
food relief. See Dept. of Indian Affairs
food scarcity. See famine and hunger
Foremost Man, 123, 235n1
Forks, 28, 89–90, 245n36
Fort à la Corne, 120, 191m, 245n36
Fort Albany, 191m
Fort Alexander, 95–96, 193m
Fort Benton, Montana, 132
    alcohol trade, 80, 82, 128
    demographics, 76
    location, 191m, 192m
    smallpox (1870s), 81, 88
    trade network, 107, 128, 132, 184
    See also I.G. Baker and Co.
Fort Carlton
    famine, 96, 146
    fish, 150
    location, 191m
    smallpox, 82t, 86–87, 89–91
    tribal relations, 55
Fort Carlton Treaty. See Treaty 6
Fort Chipewyan, 43, 51, 52, 54, 55, 191m
Fort Edmonton
    alcohol trade, 83
    famine (1870s), 96, 110
    gold rush, 75, 76
    location, 191m, 192m
    measles, 56
    smallpox, 67–68, 69, 82t, 86, 88–90
    whooping cough, 56
Fort Ellice, 65, 90–91, 95, 112, 119, 121, 191m
Fort Frances, 18
Fort la Reine, 19, 191m
Fort Macleod, 106, 112, 118, 129,
    153, 169, 179, 192m
Fort Maurepas, 19, 191m
Fort Pitt, 65, 82t, 86, 96, 131, 150, 155, 191m
Fort Prince of Wales, 17, 191m
Fort Qu'Appelle, 85, 95, 112–13, 117, 121, 191m
    See also Qu'Appelle Valley
Fort Resolution, 56, 191m

Fort Rouge, 19, 191m
Fort Simpson, 75
Fort St. John, 63, 191m
Fort St. Pierre, 18, 191m
Fort Union, 67, 191m
Fort Vermilion, 49, 74
Fort Walsh, 119
    closure, 124, 127, 141–42
    clothing shortages, 117
    food riots, 118–19
    location, 192m, 193m
    migration to, 115
    scarlet fever, 120
    sexually transmitted diseases, 154
    See also Cypress Hills; North-
        West Mounted Police
Fort Wedderburn, 54, 191m
Fort William, 191m, 192m
Frank, André Gunder, xiii
Franklin Expeditions, 56–57, 72
French fur traders. See Canadians
    (fur traders)
Frobisher, Thomas, 32
Frog Lake, 152–53, 155, 191m, 243n187
Frog Portage, 32, 71
fur trade, history
    1650s–1780s, 13–19, 26, 27–28
    1783–1820s, 41–57
    1821–1869, HBC monopoly, 59–77
    1869–1876, 90–91, 93–94
    map of trading posts, 191m
    See also Canadians (fur traders);
        Hudson's Bay Company;
        North West Company
fur trade, middleman
    1600s–1740s, 14–20
    1740s–1780s, xvii, 27–31, 33–34, 38–39, 43
    decline, 27–28, 30–31, 33–34
    military conflict, 17
    tribal relations, 29

Gaultier, Pierre. See La Vérendrye
Ghost Dance, 169–72
Girard, F.X., 138–40
Give Away Dance, 169
Gladstone, William, 76
glandular tuberculosis. See tuberculosis, bo-
    vine
Gleichen, Alberta, 175
gold rush and disease, 73, 75–76
gonorrhea. See sexually transmitted diseases
Grande Portage, 18, 48, 191m, 192m
Grandin, Vital, 87
Grant, George M., 94, 101

Grant, Peter and David, 48
Great Bear Lake region, 53, 189m
Great Slave Lake region, 51, 57, 189**m**
Green Lake, 52
Grizzly Bear's Head, Chief, 155–56, 193**m**,
    245n22, 245n26
Gros Ventre. *See* A'aninin (Fall/Gros Ventre/
    Water Fall)

Hackett, Paul, xi, 19
Hagarty, Daniel, 105, 112–13, 120, 125
Hamilton, Scott, 3
Hare, 55
hares, 53, 64, 69
Harmon, Daniel, 48, 50, 52, 53, 54, 55
Haudenosaunee (Iroquois), 5,
    13, 40, 41, 48, 190m
HBC. *See* Hudson's Bay Company
health care. *See* diseases, infectious,
    prevention and treatment
"Health Patterns and Underdevelopment"
    (Campbell), xx
Hearne, Samuel, 29–30, 33, 38
Heavy Runner, Chief, 80–81
Hector, James, 69, 74, 75
Henday, Anthony, 25, 43
Henry, Alexander, 7, 32, 46, 49
hepatitis, 2
Herring, Ann, xx
Hidatsa, 4, 66, 67, 190m
Hind Expedition, 74, 75
Hines, John, 104, 150, 164, 166
Home Farm program. *See* reserve
    system and farming
Horrall, S.W., 154
horses. *See* equestrianism
Hudson House, 32, 34, 35, 37,
    39, 40, 43, 44, 191m
Hudson's Bay Company
    1670s–1730s, 14, 17–18
    1740s–1780s, 27–36, 39–40
    1780s–1820s, 42–43, 48, 50–51, 54–57
    1821–1869, monopoly, 59–77
    1869–1876, 80, 88–90, 93–94
    1876–1885, 130–31
    agricultural settlements, 54, 61, 62
    alcohol prohibition, xviii,
        45–46, 59, 62, 83, 212n82
    alcohol trade, 45–46
    early trading posts, 14, 31
    I.G. Baker's impact on, 128, 130–31, 137–38
    impact of sale (1863), 75–76, 80, 93–94
    map of trading posts, 191m
    merger with NWC (1821), 55, 57, 59–60

records, 31
    rivalry with Canadians, 42–43
    rivalry with NWC, 48, 50–52, 54–57
    steamboats, 128, 130–31
    See also Cumberland House;
        Hudson House; Hudson's
        Bay Company, monopoly
        (1821–1869); Simpson, George
Hudson's Bay Company,
    monopoly (1821–1869)
    census, 64
    closure of posts, 59–60, 62, 66
    as de facto government,
        59–60, 62, 64, 73, 75
    free trade and, 63, 64–65, 71–72
    gold rush miners and, 73, 75, 76
    missionaries, xviii, 70–71
    overview, xviii–xix, 59–60
Hudson's Bay Company, prevention
    and treatment of diseases
    early history, 14, 17
    immunity by early exposure,
        14, 39, 208n85
    measles and whooping cough, 55–57
    quarantines, 70, 72, 104–5
    sanitation regulations, 70
    scurvy, 14
    sexually transmitted diseases, 14, 33
    smallpox, 39, 68, 84–90
    treatments, 49
    tuberculosis, 14, 49, 227n8
    vaccinations, xviii, 59, 60,
        68–70, 74, 84–86, 88–90
hunger. *See* famine and hunger
Huron, 13, 17, 190m

Icelandic immigrants, 104
I.G. Baker and Co., 129, *132*
    dishonest practices, xxi,
        115, 137–40, 151, 184
    history, xxi, 128–31
    impact on HBC, 128, 130–31, 137–38
    supplier to NWMP, 129
    supplier to reserves, xxi,
        115, 137–40, 239n84
    transportation systems, 130–31, *132*
Île-à-la-Crosse, 32, 43, 51, 56, 71, 191m
illnesses. *See* diseases, infectious
immigrants, European, 93, 104,
    108–9, 128, 192m
Indian Act
    prostitution under, 154
    religious ceremonies under, 171

James Daschuk HAS a Ph.D. in History from the University of Manitoba. He is an associate professor in the Faculty of Kinesiology and Health Studies at the University of Regina and a researcher with the Saskatchewan Population Health and Evaluation Research Unit.